JASBIR

1-2-3 FOR SCIENTISTS AND ENGINEERS

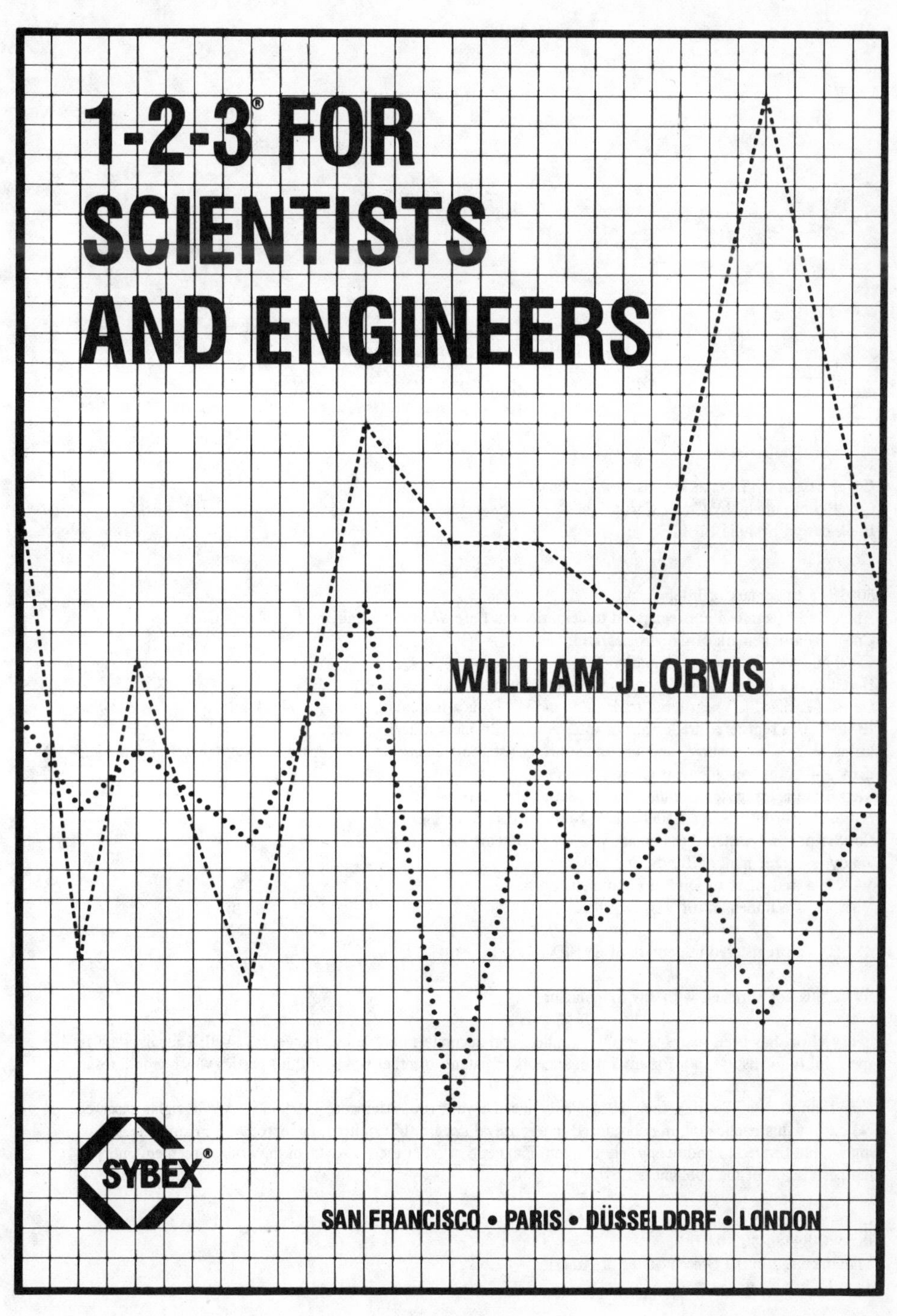
1-2-3® FOR
SCIENTISTS
AND ENGINEERS
WILLIAM J. ORVIS
SYBEX®
SAN FRANCISCO • PARIS • DÜSSELDORF • LONDON

Cover design by Thomas Ingalls + Associates
Cover photography by Casey Cartwright
Book design by Julie Bilski

8087 is a trademark of Intel Corp.
Apple and Macintosh are registered trademarks and LaserWriter is a trademark of Apple Computer Inc.
Cray-1 is a trademark of Cray Research Inc.
Excel and MS-DOS are trademarks of Microsoft Corp.
Hercules is a trademark of Hercules Computer Technology.
Hewlett-Packard is a registered trademark and HP-IV is a trademark of Hewlett-Packard Co.
IBM PC is a registered trademark of International Business Machines Inc.
Lotus, 1-2-3, Symphony, and Freelance are registered trademarks and Measure and Manuscript are trademarks of Lotus Development Corp.
MetraByte is a registered trademark of MetraByte Corp.
National Instruments is a trademark of National Instruments Corp.
PostScript is a registered trademark of Adobe Systems Inc.
Tandy is a trademark of Tandy Corp.
VAX is a trademark of Digital Equipment Corp.
VisiCalc is a trademark of VisiCorp Inc.

SYBEX is a registered trademark of SYBEX, Inc.

SYBEX is not affiliated with any manufacturer.

Every effort has been made to supply complete and accurate information. However, SYBEX assumes no responsibility for its use, nor for any infringements of patents or other rights of third parties which would result.

Copyright © 1987 SYBEX Inc., 2021 Challenger Drive #100, Alameda, CA 94501. World rights reserved. No part of this publication may be stored in a retrieval system, transmitted, or reproduced in any way, including but not limited to photocopy, photograph, magnetic or other record, without the prior agreement and written permission of the publisher.

Library of Congress Card Number: 87-61338
ISBN 0-89588-407-0
Manufactured in the United States of America
10 9 8 7 6 5 4

To Sierra–
She was born about Chapter 5 and has enriched our lives ever since.

TABLE OF CONTENTS

CHAPTER 2

CHAPTER 3

CHAPTER 6

CHAPTER 7

CHAPTER 8

PREFACE

I have been using microcomputers in my work for a number of years and prefer to use them rather than the larger mainframe computers whenever possible. Most of my computing and data analysis work has been performed using BASIC or Fortran. Since the advent of spreadsheet programs with built-in graphics, I have found myself performing more of my calculations and analyses with these.

For many years, I have been giving "hard" science presentations and papers at conferences and symposia. Last summer, I decided to do something different. Just for fun, I put together a paper on engineering with a spreadsheet. Dianne King and Rudy Langer of SYBEX found out about this paper and contacted me with an interesting offer: Would I like to write a book on this topic? I considered their proposition for about two seconds and accepted.

That evening, my wife reminded me that we had a baby due about the time that I was supposed to deliver Chapter 5. Somehow I managed to convince her that I could take care of both. Since we have two other children, we expected to, and did, have our hands full when baby Sierra arrived. However, it turned out that Sierra liked to lay across my knees while I typed. The sound of the keys clicking apparently put her to sleep. So there I sat, madly typing away until the early hours of the morning, using a newborn baby in my lap for an arm rest.

I had fun producing the examples in this book. I hope that you have as much fun using them and applying the techniques to your own problems or figuring out how to adapt other numerical methods to the spreadsheet format. If any of the examples in this book do not work as I have indicated, then please accept my apology. I have worked hard to make everything correct; however, errors will always try to sneak through.

I wish to thank Dianne King and Rudolph Langer, who offered me this project and encouraged me; Valerie Robbins, who kept me moving in the right direction; Judy Ziajka, who changed my English into something that the rest of the world could understand; and Jon Forrest, who checked all of my examples to make sure that they work. I also want to thank Olivia Shinomoto, word processing; Michelle Hoffman, production assistant; Julie Bilski, book design and layout; Stephanie Bower, proofreading; and Paula Alston, indexing.

Thanks also go to my wife, Julie, and to the rest of my family for putting up with my disappearing every evening and weekend for six months. Now that this project is completed, I plan to get to know them again.

Thank you all—it has been fun.

William J. Orvis
Livermore, California
June 1, 1987

INTRODUCTION

Scientists and engineers often perform numerical calculations. Their operations range from the simple task of determining the value of a function to the complex task of numerically integrating a differential equation—tasks that require considerable time and energy. Thus, any tool that can facilitate such calculations can increase a scientist's or engineer's productivity. Lotus 1-2-3 is one such tool, offering facilities for numerical calculations, graphics, and programmability in a single, easy-to-use package.

In the past, the slide rule was the primary tool for performing numerical calculations, and graph paper was the usual data-display device. With the advent of the hand calculator, the slide rule was quickly retired to a place of nostalgic revere (most likely the bottom of a drawer). However, the graph paper still remained.

Some scientists and engineers had access to mainframe computers and could use them for their calculations and data display. These mainframe computers had tremendous computing power, and many had impressive graphics output devices. However, individuals usually had either to hire a computer scientist (or a high school student) or to learn a computer language like FORTRAN or ALGOL to program these computers and to make the high-powered graphics work.

Microcomputers put a lot of computing power on the desktops of scientists and engineers, and the BASIC computer language included with most microcomputers provided a good environment for many numerical calculations. Many desktop computers had plotters and, with a little work, could produce reasonable graphics output. However, these computers still had to be programmed to generate and plot numbers.

In addition, even with personal computers around, most scientists and engineers still generated their numbers with an engineering calculation sheet. An engineering calculation sheet is a piece of lined paper, much like binder paper, that also has vertical lines spaced approximately every inch or so. Working with sets of numbers involves putting successive calculations in alternate columns until the final column contains the result. For example, if you want to calculate the function $y = 2x^2 + 3x$ for a list of x values, you place the x values in the first column, $2x^2$ in the second column, $3x$ in the third column, and the sum of columns 2 and 3, the final result, in column 4.

Interestingly, these engineering calculation sheets bore a remarkable resemblance to the spreadsheets that business students used when I was in school (they must have stolen the idea from the engineers). Now, you might occasionally have a beer with a business student or two, but you never involved yourself in their studies, so little was made of the these similarities. Much of this indifference was because "we" used sines, cosines, and exponentials, whereas "they" only used addition, subtraction, multiplication, division, and percentages (they got really good with percentages: percent interest, percent penalty, percent royalty, and so on).

A few years ago, the business spreadsheet was automated with the microcomputer program VisiCalc. Some of us in science and engineering immediately saw the potential of this program as an engineering tool, especially since it could calculate such scientific functions as sines, cosines, and exponentials. Since then, spreadsheet programs have grown tremendously in power and versatility, culminating in Lotus 1-2-3 (or Symphony) for the IBM PC and Microsoft Excel for the Apple Macintosh. Both of these programs have powerful spreadsheets coupled with graphics, macros, and database functions.

■ SCOPE OF THIS BOOK

In this book, you will learn how to perform science and engineering calculations using Lotus 1-2-3 spreadsheets, macros, and graphics. You will not only learn how to calculate and plot simple equations, but how to perform curve fitting; to calculate statistics, numerical derivatives, and integrals; and to solve systems of equations and one- and two-dimensional differential equations. (Note that the techniques discussed here could be applied equally well to Microsoft Excel on the Apple Macintosh.)

This book was written by a practicing scientist and engineer for other practicing scientists and engineers. Because of this, it is based on real uses of a spreadsheet as an engineering tool. Many of the problems were developed initially as part of my work or are adaptations of problems that I solved using other techniques before I became "turned on" to spreadsheets. Thus, in many cases, you will be solving real problems rather than simplified textbook problems. Because of this, a few of the problems are somewhat longer than you normally find in a textbook. In those few cases, I have included abbreviated versions of the problems that still illustrate the relevant techniques.

Again, because the problems used in this book are real science and engineering problems, and because this book is based on my own work in the science and engineering fields, many of the problems are electronics and solid state physics problems, with some astronomy thrown in for fun. If these aren't your fields, don't let that bother you, since the problems are used only to illustrate the calculation methods. The methods used to solve the problems are what are important, not the problems themselves, and these methods are easily applicable to any branch of science and engineering.

This book shows you how to apply a spreadsheet to science and engineering tasks. It is not a text for teaching you science and engineering, nor is it a text on numerical methods, so I will not discuss much of the background or mathematical justification for most of the numerical techniques described in this text. If you are interested in this background material, a number of good numerical methods books are available to sate your curiosity. I primarily depend on Curtis F. Gerald's book, *Applied Numerical Analysis,* for most of my numerical methods, though last year I picked up a copy of W. H. Press' book *Numerical Recipes,* which is also excellent.

USER BACKGROUND

To use this book, you must have a background in science, engineering, or mathematics. Although I have written this book for the practicing scientist or engineer, a college student in one of these disciplines should have no trouble understanding the problems and solutions and using them to enhance his or her studies.

You must also know how to use an IBM PC or compatible computer. If you do not know how to turn a computer on, put this book down, get a good tutorial, and play with the computer for a while. When you feel comfortable with the computer—when you can delete a file without cringing—then continue with this book.

I also assume that you know the basics of using Lotus 1-2-3. If you do not know how to start it up, move around the spreadsheet, insert data in cells, save a file, and load an old file, then study the 1-2-3 Tutorial and the 1-2-3 Reference Manual that Lotus includes with 1-2-3. The tutorial steps you through all of the basics. Once you understand these basics, then you can continue with the problems in this book.

Note though, that although I do expect you to know these basics, this book starts slowly to give you time to become comfortable with Lotus 1-2-3. Those readers with more familiarity with Lotus 1-2-3 may want to skip the first, simple problem and begin with the second problem. From there, the spreadsheets get increasingly complex.

This book also explains how to create graphics and use macros. This is because these capabilities give Lotus 1-2-3 much of its power and usefulness for science and engineering.

HARDWARE REQUIREMENTS

If you do not have the right hardware, then Lotus 1-2-3 either will not run or will not be completely functional. It requires an IBM personal computer (PC, XT, or AT) or compatible computer, but beware: It will not run on all IBM-compatible computers. If you are buying a computer, make sure it will run Lotus 1-2-3. Have the salesperson show you Lotus 1-2-3 working on the machine you are interested in (make sure that the salesperson has the same version of 1-2-3 as the one you will be using). If you already own 1-2-3, bring in your copy and try it on the computer you want to buy. Nothing will make your day like bringing home $2000 worth of computer hardware and finding out that it will not run the program for which you bought it.

Memory

You will need at least 256K of memory to run Lotus 1-2-3; however, the more memory that you have, the larger the spreadsheets that you can create. Lotus 1-2-3 can handle expanded memory options (beyond 640K) so long as they conform to the Lotus/Intel expanded memory specification. Beware: There is more than one way to expand memory beyond 640 K, and only memory that uses the Lotus/Intel specification will work.

Graphics

As you might expect, you need some special hardware to produce graphics on an IBM PC or compatible computer: You need a graphics card and a compatible monitor. There are several graphics cards on the market, so be sure to get one that works with Lotus 1-2-3. The most common are the IBM Color Graphics Adaptor for color graphics and text and the Hercules Monochrome Graphics Adaptor for high-resolution, monochrome graphics and text. IBM also makes an Enhanced Graphics Adaptor for high-resolution color graphics and text. Run the Lotus 1-2-3 Install program to see a list of currently supported graphics hardware.

For science and engineering, graphic resolution is usually more important than color. A Hercules monochrome graphics adaptor and a high-resolution, monochrome display has become a standard system for high-resolution, monochrome graphics. If you are using a color graphics adaptor, select the high-resolution, two-color driver (I like white letters on a blue background) with the Install program. If you want color and do not mind slightly lower-resolution graphics, then select the medium resolution, four-color driver. You can create more than one driver set for Lotus 1-2-3 and then specify which one to use at startup. For more information, see the Lotus 1-2-3 manual *Getting Started,* included in the Lotus 1-2-3 package.

Some IBM PC compatibles have graphics functions built in and do not need an additional graphics card. For example, the Tandy 1000 SX that I am using to write this book has the functions of the color graphics adaptor built in.

If you have only a monochrome display card, you are out of luck. With a monochrome display card, you cannot display graphics; you can display only text. The only plotting that you can do is some simple bar charts using the 1-2-3 /Range Format + (/RF+) command. Any cell that is formatted with this command will display a row of plus or minus signs, one for each positive or negative integer (that is, if you put a 3 in a cell, it will be displayed as +++ instead of the number 3). If you have a graphics card in your system, then forget about the /Range Format+ (/RF+) command.

System Used to Create the Examples

The examples in this book were run using Lotus 1-2-3 version 2.01 and MS-DOS version 3.2 on a Tandy 1000 SX computer (an IBM PC compatible) with a full load (640K) of memory, a floating-point chip, a built-in color graphics adaptor (used in high-resolution, two-color mode), and a high-resolution color monitor. Some of the problems may not run on less memory than this. The floating-point chip speeds up execution of the spreadsheet, but is not required for the problems to run. I give timing results with and without the chip installed for some of the longer running problems (see Appendix C). Many of the examples have also been run on an Apple Macintosh computer running Microsoft Excel.

■ CONVENTIONS

Many of the figures shown in this book do not show the whole spreadsheet, as some of the problems would fill many pages. In most cases I locate the important results in the upper-left corner of the spreadsheet and then show only that corner as a figure.

Lotus 1-2-3 is not case specific, so functions, variable names, and formulas can be typed using uppercase or lowercase letters. In the problem descriptions, I show all of the spreadsheet functions in uppercase, because that is how they appear in the spreadsheet. You can use either uppercase or lowercase letters for your entries, and Lotus 1-2-3 will change everything but text labels to uppercase. Macro programs are shown in lowercase, as that is how I typed them into the spreadsheet. Macros are stored as long labels in the spreadsheet and, since Lotus 1-2-3 does not change the case of text labels, it does not change the macro entries to uppercase.

■ AVAILABILITY OF EXAMPLES

If you do not want to type all of the examples but still want to be able to run them, you can obtain the examples on disk. See the insert at the end of this book for order information.

■ FOR MORE INFORMATION

References to the sources of the examples and numerical methods used in each chapter appear in a separate section, like this one, at the end of each chapter. Use the references in these sections if you want to know more about any particular example or numerical method.

Operating an IBM PC or Compatible Computer

P. Norton, *Inside the IBM PC* (Bowie, Md.: Brady, 1983).

A. Miller, *The ABC's of MS-DOS* (Alameda, Calif.: SYBEX, 1987).

J. Kamin, *MS-DOS Power User's Guide* (Alameda, Calif.: SYBEX, 1986).

Engineering with VisiCalc

S. Trost and C. Pomernacki, *VisiCalc for Science and Engineering* (Alameda, Calif.: SYBEX, 1983).

Installing Lotus 1-2-3

Lotus, *Getting Started,* release 2.01 (Cambridge, Mass. Lotus Development Corp., 1986).

Using Lotus 1-2-3

Lotus, *1-2-3 Reference Manual,* release 2.01 (Cambridge, Mass.: Lotus Development Corp., 1985).

Learning Lotus 1-2-3

Lotus, *1-2-3 Tutorial,* release 2.01 (Cambridge, Mass.: Lotus Development Corp., 1985).

C. Gilbert and L. Williams, *The ABC's of 1-2-3* (Alameda, Calif.: SYBEX, 1987).

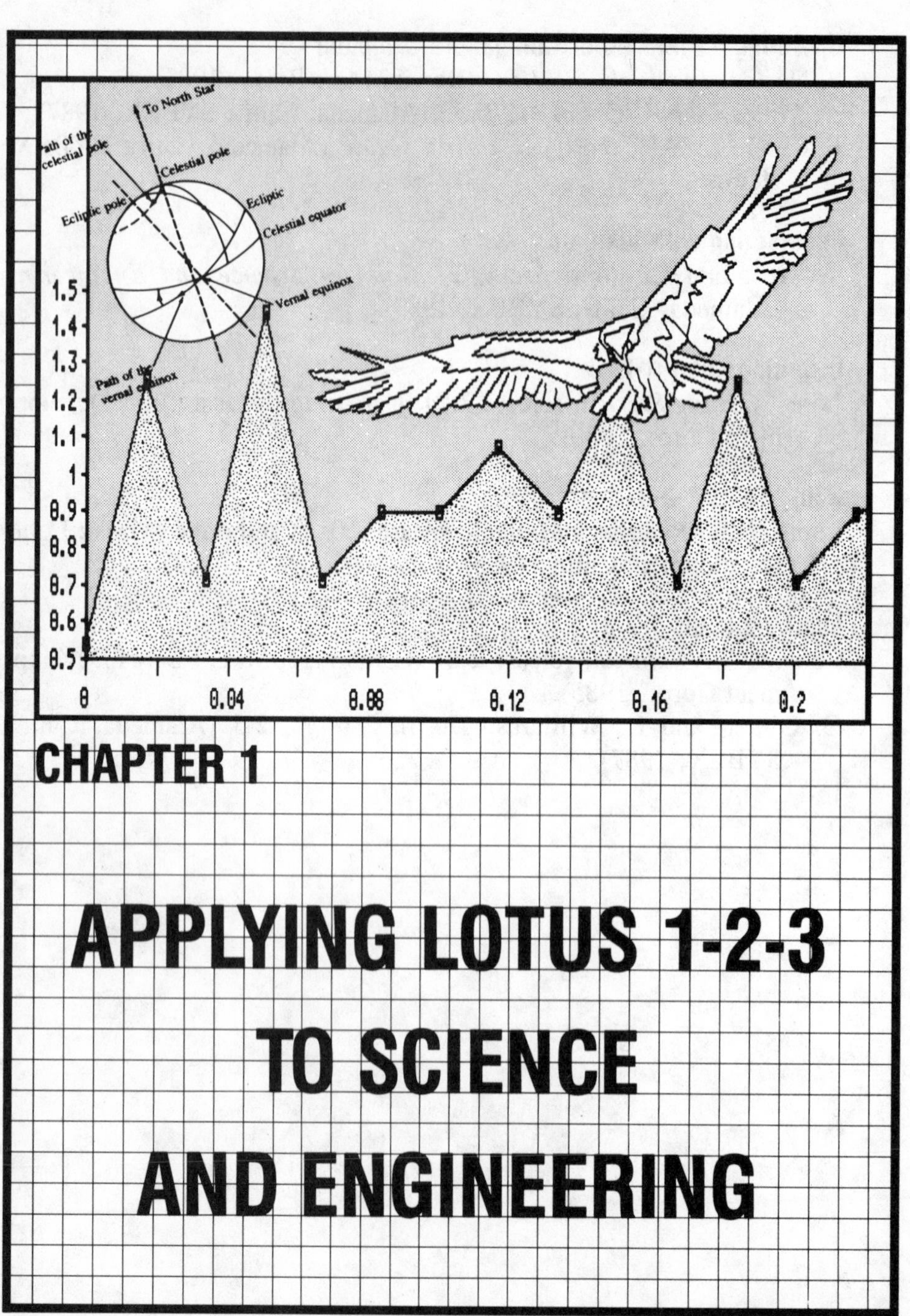

CHAPTER 1

APPLYING LOTUS 1-2-3 TO SCIENCE AND ENGINEERING

When you first saw the title of this book, you might have wondered how a "business" spreadsheet program could be used for scientific and engineering calculations. Of course, business people do use addition, subtraction, multiplication, and division, which are certainly useful to science and engineering. But they also calculate such things as the "present value of an annuity" and "compound interest," which are useful to scientists and engineers only when they want to know if they can afford the payments on a new home. What about the precision and range of the calculated numbers? Are the mathematical functions used in science and engineering available?

As you will see, Lotus 1-2-3 is more than accurate enough for most engineering calculations, and it has all of the mathematical functions of a high-level language such as FORTRAN or BASIC. And it calculates the present value of an annuity too, if you need it to do so.

NUMERIC PRECISION

The precision of a number in Lotus 1-2-3 is comparable to that of most mainframes and minicomputers. You can use up to 240 characters to type a number into a cell, but only 16 digits are maintained internally. The control panel displays only 10 digits, but you can see the extra digits by widening the column containing the cell and then formatting the cell as scientific, with 15 decimal places. My scientific calculator shows 10 digits and probably has one more internally for roundoff precision. A Cray 1 computer has about 15 digits of precision in its single-precision floating point numbers, and a VAX computer has only about 7 digits of precision in single-precision and 15 in double-precision floating-point numbers.

Lotus 1-2-3 performs all of its calculations in single-precision arithmetic. If you need extra precision, you could split a number into an upper and lower part and carry these along separately in your calculation, but this would be difficult because of the cross terms generated by many mathematical operations. Few people need this much precision. I have needed it only for celestial mechanics calculations (not using a spreadsheet). When you are integrating the orbit of an asteroid, small errors in calculating its position can add up to a large error after a few million orbits (you can place the asteroid on the wrong side of the sun).

■ NUMERIC RANGE

In addition to precision, many science and engineering calculations involve numbers with large exponents. Lotus 1-2-3 allows you to enter numbers with exponents in the range ±99, which encompasses most scientific and engineering numbers. Internally, Lotus 1-2-3 calculates exponents in the range ±308 to prevent numeric overflow during intermediate calculations. If a cell contains a number between 10^{99} and 10^{308} (or 10^{-99} and 10^{-308}), 1-2-3 will display a row of stars. However, the number will be maintained internally and can be referenced and used in calculations within another cell.

My hand calculator also handles exponents up to ±99, and I have had numeric overflow a number of times (try taking the fourth power of the inverse of the electron rest mass). The extra size of the exponents in the internal variables will significantly reduce problems with intermediate variable overflow. If a number does overflow in a cell, Lotus 1-2-3 will mark that cell and all cells that depend on the value in that cell as bad (ERR). You can sometimes rearrange your equations so that the intermediate values do not overflow; however, it is extremely unlikely that overflow will be a problem with Lotus 1-2-3. The Cray 1 handles exponents in the range ±2500, and VAX computers handle exponents in the range ±38 in single-precision arithmetic and ±308 in double-precision arithmetic. Again, as you can see, the power of Lotus 1-2-3 is comparable to that of mainframes and minicomputers.

■ A BRIEF REVIEW

I realize that you have diligently studied the Lotus 1-2-3 manual and know all about labels, relative cell references, and absolute cell references. However, we are going to briefly review them, since you must understand cell referencing to make effective use of 1-2-3's functions.

Cell Types

The cells in a Lotus 1-2-3 spreadsheet can hold more than text (labels) or numbers (values); they can also hold equations (formulas). The spreadsheet looks at the first character in a cell and uses that character to determine whether a cell contains a label or a value. If a value also contains alphanumeric text (operators, functions, and cell references), it is assumed to be a formula. The first character of a formula must be a numeric digit, a unary operator (+, −), a left parenthesis ((), or the first character of a function (@). If a formula begins with a cell reference (which starts with an alphabetic character, for example, A2), then make the first character a plus (+) sign. If a label begins with a number, then make the first character one of the label-prefix characters.

The label-prefix characters are a single quotation mark (‘), which also left aligns the text; a double quotation mark (“), which also right aligns the text; and a caret (^), which also centers the text. The label-prefix characters are not printed. The default alignment for text is left aligned.

Cell References

Values of other cells in the spreadsheet can be inserted into a formula by using cell references or cell addresses. A cell reference consists of a letter-number pair, where the letter corresponds to the column that contains the referenced cell, and the number corresponds to the row. For example, G5 corresponds to the value in the cell at column G and row 5.

Range References

Groups of cells can be specified in a function by using a range reference. A range of cells is a rectangular region on the spreadsheet. All cells within that rectangle are contained in the range (that is, there are no holes). You specify a range by using the cell references of the cells in the upper-left and lower-right corners of the rectangle, separated by one or two periods. For example, H4..J6 specifies all of the cells within the rectangle that has cell H4 in the upper-left corner and cell J6 in the lower-right corner (H4, H5, H6, I4, I5, I6, J4, J5, J6). A range reference can be as small as a single cell (H5..H5); it can also be a single row (H5..J5) or column (H5..H10).

Relative and Absolute Cell References

Cell references come in two different types: relative and absolute. Relative cell references point to cells relative to the location of the reference. Absolute cell references always point to a specific cell.

Relative Cell References

All of the cell references mentioned so far are relative cell references. Relative cell references are defined in relation to the cell that contains them. For example, if cell G5 contains the cell reference E3, the *E3* does not refer to the contents of the cell in column E and row 3 but instead points to the cell that is two columns to the left of and two rows above cell G5, which just happens to be E3. If you were to copy the contents of cell G5 into cell I8, then the cell reference would change to G6, which is two columns to the left of and two columns above cell I8.

Relative cell references are extremely handy when you are copying an equation to apply it to a set of data. If you were calculating a formula for 50 different input values, it would be tedious to type the equation 50 times. What you can do in Lotus 1-2-3 is type the equation into the first cell in a column and then copy it into the cells below that one. All of the relative cell references will be adjusted according to their relative positions. You will see how this works as we develop some spreadsheets.

Absolute Cell References

An absolute cell reference does not change when a cell is copied. It always points to a specific cell, no matter where the reference appears on the spreadsheet. Absolute cell references look much like relative cell references, except that a dollar sign ($) precedes the row and column coordinates. For example, $G$5 is an absolute reference to cell G5. Absolute cell references are useful for pointing to the coefficients in a formula. If you specify independent variables with relative cell references, you can copy an equation down a column and have it apply to all of the independent variables located in adjacent columns. Because the coefficients of the formula are the same for every copy of the formula, you can place them in a special place on the spreadsheet and then reference them in formulas by using absolute cell references. You thus need only one set of coefficients on your spreadsheet; no matter where you copy a formula that refers to them, it will still refer to them. Once you have set up your formulas this way, you can adjust a single coefficient, and all of the copies of the formula will show the results.

Absolute references may also apply to only the column or only the row coordinate, with the other coordinate being relative (mixed reference). This is achieved by placing a dollar sign before only the coordinate that you want to lock. For example, $G5 indicates that the column coordinate is locked, but the row coordinate is relative and will change if the referencing cell is copied to a different row. Reference G$5 is just the opposite; the row coordinate is locked, and the column coordinate is relative.

Range and Cell Names

You can give names to range and cell references. Then you can enter the name to reference the range or cell. This feature is useful when you use the same range reference many times. It is also useful to make some formulas more understandable. For example, the word *mass* is much more descriptive than a cell reference such as C5. You treat named ranges and cells like a replacement table. When 1-2-3 evaluates a formula, it first replaces any names with the range or cell references that they point to and then calculates the formula. Use the /Range Name (/RN) commands (Create, Delete, Labels, Reset, Table) to create, change, delete, or print named references.

You can name individual cells in two ways: by naming the cell and by naming a range containing only one cell. You can then use these names in formulas wherever a single number or cell reference is called for. You can use a named range containing only one cell in a formula where a single cell reference is required.

When you copy cells that contain named ranges into another cell, the names are replaced with their cell references and then copied, so the copied cells contain cell references rather than names. Named references are relative, so the range references in the copied cells are adjusted and no longer point to the named range. To "pin" the name to the range during a copy operation, precede the name with a dollar sign to make it absolute.

Copy versus Move

Copying cells from one place to another and moving cells to the same place may seem to be roughly the same operation. Isn't moving the contents of cell H5 to cell J7 the same as copying the contents of cell H5 into J7 and then erasing the contents of H5? The answer is yes for labels and values, but no for formulas.

As already discussed, when you copy a formula from one cell into another cell, absolute cell references do not change, and relative cell references change according to where the formula is copied. When you move the contents of a cell, Lotus 1-2-3 assumes that you are changing only the layout of your spreadsheet, not the mathematical logic. Therefore, cell references in moved cells that point to cells outside the range of moved cells do not change, and any cells that refer to moved cells are adjusted so that they point to the cells that have the same contents as the cells that they pointed to originally. A move operation should not change any of the results of your spreadsheet, unless you delete data by moving cells on top of them.

■ MATHEMATICAL OPERATORS AND FUNCTIONS

The mathematical operators and functions available in Lotus 1-2-3 are comparable to those found in most high-level languages. You will find an extensive discussion of these operators and functions, with numerous examples, in the *1-2-3 Reference Manual*. If you are still confused after reading this book and the *1-2-3 Reference Manual,* then experiment to see what the operators and functions do. Better yet, experiment even if you *do* think you know what the operators and functions do, because you may be wrong, or the operation of a function may have been changed slightly by an update of Lotus 1-2-3. As in science and engineering, the final proof is in the experiment.

Operators

Table 1.1 lists the operators available for use in Lotus 1-2-3. The mathematical operators and most of the logical operators are identical to those that you would find in a high-level programming language (such as BASIC). Some differences to note are these: A logical TRUE equals 1, and a logical FALSE equals 0; as opposed to some versions of BASIC, which use −1 for TRUE. The three logical operators are the standard Boolean operators NOT, AND, and OR. Beware: AND and OR have the same precedence during the evaluation of a formula. Be sure to include parentheses in any formulas involving Boolean operators so that the operators are evaluated in the order that you intended.

Table 1.2 contains the truth tables for these three Boolean operators. The three other common Boolean operators (NOR, NAND, and XOR) are also shown in Table 1.2, along with operator equations that define them in terms of the three supplied Boolean operators.

MATHEMATICAL OPERATORS	
Symbol	**Description**
+	Addition
−	Subtraction or negation
*	Multiplication
/	Division
^	Exponentiation
LOGICAL OPERATORS (Return True (1) or False (0))	
Symbol	**Description**
=	Equal
<>	Not equal
<	Less than
>	Greater than
<=	Less than or equal to
>=	Greater than or equal to
#NOT#	Logical negation; changes TRUE to FALSE or FALSE to TRUE
#AND#	Logical AND
#OR#	Logical OR
STRING OPERATOR	
Symbol	**Description**
&	Concatenation

Table 1.1: Operators available in Lotus 1-2-3

Mathematical and Logical Functions

The mathematical and logical functions are listed in Table 1.3. Of all the functions, these are the most important for science and engineering calculations.

BOOLEAN OPERATORS AVAILABLE IN 1-2-3

a	*b*	#NOT#*a*	*a*#AND#*b*	*a*#OR#*b*	*a*-NAND-*b*	*a*-NOR-*b*	*a*-XOR-*b*
T	T	F	T	T	F	F	F
T	F	F	F	T	T	F	T
F	T	T	F	T	T	F	T
F	F	T	F	F	T	T	F

Functional form of three other common Boolean functions not explicitly available in Lotus 1-2-3. Note that the parentheses are required, even in the last equation, because the operators #AND# and #OR# have the same precedence.

a-NAND-*b* = #NOT#(*a*#AND#*b*) = #NOT#*a*#OR##NOT#*b*

a-NOR-*b* = #NOT#(*a*#OR#*b*) = #NOT#*a*#AND##NOT#*b*

a-XOR-*b* = (*a*#AND##NOT#*b*)#OR#(*b*#AND##NOT#*a*)

Table 1.2: Truth table for the Boolean operators NOT, AND, and OR (supplied with Lotus 1-2-3) and the operators NAND, NOR, and XOR (exclusive OR) that can be obtained from them.

Trigonometric Functions

The trigonometric functions @SIN(x), @COS(x), and @TAN(x) calculate the sine, cosine, and tangent of the angle x, where x is expressed in radians. If x is expressed in degrees, then multiply it by the function @PI and then divide by 180 to convert it to radians. These functions do not yield exactly 0 or infinity when they should, except at $x = 0$. What they do yield is either an extremely small or an extremely large number. The small numbers are on the order of 10^{-16}, and the large numbers are on the order of 10^{+15}, so the results can be used in other calculations without causing an error. The exceptions to this are @SIN(0) and @TAN(0), which do yield exactly 0. Here are some examples:

@SIN(2*@PI) = −2.5E−16

@TAN(@PI/2) = 1.6E+16

@TAN(3*@PI/2) = 5.4E+15

TRIGONOMETRIC FUNCTIONS

Function	Description
@SIN(*x*)	Sine of angle *x*
@COS(*x*)	Cosine of angle *x*
@TAN(*x*)	Tangent of angle *x*
@ASIN(*x*)	Angle that is the arc sine of *x*
@ACOS(*x*)	Angle that is the arc cosine of *x*
@ATAN(*x*)	Angle that is the two quadrant, arc tangent of *x*
@ATAN2(*x*,*y*)	Angle that is the four quadrant, arc tangent of x/y
@PI	Value π (3.1415926)

EXPONENTIAL AND LOGARITHMIC FUNCTIONS

Function	Description
@EXP(*x*)	Value of **e** raised to the power *x*
@LN(*x*)	Natural logarithm (base **e**) of *x*
@EXP(1)	Value **e** (2.7182818)
@LOG(*x*)	Common logarithm (base 10) of *x*

OTHER MATHEMATICAL FUNCTIONS

Function	Description
@ABS(*x*)	Absolute value of *x*
@INT(*x*)	Integer part of *x*
@MOD(*x*,*y*)	*x* modulo *y* (the remainder of x/y)
@RAND	Random number in the range 0 to 1
@ROUND(*x*,*n*)	*x* rounded to *n* places
@SQRT(*x*)	Square root of *x*

LOGICAL FUNCTIONS

Function	Description
@TRUE	The value of logical TRUE (1)
@FALSE	The value of logical FALSE (0)
@IF(*l*,*x*,*y*)	Equal to *x* if *l* is TRUE or *y* if *l* is FALSE

Table 1.3: Mathematical and logical functions available in Lotus 1-2-3

LOGICAL TESTS

Function	Description
@ISERR(x)	Returns TRUE if x = ERR (value is an error); otherwise it returns FALSE
@ISNA(x)	Returns TRUE if x = NA (value not available); otherwise it returns FALSE
@ISNUMBER(x)	Returns TRUE if x is a number; otherwise it returns FALSE
@ISSTRING(x)	Returns TRUE if x is a string; otherwise it returns FALSE

Table 1.3: Mathematical and logical functions available in Lotus 1-2-3 *(continued)*

Inverse Trigonometric Functions

The inverse trigonometric functions @ASIN(x), @ACOS(x), @ATAN(x), and @ATAN2(x,y) calculate the arc sine, arc cosine, and the arc tangent of x, where x is in the range $-1..\ +1$ for the arc sine and arc cosine functions, and the x and y of the arc tangent functions are in the range of $\pm\infty$. The arc sine function returns an angle between $-\pi/2$ and $+\pi/2$, in radians. The arc cosine function returns an angle between 0 and π. The arc tangent function returns an angle between $-\pi/2$ and $+\pi/2$. The second arc tangent function calculates the arc tangent of x/y and puts the result in the correct quadrant. The result is in the range $-\pi$ to $+\pi$. The inverse trigonometric functions are multivalued, so use them carefully to be sure that the angle you get is the one you expect. For example, if y is the arc sine of x, then $\pi - y$ is also the arc sine of x.

Other Trigonometric Functions

The secant, cosecant, cotangent, arc secant, arc cosecant, and arc cotangent are not available as functions in Lotus 1-2-3 (they are not available in BASIC or FORTRAN either). However, any good book of mathematical tables (for example, CRC's *Standard Mathematical Tables*, 18th ed., Cleveland, Ohio: Chemical Rubber Co., 1970) will show you how to calculate them, given the set of functions 1-2-3 does provide. Table 1.4 lists the more common formulas used to define these functions in terms of the supplied functions.

STANDARD TRIGONOMETRIC FUNCTIONS	
Symbol	**Description**
SEC(*x*) = 1/@COS(*x*)	Secant of angle x
CSC(*x*) = 1/@SIN(*x*)	Cosecant of angle x
COT(*x*) = 1/@TAN(*x*)	Cotangent of angle x
INVERSE TRIGONOMETRIC FUNCTIONS	
Symbol	**Description**
ASEC(*x*) = @ATAN(@SQRT(*x*^2 − 1))	Arc secant where $x \geq 0$
ASEC(*x*) = @ATAN(@SQRT(*x*^2 − 1)) − @PI	Arc secant where $x < 0$
ACSC(*x*) = @ATAN(1/@SQRT(*x*^2 − 1))	Arc cosecant where $x \geq 0$
ACSC(*x*) = @ATAN(1/@SQRT(*x*^2 − 1)) − @PI	Arc cosecant where $x < 0$
ACOT(*x*) = @PI/2 − @ATAN(*x*)	Arc cotangent for any value x
HYPERBOLIC FUNCTIONS	
Symbol	**Description**
SINH(*x*) = 0.5*(@EXP(*x*) − @EXP(−*x*))	Hyperbolic sine of x
COSH(*x*) = 0.5*(@EXP(*x*) + @EXP(−*x*))	Hyperbolic cosine of x
TANH(*x*) = SINH(*x*)/COSH(*x*)	Hyperbolic tangent of x
INVERSE HYPERBOLIC FUNCTIONS	
Symbol	**Description**
ASINH(*x*) = @LN(*x* + @SQRT(*x*^2 + 1))	Inverse hyperbolic sine of x
ACOSH(*x*) = @LN(*x* ± @SQRT(*x*^2 − 1))	Inverse hyperbolic cosine of x (double valued)
ATANH(*x*) = 0.5*@LN((1 + *x*)/(1 − *x*))	Inverse hyperbolic tangent of x

Table 1.4: Table of formulas to calculate trigonometric functions not available in 1-2-3

Hyperbolic Functions

1-2-3 does not provide any hyperbolic functions, but these can also be calculated from their definitions. The hyperbolic functions can be defined using the exponential function and the natural logarithm function, both of which are available in Lotus 1-2-3. These functions are listed in Table 1.4.

Exponential and Logarithmic Functions

The exponential and logarithmic functions @EXP(*x*), @LN(*x*), and @EXP(1) calculate the exponential, logarithm, and base *e* of the natural logarithms. The exponential function calculates *e* to the power *x*. Theoretically, *x* can take on any value, but if *x* is greater than 230 (but less than 710), @EXP(*x*) will be greater than 10^{99}, and Lotus 1-2-3 will not be able to display the result, though it will be maintained internally and can be used in other calculations. If *x* is equal to or greater than 710, the result will be larger than 10^{308}, and the calculation will overflow, causing a value of ERR to be returned in the cell. The natural logarithm is the inverse of the exponential function (that is, *x* = @LN(@EXP(*x*))) and returns the base *e* logarithm of *x*. The value of *x* must be greater than 0, or the function will return the value ERR. The base *e* of the natural logarithm, which is approximately 2.718282, can be obtained with @EXP(1).

Logical Functions

The logical functions @TRUE and @FALSE return the logical values TRUE and FALSE. These two functions return the values 1 for TRUE and 0 for FALSE. You could just as easily use 1 or 0 in your formulas, but using these functions may make your formulas more readable. The logical IF statement @IF(*test*,*x*,*y*) calculates the value of *test*. If *test* is equal to TRUE, then @IF returns the value of *x*; if *test* is equal to FALSE, then @IF returns the value of *y*. This function actually responds simply to 0 (for FALSE) and not 0 (for TRUE). Therefore, any value of *test* other than 0 will cause the @IF statement to be TRUE and return the value *x*.

Logical Tests

1-2-3 provides four functions that test for particular types of values: @ISERR(*x*), @ISNA(*x*), @ISNUMBER(*x*), and @ISSTRING(*x*). They return TRUE if x is a value of the type for which the function is testing; otherwise they return FALSE. The @ISERR(x) function tests for x = ERR, which is returned by a formula that yields a numerical error, such as a formula that includes dividing by 0 or that contains a reference to another formula that has the value ERR. The @ISNA(x) function tests for the value NA, which stands for *not available*. A cell has the value NA when it contains the function @NA or refers to a cell that contains the value NA. You usually place @NA in cells that you have not yet filled with values, but to which functions already refer. Thus, your functions will not return a value until you replace all of the cells containing @NA. The @ISNUMBER(x) and @ISSTRING(x) functions test for x containing, respectively, a number or string.

Statistical Functions

Two types of statistical functions are available in Lotus 1-2-3: a standard set and a database set. The standard set of statistical functions operates on lists of numbers to calculate their values. The database set operates on values in a field of the records of a database that satisfy a search criterion. Table 1.5 lists these functions.

Standard Statistical Functions

The set of standard statistical functions operates on lists of data. The list input is a comma-delimited list of numbers, cell references, range references, cell names, or range names. B5,B7,B9,B12..B20,2.7,3.5, for example, is a valid list. Normally, the lists you create are not this complicated, but consist of a single range of cell references. You can also include blank cells within a range, and the statistical functions will ignore them. Cells containing labels are usually assumed to have a value of 0.

Database Statistical Functions

Database statistical functions are used to calculate statistics for selected records in a database. A database consists of records (rows) and fields (columns) and is specified with a cell-range reference that contains all of the records. Records are selected by setting up a criterion range that specifies the records wanted. The database statistical functions then operate on the values in the specified column.

STANDARD STATISTICAL FUNCTIONS

Symbol	Description
@COUNT(*list*)	Count the number of cells in *list*
@SUM(*list*)	Add all of the values in *list*
@MAX(*list*)	Find the maximum value in *list*
@MIN(*list*)	Find the minimum value in *list*
@AVG(*list*)	Average the values in *list*
@STD(*list*)	Calculate the standard deviation of the values in *list*
@VAR(*list*)	Calculate the variance of the values in *list*

DATABASE STATISTICAL FUNCTIONS

Symbol	Description
@DCOUNT(*database,offset,criterion*)	Count the number of non-blank cells in column *offset* for the records that meet the *criterion*
@DSUM(*database,offset,criterion*)	Calculate the sum of the values in column *offset* for the records that meet the *criterion*
@DMAX(*database,offset,criterion*)	Find the maximum of the values in column *offset* for the records that meet the *criterion*
@DMIN(*database,offset,criterion*)	Find the minimum of the values in column *offset* for the records that meet the *criterion*
@DAVG(*database,offset,criterion*)	Calculate the average of the

Table 1.5: Standard and database statistical functions

Symbol	Description
	values in column *offset* for the records that meet the *criterion*
@DSTD(*database,offset,criterion*)	Calculate the standard deviation of the values in column *offset* for the records that meet the *criterion*
@DVAR(*database,offset,criterion*)	Calculate the variance of the values in column *offset* for the records that meet the *criterion*

Table 1.5: Standard and database statistical functions *(continued)*

Database statistical functions are useful for preparing tables of statistical data that summarize the data in a database. For example, suppose that you have experimental data on the age of dogs and the duration of some disease. Each record contains a dog's name and age and the duration of the disease. You could set the criterion to select dogs more than 10 years old and then use the @DAVG function to average the duration column to find the average duration of the disease for dogs older than 10. We will look much more closely at how to set up a database and criteria later in this book.

The database statistical functions all have the same argument list: *database, column, criterion*. The *database* argument specifies a range of cells or a named range that contains the database records. The *column* argument specifies the offset from the first column or field of the database to the column that contains the values to be used (0 is the first column, 1 is the second column, and so on). The *criterion* argument specifies the range of cells that contain the criterion to be used in selecting records for analysis.

String Functions

The string functions, in conjunction with the concatenation operator (&), give you the capability to manipulate strings in cells, compare strings, extract substrings, and insert substrings. Many of the functions have the same names and capabilities as their BASIC counterparts. If you are familiar with BASIC, you will recognize many of these functions immediately.

The argument string can consist of a cell reference, a formula, or a literal string enclosed in quotation marks. Character positions are counted from 0 so that the first character is number 0, the second is number 1, and so on. The maximum number of characters in a string is 240. Table 1.6 lists the string functions.

FUNCTIONS THAT MANIPULATE CHARACTER CODES

Symbol	Description
@CHAR(*x*)	Returns the ASCII/LICS character for code *x*
@CODE(*str*)	Returns the ASCII/LICS code of the first character in *str*
@REPEAT(*str,n*)	Returns *str* duplicated *n* times

FUNCTIONS THAT COMPARE, FIND, AND MEASURE STRINGS

Symbol	Description
@EXACT(*str1,str2*)	Compares *str1* and *str2* and returns TRUE (1) if they are exactly the same; otherwise it returns FALSE (0)
@FIND(*sstr,str,n*)	Searches for the first occurrence of *sstr* in *str* after character *n* and returns the position
@LENGTH(*str*)	Returns the number of characters in *str*

FUNCTIONS THAT EXTRACT/REPLACE SUBSTRINGS

Symbol	Description
@LEFT(*str,n*)	Returns the left *n* characters of *str*
@RIGHT(*str,n*)	Returns the right *n* characters of *str*
@MID(*str,n,m*)	Returns *m* characters from *str* starting at character *n*

Table 1.6: String functions

Symbol	Description
@REPLACE(*str1*,*n*,*m*,*str2*)	Returns *str1* with *str2* inserted at *n* after first deleting *m* characters in *str1* starting at *n*
@TRIM(*str*)	Removes leading and trailing spaces and any double spaces

FUNCTIONS THAT CHANGE THE CASE OF CHARACTERS IN A STRING

Symbol	Description
@LOWER(*str*)	Returns *str* with all characters in lowercase
@UPPER(*str*)	Returns *str* with all characters in uppercase
@PROPER(*str*)	Capitalizes the first letter of every word in *str*

FUNCTIONS THAT EXTRACT VALUES IN A RANGE

Symbol	Description
@N(*range*)	Returns the numeric value in the upper-left corner of *range*
@S(*range*)	Returns the string value in the upper-left corner of *range*

FUNCTIONS THAT CONVERT BETWEEN STRINGS AND VALUES

Symbol	Description
@STRING(*x*,*n*)	Changes the value *x* into a string using fixed format with *n* decimal places
@VALUE(*str*)	Returns the value of the number coded in the string *str*

Table 1.6: String functions *(continued)*

Date and Time Functions

Using the date and time functions, you can not only time stamp your work with the current date, but you can also calculate with dates and times. Dates are saved in a spreadsheet as integral days starting with January 1, 1900, and extending through December 31, 2099. Subtracting the day numbers for two different dates gives you the number of days between the two dates. Time of day is stored as a time number, or the decimal fraction of the length of a day (0 is midnight, 0.5 is noon, and so on), which makes it compatible with the day numbers.

Date numbers and time numbers can be added together, and the functions will differentiate their respective parts. Date functions use only the part of the number to the left of the decimal point, and time functions use only the part of the number to the right of the decimal point. The smallest unit of time that can be manipulated with these functions is 1 second. Fractions of a second are not calculated.

If you use the date and time functions to calculate date and time numbers, you can use the Range Format command to make them appear as dates and times rather than numbers. Table 1.7 lists the date and time functions.

Financial Functions

The financial functions include the functions that let you calculate your loan payments or the rate of return on your savings account. They also include functions for figuring depreciation. Most of the formulas perform compound interest calculations. For further information about these functions, refer to one of the many books that discuss business applications of Lotus 1-2-3. Lotus 1-2-3 financial functions are summarized in Appendix A. These functions will not be discussed in this book.

Spreadsheet Functions

The spreadsheet functions are those functions that operate on the cell structure of the spreadsheet. They allow you to get the contents of cells, get cell attributes, measure the size of ranges, perform table lookups, and generate special values. Table 1.8 lists the spreadsheet functions. Table 1.9 lists the attributes of a cell that can be determined with some of these functions.

FUNCTIONS THAT RETURN DATE & TIME NUMBERS

Symbol	Description
@DATE(*yr,mo,da*)	Returns the date number for the indicated year (*yr*), month (*mo*), and day (*da*)
@DATEVALUE(*str*)	Returns the date number of the date coded in the string *str*
@NOW	Returns the date number for the current date and time
@TIME(*hr,min,sec*)	Returns the time number for the given hour (*hr*), minute (*min*), and second (*sec*)
@TIMEVALUE(*str*)	Returns the time value for the time coded in the string *str*

FUNCTIONS THAT INTERPRET DATE & TIME NUMBERS

Symbol	Description
@DAY(*n*)	Returns the day of the month of the date number *n*
@MONTH(*n*)	Returns the month of the year of the date number *n*
@YEAR(*n*)	Returns the year of the date number *n*
@HOUR(*n*)	Returns the hour of the day of the date or time number *n*
@MINUTE(*n*)	Returns the minute of the hour of the date or time number *n*
@SECOND(*n*)	Returns the second of the minute of the date or time number *n*

Table 1.7: Date and time functions

FUNCTION THAT REFERENCES CELLS INDIRECTLY

Symbol	Description
@(*ca*)	Returns the contents (value or label) of the cell whose cell reference is in the cell referenced by *ca*

FUNCTIONS THAT GET CELL ATTRIBUTES

Symbol	Description
@CELL(*att,range*)	Returns the value of the attribute specified by *att* of the upper-left cell in *range*
@CELLPOINTER(*att*)	Returns the value of the attribute specified by *att* of the currently highlighted cell

FUNCTIONS THAT GET THE SIZE OF RANGES

Symbol	Description
@COLS(*range*)	Returns the number of columns in *range*
@ROWS(*range*)	Returns the number of rows in *range*

FUNCTIONS THAT PERFORM TABLE LOOKUP

Symbol	Description
@CHOOSE(*x,v0,v1..vn*)	Returns the *x*th value in the list *v0..vn*
@HLOOKUP(*x,range,r*)	Returns the contents of the cell in row *r* and the column where *x* matches the value in the first row of *range*
@VLOOKUP(*x,range,c*)	Returns the contents of the cell in column *c* and the row where *x* matches the value in the first column of *range*
@INDEX(*range,c,r*)	Returns the contents of the cell at the intersection of row *r* and column *c* in *range*

FUNCTIONS THAT RETURN SPECIAL VALUES

Symbol	Description
@ERR	Returns the value ERR (error)
@NA	Returns the value NA (not available)

Table 1.8: Spreadsheet functions

Attribute	Description
"address"	Returns the cell address
"row"	Returns the row number
"col"	Returns a column number (1 = A, 1 = B, . . .)
"contents"	Returns the cell contents
"type"	Returns the cell type: b — Blank v — Value or formula l — Label
"prefix"	Returns the label prefix: ' — Left aligned " — Right aligned ^ — Centered Blank — Not a label
"protect"	Returns 1 if the cell is protected; otherwise it returns 0
"width"	Returns the column width
"format"	Returns the cell format: F0..F15 — Fixed format, 0 to 15 decimal places S0..S15 — Scientific format, 0 to 15 decimal places C0..C15 — Currency format, 1 to 15 decimal places G — General format D1..D9 — Date/time formats 1 to 9 T — Text format H — Hidden Blank — Cell is empty

Table 1.9: Cell attributes

■ SUMMARY

We have seen that Lotus 1-2-3 is compatible with the mathematics required for scientific and engineering calculations. It offers numeric precision and range comparable to that of mainframes and minicomputers.

It provides mathematical operators and functions comparable to those found in most high-level computer languages used for science and engineering calculations. The numbers in Lotus 1-2-3 have a precision of approximately 15 digits, a visible range of $\pm 9.99 \times 10^{\pm 99}$, and an internal range of approximately $\pm 10^{\pm 308}$. The mathematical functions include all of the expected trigonometric and logarithmic functions, plus statistics functions, string functions, time and date functions, financial functions, and spreadsheet functions. A complete alphabetical list of the 1-2-3 functions is provided in Appendix A.

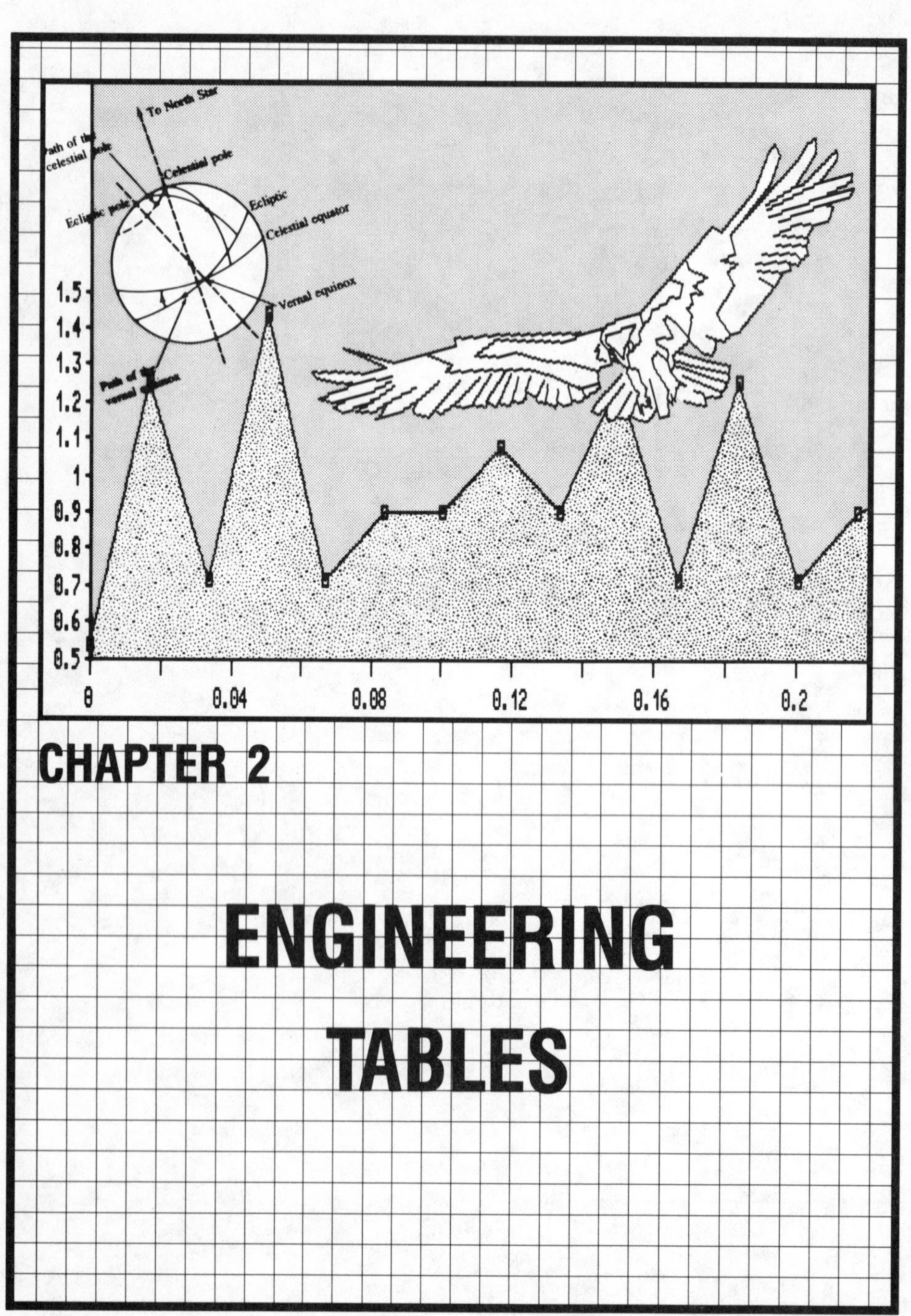

CHAPTER 2

ENGINEERING TABLES

Since you have attained this point in your reading, you must agree that Lotus 1-2-3 has the potential to be an exceptional engineering tool. Now how do you learn to put all of this power to use? Start simple, that's how. In this chapter, we will explore how to calculate values from analytical equations and how to generate engineering tables. As we develop each example, we will slowly expand our repertoire of modeling methods to use more of the power of Lotus 1-2-3.

As scientists and engineers, we frequently must perform a simple numerical task: taking an analytical equation, putting numbers into it, and calculating the result. This task is not difficult, and calculators do it well, so why resort to an expensive spreadsheet? No reason, really. I almost always use my hand calculator to calculate a single simple equation, because I will be finished before the computer even boots its operating system. However, often I want to calculate the equation with more than one set of numbers, or I want to build a table of numbers from the equation. Certainly this can be done with a calculator, but a spreadsheet is just made for problems of this type and can solve them much more quickly, easily, and accurately.

■ CALCULATING A SIMPLE ANALYTICAL EQUATION

Thermal Conductivity of Silicon The temperature dependence of the thermal conductivity of silicon can be described with a simple analytical equation for temperatures between 200 and 700 K:

$$K(T) = \frac{K_0}{(T - T_0)}$$

where $K_0 = 350$ W/cm, and $T_0 = 68$ K. Although I can calculate the value of this equation at room temperature (300 K) with my hand calculator faster than I typed the equation into the draft of this book, recalculating this equation for many temperatures takes a lot more time and is prone to errors. We will use this simple equation to examine the methods for calculating analytical equations.

Calculating a Single Value

Start with a clean spreadsheet. If you have been experimenting and have material on the spreadsheet that you want to erase, type the command /Worksheet Erase Yes (/WEY) and everything will be removed.

If you want to keep the material on the spreadsheet, then make sure that you save it by typing the command /File Save (/FS) before you erase the spreadsheet.

Let's first calculate a single value: the thermal conductivity at room temperature.

1. Move to cell B8 using the four arrow keys—Up, Down, Left, Right—or the Goto key.
2. Type **350/(300-68)**
3. Press Return.

As soon as you press Return, the number 1.508620 will appear in cell B8, which is the result you would expect if you let T equal 300 K in the thermal conductivity equation. You can check this result with your hand calculator (or your slide rule if you can find it).

You can insert other temperatures into this formula by moving the cursor to cell B8, pressing Edit, and using the editing keys (Left, Right, Backspace, Delete, Insert, and so on) to change the temperature value. When you press Return, the formula will be recalculated using the new temperature value.

This method of changing the temperature is a bit cumbersome, so let's pull the temperature out of the formula, place it in an adjacent cell, and then reference it in the formula using a cell reference.

4. Move to cell B8 and press the Edit key.
5. Replace the 300 in the formula with the cell reference **A8** and press Return.

The formula in cell B8 should now be 350/(A8-68).

6. Move to cell A8.
7. Type **300** and press Return.

As expected, B8 again has 1.508620 in it. Changing the temperature is now simple. Whatever temperature you type into A8 will be inserted into the formula in B8, and the formula will be recalculated. Using cell references instead of values in a formula is much easier than editing the formula every time you want to change values. This approach is the key to building engineering tables with Lotus 1-2-3.

Calculating a List of Values

Suppose that you want to calculate this formula every 50 degrees between 200 and 700 K. You could enter the list of temperature values in cell A8 and then write down the results of each calculation, but working with lists of data is what Lotus 1-2-3 does best.

First you need to create the list of temperatures to be inserted in the thermal conductivity formula.

8. Position the cursor in cell A8 and type the command /Data Fill (**/DF**). You will be prompted for the fill range.
9. Enter a fill range of A8..A18 either by typing the starting and ending cell references separated with a period or by highlighting the fill range.

Highlight the fill range by moving the cursor to cell A8 (if it is not already there), type a period, and then move the cursor to cell A18. If you make a mistake, press Esc to back up to a previous state. Each time you press Esc, you will back up one more level until you are in the ready mode again. This procedure will work for most commands.

10. Press Return. You will be prompted for the start number.
11. Type **200** and press Return. You will be prompted for the step.
12. Type **50** and press Return. You will be prompted for the upper limit.
13. Press Return again to accept the default upper limit.

The cells will be filled with a set of numbers ranging from 200 to 700 in steps of 50 (see cells A8 to A18 in Figure 2.1). Now you need to copy the formula in cell B8 into the cells adjacent to the temperature data.

14. Move the cursor to cell B8 and type the command /Copy (**/C**). You will be prompted for the *from* range.
15. Press Return to accept the range B8..B8. You will be prompted for the *to* range.
16. Select cells B9 to B18 as the *to* range in the same manner as you did for the /Data Fill command.
17. Press Return.

The formula is copied from cell B8 into the range of cells B9..B18, and then each formula is evaluated. If you look at the contents of cells B8..B18, you will see that the relative cell reference that you used for the temperature always adjusts itself to point to the cell immediately to the left of the cell containing the formula. Your spreadsheet should now look like Figure 2.1.

Making Coefficients Available

Suppose that you want to change the coefficients in the formula to see what happens to the thermal conductivity. You could change the values in cell B8 and then copy the new formula into the rest of the cells (copying into a cell that already has data causes the old data to be replaced by the new data). This would again be cumbersome if you want to try several different values for the coefficients. As before, a better way is to remove the coefficients from the formula and replace them with cell references.

18. In cell B8, type **$B$3/(A8-$B$4)** and press Return.
19. In cell B3, type **350** and press Return.
20. In cell B4, type **68** and press Return.

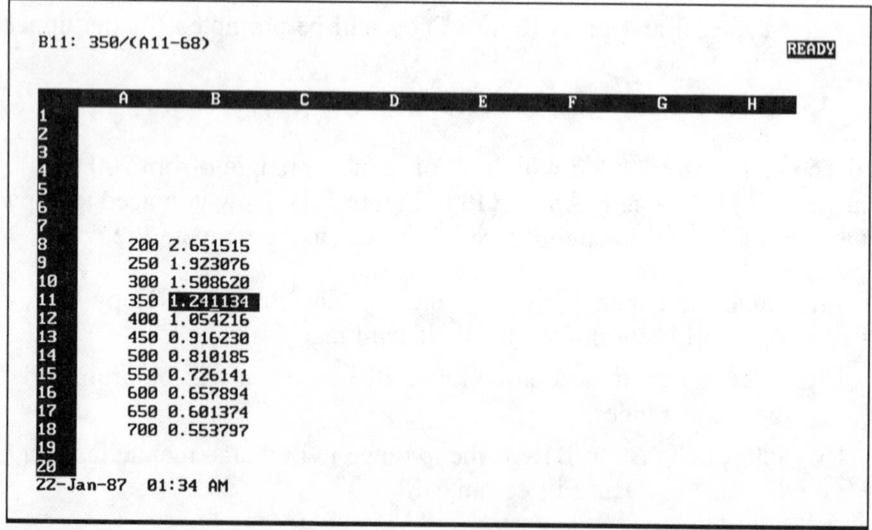

Figure 2.1: Thermal conductivity of silicon—a simple equation applied to a list of data

Note that the cell references for the coefficients are absolute cell references, so that now you can copy the formula into cells B9..B18, and the cell references will not be adjusted but will still point to the coefficients in cells B3 and B4.

21. Copy the contents of cell B8 into B9..B18, as before.

The spreadsheet should now look like Figure 2.2. You can change the values of K_0 and T_0 by changing the values of cells B3 and B4. The change will then be applied to all of the formulas in cells B8 through B18.

Dressing Up the Spreadsheet

To anyone but us, Figure 2.2 will be meaningless, and even we will have no idea what it is about in a month or two. What you need to do is dress up the spreadsheet a little with some titles so that anyone (including us) will know what is being calculated.

From now on, I will assume that you know that the Return key or one of the arrow keys must be pressed to enter a value into a cell or to complete a command. I will indicate Return key presses only when they are not obvious.

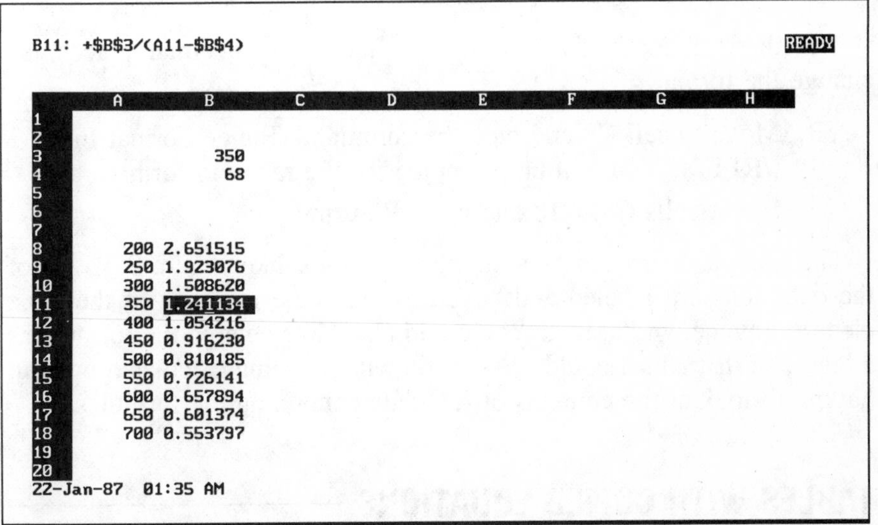

Figure 2.2: Thermal conductivity of silicon—a simple equation applied to a list of data with the coefficients of the equation pulled out

22. In cell A1, type the title **Thermal Conductivity of Silicon**

Label the coefficients with right-justified labels, using the right-justification prefix character (").

23. In cell A3, type **"K0**
24. In cell A4, type **"T0**

Draw some limit lines to make the table more readable.

25. Move to cell B4 and type the command /Worksheet Insert Column (/**WIC**) to place a blank column between the two columns of data.
26. Move to cell B4 and type the command /Worksheet Column Set-width 1 (/**WCS1**) to make the column one cell wide.
27. In cell A7, type \- to create a line of minus signs.
28. Copy the contents of cell A7 into cell C7.
29. In cell B6, type '¦
30. Copy the contents of cell B6 into cells B7..B18.

Label the columns of data.

31. In cell A6, type **" T (K)**
32. In cell C6, type **'K (W/cm-K)**

The thermal conductivity value has too many decimal places, so change the format.

33. Move to cell C8 and type the command /Range Format Fixed 2 (/**RFF2**). You will be prompted for the range to format.
34. Select cells C8..C18 and press Return.

The completed spreadsheet should now look like Figure 2.3. All of the data cells are labeled and boxed to make the meaning of the table clear to anyone who uses it. You could also have entered the formula as a label, so that a user could see exactly what is being calculated without having to look at the contents of the cells containing the formulas.

■ TABLES WITH COPIED EQUATIONS

In the last section, we created an engineering table of the thermal conductivity values for silicon. Creating tables of values like this is

```
A1: 'Thermal Conductivity of Silicon                              READY

    A    B    C         D         E         F         G         H
1   Thermal Conductivity of Silicon
2
3         K0         350
4         T0          68
5
6      T(K)   |K (W/cm-K)
7  -----------|----------
8       200   |   2.65
9       250   |   1.92
10      300   |   1.51
11      350   |   1.24
12      400   |   1.05
13      450   |   0.92
14      500   |   0.81
15      550   |   0.73
16      600   |   0.66
17      650   |   0.60
18      700   |   0.55
19
20
22-Jan-87  01:32 AM
```

Figure 2.3: Thermal conductivity of silicon—the completed spreadsheet for a simple equation

probably the second most common task of a scientist or engineer after calculating individual values of a function. Functions can be as simple as the one just described, or they can be much more complicated. In the following sections, we examine how to generate tables of this type in more detail and how to create one- and two-input tables using the /Data Table command.

The table in Figure 2.3 was made by copying the relevant formulas into the cells where the calculations were needed. This is probably the most versatile way of creating tables of values on a spreadsheet. The following sections show several engineering tables generated with this methodology.

Single-Input Tables

Precession of the North Celestial Pole Astronomy uses two common frames of reference for locating the positions of celestial objects: the equatorial system and the ecliptic system. The equatorial system is based on the orientation and rotation axis of the earth. Imagine taking a world globe with latitude and longitude lines on it, but no continents, with the same orientation as the earth. If you expand the size of that globe to infinity, you will have the celestial sphere, overlaid with the equatorial reference system. The plane of the earth's equator is also the plane of the reference system's equator and is known as the celestial equator. If you extended the axis of the earth through the north and south poles and out to the celestial sphere, its ends would form the celestial poles. The north celestial pole is near the North Star, which for centuries has been used for navigation (see Figure 2.4).

Specification of the location of a star (point *P* in Figure 2.4) in the equatorial system is much the same as specification of latitude and longitude on the earth's surface. Similar to latitude, the declination of a celestial object is the angular measure of that object's position north or south of the celestial equator (the angle from *B* to *P* in Figure 2.4). The equator is at 0 degrees, and the north and south celestial poles are at 90 degrees north or south declination. The second coordinate is similar to longitude and is known as the right ascension. The right ascension is measured in hours, minutes, and seconds from the vernal equinox (point *A* in Figure 2.4, a point in the constellation Aries) eastward to the meridian passing through the star (the angle from *A* to *B* in Figure 2.4).

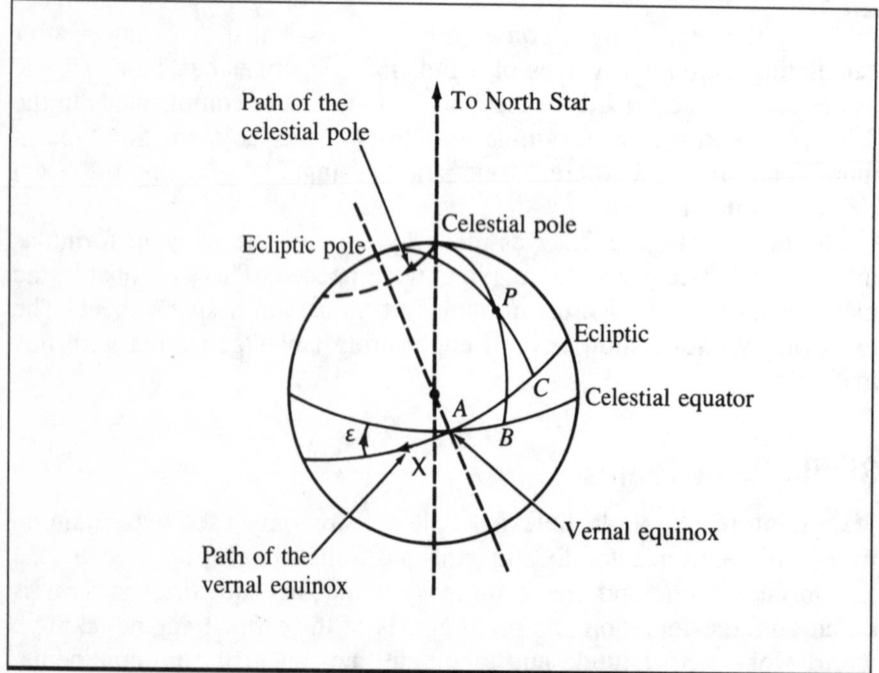

Figure 2.4: Orientation of the equatorial and ecliptic coordinate systems and the motion of the equatorial system due to precession of the earth's rotational axis

The meridian is a line from the celestial equator to the celestial pole, much like a longitude line on the earth's surface.

The second system of measurement is the ecliptic system. It is similar to the equatorial system, but it uses the plane of the earth's orbit around the sun as its basis rather than the plane of the earth's equator. If the earth's orbit is expanded to the celestial sphere, it forms a great circle among the stars known as the ecliptic. Ninety degrees above and below the ecliptic are the ecliptic poles. Measurement is in ecliptic longitude and ecliptic latitude (angles A to C and C to P respectively in Figure 2.4), which is again similar to latitude and longitude on the earth's surface, but oriented to the ecliptic rather than the equator.

The great circles that are the ecliptic and the celestial equator intersect at the vernal and autumnal equinoxes at an angle of about $23\frac{1}{2}$ degrees. This is the well-known $23\frac{1}{2}$-degree tilt of the earth with respect to the plane of its orbit and is known as the obliquity of the ecliptic.

Both of these systems are useful for different branches of astronomy; the equatorial system is useful for earth-based observational astronomy, and the ecliptic system is useful for sun-based celestial mechanics calculations. Both systems are equally relevant, being related by a simple $23\frac{1}{2}$-degree rotation of coordinate systems. Unfortunately, nature is not so simple. The relationship between these two systems is not static but variable.

The action of the sun and moon cause the rotation of the earth to wobble, like a spinning top when you give it a push sideways. This wobble is known as precession, and it causes the north pole, and hence the north celestial pole, to move in a small circle with a radius of $23\frac{1}{2}$ degrees about the north ecliptic pole. Although the plane of the ecliptic does not change, the location of the vernal equinox, which is the origin of the right ascension and the ecliptic longitude, does.

If that was not enough, the action of the planets causes precession in the ecliptic, which makes the ecliptic pole move as well. Now, if you are not an astronomer, you might think that these are really atrocious coordinate systems, wobbling around the universe as they do. But the period of this movement is about 26,000 years, which makes the movement tolerable. The following two equations calculate the annual change in the ecliptic longitude (X) and the value of the obliquity of the ecliptic (ϵ).

$$X = 50.2564'' + 0.00222''t \text{ per year}$$

$$\epsilon = 23°27'8.26'' - 0.4684''t$$

Here, *t* is the number of years since 1900. Although these changes do not cause large variations in a star's coordinates, they must be accounted for by any earth-based observatories that are fixed to this wobbly coordinate system. What you will now do is create a table of the annual change in the ecliptic longitude and the obliquity of the ecliptic every 10 years from 1900 to 2000.

1. Change the widths of columns A through J according to the following list: A = **4**, B = **6**, C = **1**, D = **11**, E = **15**, F = **4**, G = **3**, H = **1**, I = **9**, J = **2**, K = **9**
2. In cell A1, type **Precession of the North Pole**
3. In cell F1, type **For t in years after 1900**
4. In cell B3, type **Annual Precession in Longitude**
5. In cell F3, type **Obliquity of the Ecliptic**

In this example, you will type the equations as text, so that anyone reading the spreadsheet can tell what is being calculated. However, the coefficients of the equations in the text representations will be the actual values referenced in the cell formulas.

6. In cell B4, type **"X**
7. In cell C4, type **=**
8. In cell D4, type **50.2564**

The single quotation mark in cell E4 makes this a left-justified label, and the double quotation mark is the abbreviation for seconds applied to the number in cell D4. See also cells H4, J4, E5, J5, E10, H10, and J10.

9. In cell E4, type **'"** (10 spaces) **e =**
10. In cell F4, type **23°**

The degree symbol (°) is part of the DOS extended character set. On most computers, you access these characters by holding down the Alt key and typing the ASCII code number (248 in this case). Some computers require holding down Shift and Alt while typing the number. See the DOS manual for your particular computer if these methods do not work, or substitute some text for the symbol.

11. In cell G4, type **27**
12. In cell H4, type **"**
13. In cell I4, type **8.26**

14. In cell J4, type '''
15. In cell C5, type ' **+**
16. In cell D5, type **0.000222**
17. In cell E5, type ''' ***t**
18. In cell I5, type **-0.4684**
19. In cell J5, type '''
20. In cell K5, type **'*t**

Now let's enter the table headings and some lines to separate them from the data.

21. In cell B9, type \-
22. Copy the contents of cell B9 into cells C9..J9.
23. In cell C7, type '¦
24. Copy the contents of cell C7 into cells C8..C20.
25. In cell B8, type **"Date**
26. In cell D6, type ' (3 spaces) **Annual**
27. In cell D7, type **Precession in**
28. In cell D8, type ' (2 spaces) **Longitude**
29. In cell F7, type ' (2 spaces) **Obliquity of**
30. In cell F8, type ' (2 spaces) **the Ecliptic**

Enter the values of the dates to be calculated.

31. Move to cell B10 and type the command /Data Fill (**/DF**).
32. Select cells B10..B20 as the fill range.
33. Set the start value to **1900**, set the step to **10**, and accept the default ending value.

Enter the formula for the annual precession in longitude.

34. In cell D10, type **+$D$4+$D$5*(B10-1900)**
35. In cell E10, type '''

Enter the formula for the obliquity of the ecliptic. The value of the number of degrees does not change significantly over this short amount of time, so simply reference the value.

36. In cell F10, type **+ $F$4**

The number of minutes will change, so calculate the number of seconds, then divide by 60 and use the integer part as the number of minutes. The number is decreasing, so add 60 to the number of seconds and then subtract 1 from the number of minutes to eliminate negative values.

37. In cell G10, type **($G$4-1)+@INT(($I$4+$I$5*(B10-1900) +60)/60)**
38. In cell H10, type "

Calculate the number of seconds and then use the @MOD function to map them back to the range 0 to 60, since seconds in excess of 60 have been carried over into the minutes column.

39. In cell I10, type **@MOD($I$4+$I$5*(B10-1900)+60,60)**
40. In cell J10, type "'
41. Copy the values in cells D10..J10 into cells D11..J20.

Change the format of some of the cells to align them and give the correct number of decimal places.

42. Type the command /Range Format Fixed 4 (**/RFF4**) and then select cells I4..I5 to change the format of cells I4 and I5 to fixed with four decimal places.
43. Change the format of cells I10..I20 to Fixed 4 (**/RFF4**).
44. Change the format of cells D10..D20 to Fixed 4 (**/RFF4**).
45. Change the format of cells G10..G20 to Fixed 0 (**/RFF0**).

The spreadsheet should now look like the one in Figure 2.5.

Temperature Dependence of the Intrinsic Carrier Density The intrinsic carrier density of silicon is the density of electrons or holes in intrinsic silicon at equilibrium. This value is an important parameter for the modeling of silicon solid-state devices. Intrinsic silicon is defined as silicon in which the electron density equals the hole density at equilibrium. This situation is satisfied in extremely pure silicon at room temperature or in less pure silicon at higher temperatures. Holes are places in the electronic structure of silicon where an electron could be but is not. A hole can be treated as if it were an electron with a positive charge.

```
A1: [W4] 'Precession of the North Pole                                    READY

   A    B   C       D              E          F   G  H     I    J        K
1  Precession of the North Pole              For t in years after 1900
2
3        Annual Precession in Longitude      Obliquity of the Ecliptic
4          X  =      50.2564 "           e = 23° 27 '   8.2600 "
5             +   0.000222 " *t                        -0.4684 " *t
6                    Annual
7                  |Precession in              Obliquity of
8         Date  |  Longitude                  the Ecliptic
9         ------|--------------------------------------------
10        1900  |    50.2564 "               23° 27 '   8.2600 "
11        1910  |    50.2586 "               23° 27 '   3.5760 "
12        1920  |    50.2608 "               23° 26 '  58.8920 "
13        1930  |    50.2631 "               23° 26 '  54.2080 "
14        1940  |    50.2653 "               23° 26 '  49.5240 "
15        1950  |    50.2675 "               23° 26 '  44.8400 "
16        1960  |    50.2697 "               23° 26 '  40.1560 "
17        1970  |    50.2719 "               23° 26 '  35.4720 "
18        1980  |    50.2742 "               23° 26 '  30.7880 "
19        1990  |    50.2764 "               23° 26 '  26.1040 "
20        2000  |    50.2786 "               23° 26 '  21.4200 "
22-Jan-87  01:36 AM
```

Figure 2.5: Annual precession of the celestial longitude and the obliquity of the ecliptic between the years 1900 and 2000

The intrinsic carrier density (n_i) is defined with the following equation:

$$n_i = \left(4M_c\left(\frac{2\pi m_0 K}{h^2}\right)^3\right)^{1/2}\left(\frac{m_e^* m_h^*}{m_0^2}\right)^{3/4} T^{3/2} e^{-E_g/2kT}$$

The coefficients have the following values:

$M_c = 6$	The number of equivalent electron valleys in silicon
$m_0 = 0.91095 \times 10^{-30}$ kg	Electron rest mass
$k = 1.38066 \times 10^{-23}$ J/kg	Boltzmann's constant
$h = 6.62618 \times 10^{-34}$ J-s	Planck's constant
$m_e{}^* = 0.33\ m_0$	Electron effective mass
$m_h{}^* = 0.56\ m_0$	Hole effective mass

E_g is the value of the energy gap in silicon. The following equation has been fit to the experimental data for the energy gap versus temperature:

$$E_g = \left(EG0 - \frac{EG1 \cdot T^2}{T + EG2}\right)q$$

The coefficients have the following values:

$EG0 = 1.17$ eV
$EG1 = 4.73 \times 10^{-4}$ eV/K
$EG2 = 636$ K
$q = 1.60219 \times 10^{-19}$ coulombs Electron charge

You could algebraically insert the equation for the energy gap into the equation for the intrinsic carrier density. This would give you a single complicated equation for the intrinsic carrier density. It is simpler, and just as valid, to calculate the value of the energy gap separately and then insert that value into the equation for the intrinsic carrier density.

One of the first features of the intrinsic carrier density equation you may notice are the numerous constants that precede the temperature coefficients. Calculating these constants every time you use the equation will slow down the spreadsheet calculation. To make the spreadsheet more efficient, combine all of the constants into a single value and then reference that value whenever you write a formula for that equation. Name the constants to make them more readable.

1. Change the widths of columns A through F according to the following list: A = **9**, B = **9**, C = **1**, D = **9**, E = **1**, F = **12**
2. In cell A1, type **Intrinsic Carrier Density in Silicon**
3. In cell A3, type **"EG0**
4. In cell A4, type **"EG1**
5. In cell A5, type **"EG2**
6. In cell D3, type **"cons**
7. In cell B3, type **1.17**
8. In cell B4, type **4.73E-4**
9. In cell B5, type **636**

Calculate the coefficient of the intrinsic carrier density equation and change the units from 1/(m³-K) to 1/(cm³-K).

10. In cell F3, type **@SQRT(4*6*(2*@PI*0.91095E-30 *1.38066E-23/(6.62618E-34)^2)^3)*(0.33*0.56)^(.75)*1.0E-6**

Name the cells so that you can use the names in the formulas.

11. Execute the command /Range Name Labels Right (/**RNLR**) and select the labels in cells A3..A5. The names in these cells will be given to the values in the cells to the right of them.

12. The name in cell D3 is not adjacent to cell F3, where the value is, so place the cursor on cell F3 and execute the command /Range Name Create (/**RNC**). Type the name **CONS** and the cell reference **F3**.

Enter the titles and lines.

13. In cell B7, type ^**T (K)**
14. In cell D7, type **' Eg (eV)**
15. In cell F7, type ' (3 spaces) **ni (cm^-3)**
16. In cell B8, type \-
17. Copy the contents of cell B8 into cells C8..F8.
18. In cell C7, type ' ¦
19. Copy the contents of cell C7 into cells C8, C9, and E7..E9.

Enter the temperature data.

20. Type the command /Data Fill (/**DF**) and select the range B9..B19; then type **300** as the starting value and **50** as the step.

Enter the energy gap equation. Note that you do not enter the range names for EG1 and EG2 since these are valid cell references. If you were to enter them in the equation, the values in cells EG1 and EG2 would be used instead of the values in cells B4 and B5 that you named *EG1* and *EG2*. When you press return, the cell references will be replaced with the correct range names. Be careful when you do this so that the values that you want in a cell are the ones that actually get inserted.

21. In cell D9, type **+$EG0-$B$4*B9^2/(B9+$B$5)**

Enter the formula for the intrinsic carrier equation, using the values of the temperature and the energy gap.

22. In cell F9, type **+$CONS*(@SQRT(B9)^3)*@EXP (-D9*1.60219E-19/(2*1.38066E-23*B9))**
23. Copy the contents of cells C9..F9 into cells C10..F19.
24. Set the format of cells D9..D19 to Fixed 2 (/**RFF2**).
25. Set the format of cells F9..F19 to Scientific 2 (/**RFS2**).

The spreadsheet should now look like that in Figure 2.6.

```
A1: [W9] 'Intrinsic Carrier Density in Silicon                              READY

     A        B  C  D  E     F            G          H          I
1   Intrinsic Carrier Density in Silicon
2
3        EG0      1.17       cons    3.3341E+15
4        EG1 0.000473
5        EG2       636
6
7             T (K)  | Eg (eV)  |    ni (cm^-3)
8         -----------|----------|------------
9               300  |     1.12 |    6.21E+09
10              350  |     1.11 |    2.18E+11
11              400  |     1.10 |    3.28E+12
12              450  |     1.08 |    2.79E+13
13              500  |     1.07 |    1.58E+14
14              550  |     1.05 |    6.70E+14
15              600  |     1.03 |    2.26E+15
16              650  |     1.01 |    6.44E+15
17              700  |     1.00 |    1.60E+16
18              750  |     0.98 |    3.54E+16
19              800  |     0.96 |    7.18E+16
20
22-Jan-87  01:42 AM
```

Figure 2.6: Intrinsic carrier density in silicon

Hyperbolic Functions In Chapter 1, you saw how to calculate the hyperbolic functions using the available exponential and logarithmic functions. In this next example, you will use those equations to calculate the values of the hyperbolic functions for several different arguments. You will also calculate the inverse hyperbolic functions to see if we get the original argument back.

1. Change the widths of columns A through P according to the following list: A = **7**, B = **1**, C = **9**, D = **1**, E = **7**, F = **1**, G = **9**, H = **1**, I = **8**, J = **1**, K = **8**, L = **1**, M = **9**, N = **1**, O = **7**, P = **1**
2. In cell A1, type **Hyperbolic Functions**
3. In cell A3, type **^x**
4. In cell A4, type **\-**
5. Copy the contents of cell A4 into cells B4..P4.
6. In cell B3, type **I**
7. Copy the contents of cell B3 into cells B4, B5, F3..F5, L3..L5, P3..P5.
8. In cell C3, type **^SINH(x)**
9. In cell E3, type **^ASINH**
10. In cell G3, type **^COSH(x)**

The arc hyperbolic cosine is double valued, so calculate both values.

11. In cell I3, type **^ACOSH+**
12. In cell K3, type **^ACOSH-**
13. In cell M3, type **^TANH(x)**
14. In cell O3, type **^ATANH**
15. In cells A5..A19, type the following values: **−5, −4, −3, −2, −1, −0.5, −0.1, 0, 0.1, 0.5, 1, 2, 3, 4, 5**
16. In cell C5, type **0.5*(@EXP(A5)-@EXP(-A5))**
17. In cell E5, type **@LN(C5+@SQRT(C5^2+1))**
18. In cell G5, type **0.5*(@EXP(A5)+@EXP(-A5))**
19. In cell I5, type **@LN(G5+@SQRT(G5^2-1))**
20. In cell K5, type **@LN(G5-@SQRT(G5^2-1))**
21. In cell M5, type **+C5/G5**
22. In cell O5, type **0.5*@LN((1+M5)/(1-M5))**
23. Copy the contents of cells B5..P5 into cells B6..P19.
24. Format cells A5..A19, C5..C19, E5..E19, G5..G19, I5..I19, K5..K19, and O5..O19 as Fixed 2 (/**RFF2**).
25. Format cells M5..M19 as Fixed 4 (/**RFF4**).

Your spreadsheet should now look like that in Figure 2.7. Note that the inverse hyperbolic functions do return the original arguments. The inverse hyperbolic cosine is double valued and returns plus and minus the original arguments. For the arguments ±5, the format of the hyperbolic tangent has too few decimal places to accurately display the number. However, Lotus 1-2-3 maintains the number internally, so the inverse function that uses it gives the correct value.

Two-Input Tables

The previous examples all have one independent variable (the input) and one or more dependent variables (the output or result of the equation). Often equations have two or more input variables, which must be handled separately. There are two ways to handle equations with two input variables. One is to put the input variables in parallel columns. The other is to use a square array with one variable in a column on the left side and the other in a row along the top. In the next two examples, we will examine both methods.

A1: [W7] 'Hyperbolic Functions READY

1 Hyperbolic Functions

	x	SINH(x)	ASINH	COSH(x)	ACOSH+	ACOSH-	TANH(x)	ATANH
5	-5.00	-74.20	-5.00	74.21	5.00	-5.00	-0.9999	-5.00
6	-4.00	-27.29	-4.00	27.31	4.00	-4.00	-0.9993	-4.00
7	-3.00	-10.02	-3.00	10.07	3.00	-3.00	-0.9951	-3.00
8	-2.00	-3.63	-2.00	3.76	2.00	-2.00	-0.9640	-2.00
9	-1.00	-1.18	-1.00	1.54	1.00	-1.00	-0.7616	-1.00
10	-0.50	-0.52	-0.50	1.13	0.50	-0.50	-0.4621	-0.50
11	-0.10	-0.10	-0.10	1.01	0.10	-0.10	-0.0997	-0.10
12	0.00	0.00	0.00	1.00	0.00	0.00	0.0000	0.00
13	0.10	0.10	0.10	1.01	0.10	-0.10	0.0997	0.10
14	0.50	0.52	0.50	1.13	0.50	-0.50	0.4621	0.50
15	1.00	1.18	1.00	1.54	1.00	-1.00	0.7616	1.00
16	2.00	3.63	2.00	3.76	2.00	-2.00	0.9640	2.00
17	3.00	10.02	3.00	10.07	3.00	-3.00	0.9951	3.00
18	4.00	27.29	4.00	27.31	4.00	-4.00	0.9993	4.00
19	5.00	74.20	5.00	74.21	5.00	-5.00	0.9999	5.00

24-Jan-87 01:55 PM

Figure 2.7: Hyperbolic and inverse hyperbolic functions

Van der Waals Equation of State You may remember this problem from freshman physics. The van der Waals equation of state is a modification of the ideal gas law. The ideal gas law shows the relationship of the pressure (p), volume (V), and temperature (T) of an ideal gas. This law is relatively accurate for most gases at low densities, but not at higher densities. It is stated as follows:

$$pV = \mu RT$$

where μ is the number of moles of gas, and R is the universal gas constant. To develop this equation, the volume of the individual gas molecules and the range of the intermolecular forces were ignored. This equation works well for low-density gases, but it becomes less and less accurate as density increases. In a real gas, molecules have a definite volume, and the intermolecular forces are not localized to the volume of the molecules.

In an attempt to better model the behavior of a real gas, J. D. van der Waals modified the ideal gas law to account for these facts. His modified equation of state takes the following form:

$$\left(p + \frac{a}{v^2}\right)(v - b) = RT$$

where v is the volume per mole (V/μ), and a and b are constants derived from experiments. For carbon dioxide gas, the constants have these values:

a = 3.59 l^2-atm/mole^2
b = 0.0427 l/mole

This equation has three variables, any one of which could be solved for in terms of the other two. In this next example, you calculate the pressure for different volume and temperature values.

1. Change the widths of columns A through F according to the following list: A = **9**, B = **1**, C = **12**, D = **1**, E = **9**, F = **1**
2. In cell A1, type **Van der Waals Equation of State**
3. In cell A3, type **"a =**
4. In cell C3, type **3.59**
5. In cell E3, type **l^2atm/mole^2**
6. Give cell C3 the name **A**.
7. In cell A4, type **"b =**
8. In cell C4, type **0.0427**
9. In cell E4, type **l/mole**
10. Give cell C4 the name **B**.
11. In cell A6, type **^T (K)**
12. In cell B6, type **:**
13. In cell C6, type **^v (l/mole)**
14. In cell D6, type **' ¦**
15. In cell E6, type **^P (atm)**
16. In cell F6, type **' ¦**
17. Copy the contents of cell B6 into cells B7..B33.
18. Copy the contents of cell D6 into cells D7..D33.
19. Copy the contents of cell F6 into cells F7..F33.
20. In cell A7, type **\ =**
21. Copy the contents of cell A7 into cells B7..F7.
22. In cell A8, type **264**
23. Copy the contents of cell A8 into cells A9..A15.

24. Move to cell C8 and type the command /Data Fill (/**DF**). Select the range C8..C15 and enter a start value of **0.05** and a step value of **0.05**.

Enter the van der Waals equation, solved for the pressure value. Convert the universal gas constant from J/mole-K to l-atm/mole-K with the factor 101.3.

25. In cell E8, type **(8.3143/101.3)*A8/(C8-$B)-$A/(C8^2)**
26. Copy the contents of cell E8 into cells E9..E33.
27. In cell A16, type **\=**
28. Copy the contents of cell A16 into cells B16..F16.
29. In cell A17, type **304**
30. Copy the contents of cell A17 into cells A18..A24.
31. Copy the contents of cells C8..C15 into cells C17..C24.
32. In cell A25, type **\=**
33. Copy the contents of cell A25 into cells B25..F25.
34. Copy the contents of cells C8..C15 into cells C26..C33.
35. In cell A26, type **344**.
36. Copy the contents of cell A26 into cells A27..A33.
37. In cell A34, type **\=**
38. Copy the contents of cell A34 into cells B34..F34.
39. Change the format of cells C8..C33 to Fixed 2 (/**RFF2**).
40. Change the format of cells E8..E33 to Fixed 1 (/**RFF1**).

The spreadsheet should now look like Figure 2.8. Note that for many values of the different variables, this spreadsheet could get quite long and difficult to understand. A more efficient way to set up two-input tables is to have one variable in a column and the second variable in a row. The next example will show that type of setup.

Absolute Magnitude of a Star In astronomy, the apparent brightness of a star is measured in magnitudes. This system of measurement was first used by Hipparchus, an early Middle Eastern astronomer. He called the brightest stars in the sky *first magnitude* and the dimmest visible ones *sixth magnitude*. Differences in magnitude were determined by the difference in brightness a person could discern between two stars. Since

```
A1: 'Van der Waals Equation of State                                 READY

         A    B      C        D      E      F   G     H    I     J     K    L    M
1   Van der Waals Equation of State
2
3        a =         3.59   l^2atm/mole^2
4        b =       0.0427   l/mole
5
6     T (K)   : v (l/mole) | P (atm) |
7   ===============================
8        264 :         0.05 |   1532.2 |
9        264 :         0.10 |     19.2 |
10       264 :         0.15 |     42.4 |
11       264 :         0.20 |     48.0 |
12       264 :         0.25 |     47.1 |
13       264 :         0.30 |     44.3 |
14       264 :         0.35 |     41.2 |
15       264 :         0.40 |     38.2 |
16  ===============================
17       304 :         0.05 |   1982.0 |
18       304 :         0.10 |     76.4 |
19       304 :         0.15 |     73.0 |
20       304 :         0.20 |     68.9 |
01-Jan-80   12:56 AM
```

Figure 2.8: Van der Waals equation of state

```
A21: 304                                                             READY

         A    B      C        D      E      F   G     H    I     J     K    L    M
21       304 :         0.25 |     62.9 |
22       304 :         0.30 |     57.1 |
23       304 :         0.35 |     51.9 |
24       304 :         0.40 |     47.4 |
25  ===============================
26       344 :         0.05 |   2431.7 |
27       344 :         0.10 |    133.7 |
28       344 :         0.15 |    103.6 |
29       344 :         0.20 |     89.7 |
30       344 :         0.25 |     78.8 |
31       344 :         0.30 |     69.8 |
32       344 :         0.35 |     62.6 |
33       344 :         0.40 |     56.6 |
34  ===============================
35
36
37
38
39
40
01-Jan-80   12:58 AM
```

Figure 2.8: Van der Waals equation of state *(continued)*

that time, the magnitude scale has been formalized mathematically for more precise measurement. Currently, a difference in magnitude of 5 is equal to a difference in brightness of 100. This leads to a simple formula for the relative magnitude of any two stars based on their measurable difference in brightness:

$$(m_2 - m_1) = \frac{1}{0.4} \operatorname{Log}\left(\frac{b_1}{b_2}\right)$$

where m_1 and m_2 are the magnitudes of the two stars, and b_1 and b_2 are the brightness values for the two stars. With at least one star as a standard, the magnitude of any other star can be calculated from its brightness relative to the standard.

The magnitude of objects visible from the earth ranges from −26.7 for the sun to +23 for the dimmest object discernable in the 200-inch Hale telescope. Two of the brightest stars are Sirius, with a magnitude of −1.58, and Vega, with a magnitude of +0.14. After astronomers agreed on a zero point for the magnitude system, they found that some stars were brighter. Thus, the sun as well as some of the brighter stars have a negative magnitude.

What we have discussed thus far is the apparent magnitude of a star: the brightness of a star as we see it from the earth's surface. This apparent brightness depends on the actual brightness of the star and the distance of the star from the earth. Apparent magnitude does not tell us much about a star's characteristics, nor does it allow us to make meaningful comparisons between stars. To remedy this, astronomers have defined the absolute magnitude; the magnitude that a star would have if it were 10 parsecs (192 trillion miles) from earth. Using absolute magnitudes, the brightness of different stars can be compared. The relationship between apparent magnitude and absolute magnitude is

$$M = m + 5 - 5 \operatorname{Log}(r)$$

where M is the absolute magnitude, m is the apparent magnitude, and r is the distance to the star in parsecs. In 1913, Hertzsprung in Germany and Russell in the United States compared the absolute magnitude with the spectral class (essentially the color) of stars and came up with a nearly linear relationship. The now classic Hertzsprung-Russell diagram allows astronomers to determine the absolute magnitude of a star from its spectral class. Knowing the absolute magnitude and the apparent magnitude, you can use the preceding equation to calculate the distance to a star.

In this example, you will create a table of distances, based on the absolute and relative magnitudes of a star. First, you must solve the preceding equation for the distance value.

$$r = 10\left(\frac{5 + m - M}{5}\right)$$

Create a two-input table with apparent magnitude on the left, absolute magnitude on the top, and distance in the body.

1. Set the widths of columns A to N according to the following list: A = **10**, B = **4**, C = **1**, D..N = **9**
2. In cell A1, type **Distance to a star based on its absolute and apparent magnitudes**
3. In cell B2, type **Distance in parsecs (1 parsec = 3.26 light-years)**
4. In cell G3, type **Absolute Magnitude**
5. In cell A9, type **Apparent**
6. In cell A10, type **Magnitude**
7. In cell C5, type **\-**
8. Copy the contents of cell C5 into cells C5..N5.
9. In cell C6, type **‘¦**
10. Copy the contents of cell C6 into cells C7..C20.
11. Use the command /Data Fill (/**DF**) to fill cells D4..N4 with the set of integers from −5 to 15 in steps of 2.
12. Use the command /Data Fill (/**DF**) to fill cells B6..B20 with the set of integers from −5 to 23 in steps of 2.
13. In cell D6, type **10^((5+$B6-D$4)/5)**
14. Copy the contents of cell D6 into cells D6..N20.
15. Set the format of cells D6..N20 to scientific format 1 (**/RFS1**).

The spreadsheet should now look like Figure 2.9. Note the use of mixed cell references in the formula. These keep the arguments pointing to the correct row or column when the cells are copied into the rectangular body of the table.

Multi-Input, Multicolumn Tables

Many functions have more than one or two inputs. Tables of these functions cannot be created on the spreadsheet in the simple rectangular format used in the previous example. Instead, they can be handled in

```
A1: [W10] 'Distance to a star based on its absolute and apparent magnitudes READY

      A          B C      D          E          F          G          H          I
 1  Distance to a star based on its absolute and apparent magnitudes.
 2               Distance is in parsecs (1 parsec = 3.26 light-years)
 3                                            Absolute Magnitude
 4                          -5         -3         -1          1          3          5
 5               ---------------------------------------------------------------------
 6                -5 | 1.0E+01    4.0E+00    1.6E+00    6.3E-01    2.5E-01    1.0E-01
 7                -3 | 2.5E+01    1.0E+01    4.0E+00    1.6E+00    6.3E-01    2.5E-01
 8                -1 | 6.3E+01    2.5E+01    1.0E+01    4.0E+00    1.6E+00    6.3E-01
 9  Apparent       1 | 1.6E+02    6.3E+01    2.5E+01    1.0E+01    4.0E+00    1.6E+00
10  Magnitude      3 | 4.0E+02    1.6E+02    6.3E+01    2.5E+01    1.0E+01    4.0E+00
11                 5 | 1.0E+03    4.0E+02    1.6E+02    6.3E+01    2.5E+01    1.0E+01
12                 7 | 2.5E+03    1.0E+03    4.0E+02    1.6E+02    6.3E+01    2.5E+01
13                 9 | 6.3E+03    2.5E+03    1.0E+03    4.0E+02    1.6E+02    6.3E+01
14                11 | 1.6E+04    6.3E+03    2.5E+03    1.0E+03    4.0E+02    1.6E+02
15                13 | 4.0E+04    1.6E+04    6.3E+03    2.5E+03    1.0E+03    4.0E+02
16                15 | 1.0E+05    4.0E+04    1.6E+04    6.3E+03    2.5E+03    1.0E+03
17                17 | 2.5E+05    1.0E+05    4.0E+04    1.6E+04    6.3E+03    2.5E+03
18                19 | 6.3E+05    2.5E+05    1.0E+05    4.0E+04    1.6E+04    6.3E+03
19                21 | 1.6E+06    6.3E+05    2.5E+05    1.0E+05    4.0E+04    1.6E+04
20                23 | 4.0E+06    1.6E+06    6.3E+05    2.5E+05    1.0E+05    4.0E+04
21-Jun-87   11:29 PM
```

Figure 2.9: Distance to a star based on its absolute and relative magnitudes

```
J1:                                                                     READY

        J          K          L          M          N          O          P          Q
 1
 2
 3
 4            7          9         11         13         15
 5    -----------------------------------------------------
 6    4.0E-02    1.6E-02    6.3E-03    2.5E-03    1.0E-03
 7    1.0E-01    4.0E-02    1.6E-02    6.3E-03    2.5E-03
 8    2.5E-01    1.0E-01    4.0E-02    1.6E-02    6.3E-03
 9    6.3E-01    2.5E-01    1.0E-01    4.0E-02    1.6E-02
10    1.6E+00    6.3E-01    2.5E-01    1.0E-01    4.0E-02
11    4.0E+00    1.6E+00    6.3E-01    2.5E-01    1.0E-01
12    1.0E+01    4.0E+00    1.6E+00    6.3E-01    2.5E-01
13    2.5E+01    1.0E+01    4.0E+00    1.6E+00    6.3E-01
14    6.3E+01    2.5E+01    1.0E+01    4.0E+00    1.6E+00
15    1.6E+02    6.3E+01    2.5E+01    1.0E+01    4.0E+00
16    4.0E+02    1.6E+02    6.3E+01    2.5E+01    1.0E+01
17    1.0E+03    4.0E+02    1.6E+02    6.3E+01    2.5E+01
18    2.5E+03    1.0E+03    4.0E+02    1.6E+02    6.3E+01
19    6.3E+03    2.5E+03    1.0E+03    4.0E+02    1.6E+02
20    1.6E+04    6.3E+03    2.5E+03    1.0E+03    4.0E+02
21-Jun-87   11:29 PM
```

Figure 2.9: Distance to a star based on its absolute and relative magnitudes *(continued)*

several ways. One way is to put different variables in alternate columns, with the function value in the last column, as in the van der Waals equation in Figure 2.8. A second way is to put one of the variables in a row and the others in alternate columns, which tends to compact the table.

How you set up a particular table depends on what you are calculating and how you want to view the results.

Electron Mobility in Silicon This example calculates the electron mobility in silicon given the electric field, doping density, and temperature. This formula uses three input values to get the one output value. You will set up this example using three columns for the independent variables, two columns for intermediate values, and one column for the calculated mobility values.

The mobility equation was developed for use in large-scale semiconductor transient code. It consists of the curve fits of mobility versus electric field, doping density, and temperature. It is expressed as follows:

$$\mu_0 = \frac{\mu_{max} - \mu_{min}}{1 + (N/N_r)^{\alpha}} + \mu_{min}$$

$$E_c = \frac{2.319V_m}{(1 + 0.8\exp(T/600))\mu_0(T/T_0)^{\delta}}$$

$$\mu = \frac{\mu_0(T/T_0)^{-\delta}}{(1 + (E/E_c)^{\beta})^{1/\beta}}$$

The coefficients have the following values:

$\mu_{max} = 0.1330\ \mathrm{m^2/V\text{-}s}$
$\mu_{min} = 0.0065\ \mathrm{m^2/V\text{-}s}$
$N_r = 8.5 \times 10^{22}\ \mathrm{m^{-3}}$
$V_m = 1.1 \times 10^5\ \mathrm{m/s}$
$\alpha = 0.72$
$\beta = 2$
$\delta = 2.42$
$T_0 = 300\ \mathrm{K}$

Here, N is the net positive doping density (that is, donor density − acceptor density) in inverse cubic meters, T is the temperature in kelvins, E is the electric field in volts per meter, and μ is the electron mobility in meters squared per volt-second. The formula is in three parts, which you could combine to get a single formula. However, it is much simpler to assemble the table in columns and then calculate each part of the formula in a separate column.

1. Change the default column width to 10 with the command /Worksheet Global Column-width 10 (/**WGC10**).
2. In cell A1, type **Electron Mobility in Silicon**
3. In cell A3, type **"μmax**

The μ is part of the DOS extended character set and is created by holding down Alt and typing **230** on the keypad. Some computers require you to hold down both Shift and Alt. Consult your DOS manual if Alt-230 does not work.

4. In cell B3, type **0.133**
5. In cell D3, type **"alpha**
6. In cell E3, type **0.72**
7. In cell A4, type **"μmin**
8. In cell B4, type **0.0065**
9. In cell D4, type **"beta**
10. In cell E4, type **2**
11. In cell A5, type **"Nr**
12. In cell B5, type **8.5E22**
13. In cell D5, type **"delta**
14. In cell E5, type **2.42**
15. In cell A6, type **"Vm**
16. In cell B6, type **1.1E5**
17. In cell D6, type **"T0**
18. In cell E6, type **300**
19. In cell A8, type **^Doping**
20. In cell A9, type **^Density**
21. In cell A10, type **^(m^-3)**
22. In cell B8, type **^Temp.**
23. In cell B10, type **^(K)**
24. In cell C8, type **^Electric**
25. In cell C9, type **^Field**
26. In cell C10, type **^(V/m)**
27. In cell D8, type **^μ0**

28. In cell D10, type **^(m^2/V-s)**
29. In cell E8, type **^Ec**
30. In cell E10, type **^(V/m)**
31. In cell F8, type **^μ**
32. In cell F10, type **^(m^2/V-s)**
33. In cells A11..F11, type/copy **\-**

By type/copy, I mean that you should type the value or formula into the first cell of the range and then copy it into the rest of the range.

34. In cells A12..A19, type/copy **1.0E19**
35. In cells B12..B15, type/copy **300**
36. In cells B16..B19, type/copy **600**
37. In cells C12..C15, type **1E4, 1E5, 1E6, 1E7**
38. Copy cells C12..C15 into cells C16..C19.
39. Use the command /Range Name Labels Right (**/RNLR**) to name cells B3..B6 and E3..E6 with the labels in cells A3..A6 and D3..D6.
40. In cells D12..D19, type/copy **($μMAX-$μMIN)/(1+(A12/$NR)^$ALPHA)+$μMIN**
41. In cells E12..E19, type/copy **2.319*$VM/((1+0.8*@EXP(B12/600))*D12*(B12/$T0)^$DELTA)**
42. In cells F12..F19, type/copy **(D12*(B12/$T0)^$DELTA)/((1+(C12/E12)^$BETA)^(1/$BETA)**
43. Format cells C12..C19 as Scientific 0 (**/RFS0**).
44. Format cells D12..F19 as Scientific 3 (**/RFS3**).
45. Format cells B12..B19 as Fixed 0 (**/RFF0**).
46. Copy cells A12..F19 to cells A21..F28.
47. In cells A21..A28, type/copy **1.0E21**
48. Fix the labels by moving to cell A12 and executing the command /Worksheet Titles Horizontal (**/WTH**).

The spreadsheet should now look like that in Figure 2.10. Since you have locked in the titles, pressing the PgUp and PgDn keys will flip between the two blocks of the table. More blocks can be added for different doping densities, and they will also scroll under the labels fixed at the top.

```
A1: 'Electron Mobility in Silicon                                READY

     A         B          C          D          E          F         G
1  Electron Mobility in Silicon
2
3       μmax      0.133                alpha       0.72
4       μmin     0.0065                 beta          2
5         Nr   8.50E+22                delta       2.42
6         Vm     110000                   T0        300
7
8     Doping     Temp.    Electric      μ0          Ec          μ
9     Density               Field
10    (m^-3)      (K)       (V/m)   (m^2/V-s)     (V/m)    (m^2/V-s)
11 ---------------------------------------------------------------
12   1.00E+19       300      1E+04 1.328E-01 8.282E+05 1.328E-01
13   1.00E+19       300      1E+05 1.328E-01 8.282E+05 1.319E-01
14   1.00E+19       300      1E+06 1.328E-01 8.282E+05 8.472E-02
15   1.00E+19       300      1E+07 1.328E-01 8.282E+05 1.096E-02
16   1.00E+19       600      1E+04 1.328E-01 1.130E+05 7.080E-01
17   1.00E+19       600      1E+05 1.328E-01 1.130E+05 5.324E-01
18   1.00E+19       600      1E+06 1.328E-01 1.130E+05 7.984E-02
19   1.00E+19       600      1E+07 1.328E-01 1.130E+05 8.035E-03
20
01-Jan-80  01:09 AM
```

Figure 2.10: Electron mobility in silicon

```
A21: 1.0000000E+21                                               READY

     A         B          C          D          E          F         G
21   1.00E+21       300      1E+04 1.280E-01 8.591E+05 1.280E-01
22   1.00E+21       300      1E+05 1.280E-01 8.591E+05 1.272E-01
23   1.00E+21       300      1E+06 1.280E-01 8.591E+05 8.344E-02
24   1.00E+21       300      1E+07 1.280E-01 8.591E+05 1.096E-02
25   1.00E+21       600      1E+04 1.280E-01 1.173E+05 6.828E-01
26   1.00E+21       600      1E+05 1.280E-01 1.173E+05 5.214E-01
27   1.00E+21       600      1E+06 1.280E-01 1.173E+05 7.981E-02
28   1.00E+21       600      1E+07 1.280E-01 1.173E+05 8.035E-03
29
30
31
32
33
34
35
36
37
38
39
40
01-Jan-80  01:11 AM
```

Figure 2.10: Electron mobility in silicon *(continued)*

■ THE TABLE FUNCTION

Lotus 1-2-3 has a command for producing one- and two-input tables from a single copy of a formula instead of copying the formula into every cell. The single-input table command /Data Table 1 (/DT1) actually calculates a table for several single-input formulas in adjacent columns. The two-input table command /Data Table 2 (/DT2) calculates a two-input table only for a single formula.

Using the /Data Table command has several advantages over copying equations. First, with the command you need only one copy of a formula. This saves some typing and allows you to quickly alter a formula and see the results in the table. The second advantage is that the table is not recalculated every time the rest of the spreadsheet is recalculated. It is only recalculated when you press the Table key. If a table is large, it may take a long time to calculate. Unless you set the spreadsheet's recalculation mode to manual (/WGRM), every time you make a change in a cell, the whole spreadsheet is recalculated. Thus, making part of the spreadsheet a data table saves you time.

Disadvantages to using a data table are that you must use a single formula, rather than a set of formulas, for the function, and you cannot use limit lines to visually delineate the table structure. You can add limit lines by first calculating the table, executing the command /Data Table Reset (/DTR), and then inserting the limit lines, but then you can no longer recalculate values in the table.

Though it is largely a matter of preference, I find that I rarely use the table commands. The time required to set up tables using copied equations is about the same as that required to set up tables using the table commands, so there is no advantage there. The speed with which the table is calculated is also about the same for both methods. I find that I often change individual equations or groups of equations to better handle a part of the range of the input variable, and this cannot be done with the table commands. Also, the equations that I calculate are usually not available as a single formula, but as a set of formulas, each calculating an intermediate value leading to the final result. Now, I could probably do all of the algebra to make these into single formulas, but the equations would quickly become unwieldly. I use the computer to decrease the amount of work that I need to do.

Single-Input Tables

To create a single-input table using the /Data Table 1 command (/DT1), you must set up the spreadsheet. First, enter the list of input values in the column immediately to the left of the body of the data table. Second, select a convenient cell outside of the table to use as the input cell. Use this cell in your formulas for the input variable. Third, enter the formula to be evaluated in a cell one row above the body of the table. You can calculate several single-input tables at the same time, so long as they use the same set of input data. Just put the formulas in adjacent columns.

You can now execute the /Data Table 1 (/DT1) command. Make the input range the whole data table, including the cells containing the input values and the formulas, but not the input cell. Select the chosen input cell, and the table will be calculated: The input values are inserted into the input cell, the formula is calculated, and the result is listed in the column below the formula and in the same row as the input value.

Stress and Deflection in a Cantilever Beam Calculating stress and strain in beams is a common requirement in mechanical and civil engineering. In most cases, standard beams can be modeled with a set of simple analytical equations. Lists of these equations for different beams and methods of support can be found in a number of handbooks.

Stress (s) in a cantilever beam with a single-point load (Figure 2.11) can be calculated at any point x with the following equation:

$$S = \frac{W}{Z}(l - x) \qquad (\text{for } x < l)$$

Here, W is the applied load, l is the location of the load, and Z is the section modulus of the beam. The deflection (y) of the beam is calculated using

$$y = \frac{Wx^2}{6EI}(3l - x) \qquad (\text{for } x < l)$$

$$y = \frac{Wl^2}{6EI}(3x - l) \qquad (\text{for } x > l)$$

where E is the modulus of elasticity, and I is the moment of inertia.

Suppose that you have a 12-foot cantilever beam with a 15,000-pound load located 2 feet from the end and you want to calculate the stress in the beam and the deflection at every point. You have selected a type W 12 × 53 beam, which is a form of I-beam 12 inches deep with a weight of 53 pounds per foot. A beam of this type has a section modulus (Z) of 70.7 in^3, a moment of inertia (I) of 426 in^4, and a modulus of elasticity (E) of 2.9×10^7 psi.

You will now create an engineering table that shows the stress and deflection of the cantilever beam every foot along its length. Actually,

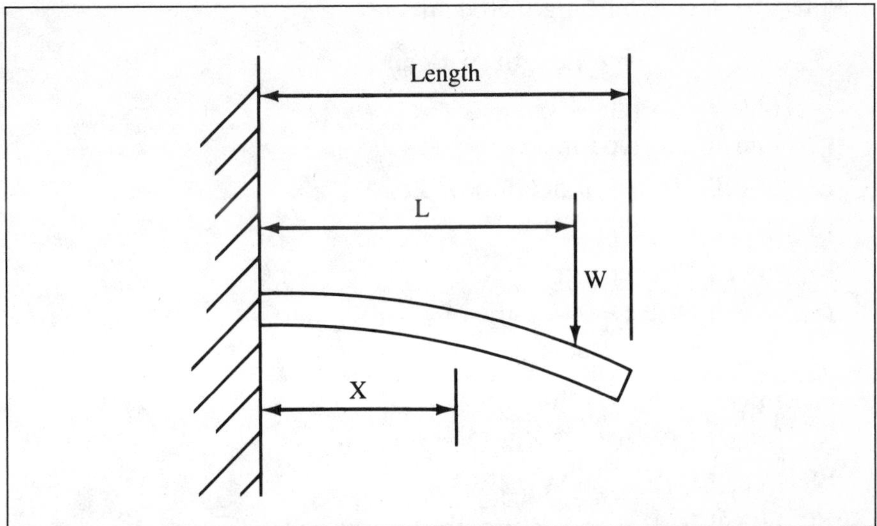

Figure 2.11: Cantilever beam with a single-point load

this table will be two engineering tables applied to the same set of input data with the /Data Table 1 (/DT1) command. The first table is the stress calculation, and the second is the deflection calculation.

1. Set the widths of columns A through G according to the following list: A = **9**, B = **4**, C = **9**, D = **9**, E = **3**,F = **19**, G = **9**
2. In cell A1, type **Cantilever Beam**
3. In cell C3, type ^**Stress**
4. In cell C4, type ^**(psi)**
5. In cell D3, type ^**Deflection**
6. In cell D4, type ^**(in)**

Mark the locations of the input cell to emphasize its location in this example. This marking is not necessary for the execution of the table command or for understanding the table. You would probably not mark the input cell locations in your own spreadsheets once you understand the operation of the table command.

7. In cell A6, type ^^^**input**^^
8. In cell A7, type ^**cell**

Enter the data describing the beam.

9. In cell F8, type **Length of Beam**
10. In cell G8, type **144**
11. In cell H8, type **in**
12. In cell F9, type **Location of Load**
13. In cell G9, type **120**
14. In cell H9, type **in**
15. In cell F10, type **Weight of Load**
16. In cell G10, type **15000**
17. In cell H10, type **lbs**
18. In cell F12, type **Beam Designation**
19. In cell G12, type **W 12 x 53**
20. In cell F13, type **Section modulus**
21. In cell G13, type **70.7**
22. In cell H13, type **in^3**
23. In cell F14, type **Moment of Inertia**
24. In cell G14, type **426**
25. In cell H14, type **in^4**
26. In cell F15, type **Modulus of**
27. In cell F16, type **"Elasticity**
28. In cell G16, type **2.9E7**
29. In cell H16, type **psi**
30. In cell A10, type **Distance**
31. In cell A11, type **from Wall**
32. In cell A12, type **^(in)**

Enter the input data for the calculation. You will calculate the stress and deflection every 12 inches along the beam.

33. Move to cell B6, execute the command /Data Fill (**/DF**), set the range as B6..B18, enter the start value as **0**, and enter the step as **12**.
34. Name cells G9, G10, G13, G14, and G16 as **L**, **W**, **Z**, **I**, **E**.

This problem uses two stress and two deflection equations: stress and deflection equations for *x* between the wall and the location of the weight, and stress and deflection equations for *x* beyond the location of the weight. Use the logical IF statement to select the correct equations for the input range.

35. In cell C5, type **@IF(A5<L,(W/Z)*(L-A5),0)**
36. In cell D5, type **@IF(A5 < L,(W*A5^2)*(3*L-A5)/(6*E*I), (W*A5^2)*(3*A5-L)/(6*E*I))**

The table is now set up for execution of the /Data Table 1 (/DT1) command. Note that the range of the table includes the column of input values and the formulas, but not the input cell.

37. Move to cell B5 and type the command /Data Table 1 (**/DT1**), set the table range as B5..D18, and enter the input cell as **A5**.
38. Format cells C5..C18 as Fixed 0 (**/RFF0**).
39. Format cells D5..D18 as Fixed 4 (**/RFF4**).
40. Format cell G16 as Scientific 2 (**/RFS2**).

Hide the values calculated by the formulas at the top of the columns.

41. Format cells C5 and D5 as Hidden (**/RFH**).

The spreadsheet should now look like Figure 2.12. If you look at any of the cells in the body of the table, you will see that they are all values rather than formulas. These values can now be used in other formulas.

Two-Input Tables

The two-input table command works much the same as the one-input table command. You enter the values of the first input variable in the column immediately to the left of the body of the table, and you put the second input variable in the row immediately above the body of the table. In this case, you place the formula at the intersection of the row and column containing the input variables. You then define two input cells outside of the table area and reference them in the function.

Linear Variable Differential Transformer Several years ago, I worked on reactor instrumentation at the Idaho National Engineering Laboratory. At this laboratory, nuclear reactors and reactor components are

```
A1: 'Cantilever Beam                                                        READY

      A       B       C        D       E          F              G          H
1  Cantilever Beam
2
3                   Stress   Deflection
4                   (psi)      (in)
5
6  ^^input^^   0    25460    0.0000
7    cell     12    22914    0.0101
8             24    20368    0.0392    Length of Beam             144 in
9             36    17822    0.0850    Location of Load           120 in
10 Distance   48    15276    0.1455    Weight of Load           15000 lbs
11 from Wall  60    12730    0.2186
12   (in)     72    10184    0.3021    Beam Designation    W 12 x 53
13            84     7638    0.3941    Section Modulus          70.7 in^3
14            96     5092    0.4924    Moment of Inertia         426 in^4
15           108     2546    0.5948    Modulus of
16           120        0    0.6994         Elasticity 2.90E+07 psi
17           132        0    0.9732
18           144        0    1.3092
19
20
01-Jan-80  01:14 AM
```

Figure 2.12: Stress and deflection in a cantilever beam

stressed to failure in order to determine the nominal failure levels. As fuel rods are heated and cooled, their length changes. Rod length also changes drastically when a fuel rod breaks, which often happens in the destructive tests. To measure the change in length, we used a linear variable differential transformer, or LVDT.

A linear variable differential transformer consists of two identical secondary coils of wire spaced symmetrically about a primary coil. The secondary coils are wired in a series-opposed circuit. When the primary coil is excited with an AC source, the magnetic field is coupled to the secondary coils through a movable core. If the core is centered in the device, the coupling to each of the secondary coils is identical. Since they are wired in a series-opposed configuration, the resultant voltage is zero. If the movable core is displaced in either direction, a differential voltage is produced. The series-opposed configuration also helps to reduce thermal and radiation-induced noise.

We calibrated these LVDT devices at several different temperatures and performed linear curve fits on the voltage versus displacement data. Then we fit the coefficients of the curve fit to a linear function of the temperature to get the temperature sensitivity. Combining these curve fits resulted in the calibration equation

$$x = a_0 + a_1 V + a_2(T - 608) + a_3 V(T - 608)$$

where x is the fuel-rod value elongation in millimeters, V is the transducer voltage, and T is the transducer temperature in kelvins. For a particular device, we found the coefficients to be

$$\begin{aligned} a_0 &= 0.3347 \text{ mm} \\ a_1 &= 10.6592 \text{ mm/V} \\ a_2 &= -2.19701 \times 10^{-3} \text{ mm/K} \\ a_3 &= -6.32662 \times 10^{-4} \text{ mm/K}-\text{V} \end{aligned}$$

Use these values to create a table showing fuel-rod elongation versus transducer voltage and temperature.

1. Change the widths of columns A through G according to the following list: A = **13**, B = **9**, C = **9**, D = **9**, E = **9**, F = **9**, G = **9**
2. In cell A1, type **LVDT Calibration Table**
3. In cell D2, type **^a0**
4. In cell E2, type **^a1**
5. In cell F2, type **^a2**
6. In cell G2, type **^a3**
7. In cell B3, type **Coefficients**
8. In cell D3, type **0.3347**
9. In cell E3, type **10.6592**
10. In cell F3, type **-2.19701E-3**
11. In cell G3, type **-6.32662E-4**
12. In cell A5, type **Fuel rod elongation in millimeters.**
13. In cell C6, type **Transducer Temperature (K)**

Enter the values for the second input across the top of the table. These four instructions could also be performed with a /Data Fill (/DF) command, but it is often faster to just enter the values if the list is short and the values are simple to type.

14. In cell C7, type **300**
15. In cell D7, type **400**
16. In cell E7, type **500**
17. In cell F7, type **600**
18. In cell A8, type **^^^input 1**

19. In cell A10, type ^^^**input 2**
20. In cell A12, type ^**Transducer**
21. In cell A13, type ^**Voltage**
22. In cell A14, type ^(V)

Enter the values for the first input in a column on the left side of the table.

23. Move to cell B8 and execute the command /Data Fill (/**DF**), select cells B8..B20 as the range and enter a starting value of **1.2**, a step value of **-0.2**, and an ending value of **-1.2**.

Enter the two-input functions in the table at the intersection of the column containing the first input variables and the row containing the second input variables.

24. In cell B7, type **+D3+E3*A7+F3*(A9-608)+G3*(A9-608)*A7**

Create the table with the /Data Table 2 (/DT2) command.

25. Type the command /Data Table 2 (/**DT2**), select cells B7..F20 as the range, and enter **A7** as input 1 and **A9** as input 2.
26. Format cells B8..B20 as Fixed 1 (/**RFF1**).
27. Format cells C8..F20 as Fixed 2 (/**RFF2**).

Hide the contents of the cell containing the formula so that it will not detract from the rest of the table.

28. Format cell B7 as Hidden (/**RFH**).

Your spreadsheet should now look like that in Figure 2.13, Again, if you look in the body of the table, the cells all contain values. If you change one of the values in an input row or column or change the table formula, the table will not be updated. Even if you press the Calc key, the table will not be updated. The table will only be updated when you press the Table key.

If you want to add lines to the bottom or right of the table, you must reexecute the /Data Table (/DT) command to cause them to be used. If you insert rows or columns using the /Worksheet Insert Row (/WIR) or /Worksheet Insert Column (/WIC) commands, and if you insert those rows or columns between the first and last rows or columns of the table,

```
A1: [W13] 'LVDT Calibration Table                                        READY

      A          B        C         D         E         F         G
1   LVDT Calibration Table
2                                  a0        a1        a2        a3
3                Coefficients:    0.3347   10.6592  -0.00219  -0.00063
4
5   Fuel rod elongation in millimeters
6                           Transducer Temperature (K)
7                            300       400       500       600
8     ^^input 1      1.2    14.04     13.74     13.45     13.15
9                    1.0    11.87     11.58     11.30     11.02
10    ^^input 2      0.8     9.69      9.42      9.15      8.88
11                   0.6     7.52      7.27      7.01      6.75
12   Transducer      0.4     5.35      5.11      4.86      4.62
13     Voltage       0.2     3.18      2.95      2.72      2.49
14       (V)         0.0     1.01      0.79      0.57      0.35
15                  -0.2    -1.16     -1.37     -1.57     -1.78
16                  -0.4    -3.33     -3.52     -3.72     -3.91
17                  -0.6    -5.50     -5.68     -5.86     -6.05
18                  -0.8    -7.67     -7.84     -8.01     -8.18
19                  -1.0    -9.84    -10.00    -10.16    -10.31
20                  -1.2   -12.01    -12.16    -12.30    -12.44
01-Jan-80  01:18 AM
```

Figure 2.13: LVDT calibration data

they will be included in the table and will be filled with values when you press the Table key.

■ FUNCTION CALCULATORS

Function calculators are similar to the first equation discussed in this chapter. One or several input values are placed in a formula, and one or several results are calculated. This is in contrast to the tables of values that you have been calculating in the rest of this chapter. In a function calculator, you have an input area where the user types the input values and an output area where the results are calculated and presented. You can also protect parts of the function calculator so that users can enter values only in the input area and not elsewhere on the spreadsheet.

A Simple Function Calculator

A function calculator need not be complex. In this first example, you will create a function calculator that has a single input value and a single output value calculated with a single simple formula.

Julian Day Calculator One of the principal tasks of astronomers is recording the dates and times of events, measurements, and sightings.

Although this can be done using conventional days, months, and years, the irregularity of months and years makes calculations difficult. If you need to know the difference in time between two events, you must take into account the lengths of the years (that is, how many were regular years, and how many were leap years) and the lengths of the months between the events.

Needless to say, astronomers do not want to spend time calculating the lengths of months and years when there is a clear night sky and the seeing (the amount of twinkle) is good. Therefore they use a system of time measurement known as the Julian day, proposed by Joseph Scalinger in 1582. The Julian day calendar consists of consecutively numbered days starting with January 1, 4713 BC. (I do not have any idea why Scalinger chose this particular date, but it is well before any accurately recorded history). To find the difference in time between two events, you simply subtract their Julian days.

Time of day has also been incorporated into the Julian day calendar using decimal fractions of a day. Since astronomers generally work at night, the Julian day has been defined to start at noon rather than midnight. Therefore, midnight between 12/31/79 and 1/1/80 is Julian Day 2,444,239.5.

Julian days work well with the date and time functions supplied with Lotus 1-2-3, since they also work with consecutive days and fractions of days. All you need to do is add the offset from a known date. These functions should be used with care, since Lotus 1-2-3 counts a day for February 29, 1900, even though 1900 was not a leap year, and Lotus 1-2-3 does not calculate days before January 1, 1900, or after December 31, 2099. Therefore, a table created with the date functions is valid between March 1, 1900, and December 31, 2099.

In this example, you will create a simple function calculator that converts a standard date into a Julian day.

1. Set the width of column A as **12** and of column B as **11**.
2. In cell A1, type **Julian Day Calculator**
3. In cell A3, type **Input the date to be converted as 'MM/DD/YY**
4. In cell A4, type **The date must be between 3/1/00 and 12/31/199**
5. In cell A6, type **"Date:**
6. In cell A8, type **"Julian Day:**

The afternoon of 1/1/80 is in Julian day 2,444,240. Use that date to synchronize the Julian day calendar with the Lotus 1-2-3 calendar functions.

7. In cell B8, type **@DATEVALUE(B6)-@DATEVALUE("1/1/80")+2444240**
8. Format cell B8 as ,0 by entering **/RF,0**
9. In cell A10, type **Julian days go from noon to noon rather than midnight to midnight,**
10. In cell A11, type **so this is the Julian day of the evening of the date specified**
11. In cell A12, type **in the input cell. The Julian day calendar starts at noon on Jan. 1, 4713 BC.**

The text in cells A10..A12 looks a bit ragged. To form a compact paragraph at the bottom of the spreadsheet, reformat the paragraph using the /Range Justify (/RJ) command. The text to be justified must be in a single column. The range you select in this command determines the width of the text when it is justified.

12. Type the command /Range Justify (/**RJ**) and select the range A10..D18.

Since you may want to give this spreadsheet to others, you should protect it so that users do not ruin all of your hard work. You cannot protect the whole spreadsheet; otherwise, you could not enter the date to be converted into a Julian day. Use the command /Range Unprotect (/RU) to mark some cells as not protected. Then use the command /Worksheet Global Protection Enable (/WGPE) to protect the rest of the spreadsheet. These commands can be executed in any order, and the result will be the same. The /Range Unprotect (/RU) command also makes the text in the cell a different color to set it off from the protected cells. If you try to change a protected part of the spreadsheet, an error will occur. To recover from this error condition, press Esc.

13. Move to cell B6 and type the command /Range Unprotect (/**RU**) and select B6..B6 as the range.
14. Type the command /Worksheet Global Protection Enable (/**WGPE**).

Enter a date in cell B6, prefaced with a single quotation mark (') to make it a label, and the Julian day will appear in cell B8. For example, if you enter '1/19/87, the spreadsheet will look like Figure 2.14.

A Complicated Function Calculator

Thermoelectric Cooler A thermoelectric cooler is a solid-state heat pump. It is a semiconductor device that uses electrons to carry heat from one side of a device to the other. When you apply a voltage to a thermoelectric cooler, one side of it gets hot, and the other side gets cold, the opposite of what happens in a thermocouple. In fact, if you drive a thermoelectric cooler with heat on one side and cold on the other, it will generate an electric current. If you reverse the current through the thermoelectric cooler, the opposite sides of the device will be heated and cooled.

Thermoelectric coolers have been used for a number of years to cool small, restricted spaces, such as a single integrated circuit in the middle of a large circuit board. More recently, they have been used to heat or cool ice chests so that you can have hot food and cold beer at a picnic.

A few years ago, I taught an engineering design class on direct energy conversion that included a section on thermoelectric coolers. One

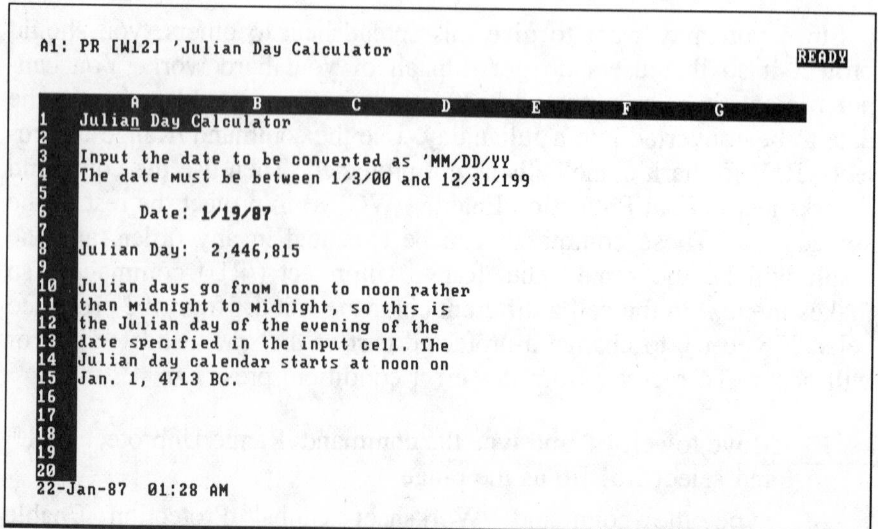

Figure 2.14: A Julian day function calculator

class assignment was to design a thermoelectric cooler and calculate all of the relevant design and operational parameters. We will use this problem to demonstrate a complicated function calculator.

The input parameters for a thermoelectric cooler consist of material parameters and device parameters. The material parameters consist of the Seebeck coefficient (α), the resistivity (ρ), and the figure of merit (Z), for the n-type and p-type materials that make up the two legs of the cooler. Table 2.1 lists the data for the n-type and p-type semiconductors commonly used in thermoelectric coolers.

The thermal conductivities (λ) of the materials can be calculated using

$$\lambda = \frac{\alpha^2}{\rho Z}$$

and the junction Seebeck coefficient,

$$\alpha = |\alpha_n| + |\alpha_p|$$

The device parameters start with the ratios of the areas to the lengths of the n and p legs of the thermoelectric cooler: γ_n and γ_p. These are design parameters, and if they are in the following ratio, they optimize the coefficient of performance (β):

$$\frac{\gamma_n}{\gamma_p} = \left(\frac{\rho_n \lambda_p}{\rho_p \lambda_n}\right)^{1/2}$$

The figure of merit for the junction is calculated with

$$Z = \frac{\alpha^2}{RK}$$

Parameter	n-type	p-type
Composition	75% Bi^2Te^3	25% Bi^2Te^3 25% Bi^2Se^3 75% Sb^2Te^3
Seebeck coeff (α)	-1.65×10^{-4}	2.10×10^{-4}V/K
Resistivity (ρ)	1.05×10^{-3}	9.8×10^{-4}ohm-cm
Figure of merit (Z)	2.0×10^{-3}	$3.5 \times 10^{-3}(K)^{-1}$

Table 2.1: Material parameters for a thermoelectric cooler

where R is the device resistance, and K is the device thermal conductance. The device resistance is calculated with

$$R = \frac{\rho_n}{\lambda_n} + \frac{\rho_p}{\lambda_p}$$

$$K = \lambda_n \gamma_n + \lambda_p \gamma_p$$

The figure of merit is optimized using

$$Z^* = \frac{\alpha^2}{[(\rho_n \lambda_n)^{1/2} + (\rho_p \lambda_p)^{1/2}]^2}$$

The driving current is another design parameter, and the value that optimizes the coefficient of performance is

$$I = \frac{\alpha \Delta T}{R[(1 + Z^* T_{av})^{1/2} - 1]}$$

where T_{av} is the average, and Δ_T is the temperature difference of the hot (T_h) and cold (T_c) junction temperatures.

The rates at which heat is pumped out of the cold junction is

$$q = \alpha T_c I - \tfrac{1}{2} I^2 R - K \Delta T$$

The coefficient of performance is the ratio of the heat pumped out of the cold junction to the electrical energy required to pump it:

$$\beta = \frac{\alpha T_c I - \frac{1}{2} I^2 R - K \Delta T}{\alpha T_c \Delta T + I^2 R}$$

The maximum value of β is found by inserting the optimized values of I, K, and R:

$$\beta_{max} = \frac{T_c}{\Delta T} \left[\frac{(1 + Z^* T_{av})^{1/2} - T_n/T_c}{(1 + Z^* T_{av})^{1/2} - 1} \right]$$

Finally, the power input into the device is

$$P = \alpha I \Delta T + I^2 R$$

If the device was completely optimized, this would equal the optimized power input:

$$P = \frac{q}{\beta_{max}}$$

Now, using this jumble of equations, you will create a function calculator that calculates all of the device parameters. You will calculate two sets of values: one for input device parameters and one for optimized values of the device parameters. First, you will enter the material type and material parameters from Table 2.1.

1. Set the widths of columns A through E using the following list: A = **16**, B = **11**, C = **12**, D = **11**, E = **9**.
2. In cell A1, type **Thermoelectric Cooler Calculator**
3. In cell A2, type **n-type: 75% Bi2Te3 25% Sb2Te3 p-type: 25% Bi2Te3 75% Sb2Te3**

In cell A3, you will type a long label that overlaps several other cells. When the number is typed in cell B3, all but the beginning of the long label will be hidden. This allows you to make descriptive material available to a spreadsheet user without cluttering the spreadsheet with excessive text. The user can view the descriptive material by moving the cursor to the appropriate cell, which displays the cell's contents in the control panel.

4. In cell A3, type ' (8 spaces) **alpha =** (3 spaces) **Material Seebeck Coefficient**
5. In cell B3, type **-1.65E-4**
6. In cell C3, type **V/K**
7. In cell D3, type **2.1E-4**
8. In cell E3, type **V/K**
9. In cell A4, type ' (10 spaces) **Rho =** (3 spaces) **Material Resistivity**
10. In cell B4, type **1.05E-3**
11. In cell C4, type **ohm-cm**
12. In cell D4, type **9.8E-4**
13. In cell E4, type **ohm-cm**
14. In cell A5, type ' (12 spaces) **Z =** (3 spaces) **Material Figure of Merit**
15. In cell B5, type **2.0E-3**
16. In cell C5, type **'1/K**
17. In cell D5, type **3.5E-3**
18. In cell E5, type **'1/K**

Calculate the thermal conductivities.

19. In cell A6, type ‘ (7 spaces) **lambda =** (3 spaces) **Material Thermal Conductivity**
20. In cell B6, type **+B3^2/(B4*B5)**
21. In cell C6, type **watt/cm-K**
22. In cell D6, type **+D3^2/(D4*D5)**
23. In cell E6, type **watt/cm-K**

Enter the hot and cold junction temperatures. Assume that you want to keep the cold junction at freezing (273 K) and the hot junction at 327 K so that the average is room temperature (300 K).

24. In cell A7, type ‘ **T-hot,T-cold =** (3 spaces) **Hot leg and cold leg temperatures**
25. In cell B7, type **327**
26. In cell C7, type **K**
27. In cell D7, type **273**
28. In cell E7, type **K**

Now enter the area-to-length ratios. The optimized value of γ_p is calculated in cell D13.

29. In cell A8, type ‘ (8 spaces) **gamma =** (3 spaces) **Ratio of the leg area to leg length**
30. In cell B8, type **1**
31. In cell C8, type **cm**
32. In cell D8, type **1**
33. In cell E8, type **cm**
34. In cell A9, type ‘ (10 spaces) **Tav =** (3 spaces) **Average temperature**
35. In cell B9, type **(B7+D7)/2**
36. In cell C9, type **K**
37. In cell A10, type ‘ (7 spaces) **Alpha =** (3 spaces) **Junction Seebeck coefficient**
38. In cell B10, type **@ABS(B3)+@ABS(D3)**
39. In cell B12, type **General Values**
40. In cell D12, type **Optimized Values**

41. In cell A13, type ‘ (4 spaces) **gamma opt =** (3 spaces) **Optimized p-type A/l ratio using the n-type A/l**
42. In cell B13, type ‘
43. In cell D13, type **@SQRT(B4*D6/(D4*B6))**
44. In cell E13, type **cm**
45. In cell A14, type ‘ (12 spaces) **Z =** (3 spaces) **Junction figure of merit**
46. In cell B14, type **+B10^2/(B15*B16)**
47. In cell C14, type **‘1/K**
48. In cell D14, type **+B10^2/((@SQRT(B4*B6)+@SQRT (D4*D6))^2)**
49. In cell E14, type **‘1/K**
50. In cell A15, type ‘ (12 spaces) **K =** (3 spaces) **Device thermal conductance**
51. In cell B15, type **+B6*B8+D6*D8**
52. In cell C15, type **watt/K**
53. In cell D15, type **+B6*B8+D6*D13**
54. In cell E15, type **watt/K**
55. In cell A16, type ‘ (12 spaces) **R =** (3 spaces) **Device resistance**
56. In cell B16, type **+B4/B8+D4/D8**
57. In cell C16, type **ohms**
58. In cell D16, type **+B4/B8+D4/D13**
59. In cell E16, type **ohms**

In the unoptimized calculation, the value of I is an input parameter. In the optimized calculation, it is calculated.

60. In cell A17, type ‘ (12 spaces) **I =** (3 spaces) **Device current**
61. In cell B17, type **29**
62. In cell C17, type **amps**
63. In cell D17, type **+B10*(B7-D7)/(D16*(@SQRT(1+D14* B9)-1))**
64. In cell E17, type **amps**
65. In cell A18, type ‘ (11 spaces) **qc =** (3 spaces) **Heat flow into the cold side**

66. In cell B18, type **+B10*D7*B17-0.5*B17^2*B16-B15*(B7-D7)**
67. In cell C18, type **watt**
68. In cell D18, type **+B10*D7*D17-0.5*D17^2*D16-D15*(B7-D7)**
69. In cell E18, type **watt**
70. In cell A19, type ' (9 spaces) **beta =** (3 spaces) **Coefficient of performance**
71. In cell B19, type **(B10*D7*B17-0.5*B17^2*B16-B15*(B7-D7))/(B10*B17*(B7-D7)+B17^2*B16)**
72. In cell D19, type **(D7/(B7-D7))*(@SQRT(1+D14*B9)-B7/D7)/(@SQRT(1+D14*B9)+1)**
73. In cell A20, type ' (12 spaces) **P =** (3 spaces) **Input power**
74. In cell B20, type **+B10*B17*(B7-D7)+B17^2*B16**
75. In cell C20, type **watt**
76. In cell D20, type **+D18/D19**
77. In cell E20, type **watt**
78. Format cells B3..B6, B10, B14..B16,D3..D6, and D14..D16 as Scientific 3 (/**RFS3**).
79. Format cells B17..B20, D13, and D17..D20 as Fixed 3 (/**RFF3**).
80. Unprotect cells A2, B3..B5, B7, B8, B17, D3..D5, D7 and D8 with the /Range Unprotect (/**RU**) command.
81. Protect the spreadsheet with the /Worksheet Global Protection Enable (/**WGPE**) command.

The worksheet should now look like Figure 2.15 with the unprotected cells highlighted (so that you can change their values) and the rest of the cells protected.

■ SUMMARY

This chapter probably covers at least 50 percent of the spreadsheet techniques that a practicing scientist or engineer normally uses in the course of work. Let's face it, much of the numerical work of science

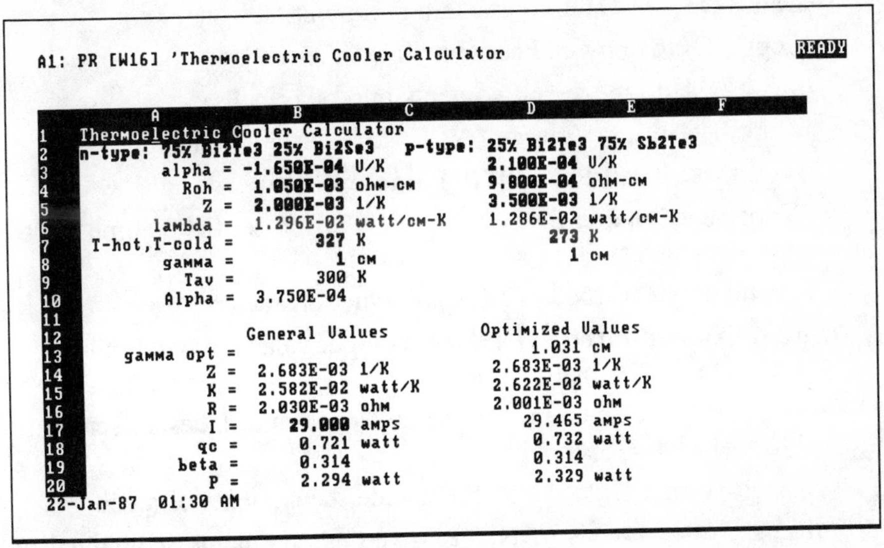

```
A1: PR [W16] 'Thermoelectric Cooler Calculator                                READY

           A             B           C              D           E        F
1   Thermoelectric Cooler Calculator
2   n-type: 75% Bi2Te3 25% Bi2Se3   p-type: 25% Bi2Te3 75% Sb2Te3
3          alpha = -1.650E-04 V/K              2.100E-04 V/K
4            Roh =  1.050E-03 ohm-cm           9.800E-04 ohm-cm
5              Z =  2.000E-03 1/K              3.500E-03 1/K
6         lambda =  1.296E-02 watt/cm-K        1.286E-02 watt/cm-K
7   T-hot,T-cold =        327 K                      273 K
8          gamma =          1 cm                       1 cm
9            Tav =        300 K
10         Alpha =  3.750E-04
11
12                General Values           Optimized Values
13     gamma opt =                                 1.031 cm
14             Z =  2.683E-03 1/K              2.683E-03 1/K
15             K =  2.582E-02 watt/K           2.622E-02 watt/K
16             R =  2.030E-03 ohm              2.001E-03 ohm
17             I =     29.000 amps                29.465 amps
18            qc =      0.721 watt                 0.732 watt
19          beta =      0.314                      0.314
20             P =      2.294 watt                 2.329 watt
22-Jan-87  01:30 AM
```

Figure 2.15: A calculator for analyzing a thermoelectric cooler

and engineering (but not all—luckily) involves putting simple numbers into relatively simple equations and calculating the results. As this chapter has demonstrated, the spreadsheet format is quite amenable to this type of work. All that is missing is graphic presentation of the data, which we will discuss in the next chapter.

In this chapter, we have explored many ways to create engineering tables and formula calculators. Hopefully, this exploration has given you a strong start in solving your own problems with Lotus 1-2-3. As you use the spreadsheet and gain experience with it, you will find many more ways to calculate and present useful results.

Engineering tables allow you to calculate single or multiple values from scientific and engineering equations. Function calculators calculate values for complex sets of equations. With them, you can model a complex system and then play "what if" games with the system parameters and immediately see the results. While creating these tables and calculators, you have used many of the commands and techniques that simplify spreadsheet creation and define how the completed spreadsheet will look. Specifically, this chapter has presented the following commands:

Worksheet Erase Yes (/WEY) to erase the spreadsheet

/Data Fill (/DF) to fill a range with sequential numbers

/Data Table 1 (/DT1) to create a single input table

/Data Table 2 (/DT2) to create a two input table

/Copy (/C) to copy cell contents into other cells

/Move (/M) to move cell contents into other cells

/Worksheet Insert Column (/WIC) to insert a column

/Worksheet Insert Row (/WIR) to insert a row

/Worksheet Column Set-width *n* (/WCS*n*) to set the column width to *n* characters

\- to fill a cell with dashes (or any other characters)

/Range Format Fixed *n* (/RFF*n*) to output values in fixed-point format with *n* decimal places

/Range Format Scientific *n* (/RFS*n*) to output values in scientific format with *n* decimal places

/Range Format Hidden (/RFH) to hide the contents of a cell

/Range Name Labels (/RNL) to give cells the names contained in labels in adjacent cells

/Range Name Create (/RNC) to create a name for a range of cells

/Worksheet Global Column-width *n* (/WGC*n*) to set the default width of all columns in the worksheet

/Worksheet Global Recalculation Manual (/WGRM) to stop automatic recalculation of the worksheet

/Range Unprotect (/RU) to unprotect a range of cells

These commands and their variations will do most of what you need to create a spreadsheet with Lotus 1-2-3. In the next few chapters, you will explore a number of other commands as well as some variations of those discussed here.

■ FOR MORE INFORMATION

For further information about the topics in this chapter, you can consult the following sources.

Thermal Conductivity

E. L. Heasell, "The Heat Flow Problem in Silicon," *IEEE Trans. on Elec. Dev., ED-25* 12 (Dec. 1978):1382.

Precession of the North Celestial Pole

A. E. Roy, *The Foundations of Astrodynamics* (New York: Macmillan, 1969), p. 53.

Temperature Dependence of the Intrinsic Carrier Density

S. M. Sze, *Physics of Semiconductor Devices,* 2nd ed. (New York: Wiley, 1981), p. 19.

Van der Waals Equation of State

D. Halliday and R. Resnick, *Physics* (New York: Wiley, 1967), pp. 611–615.

Absolute Magnitude of a Star

D. S. Birney, *Modern Astronomy* (Boston: Allyn & Bacon, 1969), pp. 168–174.

Electron Mobility in Silicon

W. J. Orvis, *Semiconductor Device Modeling with BURN42: A One-Dimensional Code for Modeling Solid State Devices,* UCID-20602 (Livermore, Calif.: Lawrence Livermore National Laboratory, 1985), p. 8.

D. M. Canghey and R. E. Thomas, "Carrier Mobilities in Silicon Empirically Related to Doping and Field," *Proc. IEEE* (Dec. 1967):2192.

C. Jacoboni et al., "A Review of Some Charge Transport Properties of Silicon," *Solid State Electronics* 20 (1977):77.

Stress and Deflection in a Cantilever Beam

E. Oberg, F. D. Jones, and H. L. Horton, *Machinery's Handbook,* 20th ed. (New York: Industrial Press, 1978).

T. Baumeister, E. Avallone, and T. Baumeister III, *Standard Handbook for Mechanical Engineers* (New York: McGraw-Hill, 1979).

Julian Days

G. Ottewell, *The Astronomical Companion,* published by the author at Furman University, Greenville, S.C. 1979, p. 23.

Thermoelectric Coolers

S. W. Angrist, *Direct Energy Conversion,* 4th ed. (Boston: Allyn & Bacon, 1982), pp. 148–153.

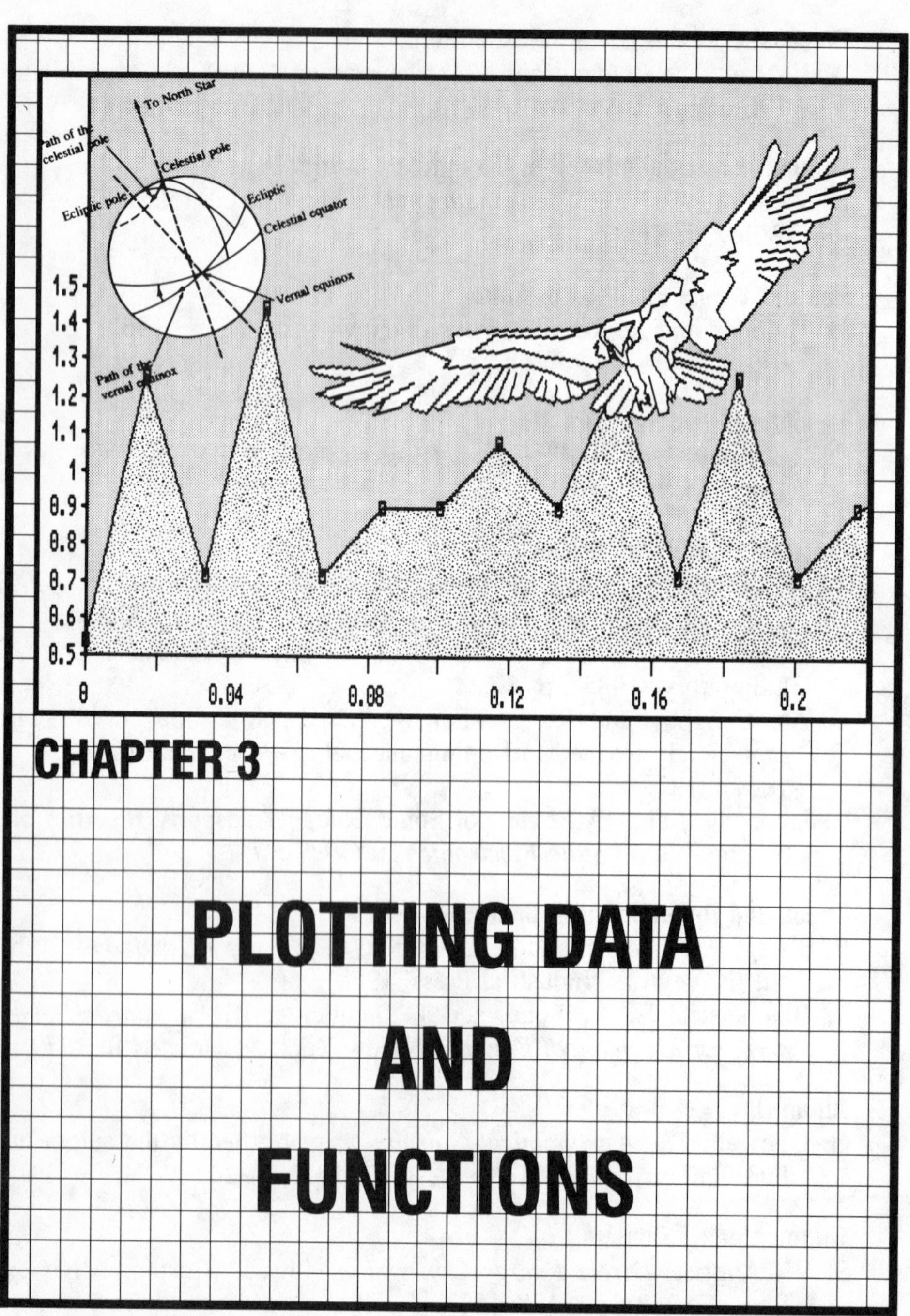

CHAPTER 3

PLOTTING DATA AND FUNCTIONS

Once we have generated a set of numbers, our next task usually is to analyze them. The simplest form of analysis is to plot the numbers and see what kind of a curve they form, if any. A lot of good scientific information has been obtained by simply looking at the shape of a plot of data. In this chapter, we will examine the plotting capabilities of Lotus 1-2-3 and how to adapt them to scientific and engineering uses.

THE GRAPH COMMAND

You can easily create plots with Lotus 1-2-3. Using the /Graph (/G) command menu, you select the data ranges to be plotted and the plot type. Then you can display the graph by using the View command (V) from the graph menu or pressing the Graph key in ready mode.

When you execute the /Graph (/G) command, the following Graph menu is displayed:

```
Type X A B C D E F Reset View Save Options Name Quit
```

Note that the /Graph command is different from the other commands in this book so far. When you execute one of the Graph commands, you do not return to the ready mode as you do with /Move (/M) or /Copy (/C); instead, you return to the Graph menu. To exit the Graph menu, use the Quit (Q) command or press Esc.

Plot Types

Executing the Type (T) command allows you to select the type of plot to be created. Five different plot types are available: line plots, bar charts, stacked bar charts, pie charts, and X-Y plots (see page 112 in the Lotus *1-2-3 Reference Manual* for examples). Only the last plot type, the X-Y plot, is really useful for science and engineering purposes. All of the others are primarily business and administrative tools. In fact, only the X-Y plot actually plots the *x* range of data. All of the other plot types use the *x* data for labels. No matter what the values of the *x* coordinates, all of the data points are equally spaced in the *x* direction. You do not even have to use values for the *x* data, but can use labels (for example, Jan., Feb., Expenses, and so on). Unless all of your data is equally spaced and ordered, these other plot types are not of much use for scientific and engineering tasks.

The X-Y plot type is a true X-Y plot using linear scales, where both the *x* and *y* coordinate values are used to plot the position of the point. The *x*-range data must all be values and not labels. You can plot data versus labels if you want to, but all of the data will be stacked at $x = 0$. This happens because the value of a label is 0.

Setting Data Ranges

Once you have set the type of plot (here, the X-Y plot type), you must specify what data on the spreadsheet to plot. You do this with the Graph commands: X A B C D E F. Use the X command to enter the range of data on the spreadsheet to use for the *x* coordinates. Use commands A through F to set the ranges of data to use for the *y* coordinates. Thus, you can have up to six separately formatted plots on one graph, so long as they use the same *x* range data (you will see later how to get around this restriction). Lotus 1-2-3 will prompt you to select a range in the same manner as it prompted you for ranges in the /Copy and /Move commands (/C and /M). You can either type the starting and ending values of the range separated with a period or select the range using the cursor-movement keys.

Setting Plot Options

Once you have selected the plot type and data ranges, you can view the plot with the View (V) command while in the Graph menu or by pressing the Graph key while in ready mode. What you will see is a plot of the *x* and *y* data with no axis labels or titles. To add labels to the graph and axes and to change the display method, you execute the Options (O) command. Executing this command results in another menu of commands:

```
Legend  Format  Titles  Grid  Scale  Color  B&W
Data-labels  Quit
```

As with the Graph menu, executing a command from the Graph Options menu returns to this menu. To return to the Graph menu, use the Quit (Q) command or the Esc key.

Legend

Each of the six possible plots on a graph uses a different symbol to mark the data points. The Legend (L) command allows you to associate text with these marker symbols to identify the plots. This text is then printed along the bottom of the plot beside the marker symbols used on the plot.

Format

The Format (F) command allows you to set the format of the six plots on the graph. The possible formats are *line, symbol, both,* or *neither*. You use the *neither* option when you are going to mark the plot with data labels.

Titles

Each graph can have a two-line title along the top. Use the Titles (T) command to specify the text for titles and for the labels of the x and y axes.

Grid

The default grid has tick marks around the edge, but no grid lines within the graph body. Use the Grid (G) command to plot horizontal or vertical, or both, sets of grid lines.

Scale

Normally, Lotus 1-2-3 looks at the data being plotted and automatically selects plot limits that will contain the whole plot. If you want to specify particular plot limits, use the Scale (S) command. You can also use the Scale command to specify the format of the numbers printed along the x and y axes and whether the scale indicator is printed. The formats allowed are the same as those available with the /Range Format (/RF) command.

The scale indicator is a word printed along an axis to specify the multiplier to use on the axis values (thousands, millions, billions, and so on). If you execute Indicator No (IN), then the values on that axis may be in error by some power of 10, and you will need to specify the multiplier in the axis label.

Color or B&W

When you are operating in high resolution, two-color mode (determined by the driver set selected with the setup program), the Color (C) and B&W (B, Black and White) commands control only the shading of bars in bar charts and of slices in pie charts. Be sure to execute the B&W command when you use this mode, or you will not be able to tell one bar on a bar chart from another. If you are using color graphics mode, then you can pick either color or B&W, depending on what looks best.

Data Labels

The Data-labels (D) command can be used to specify a set of labels to be printed at each data point. The labels to use are entered as a range on the spreadsheet. The first label in the range is associated with the first data point, the second label with the second data point, and so forth. If you want to label only some of the data points, you must have blank cells in the label range opposite the data points that will not have labels. The labels can be put to either side of the data points or above, below, or centered on the data points. As already noted, you can use the Format (F) command to eliminate the lines or symbols from the plot so that the only markers are those that you specify with the Data-labels (D) command.

Viewing the Plot

When you want to see what the plot looks like, press the View (V) command while in the Graph menu, and the plot will be displayed. Press any key to return to the Graph menu. If you are in ready mode, press the Graph key to switch between the graph and the spreadsheet. That way, you can change the spreadsheet data and then immediately look at the graph of that data to see the effect of the change.

Naming and Saving

Lotus 1-2-3 can have only one current graph at a time, but several graphs can be attached to a spreadsheet. Use the Name Create (NC) command to name a graph and attach it to a spreadsheet. Use the Name Use (NU) command to use a previously saved graph and make it the current graph. Actually, you are not saving a graph, but are saving the graph settings (type, x and y ranges, labels, and so on). If you change the spreadsheet contents, a recalled graph will show the changes.

The Save (S) command in the Graph menu saves a copy of the graph in a file with the extension .PIC. You cannot recall this graph into Lotus 1-2-3. It can only be printed with the Lotus PrintGraph program included with Lotus 1-2-3. If you want to save a graph for later recall into Lotus 1-2-3, use the Name commands described in the preceding paragraph.

A simpler way to get a copy of a graph is with a graphics screen dump to the printer. The quality is not as good, but the process is much faster. To do this, you must execute the DOS command GRAPHICS before loading Lotus 1-2-3. A graphics screen can then be dumped to the printer using Shift-Print.

■ PLOTTING AN ENGINEERING TABLE

The following example demonstrates how to create graphs of engineering functions.

Resistivity of Silicon A plot of the resistivity of silicon versus temperature is a multivalued curve that peaks at some temperature between 300 and 1000 K, depending on the doping density. This curve is important to solid-state device engineering because the change in the curve slope from positive to negative can cause a semiconductor device to go into a state known as thermal second breakdown.

At low temperatures, the resistance of silicon increases with temperature. Thus, any heating of a device due to high currents is self-limiting because the increasing resistance stops the current and stops the heating. If, on the other hand, the temperature of a device passes a threshold value, then resistance starts to decrease with temperature. As resistance decreases, more current can flow, which increases the heating and decreases the resistance even more. This effect grows exponentially and is known as thermal second breakdown in semiconductor devices.

The resistivity of silicon due to electron motion (we will ignore hole motion in this example) is defined with the following equation:

$$\rho = \frac{1}{qn\mu}$$

where ρ is the resistivity in ohm-meters, q is the charge on an electron, n is the electron density, and μ is the electron mobility. The electron equilibrium density in doped silicon can be obtained from this equation:

$$n = \frac{1}{2}\left[N + \sqrt{N^2 + 4n_i^2}\right]$$

where N is the doping density in m^{-3}, and n_i is the intrinsic carrier density. You calculated the intrinsic carrier density in the last chapter. You also calculated the mobility for all fields, temperatures, and doping densities. However, for this problem, you are dealing with low fields and doping densities, so the mobility equation can be approximated with

$$\mu = \mu_0\left(\frac{T}{T_0}\right)^{-2.42}$$

which is much simpler than the formula that you calculated in the last chapter. If you have the intrinsic carrier density problem available from the last chapter, you can use it as a starting point for this problem. Otherwise, you will have to enter it again.

In this example you will calculate the resistivity of silicon versus temperature for three different doping densities (1.0×10^{13}, 1.5×10^{13}, and 1.0×10^{14} cm^{-3}). You may want to turn off global recalculation with the command /Worksheet Global Recalculation Manual (/WGRM) while you are entering this spreadsheet and then, when you are done, turn it back on with the /Worksheet Global Recalculation Automatic (/WGRA) command. You can recalculate the spreadsheet at any time by pressing the Calc key.

1. Set the cell widths according to the following list: A = **9**, B = **9**, C = **9**, D = **12**, E = **10**, F..N = **9**
2. In cell A1, type **Resistivity of Silicon vs. Temperature**
3. In cell A3, type **"EG0**
4. In cell B3, type **1.17**
5. In cell A4, type **"EG1**
6. In cell B4, type **4.73E-4**
7. In cell A5, type **"EG2**
8. In cell B5, type **636**
9. In cell C3, type **"CONS**
10. In cell D3, type **@SQRT(4*6*(2*@PI*0.91095E-30 *1.38066 E-23/(6.62618E-34^2))^3)*(0.33*0.56)^(0.75)*1E-6**

11. In cell C4, type **“Q**
12. In cell D4, type **1.6E-19**
13. In cell E2, type **“μ0**
14. In cell F2, type **1330**
15. In cell E3, type **“T0**
16. In cell F3, type **300**
17. In cell E4, type **“GAMMA**
18. In cell F4, type **2.42**
19. In cell B6, type **^T**
20. In cell B7, type **^(K)**
21. In cell C6, type **^Eg**
22. In cell C7, type **^(eV)**
23. In cell D6, type **^ni**
24. In cell D7, type **^(cm^-3)**
25. In cell E6, type **^μ**
26. In cell E7, type **^(cm^2/V-s)**
27. In cell F6, type **^n**
28. In cell F7, type **^(cm^-3)**
29. In cell G6, type **^rho**
30. In cell G7, type **^(ohm-cm)**
31. In cell H6, type **^n**
32. In cell H7, type **^(cm^-3)**
33. In cell I6, type **^rho**
34. In cell I7, type **^(ohm-cm)**
35. In cell J6, type **^n**
36. In cell J7, type **^(cm^-3)**
37. In cell K6, type **^rho**
38. In cell K7, type **^(ohm-cm)**
39. In cell E5, type **Doping:**
40. In cell F5, type **1E13**
41. In cell G5, type **‘(cm^-3)**
42. In cell H5, type **1.5E13**

43. In cell I5, type **'(cm^-3)**
44. In cell J5, type **1E14**
45. In cell K5, type **'(cm^-3)**
46. In cells B8..K8, type/copy **\-**
47. Name cells B3..B5, D3, D4, F2..F4 with the labels in cells A3..A5, C3, C4, E2..E4 with the /Range Name Labels Right (/**RNLR**) command.
48. In cells B9..B19, use the /Data Fill (/**DF**) command with a starting value of **300** and a step of **20**.
49. In cell C9, type **+$B$3-$B$4*B9^2/(B9+$B$5)**

Note that I have not used the names for the constants (EG1 and EG2) in this equation, because they are the same as valid cell references. After I have typed the cell references, Lotus 1-2-3 inserts the cell names. I do not need to do this in the rest of the formulas as they do not contain cell names that are also valid cell references.

50. In cell D9, type **+$CONS*@SQRT(B9^3)*@EXP(-C9* 1.60219E-19 /(2*1.38066E-23*B9))**
51. In cell E9, type **+$μ0*(B9/$T0)^(-$GAMMA)**
52. In cell F9, type **0.5*(F$5+@SQRT(F$5^2+4*$D9^2))**
53. In cell G9, type **1/($Q*F9*$E9)**
54. Copy cells F6..G9 into cells H6..I9 and cells J6..K9.
55. Copy cells C9..K9 into cells C10..K19.

If you earlier turned off automatic recalculation, then turn it on again now or press the Calc key whenever you make a change to the spreadsheet. The spreadsheet should look like that in Figure 3.1 minus the labels in columns L..N.

You are now ready to plot these three sets of data.

56. Execute the /Graph (/**G**) command to get the Graph menu.
57. Execute the Type XY (**TX**) command to select an X-Y plot type.
58. Execute the X (**X**) command and select B9..B19 as the *x* range.
59. Execute the A (**A**) command and select G9..G19 as the first set of *y* data to plot.
60. Execute the View (**V**) command to see the plot.

```
A1: [W9] 'Resistivity of Silicon vs. Temperature                    READY

        A        B        C         D          E         F         G
1   Resistivity of Silicon vs. Temperature
2                                              µ0        1330
3      EG0      1.17     CONS  3.3341E+15      T0         300
4      EG1  0.000473        Q  1.6000E-19   GAMMA        2.42
5      EG2       636                      Doping:     1.0E+13 (cm^-3)
6                  T       Eg        ni         µ          n       rho
7                (K)     (eV)   (cm^-3)  (cm^2/V-s) (cm^-3) (ohm-cm)
8            ------------------------------------------------------------
9                300     1.12   6.2E+09    1.3E+03  1.0E+13  4.7E+02
10               320     1.12   2.9E+10    1.1E+03  1.0E+13  5.5E+02
11               340     1.11   1.2E+11    9.8E+02  1.0E+13  6.4E+02
12               360     1.11   4.0E+11    8.6E+02  1.0E+13  7.3E+02
13               380     1.10   1.2E+12    7.5E+02  1.0E+13  8.2E+02
14               400     1.10   3.3E+12    6.6E+02  1.1E+13  8.6E+02
15               420     1.09   8.2E+12    5.9E+02  1.5E+13  7.3E+02
16               440     1.08   1.9E+13    5.3E+02  2.4E+13  4.8E+02
17               460     1.08   4.1E+13    4.7E+02  4.6E+13  2.9E+02
18               480     1.07   8.2E+13    4.3E+02  8.7E+13  1.7E+02
19               500     1.07   1.6E+14    3.9E+02  1.6E+14  9.9E+01
20
21-Feb-87   11:34 PM
```

Figure 3.1: Resistivity of silicon versus temperature

```
O1:                                                                 READY

        H        I        J        K        L        M        N        O
1
2
3
4
5    1.5E+13 (cm^-3)   1.0E+14 (cm^-3)
6          n      rho        n      rho
7    (cm^-3) (ohm-cm)  (cm^-3) (ohm-cm)
8   -------------------------------------
9    1.5E+13  3.1E+02  1.0E+14  4.7E+01
10   1.5E+13  3.7E+02  1.0E+14  5.5E+01
11   1.5E+13  4.2E+02  1.0E+14  6.4E+01
12   1.5E+13  4.9E+02  1.0E+14  7.3E+01 1.0E14    1.5E13           1.0E13 (cm
13   1.5E+13  5.5E+02  1.0E+14  8.3E+01
14   1.6E+13  6.0E+02  1.0E+14  9.4E+01
15   1.9E+13  5.7E+02  1.0E+14  1.1E+02
16   2.8E+13  4.3E+02  1.0E+14  1.1E+02
17   4.9E+13  2.7E+02  1.1E+14  1.2E+02
18   9.0E+13  1.6E+02  1.5E+14  1.0E+02
19   1.7E+14  9.7E+01  2.2E+14  7.5E+01
20
21-Feb-87   11:35 PM
```

Figure 3.1: Resistivity of silicon versus temperature *(continued)*

You should see the graph shown in Figure 3.2, with the first set of data plotted on it. Now plot the other sets of data.

61. Execute the B (**B**) command and select cells I9..I19 as the second set of *y* data to plot.

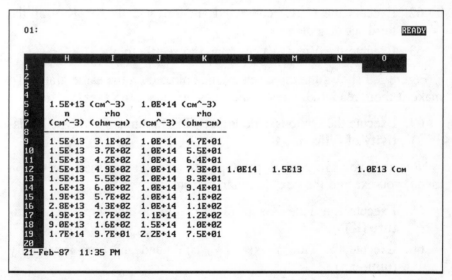

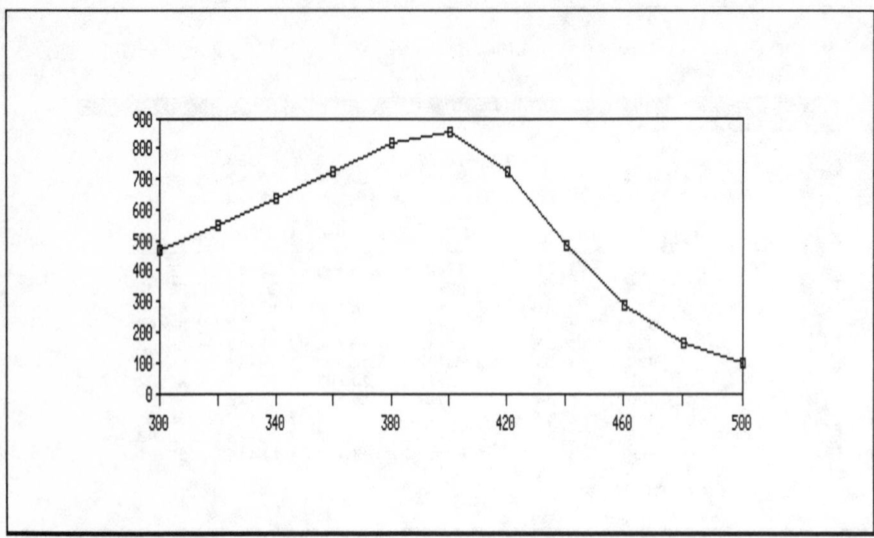

Figure 3.2: Graph with one plot

62. Execute the C (C) command and select cells K9..K19 as the third set of *y* data to plot.
63. Execute the View (V) command to see the plot.

Figure 3.3 shows the three sets of data plotted on the same graph. To make it more readable, enter some titles and label the axes.

64. Execute the Options Title First (OTF) command and type **Resistivity of Silicon**

Note that you are now in the Options menu rather than the Graph menu; you execute the next commands from there.

65. Execute the Title X-axis (TX) command and type **Temperature (K)**
66. Execute the Title Y-axis (TY) command and type **Resistivity (ohm-cm)**
67. Execute the Quit (Q) command to return to the Graph menu.
68. Execute the View (V) command to see the plot.

The plot should now look like that in Figure 3.4. All that is necessary is to label the three different plots to differentiate them. There are two ways to mark them: You can use the Options Legend (OL) command

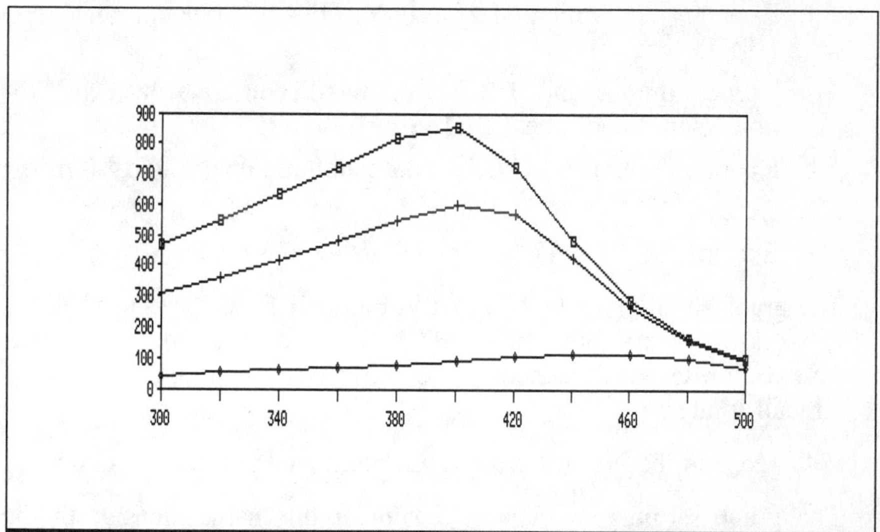

Figure 3.3: Graph with three plots

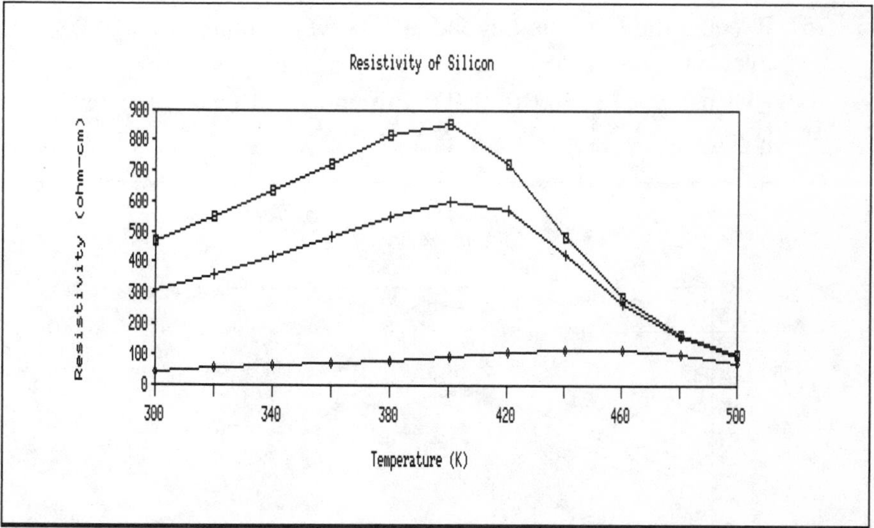

Figure 3.4: Graph with titles

and type a legend for each label, which will be inserted at the bottom of the graph, or you can create some data labels and attach them to three of the data points, which will place the labels on the graph itself. Try both methods here to compare the results. Label the plots with the doping density that was used to create them.

69. Execute the Options Legend A (**OLA**) command and type **1.0E13 (cm^-3)**
70. Execute the Legend B (**LB**) command (you are still in the Options menu) and type **1.5E13 (cm^-3)**
71. Execute the Legend C (**LC**) command and type **1.0E14 (cm^-3)**
72. Execute the Quit (**Q**) command to return to the Graph menu.
73. Execute the View (**V**) command to see the graph.

The graph should now be like that in Figure 3.5, which is not bad for your working papers, but you should probably dress it up a little more before you present it to someone else. First save this graph so that you can recall it later.

74. Execute the Name Create (**NC**) command and type **FIG3-5**

The graph settings are now saved under this name along with the spreadsheet so that you can recall them later. To use data labels instead of a legend, you first need to get rid of the existing legends.

75. Execute the Options Legend A (**OLA**) command and backspace over the existing legend.
76. Execute the Legend B (**LB**) command and backspace over that legend.

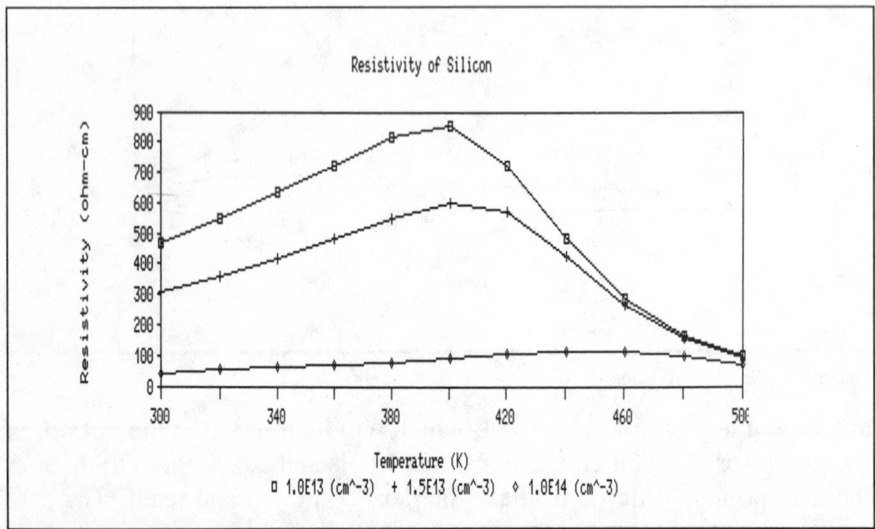

Figure 3.5: Resistivity of silicon versus temperature and doping density, with a legend.

77. Execute the Legend C (**LC**) command and backspace over the last legend.

Data labels are attached to a set of data points in a data range in the same manner as another set of data would be. To insert the data labels, you must go back to the spreadsheet and enter the labels in some cells. You then return to the Graph menu and attach the labels with the Options Data-labels (**OD**) command.

78. Execute the Quit (**Q**) command to return to ready mode.
79. In cell L12, type **'1.0E14**
80. In cell M12, type **'1.5E13**
81. In cell N12, type ' (8 spaces) **1.0E13 (cm^-3)**
82. Execute the /Graph Options (**/GO**) command to return to the Options menu.
83. Execute the Data-labels A (**DA**) command and select N9..N19 as the label range and enter Below (**B**) as the location.
84. Execute the B (**B**) command (you are still in the Data-labels menu), select M9..M19 as the label range, and enter Below (**B**) as the location.
85. Execute the C (**C**) command, select cells L9..L19 as the label range, and enter Above (**A**) as the location.
86. Execute the Quit Quit (**QQ**) command to return to the Graph menu.
87. Execute the View (**V**) command to see the plot.

The graph should now look like that in Figure 3.6, which looks much more professional than the previous graph. The problem with this method of labeling is that if you change the plots, the labels may no longer be in appropriate locations and may need to be moved. Note that when you selected the cell ranges for the data labels, you selected a lot of blank cells. The labels are matched one for one with the data points, so you need three blank cells in the beginning of the ranges to place labels on the fourth data points. Save this graph and recall the previous one for comparison.

88. Execute Name Create (**NC**) and type **FIG3-6**
89. Execute Name Use (**NU**) and select FIG3-5.

The graph with a legend is now displayed. You can use the Name Use (NU) command to switch back and forth between the two graphs.

■ LOG AND SEMILOG GRAPHS

The X-Y plot type only has linear axes, so plotting functions on logarithmic or semilogarithmic axes poses a small problem. The way to get around this restriction is to calculate the logarithm of the data and plot this instead of the original data. Be sure to note this approach in the axes labels.

Electron Avalanche Coefficient in Silicon When a voltage is applied across a semiconductor device, electrons in the semiconductor material are accelerated. If the voltage is high enough, the electrons are accelerated to the point where they can generate additional electrons through impact ionization. Device designers usually like to keep avalanche out of their devices, except in special devices, such as avalanche transistors.

The avalanche rate can be calculated with empirical equations that have been fit to experimental data. For example, you can calculate the silicon avalanche coefficient versus electric field and temperature with

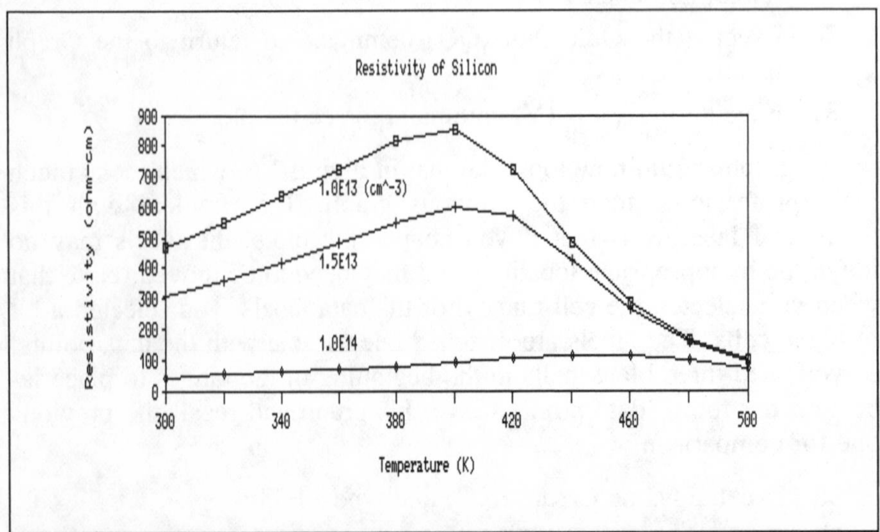

Figure 3.6: Resistivity of silicon versus temperature and doping density, with data labels.

the following equation, using the coefficients in Table 3.1:

$$\alpha = AVN1 \exp\left[\frac{AVN2 + AVN3(T - 300)}{|E|}\right]$$

Here, α is in m^{-1}, T is the temperature in kelvins, and E is the electric field in V/m. The avalanche rate can then be calculated by multiplying this coefficient times the electron density and the electron velocity.

In this example, you will calculate the avalanche coefficients versus electric field at 300, 600, and 900 K.

1. Set the column widths according to the following list: A = **12**, B = **12**, C = **7**, D = **12**, E = **7**, F = **12**, G = **7**
2. In cell A1, type **Electron Avalanche Coefficients in Silicon**

Create the table of values for use in the avalanche coefficient equation. Each set of coefficients is for a different range of electric field values.

3. In cell A3, type **"E (V/m)**
4. In cell A4, type **0**
5. In cell A5, type **2.4E7**
6. In cell A6, type **4.2E7**
7. In cell B3, type **"AVN1 (1/m)**
8. In cell B4, type **2.6E8**
9. In cell B5, type **6.2E7**
10. In cell B6, type **5.0E7**
11. In cell D3, type **"AVN2 (V/m)**
12. In cell D4, type **1.43E8**
13. In cell D5, type **1.08E8**

E(V/m)	AVN1 (m^{-1})	AVN2 (V/m)	AVN3 (V/m − K)
$E < 2.4 \times 10^7$	2.6×10^8	1.43×10^8	1.3×10^5
$2.4 \times 10^7 < E < 4.2 \times 10^7$	6.2×10^7	1.08×10^8	1.3×10^5
$E > 4.2 \times 10^7$	5.0×10^7	9.90×10^7	1.3×10^5

Table 3.1: Coefficients for the electron avalanche coefficient equation

14. In cell D6, type **9.9E7**
15. In cell F3, type **"AVN3 (V/m-K)**
16. In cell F4, type **1.3E5**
17. In cell F5, type **1.3E5**
18. In cell F6, type **1.3E5**

Name the cells in the table.

19. Name cells A5 and A6 as **ECUT1** and **ECUT2**.
20. Name cells B4..B6 as **AVN11**, **AVN12**, and **AVN13**.
21. Name cells D4..D6 as **AVN21**, **AVN22**, and **AVN32**.
22. Name cells F4..F6 as **AVN31**, **AVN32**, and **AVN33**.
23. Name the whole table A4..F6 as **COEFFS**.

Create the avalanche coefficient table.

24. In cell A8, type **"T =**
25. In cell B8, type **300**
26. In cell C8, type **'(K)**
27. In cell D8, type **600**
28. In cell E8, type **'(K)**
29. In cell F8, type **900**
30. In cell G8, type **'(K)**
31. In cell A9, type **"E (V/m)**
32. In cell B9, type **"alpha (1/m)**
33. In cell C9, type **^Log**
34. In cells A10..C10, type/copy **\-**
35. Execute the /Data Fill (**/DF**) command on the cell range A11..A30 with a start value of **5.0E + 06**, a step value of **5.0E + 06**, and a stop value of **1.0E8**.

There are two ways to select the correct values from the table according to the applied field. The first is to use nested @IF functions; two nested @IF functions break the problem into three ranges. The second method is to use the @VLOOKUP function, which scans the table automatically. The @LOOKUP function yields a more compact equation than the nested @IF functions, especially if the table includes more than two ranges. Use whatever works best for you. You will use both methods in this example.

First, use the nested @IF function method.

36. In cell B11, type **@IF($A11 > $ECUT1, @IF($A11>$ECUT2,$AVN13,$AVN12),$AVN11)* @EXP(-(@IF($A11>$ECUT1, @IF($A11>$ECUT2,$AVN23,$AVN22),$AVN21)+ @IF($A11>$ECUT1, @IF($A11>$ECUT2,$AVN33,$AVN32),$AVN31)* (B$8-300))/$A11)**
37. In cell C11, type **@LOG(B11)**

Now use the lookup function method.

38. In cell D11, type **@VLOOKUP($A11,$COEFFS,1)* @EXP(-(@VLOOKUP($A11,$COEFFS,3)+ @VLOOKUP($A11,$COEFFS,5)* (B$8-300))/$A11)**
39. In cell E11, type **@LOG(D11)**
40. Copy cells B9..C10 to D9..E10.

Use the @LOOKUP function for the rest of the spreadsheet.

41. Copy cells D9..E11 to F9..G11.
42. Copy cells B11..G11 to B12..G30.

This completes the spreadsheet, which should look like that in Figure 3.7. This spreadsheet calculates the electron avalanche coefficient versus electric field for the temperatures 300, 600, and 900 K, listed along the top.

As you can see, the values of the avalanche coefficient span many orders of magnitude, which would be difficult to plot on a linear scale. You have also calculated the common logarithms for all of these values, which are much more reasonable values to plot.

43. Execute the /Graph (**/G**) command to go to the Graph menu.

Select the X-Y graph type and set the ranges of the x and y data.

44. Execute the Type XY (**TX**) command to select the X-Y graph type.
45. Execute the X (**X**) command with a range of A11..A30 to set the x range.

A1: [W12] 'Electron Avalanche Coefficients in Silicon READY

	A	B	C	D	E	F	G
1	Electron Avalanche Coefficients in Silicon						
2							
3	E (V/m)	AVN1 (1/m)		AVN2 (V/m)		AVN3 (V/m-K)	
4	0.00E+00	2.60E+08		1.43E+08		1.30E+05	
5	2.40E+07	6.20E+07		1.08E+08		1.30E+05	
6	4.20E+07	5.00E+07		9.90E+07		1.30E+05	
7							
8	T =	300 (K)		600 (K)		900 (K)	
9	E (V/m)	alpha (1/m)	Log	alpha (1/m)	Log	alpha (1/m)	Log
10	------------	------------	------------	------------	------------	------------	------------
11	5.00E+06	9.87E-05	-4.01	4.04E-08	-7.39	1.66E-11	-10.78
12	1.00E+07	1.60E+02	2.20	3.24E+00	0.51	6.56E-02	-1.18
13	1.50E+07	1.88E+04	4.27	1.40E+03	3.15	1.04E+02	2.02
14	2.00E+07	2.04E+05	5.31	2.90E+04	4.46	4.13E+03	3.62
15	2.50E+07	8.25E+05	5.92	1.73E+05	5.24	3.64E+04	4.56
16	3.00E+07	1.69E+06	6.23	4.62E+05	5.66	1.26E+05	5.10
17	3.50E+07	2.83E+06	6.45	9.30E+05	5.97	3.05E+05	5.48
18	4.00E+07	4.17E+06	6.62	1.57E+06	6.20	5.93E+05	5.77
19	4.50E+07	5.54E+06	6.74	2.33E+06	6.37	9.79E+05	5.99
20	5.00E+07	6.90E+06	6.84	3.16E+06	6.50	1.45E+06	6.16

18-Feb-87 11:13 PM

Figure 3.7: The electron avalanche coefficients in silicon versus electric field and temperature

A21: (S2) [W12] 55000000 READY

	A	B	C	D	E	F	G
21	5.50E+07	8.26E+06	6.92	4.07E+06	6.61	2.00E+06	6.30
22	6.00E+07	9.60E+06	6.98	5.01E+06	6.70	2.62E+06	6.42
23	6.50E+07	1.09E+07	7.04	5.98E+06	6.78	3.28E+06	6.52
24	7.00E+07	1.22E+07	7.08	6.96E+06	6.84	3.99E+06	6.60
25	7.50E+07	1.34E+07	7.13	7.94E+06	6.90	4.72E+06	6.67
26	8.00E+07	1.45E+07	7.16	8.91E+06	6.95	5.47E+06	6.74
27	8.50E+07	1.56E+07	7.19	9.86E+06	6.99	6.23E+06	6.79
28	9.00E+07	1.66E+07	7.22	1.08E+07	7.03	7.00E+06	6.84
29	9.50E+07	1.76E+07	7.25	1.17E+07	7.07	7.76E+06	6.89
30	1.00E+08	1.86E+07	7.27	1.26E+07	7.10	8.52E+06	6.93
31							
32							
33							
34							
35							
36							
37							
38							
39							
40							

18-Feb-87 11:14 PM

Figure 3.7: The electron avalanche coefficients in silicon versus electric field and temperature *(continued)*

46. Execute the A (**A**) command with a range of C11..C30 to set the *y* range for the first plot.
47. Execute the B (**B**) command with a range of E11..E30 to set the *y* range for the second plot.

48. Execute the C (**C**) command with a range of G11..G30 to set the *y* range for the third plot.

Create a legend to identify which plot is which.

49. Execute the Options Legend A (**OLA**) command and type **T = 300 K**
50. Execute the Legend B (**LB**) command (you are still in the Options menu) and type **T = 600 K**
51. Execute the Legend C (**LC**) command and type **T = 900 K**

At this point I looked at the plot and decided that the automatically selected endpoints for the *y* axis were not appropriate, so let's change to manual mode and set them.

52. Execute the Scale Y Manual (**SYM**) command.
53. Execute the Lower (**L**) command with a value of **2** to set the lower *y*-plot limit.
54. Execute the Upper (**U**) command with a value of **10** to set the upper *y*-plot limit.
55. Execute the Quit (**Q**) command to return to the Options menu.
56. Execute the Scale X Indicator No (**SXIN**) command to turn off the indicator on the *x* axis.
57. Execute the Quit (**Q**) command to return to the Options menu.

Label the graph and axes.

58. Execute the Titles First (**TF**) command and type **Electron Avalanche Coefficient**
59. Execute the Titles Second (**TS**) command and type **Silicon**
60. Execute the Titles X-axis (**TX**) command and type **Electric Field (x10^6 V/m)**
61. Execute the Titles Y-axis (**TY**) command and type **Log (Avalanche Coeff.) Log(1/m)**
62. Execute the Quit (**Q**) command to return to the Graph menu.
63. Execute the Name Create (**NC**) command and type **FIG3-8**

You can look at the graph using the View (**V**) command. If everything looks good, then you need to execute the Quit (**Q**) command to return to ready mode. From ready mode, you can always recall the graph by pressing the Graph key.

64. Execute the View (V) command to see the graph.
65. Execute the Quit (Q) command to return to ready mode.

The completed graph is shown in Figure 3.8. This graph is a semilog graph plotted on linear axes. Creating an x axis semilog graph or a log-log graph uses similar methods. If you do not like having the log calculations in the middle of your spreadsheet, you can easily move them to one side and hide them.

■ THREE-DIMENSIONAL PLOTS

Lotus 1-2-3 was not intended for creating three-dimensional graphs of data. However, that will not stop us. By plotting consecutive slices through the data and offsetting them an appropriate amount, you can produce a reasonable three-dimensional plot.

Lotus 1-2-3 can have only six separate plots on any one graph, so unless you have only six slices of data to plot, you cannot generate the plots in the usual way. Lotus 1-2-3 does allow you to have an almost unlimited number of data points in any one plot, however. Using this feature, you can string all of the sections of data together into one plot, with each section of data offset a certain amount.

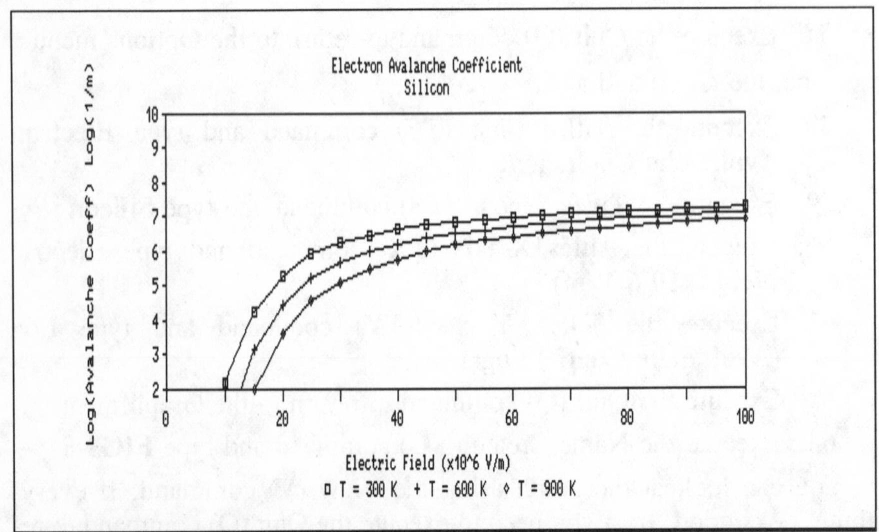

Figure 3.8: The electron avalanche coefficient in silicon for three different temperatures: a semilog plot

First, you define a new rectangular coordinate system u, v, and w. You plot the u axis horizontally, the v axis at an angle ϕ, and the w axis vertically (see Figure 3.9). Next you map these three axes onto the two-dimensional (X-Y) screen. You do this with the following transform:

$$x = u + v\cos(\phi)$$ Þ)

$$y = w + v\sin(\phi)$$ Þ)

To plot any three-dimensional data point (u, v, w), you just insert it into these transform equations and calculate the two-dimensional (X-Y) data point.

Next, you need to put all of the data into three columns on the spreadsheet so that you can map them into two columns that can then be plotted as an X-Y data set. Data for this type of plot normally comes in the form of slices through the domain to be plotted. Each slice goes from one boundary to the other. You can stack these data sets head to tail, where the first data point of one section comes after the last data point of the previous section. A problem with this approach is that a line will be drawn from the last data point of each section to the first data point of the next section. These lines will usually cut across the middle of the graph, which is definitely not what you want. In Lotus 1-2-3, if a data point is missing in the middle of a data range, then no data marker or lines are drawn to that point. Therefore, if you insert a blank line between the data sets, the return lines will not be drawn. Note that the line must be truly blank and not filled with blank labels, since a blank label has a value of 0.

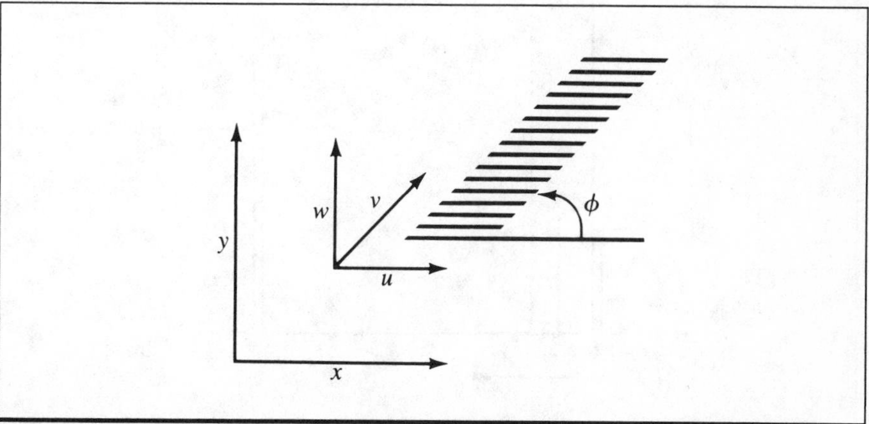

Figure 3.9: Mapping the three-dimensional axes onto the two-dimensional plotting surface

Temperature Profile in an Overstressed Silicon Diode When a small silicon diode is pulsed with a high power pulse of electricity, it heats up. If it heats up too much, it will be damaged. Of course, if you really pour on the power you will see smoke and fire where the diode used to be, and there will not be much question that it failed. On the other hand, if you use only a small amount of power, the diode may only be degraded and may still operate, at least for a while.

One way to evaluate the damage that a diode sustains is to mathematically model its operation to see where damaging heating occurs. This type of modeling is usually done on a Cray- or VAX-sized computer; however, the analysis of the results can be done on a desktop computer.

The data in Table 3.2 comes from just such a diode simulation and shows the temperature at different positions in the diode. The data is in the form of *y* and *z* position data and *T* temperature data.

The data at $y = 0$ is the centerline of the device (that is, only half of the diode was modeled). The bottom conductor is at $z = 130$ microns and covers the entire bottom of the diode. The top conductor is at $z = 0$ and extends from $y = 0$ to $y = 40$ microns. The diode junction, where all of the action takes place, is at $z = 10$ microns and extends from $y = 0$ to about 50 microns (Figure 3.10).

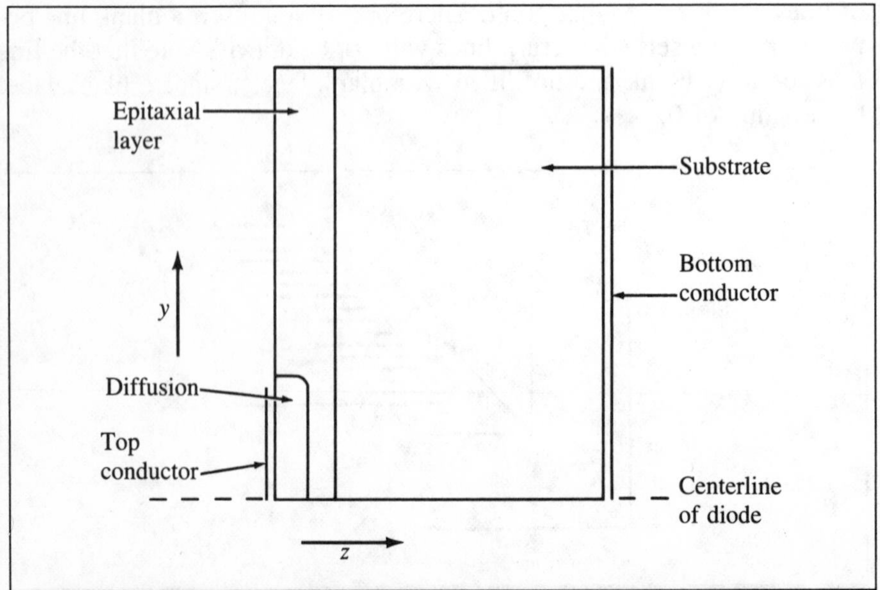

Figure 3.10: Layout of the small signal diode used to generate the temperature data

	y(μ)														
T(K)	0	10	20	30	35	40	43.3	46.6	50	55	60	110	155	200	250
z(μ)															
0	300	300	300	300	300	300	486	329	308	303	301	300	300	300	300
1	425	429	441	474	528	779	414	327	307	302	301	300	300	300	300
2	462	465	478	512	569	766	419	332	309	303	301	300	300	300	300
3	463	465	476	505	554	659	448	342	312	303	301	300	300	300	300
4	453	456	466	495	542	659	461	352	316	304	301	300	300	300	300
5	440	443	453	480	522	617	459	360	320	305	301	300	300	300	300
6	424	426	435	460	497	572	451	365	324	306	301	300	300	300	300
7	405	407	415	436	467	527	443	370	328	308	301	300	300	300	300
8	389	390	397	416	443	496	440	377	333	309	301	300	300	300	300
9	380	382	388	406	430	482	442	384	338	311	301	300	300	300	300
10	381	383	389	407	430	480	448	392	344	313	302	300	300	300	300
11	385	387	395	413	435	480	452	398	350	316	302	300	300	300	300
12	391	393	401	420	439	476	451	403	356	319	302	300	300	300	300
13	376	378	384	400	415	449	440	404	360	322	303	300	300	300	300
14	444	447	457	477	494	518	492	442	385	333	305	300	300	300	300
15	444	448	459	484	503	520	493	449	399	349	323	301	300	300	300
16	344	346	354	373	391	414	410	397	376	352	338	302	300	300	300
17	331	333	339	354	369	386	386	378	365	348	335	302	300	300	300
18	330	332	337	351	363	375	375	369	359	344	333	302	300	300	300
19	330	331	337	349	359	368	367	362	353	341	331	302	300	300	300
20	330	331	336	347	355	362	361	356	348	337	328	302	300	300	300
31	325	325	327	329	330	329	328	326	323	319	314	302	300	300	300
42	319	319	319	319	318	317	316	315	314	312	309	302	300	300	300
53	315	315	314	314	313	312	311	311	310	309	307	302	300	300	300
64	312	312	311	310	310	309	309	308	308	307	306	301	300	300	300
75	310	310	309	308	308	308	307	307	306	306	305	301	300	300	300
86	308	308	308	307	307	307	306	306	306	305	305	301	300	300	300
97	307	307	307	306	306	306	306	305	305	305	304	301	300	300	300
108	307	307	306	306	306	305	305	305	305	304	304	301	300	300	300
119	306	306	306	306	305	305	305	305	305	304	304	301	300	300	300
130	300	300	300	300	300	300	300	300	300	300	300	300	300	300	300

Table 3.2: Temperature data versus position in a small signal diode

As you can tell from Table 3.2, a large amount of data goes into this worksheet. The *y*, *z*, and *T* data goes into three parallel columns, and this data is then mapped onto the X-Y plane in two more columns, which are then plotted. If you do not want to type all of this data, I supply alternative data for an interesting graph.

1. Set the column widths according to the following list: A = **9**, B = **9**, C = **9**, D = **11**, E = **9**, F = **9**, G = **9**
2. In cell A1, type **Temperature Profile in an Overstressed Silicon Diode**
3. In cell D2, type **"Plot Angle:**
4. In cell E2, type **60**

You need both the sine and cosine of the plot angle in every mapping, and there is no sense in recalculating them again and again (transcendental functions such as sine and cosine are slow compared to simple multiplication or addition), so calculate them here and use the numbers in the rest of the worksheet. Convert the degrees to the radian measure needed by the functions.

5. In cell F2, type **@SIN(E2*@PI/180)**
6. In cell G2, type **@COS(E2*@PI/180)**
7. In cell A3, type **"Y (μ)**
8. In cell B3, type **"Z (μ)**
9. In cell C3, type **"T (K)**
10. In cell D3, type **"x**
11. In cell E3, type **"y**

Insert the *y* values.

12. In cells A4..A34, type/copy **0**
13. In cells A36..A66, type/copy **10**
14. In cells A68..A98, type/copy **20**
15. In cells A100..A130, type/copy **30**
16. In cells A132..A162, type/copy **35**
17. In cells A164..A194, type/copy **40**
18. In cells A196..A226, type/copy **43.3**
19. In cells A228..A258, type/copy **46.6**

20. In cells A260..A290, type/copy **50**
21. In cells A292..A322, type/copy **55**
22. In cells A324..A354, type/copy **60**
23. In cells A356..A386, type/copy **110**
24. In cells A388..A418, type/copy **155**
25. In cells A420..A450, type/copy **200**
26. In cells A452..A482, type/copy **250**

Enter the *z* data values. Type one set and then copy it into the rest of the data ranges.

27. In cells B4..B34, B36..B66, B68..B98, B100..B130, B132..B162, B164..B194, B196..B226, B228..B258, B260..B290, B292..B322, B324..B354, B356..B386, B388..B418, B420..B450, and B452..B482, type/copy this list of data into each cell range: **0, 1, 2, 3, 4, 5, 6, 7, 8, 9, 10, 11, 12, 13, 14, 15, 16, 17, 18, 19, 20, 31, 42, 53, 64, 75, 86, 97, 108, 119, 130**

Enter the temperature data. Be sure that you put the correct temperature value with each *y*, *z* value; do not forget the blank lines between the sets of data. If you accidentally type something in a cell that should be blank, use the /Range Erase (/RE) command to clear it. If you do not want to type the 464 data values, then plot the function in alternate step 28A.

28. Using the data in Table 3.2, type the 464 temperature values into cells C4..C482.

28A. In cells C4..C482, type/copy **300+500*@COS(A4*3*@PI/250)*@COS(B4*3*@PI/130)*@EXP(-A4/62)*@EXP(-B4/33)**

Enter the mapping functions.

29. In cells D4..D468, type/copy **+B4+A4*$G$2**
30. In cells E4..E468, type/copy **+C4+A4*$F$2**
31. Use the /Range Erase (/**RE**) command to erase the data copied into the blank lines at rows 35, 67, 99, 131, 163, 195, 227, 259, 291, 323, 355, 387, 419, and 453.

Draw lines around the edges of the plot of the data at the minimum temperature (300 K) for a visual queue to the perspective of the graph.

32. In cells D483, D484, E483, and E484 respectively, type the values **130, 0, 300, 300**
33. In cell D485, type **0+250*$G$2**
34. In cell D486, type **130+250*$G$2**
35. In cells E485 and E486, type **300+250*$F$2**

The worksheet should now look like that in Figure 3.11, or 3.12 if you plotted the alternate function. You are now ready to plot the data in columns D and E.

36. Execute the /Graph X (**/GX**) command and select cells D4..D486.
37. Execute the A (**A**) command and select cells E4..E486.
38. Execute the Options Titles First (**OTF**) command and type **Temperature Profile in a Silicon Diode**
39. Execute the Titles X-axis (**TX**) command and type **z (microns)**
40. Execute the Titles Y-axis (**TY**) command and type **Temperature (K)**
41. Execute the Format A Lines (**FAL**) command to use lines only.
42. Execute the Quit Quit Quit (**QQQ**) command to return to ready mode.

A1: 'Temperature Profile in an Overstressed Silicon Diode READY

	A	B	C	D	E	F	G
1	Temperature Profile in an Overstressed Silicon Diode						
2			Plot Angle:		60	0.866025	0.5
3	y (μ)	z (μ)	T (K)	x	y		
4	0	0	300	0	300		
5	0	1	425	1	425		
6	0	2	462	2	462		
7	0	3	463	3	463		
8	0	4	453	4	453		
9	0	5	440	5	440		
10	0	6	424	6	424		
11	0	7	405	7	405		
12	0	8	389	8	389		
13	0	9	380	9	380		
14	0	10	381	10	381		
15	0	11	385	11	385		
16	0	12	391	12	391		
17	0	13	376	13	376		
18	0	14	444	14	444		
19	0	15	444	15	444		
20	0	16	344	16	344		

18-Feb-87 11:27 PM

Figure 3.11: Temperature profile in an overstressed silicon diode

A21: 0 READY

	A	B	C	D	E	F	G
21	0	17	331	17	331		
22	0	18	330	18	330		
23	0	19	330	19	330		
24	0	20	330	20	330		
25	0	31	325	31	325		
26	0	42	319	42	319		
27	0	53	315	53	315		
28	0	64	312	64	312		
29	0	75	310	75	310		
30	0	86	308	86	308		
31	0	97	307	97	307		
32	0	108	307	108	307		
33	0	119	306	119	306		
34	0	130	300	130	300		
35							
36	10	0	300	5	308.6602		
37	10	1	429	6	437.6602		
38	10	2	465	7	473.6602		
39	10	3	465	8	473.6602		
40	10	4	456	9	464.6602		

18-Feb-87 11:29 PM

Figure 3.11: Temperature profile in an overstressed silicon diode *(continued)*

A467: 250 READY

	A	B	C	D	E	F	G
467	250	15	300	140	516.5063		
468	250	16	300	141	516.5063		
469	250	17	300	142	516.5063		
470	250	18	300	143	516.5063		
471	250	19	300	144	516.5063		
472	250	20	300	145	516.5063		
473	250	31	300	156	516.5063		
474	250	42	300	167	516.5063		
475	250	53	300	178	516.5063		
476	250	64	300	189	516.5063		
477	250	75	300	200	516.5063		
478	250	86	300	211	516.5063		
479	250	97	300	222	516.5063		
480	250	108	300	233	516.5063		
481	250	119	300	244	516.5063		
482	250	130	300	255	516.5063	250	
483				130	300		
484				0	300		
485				125	516.5063		
486				255	516.5063		

18-Feb-87 11:32 PM

Figure 3.11: Temperature profile in an overstressed silicon diode *(continued)*

A1: 'Temperature Profile in an Overstressed Silicon Diode READY

	A	B	C	D	E	F	G
1	Temperature Profile in an Overstressed Silicon Diode						
2				Plot Angle:	60	0.866025	0.5
3	y (μ)	z (μ)	T (K)	x	y		
4	0	0	800	0	800		
5	0	1	783.8015	1	783.8015		
6	0	2	765.6587	2	765.6587		
7	0	3	745.7945	3	745.7945		
8	0	4	724.4291	4	724.4291		
9	0	5	701.7787	5	701.7787		
10	0	6	678.0545	6	678.0545		
11	0	7	653.4617	7	653.4617		
12	0	8	628.1987	8	628.1987		
13	0	9	602.4561	9	602.4561		
14	0	10	576.4163	10	576.4163		
15	0	11	550.2526	11	550.2526		
16	0	12	524.1290	12	524.1290		
17	0	13	498.1996	13	498.1996		
18	0	14	472.6083	14	472.6083		
19	0	15	447.4883	15	447.4883		
20	0	16	422.9624	16	422.9624		

30-May-87 09:55 PM

Figure 3.12: Alternative function for a three-dimensional graph

A21: 0 READY

	A	B	C	D	E	F	G
21	0	17	399.1425	17	399.1425		
22	0	18	376.1297	18	376.1297		
23	0	19	354.0143	19	354.0143		
24	0	20	332.8761	20	332.8761		
25	0	31	177.6231	31	177.6231		
26	0	42	160.6203	42	160.6203		
27	0	53	223.3098	53	223.3098		
28	0	64	294.7922	64	294.7922		
29	0	75	334.1610	75	334.1610		
30	0	86	336.8692	86	336.8692		
31	0	97	319.3676	97	319.3676		
32	0	108	300.4579	108	300.4579		
33	0	119	290.5146	119	290.5146		
34	0	130	290.2699	130	290.2699		
35			800				
36	10	0	695.6407	5	704.3010		
37	10	1	682.8232	6	691.4834		
38	10	2	668.4671	7	677.1274		
39	10	3	652.7489	8	661.4092		
40	10	4	635.8429	9	644.5032		

30-May-87 09:56 PM

Figure 3.12: Alternative function for a three-dimensional graph *(continued)*

A469: 250 READY

	A	B	C	D	E	F	G
469	250	17	298.2417	142	514.7481		
470	250	18	298.6498	143	515.1562		
471	250	19	299.0420	144	515.5484		
472	250	20	299.4169	145	515.9233		
473	250	31	302.1702	156	518.6766		
474	250	42	302.4717	167	518.9781		
475	250	53	301.3600	178	517.8663		
476	250	64	300.0923	189	516.5987		
477	250	75	299.3941	200	515.9005		
478	250	86	299.3461	211	515.8525		
479	250	97	299.6565	222	516.1628		
480	250	108	299.9918	233	516.4982		
481	250	119	300.1682	244	516.6745		
482	250	130	300.1725	255	516.6789	250	
483				130	300		
484				0	300		
485				125	516.5063		
486				255	516.5063		
487							
488							

30-May-87 09:57 PM

Figure 3.12: Alternative function for a three-dimensional graph *(continued)*

Add some labels to mark the *y* axis.

43. In cell F354, type '(5 spaces) **60**
44. In cell F418, type '(5 spaces) **155** (4 spaces) **y (microns)**
45. In cell F482, type '(5 spaces) **250**
46. Execute the /Graph Options Data-labels A (**/GODA**) command and select F4..F486 as the label range and Centered (C) for the alignment.
47. Execute the Quit Quit Name Create (QQNC) command and type the name **Fig3-13**
48. Execute the Quit (**Q**) command to return to ready mode.
49. Press the Graph key to view the graph.

The three-dimensional graph should look like that in Figure 3.13, unless you plotted the alternate function, in which case it will look like Figure 3.14. You can change the value of the plot angle and see how this changes the view of the three-dimensional graph.

■ DRAWING PICTURES

Although the graphics capability of Lotus 1-2-3 is primarily designed to plot data generated on a spreadsheet, it actually does not matter

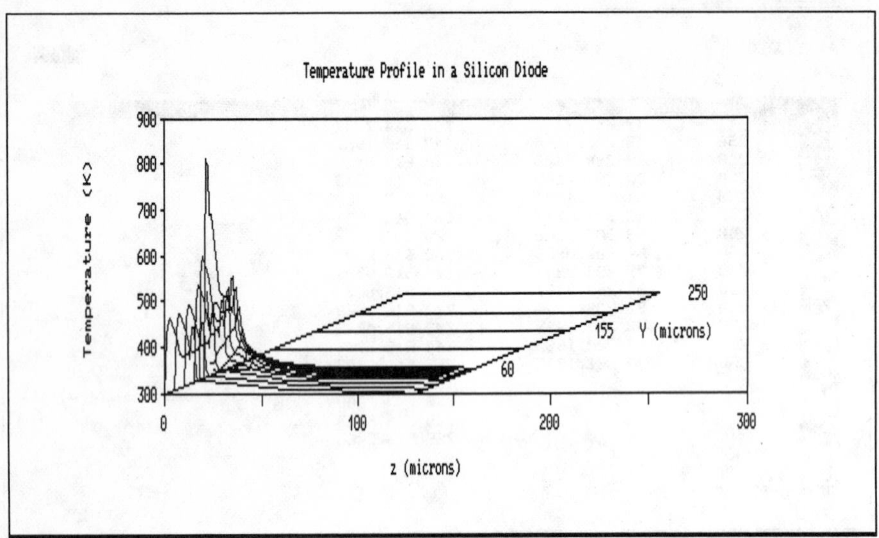

Figure 3.13: Temperature profile in an overstressed silicon diode: a three-dimensional plot

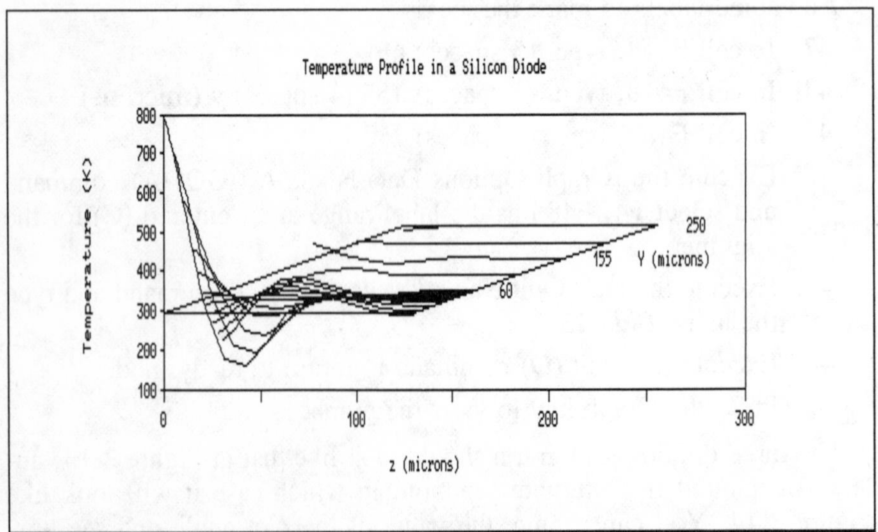

Figure 3.14: Three-dimensional plot of the alternate function

where the data comes from. In fact, you can use the graphics capability to draw figures on the screen. Figure 3.15 is a segmented line drawing created with approximately 350 data pairs that form 53 discrete line segments. It took me one evening to digitize the drawing by hand and type the data pairs into the spreadsheet, which is not an unreasonable amount of time to produce a figure of this complexity. Of course this does not include the amount of time that my wife spent drawing the original figure. As you can see, you can create a complicated line drawing in a reasonable amount of time using Lotus 1-2-3.

Drawing figures on graphs can help you illustrate the function being plotted. For example, if you are plotting the output of an electronic circuit, a simple drawing of the circuit in the corner of your graph can make the results much more meaningful to readers.

Since you can only have one set of *x* values on a graph, any drawing must be a continuation of the plot. However, since Lotus 1-2-3 will not plot empty cells, you can make the *x* values of the drawing follow the *x* values of your plot. Put the *y* values of the plot in the next column, and the *y* values of the drawing in a third. Put the data labels for the drawing in a fourth column.

Delyiannis Bandpass Filter The Delyiannis bandpass filter is an active electronic filter network that passes frequencies within only a particular range and filters out all others. Figure 3.16 shows the circuit diagram. The transfer function, the ratio of the output to the input, is defined with

Figure 3.15: An Osprey in flight, by Julie Stephens Orvis, D.V.M.

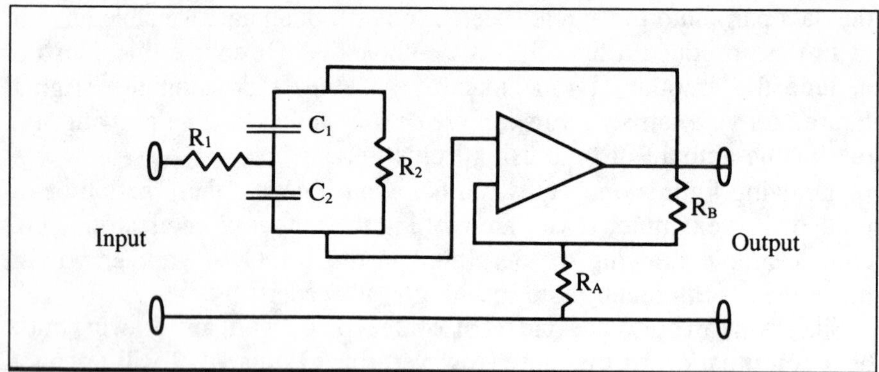

Figure 3.16: Delyiannis bandpass circuit diagram

the following equation:

$$|G(i\omega)| = \frac{\dfrac{\omega}{R_1 C_2(1 - 1/k)}}{\sqrt{(\omega_p^2 - \omega^2) + \omega^2(\omega_p/Q_p)^2}}$$

Here, ω is the angular frequency.

$$k = 1 + \frac{R_A}{R_B}$$

$$\omega_p^2 = \frac{1}{R_1 R_2 C_1 C_2}$$

$$\frac{\omega_p}{Q_p} = \frac{1}{R_2 C_1} + \frac{1}{R_2 C_2} + \frac{1}{k - 1}\frac{1}{R_1 C_2}$$

Let $C_1 = C_2 = 1\ \mu$f, $R_1 = R_2 = R_B = 10$ ohms, and $R_A = 32$ ohms, which yields a bandpass frequency centered on 100 kHz. You will plot the transfer function and then draw the circuit on the graph.

1. Set the column widths according to the following list: A = **10**, B = **9**, C = **1**, D = **9**, E = **9**, F = **1**, G = **9**, H = **9**
2. In cell A1, type **Delyiannis Bandpass Circuit**
3. In cell A3, type **"RES1**
4. In cell A4, type **"RES2**
5. In cell B3, type **10**
6. In cell B4, type **10**

7. In cell D3, type **“CAP1**
8. In cell D4, type **“CAP2**
9. In cell E3, type **1E-6**
10. In cell E4, type **1E-6**
11. In cell G3, type **“RESA**
12. In cell G4, type **“RESB**
13. In cell H3, type **32**
14. In cell H4, type **10**
15. Name cells B3, B4, E3, E4, H3, and H4 as **RES1**, **RES2**, **CAP1**, **CAP2**, **RESA**, and **RESB**. These names are in the labels to their left, so use the /Range Name Labels Right (**/RNLR**) command.
16. In cell A6, type **“K**
17. In cell B6, type **1+$RESA/$RESB**
18. In cell D6, type **“WP**
19. In cell E6, type **@SQRT(1/($RES1*$RES2*$CAP1*$CAP2))**
20. In cell G6, type **“WPQP**
21. Name cells B6, E6, and H6 respectively, as **K**, **WP**, and **WPQP**.
22. In cell H6, type **1/($RES2*CAP1)+1/(RES2*CAP2) -(1/(K-1))*(1/(RES1*CAP2))**
23. In cell A8, type **“Frequency**
24. In cell B8, type **“G(s)**
25. In cells C8..C135, type/copy **‘`**
26. In cell D8, type **‘Circuit**
27. In cell E8, type **‘Labels**
28. In cells F8..F135, type/copy **‘`**
29. In cell G8, type **‘Comments**
30. In cells A9, B9, D9, E9, and G9 type **\-**
31. Execute the /Data Fill (**/DF**) command and select cells A10 ..A50, with a starting value of **1E4**, a step value of **1E4**, and an ending value of **4.1E5**.
32. In cells B10..B50, type/copy **(A10/($RES1*$CAP2*(1-1/$K))) /@SQRT(($WP^2-A10^2)^2+$WPQP^2*A10^2)**

33. In cell G10, type **'Begin filter calculation**
34. In cell G50 type **'End filter calculation**
35. Format cells A10..A135, E3, E4, E6, and H6 as Scientific 2 (**S2**).
36. Format cells B10..B50 as Fixed (**F2**).

This completes the data entry for the transfer function plot. Now enter the data for the drawing. I sketched the circuit on grid paper first and then determined the X-Y coordinates of the lines to type into the spreadsheet. Such drawing must be done in the scale of the plot already on the graph. Alternately, I could have determined the X-Y pairs on a regular grid (say 100 by 100) and then used a simple function to map the values onto the scale of the plot on the graph.

The data for the drawing is in Table 3.3. If you do not want to type this much data for an example, then just type 10 or 20 lines. The spreadsheet and graph can still be formed, although the drawing will be incomplete.

37. Fill cells A52..G135 according to Table 3.3.

Cell	Contents	Cell	Contents	Cell	Contents
				G52	**'Begin circuit plot**
A54	**50000**	D54	**0.1**	E54	**'O**
				G54	**'Ground line**
A55	**300000**	D55	**0.1**	E55	**'O**
A57	**230000**	D57	**0.1**	G57	**'Resistor A**
A58	**230000**	D58	**0.12**		
A59	**235000**	D59	**0.13**		
A60	**225000**	D60	**0.14**		
A61	**235000**	D61	**0.15**	E61	'(4 spaces) **RA**
A62	**225000**	D62	**0.16**		
A63	**235000**	D63	**0.17**		
A64	**230000**	D64	**0.18**		
A65	**230000**	D65	**0.2**		
A67	**200000**	D67	**0.24**	G67	**'Operational amplifier**

Table 3.3: Delyiannis bandpass circuit: circuit diagram

Cell	Contents	Cell	Contents	Cell	Contents
A68	**250000**	D68	**0.3**		
A69	**200000**	D69	**0.36**		
A70	**200000**	D70	**0.24**		
A72	**200000**	D72	**0.27**	G72	**'Resistor B and wire**
A73	**190000**	D73	**0.27**	G73	**'from input network**
A74	**190000**	D74	**0.2**	G74	**'to operational amplifier**
A75	**280000**	D75	**0.2**		
A76	**280000**	D76	**0.22**		
A77	**285000**	D77	**0.23**		
A78	**275000**	D78	**0.24**		
A79	**285000**	D79	**0.25**	E79	'(4 spaces) **RB**
A80	**275000**	D80	**0.26**		
A81	**285000**	D81	**0.27**		
A82	**280000**	D82	**0.28**		
A83	**280000**	D83	**0.42**		
A84	**125000**	D84	0.42		
A85	**125000**	D85	0.39		
A87	**100000**	D87	0.35	G87	**'Resistor 2**
A88	**100000**	D88	0.39		
A89	**150000**	D89	0.39		
A90	**150000**	D90	0.33		
A91	**145000**	D91	0.32		
A92	**155000**	D92	0.31	E92	'(4 spaces) **R2**
A93	**145000**	D93	0.3		
A94	**155000**	D94	0.29	G101	**'Capacitor 1**
A95	**145000**	D95	0.28		
A96	**150000**	D96	0.27		
A97	**150000**	D97	0.21		
A98	**100000**	D98	0.21		
A99	**100000**	D99	0.25		
A101	**85000**	D101	0.25		
A102	**115000**	D102	0.25		

Table 3.3: Delyiannis bandpass circuit: circuit diagram *(continued)*

Cell	Contents	Cell	Contents	Cell	Contents
A104	**85000**	D104	**0.26**		
A105	**115000**	D105	**0.26**	E105	**'(4 spaces) C1**
A107	**85000**	D107	**0.34**	G107	**'Capacitor 2**
A108	**115000**	D108	**0.34**		
A110	**85000**	D110	**0.35**		
A111	**115000**	D111	**0.35**	E111	**'(4 spaces) C2**
A113	**50000**	D113	**0.3**	E113	**'O**
				G113	**'Resistor 1**
A114	**60000**	D114	**0.3**		
A115	**65000**	D115	**0.31**		
A116	**70000**	D116	**0.29**		
A117	**75000**	D117	**0.31**		
A118	**80000**	D118	**0.29**		
A119	**85000**	D119	**0.31**		
A120	**90000**	D120	**0.3**		
A121	**100000**	D121	**0.3**		
A123	**250000**	D123	**0.3**	G123	**'Output terminal**
A124	**300000**	D124	**0.3**	E124	**'O**
A126	**100000**	D126	**0.26**	G126	**'Wire from C1 to C25**
A127	**100000**	D127	**0.34**		
A129	**125000**	D129	**0.21**	G129	**'Wire from input network**
A130	**125000**	D130	**0.18**	G130	**'to operational amplifier**
A131	**180000**	D131	**0.18**		
A132	**180000**	D132	**0.33**		
A133	**200000**	D133	**0.33**		
A135	**75000**	D135	**0.35**	E135	**'R16**
				G135	**'Label for resistor**

Table 3.3: Delyiannis bandpass circuit: circuit diagram *(continued)*

The spreadsheet should look like Figure 3.17.You are now ready to plot this data on a graph.

38. Execute the /Graph Type X-Y (/**GTX**) command.
39. Execute the X (**X**) command and select cells A10..A135 as the *x* data.
40. Execute the A (**A**) command and select cells B10..B50 as plot A.
41. **Execute the B (B) command and select cells D10..D135 as plot B.** plot B.

Note that you are selecting different numbers of data cells for the *A* and *B* data ranges. Lotus 1-2-3 will pair each *X* value with each *A* or *B* data value in order. Since the *A*-range data cells match the first of the *X*-range data cells, you need select only the actual *A*-range data (B10..B50). The *B*-range data cells must match the last group of the *X*-range data cells, so you must select a large group of blank cells at the beginning of the *B*-range data. These blank cells will not be plotted but will serve to align the *B*-range data cells with the correct *X*-range data cells. The same is true for the data labels that will be used with the *B* range.

```
A1: [W10] 'Delyiannis Bandpass Circuit                                    READY

         A          B   C    D          E    F    G           H         I
1   Delyiannis Bandpass Circuit
2
3        RES1        10       CAP1 1.00E-06        RESA          32
4        RES2        10       CAP2 1.00E-06        RESB          10
5
6           K       4.2         WP 1.00E+05        WPQP 1.69E+05
7
8   Frequency     |G(s)| |Circuit  Labels      |Comments
9   -----------------------------------------------|---------
10   1.00E+04      0.13 |                      |Begin filter calculation
11   2.00E+04      0.26 |                      |
12   3.00E+04      0.38 |                      |
13   4.00E+04      0.49 |                      |
14   5.00E+04      0.58 |                      |
15   6.00E+04      0.66 |                      |
16   7.00E+04      0.71 |                      |
17   8.00E+04      0.75 |                      |
18   9.00E+04      0.77 |                      |
19   1.00E+05      0.78 |                      |
20   1.10E+05      0.77 |                      |
30-May-87  10:24 PM
```

Figure 3.17: Delyiannis bandpass circuit transfer function and circuit diagram spreadsheet

Label the graph and its axes.

42. Execute the Options Titles First (**OTF**) command and type **Delyiannis Bandpass Circuit**
43. Execute the Titles X-axis (**TX**) command and type **Frequency (Hz)**
44. Execute the Titles Y-axis (**TY**) command and type **Transfer function**

Change the *x* and *y* axis scales to manual so that you can fix them at particular values. The drawing must be done in the scale of the data plot. If you allowed the axes to change automatically, the drawing would be distorted. Make sure that you have the plot in the form that you want it before you do the drawing; otherwise you may have to transform the drawing data to some new set of graph limits.

45. Execute the Scale Y-scale Manual (**SYM**) command.
46. Execute the Lower (**L**) command and type **0**
47. Execute the Upper (**U**) command and type **0.8**
48. Execute the Quit (**Q**) command to return to the Options menu.
49. Execute the Scale X-scale Manual (**SXM**) command.

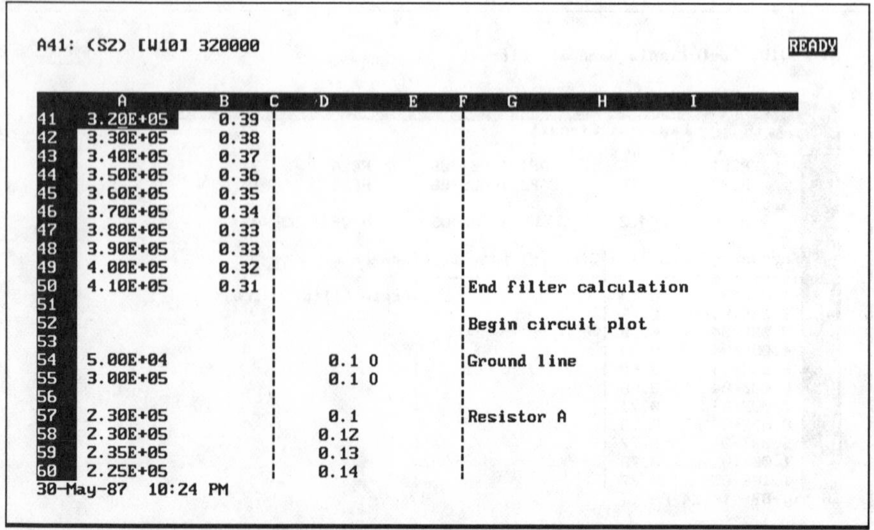

A41: (S2) [W10] 320000 READY

	A	B	C	D	E	F	G	H	I
41	3.20E+05	0.39							
42	3.30E+05	0.38							
43	3.40E+05	0.37							
44	3.50E+05	0.36							
45	3.60E+05	0.35							
46	3.70E+05	0.34							
47	3.80E+05	0.33							
48	3.90E+05	0.33							
49	4.00E+05	0.32							
50	4.10E+05	0.31				End filter calculation			
51									
52						Begin circuit plot			
53									
54	5.00E+04			0.1 0		Ground line			
55	3.00E+05			0.1 0					
56									
57	2.30E+05			0.1		Resistor A			
58	2.30E+05			0.12					
59	2.35E+05			0.13					
60	2.25E+05			0.14					

30-May-87 10:24 PM

Figure 3.17: Delyiannis bandpass circuit transfer function and circuit diagram spreadsheet *(continued)*

50. Execute the Lower (**L**) command and type **0**
51. Execute the Upper (**U**) command and type **5E5**
52. Execute the Quit (**Q**) command return to the Options menu.

These data labels identify the circuit components and put small circles at the ends of the wires.

53. Execute the Data-labels B (**DB**) command, select cells E10..E135, and select Centered (**C**).
54. Execute the Quit (**Q**) command to return to the Graph menu.

Turn off the data markers on the drawing.

55. Execute the Format B Lines (**FBL**) command to plot the drawing without data markers.
56. Execute the Quit (**Q**) command to return to the Graph menu.
57. Execute the Name Create (**NC**) command and type **Fig3-18**
58. Execute the Quit (**Q**) command to return to ready mode.

The graph should now look like Figure 3.18, with the transfer function data and the circuit plotted on the same graph. If you did not enter all of the data in Table 3.3, then the drawing will be missing some parts.

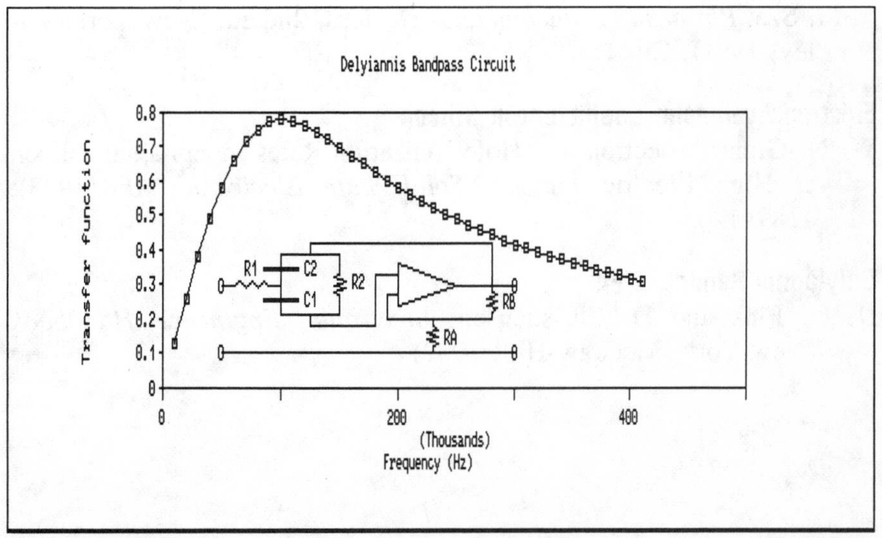

Figure 3.18: Delyiannis bandpass transfer function and circuit—data plot with drawing

■ SUMMARY

In this chapter, you have created plots of spreadsheet data and have enhanced those plots with data labels, markers, legends, and titles. You have also learned how to save these graphs for later recall. In addition to examining these normal plotting functions, you have explored ways to use the Lotus 1-2-3 graphics capability for other common science and engineering graphics tasks, such as creating semilog, log, and three-dimensional plots. You have also seen how to enhance these plots with simple drawings.

Using the techniques explored in this chapter plus a little ingenuity, you should be able to manage most of your data plotting and presentation tasks. For any new plot type (such as polar), create a linear transform to transform your data to the linear X-Y axes in Lotus 1-2-3. Plot your data and then use the drawing capability to add any required axis lines or labels.

■ FOR MORE INFORMATION

For more information about the topics in this chapter, you can consult the following sources.

Resistivity of Silicon

S. M. Sze, *Physics of Semiconductor Devices,* 2nd ed. (New York: Wiley, 1981), Ch. 1.

Electron Avalanche Coefficient in Silicon

W. N. Grant, "Electron and Hole Ionization Rates in Epitaxial Silicon at High Electric Fields," *Solid State Electronics* 16 (1973): 1189–1203.

Delyiannis Bandpass Filter

D. G. Fink and D. Christiansen, *Electronics Engineers' Handbook* (New York: McGraw-Hill, 1982).

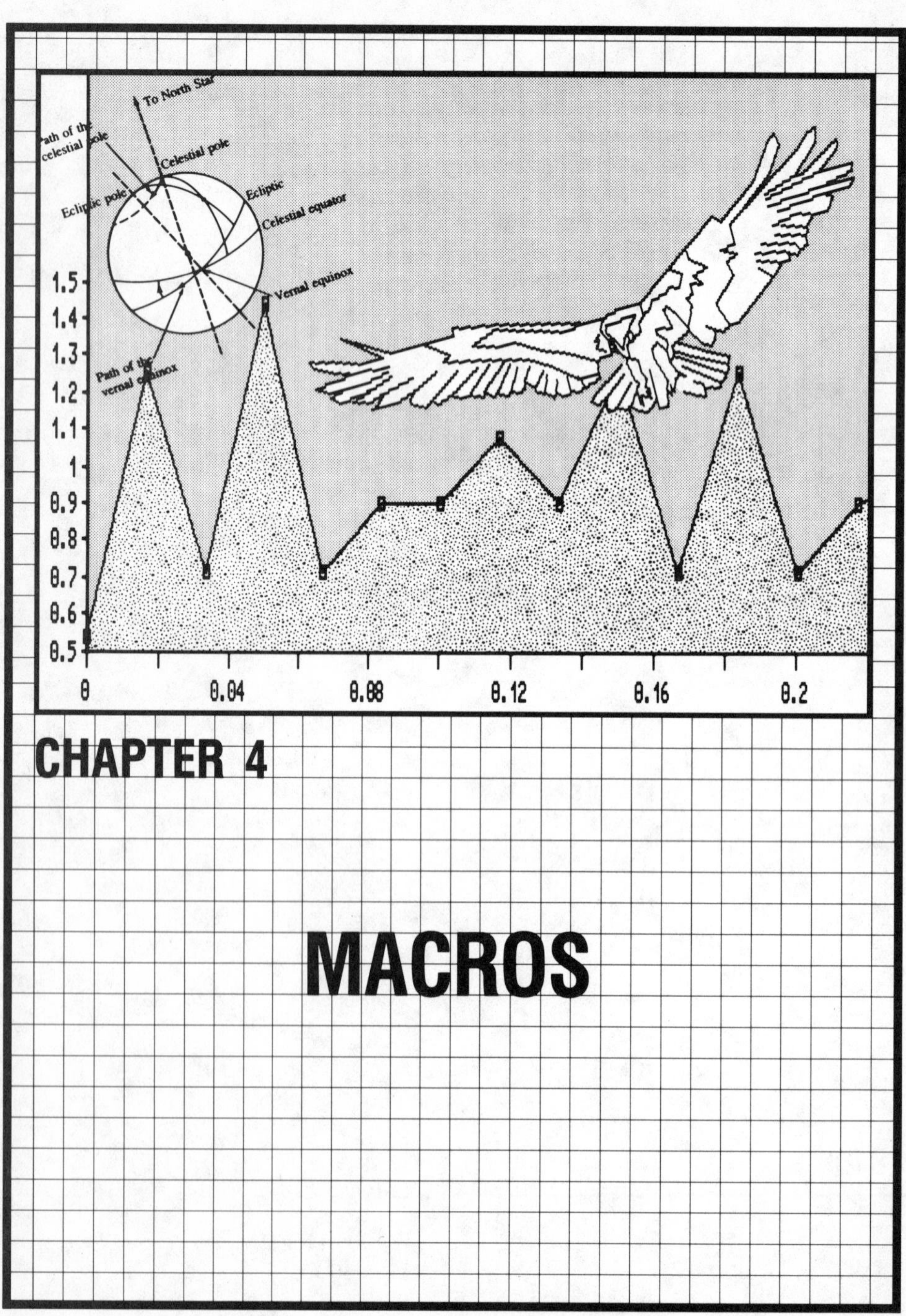

CHAPTER 4

MACROS

The word *macro* is one of the most overused computer words. A macro can be loosely defined as a capability to combine many actions (keystrokes, mouse clicks, and so on) into a few actions. Many programs offer some sort of macro capability. There are keyboard macro programs, which allow you to store sequences of keystrokes to be recalled with a single keystroke. There are programming macros, available in most programming languages, which allow you to insert large, predefined blocks of code into a program with a single reference. And there are Lotus 1-2-3 macros.

In Lotus 1-2-3, macros are combinations of spreadsheet commands and keystrokes that can be executed with one or a few keystrokes. They were originally designed to automate spreadsheet creation by allowing users to store keystrokes and then play them back with a single command. They have evolved into a programming language with the capability to perform loops, subroutines, jumps, conditional (IF) statements, assignments (of values or labels to cells), and file access.

MACRO BASICS

So far as the spreadsheet is concerned, a macro is just a set of named labels, so when the spreadsheet is recalculated, the macro is not disturbed. You type a macro into a single cell or a column of cells. When you invoke a macro, it is read by Lotus 1-2-3 from the top down and left to right. Macro execution continues down a column until a blank cell, a {QUIT} command, or a {RETURN} command is reached.

For a macro to be executed, the first cell in the macro must be named. Lotus 1-2-3 will accept only the names \A through \Z, plus the special name \0 (zero) for macros. Thus you can have 26 regular macros and 1 special macro. To invoke a macro, hold down the macro key (Alt on most keyboards) and press the letter that corresponds to the first cell in the macro. The special macro (\0) is the autoexecute macro. This macro executes automatically when you load the spreadsheet. The name restrictions just discussed apply only to macro execution from the keyboard. Macro subroutines and branch addresses (places you branch to) can have any valid cell name.

The macro section of the *Lotus 1-2-3 Reference Manual* contains an extensive description of the various macro commands and capabilities.

You should read that section to learn about using macros in general and to learn the details of particular macro commands. I will only briefly discuss macros here. The commands are also listed in Appendix B.

■ MACROS TO AUTOMATE SPREADSHEETS

The most basic set of macro commands are simply keystrokes. Macro commands are typed exactly as if you were typing the commands and text into the spreadsheet. The only differences are that you must prefix the commands with a single quotation mark to make them labels and that you must use the key equivalents in Table 4.1 in place of all of the special keys, including Return (or Enter). For example, a macro to copy the contents of cells A2..A5 into cells C3..C6 is

```
'/CA2.A5~C3.C6~
```

where ~ is the key equivalent of Return. Simple, isn't it?

The main purposes of these commands are to save you keystrokes when you have to type repetitive commands and to create automatic spreadsheets for people who are not expert users of Lotus 1-2-3. They are also good for amazing your friends, as spreadsheets appear to create themselves without anyone touching the keyboard.

■ MACROS AS A PROGRAMMING LANGUAGE

The advanced macro commands in Table 4.2 give you most of the capabilities of a high-level computer programming language. All of the commands that you would expect to find in a high-level language are available.

Variables

In the macro language, spreadsheet cells are the variables used to store the values or labels used in your calculations. You should use named cells and named ranges in a macro rather than actual cell references. Whenever you reorganize a spreadsheet using the /Copy and /Move commands, any cell references that refer to the moved cells are

Key	Macro key equivalents
Abs	{abs}
Backspace	{bs} or {backspace}
Big left	{bigleft}
Big right	{bigright}
Calc	{calc}
Delete	{delete}
Delete	{del}
Down arrow	{down}
Edit	{edit}
End	{end}
Esc	{esc} or {escape}
Goto	{goto}
Graph	{graph}
Home	{home}
Left arrow	{left}
Name	{name}
Page down	{pgdn}
Page up	{pgup}
Query	{query}
Right arrow	{right}
Table	{table}
Up arrow	{up}
Window	{window}
Left brace	{{ }
Right brace	{ }}
Character ~	{~}
Return or Enter	~

Table 4.1: Macro key equivalents

Macro command	Function
{?}	Wait for keyboard input
{BEEP}	Sound keyboard bell
{BLANK}	Erase a cell or cells
{BRANCH}	Continue execution at a specified cell
{BREAKOFF}	Disable the Break key
{BREAKON}	Enable the Break key
{CLOSE}	Close a disk file
{CONTENTS}	Change cell contents into a label
{DEFINE}	Specify location of subroutine arguments
{DISPATCH}	Continue execution at the cell specified by the contents of a cell
{FILESIZE}	Get the size of a disk file
{FORBREAK}	Cause early termination of a {FOR} loop
{FOR}	Loop control
{GETLABEL}	Keyboard input; get a label
{GETNUMBER}	Keyboard input; get a value
{GETPOS}	Get the current position in a disk file
{GET}	Keyboard input; get a character
{IF}	Conditional execution of a statement
{INDICATE}	Change the indicator
{LET}	Set the contents of a cell
{LOOK}	Check whether a key has been pressed
{MENUBRANCH}	Create a custom menu
{MENUCALL}	Use a custom menu
{ONERROR}	Trap error conditions in a subroutine
{OPEN}	Open a disk file
{PANELOFF}	Disable control panel updating
{PANELON}	Enable control panel updating

Table 4.2: Advanced macro commands

Macro command	Function
{PUT}	Set the contents of a cell in a range
{QUIT}	End macro operation
{READLN}	Read a line from the disk file
{READ}	Read characters from a disk file
{RECALCCOL}	Recalculate column by column
{RECALC}	Recalculate row by row
{RESTART}	Break out of a subroutine call chain
{RETURN}	Return from a subroutine
{routine-name}	Call a subroutine
{SETPOS}	Set the current position in a disk file
{WAIT}	Suspend macro operation
{WINDOWSOFF}	Suspend screen updating
{WINDOWSON}	Enable screen updating
{WRITELN}	Write a line of text to the disk file
{WRITE}	Write characters to the disk file

Table 4.2: Advanced macro commands *(continued)*

adjusted to point to the cells in the new location. Since the macro commands are labels, any cell references contained in them would not be adjusted. Thus, if you use cell references rather than named ranges, your macro may not work after you rearrange the spreadsheet.

Input and Output Operations

You use the commands {?}, {GET}, {GETLABEL}, {GETNUMBER}, and {LOOK} to perform keyboard input and output (I/O) operations. These commands allow you to get a single character, a line of text, or a value from the keyboard. You can also get input by creating a custom menu with {MENUBRANCH} and {MENUCALL}.

You can access data in ASCII disk files with the {OPEN}, {CLOSE}, {READ}, {WRITE}, {GETPOS}, {SETPOS}, {READLN}, and {WRITELN} commands. You can also get the file size with {FILESIZE}. These commands allow you to open and close text files and read and write data one character or line at a time.

Program Flow Control

You control the flow of operations in a macro with loop commands, jumps, conditionals, and subroutine calls. Loops are controlled with the {FOR} and {FORBREAK} commands. The {FOR} command repeatedly executes a macro a specified number of times. You can execute an unconditional jump, similar to GOTO in FORTRAN or BASIC, with the {BRANCH} and {DISPATCH} commands. The {IF} command controls conditional calculations. You can call a subroutine by placing its name in braces: {*subroutine-name*}. Subroutines return to the calling routine when they encounter a {RETURN} command or a blank line. You use the {DEFINE} command to specify where subroutine parameters are stored. The remaining commands are {QUIT} to terminate a macro and {RESTART} to break out of a subroutine call chain.

Assignment

You can change the contents of cells with the {LET} and {PUT} commands. The {LET} command assigns values or labels to a specific cell. The {PUT} command assigns a value to a cell in a range. The first argument of the {LET} or {PUT} command must be a specific cell address. It cannot be a formula that evaluates a cell address. This is unfortunate, because it makes it difficult to perform the same operation on a series of cells with a loop command. To operate on a group of cells with the same command, you must name those cells and use the {PUT} command to step through the cells in the range.

Recalculation

You control recalculation of the spreadsheet with the macro commands {RECALC}, which causes recalculation row by row, and {RECALCCOL}, which causes recalculation column by column. You also control recalculation with the macro key equivalent {calc}, which causes recalculation in the order set with the /Spreadsheet Global Recalculation (/WGR) command. Executing {calc} is the same as pressing the Calc key.

Environment Control

You control the spreadsheet environment with {BREAKON}, {BREAKOFF}, {ONERROR}, {WAIT}, {INDICATE}, {PANELON}, {PANELOFF}, {WINDOWSON}, and {WINDOWSOFF}. Normally, you can use the Break key to suspend a macro, but the {BREAKOFF} command disables it. Beware of this, because if you disable the Break key and your macro gets into an infinite loop, the only way to stop the macro is to reboot the computer. The {BREAKON} command reenables the Break key.

The {WAIT} command suspends macro operation for a specified length of time. The {INDICATE} command changes the value of the indicator in the upper-right corner of the screen. The {PANELON}, {PANELOFF}, {WINDOWSON}, and {WINDOWSOFF} commands restore or suppress control panel or screen updating during macro operation. Window updating is a slow process that occurs every time the spreadsheet is updated. Turning it off while a macro is running often speeds up the macro, especially if that macro must perform many spreadsheet update operations. Turning off window updating will not change the results of a macro, as the underlying data is always updated.

Syntax

A macro command starts with a left brace ({) and the command keyword. If the command has no arguments, then it is followed by a right brace (}); for example, {PANELOFF}. If the command does have arguments, they are in a comma-delimited list, separated from the keyword by a single space and terminated with a right brace; for example, {LET B7,–275.5}. Make sure that there are no other spaces in the macro command. The contents of the arguments are different for each command and are listed in the *1-2-3 Reference Manual* and in Appendix B. Often, one of the arguments is the spreadsheet location where the command is to act. This argument must be a cell reference, range reference, or range name. Unfortunately, it cannot be an equation that evaluates a valid reference.

■ MACRO LAYOUT

It is customary, though not required, to lay out macros in a three-column format. The first column is used to label the named cells in the macro. For any cells that you name in the second column, put their name next to them in the first column. The names consist of the macro names and any named cells used for data storage. The second column contains the macro and the named ranges for data storage (separated from the end of the macro by at least one blank line). The third column is for comments.

■ FUNCTION MACROS

Factorial Calculator Macros can be used to calculate functions that are not available in Lotus 1-2-3 and that cannot be created from the existing functions. For example, the factorial function is not available. The factorial of n is

$$n! = 1 \cdot 2 \cdot 3 \cdots (n - 1)n$$

which can be calculated with a simple loop. Here you will calculate the factorial for a column of numbers, so you need a second loop over the number of cells in a column.

In the following spreadsheet, you will calculate the factorial of the integers 1 to 11. Just for fun, you will create the whole spreadsheet with a macro. Normally, you would lay out the spreadsheet by hand and use the macro to calculate the factorial function.

1. Set the widths of columns A through F using the following list: A = **9**, B = **9**, C = **3**, D = **6**, E = **26**, and F = **9**
2. In cell D1, type **Macro to create the factorial table**

This is the start of the macro. Put a label in cell D2 so you know the name of the macro that starts in cell E2. Comments will be in column F.

3. In cell D2, type **'\a**

The commands in cell E2 start with a single quotation mark, making them labels. Next comes the keyboard commands that you would have to type to erase cells A1..B16; that is /Range Erase A1.B16 Return.

4. In cell E2, type **'/rea1.b16~**
5. In cell F2, type **Clear the table**
6. Name cell E2 as **\A**.

In cell E3, you will use the key equivalents {goto} and ˜ , which is the same as pressing the Goto and Return keys. The {goto} command is followed by the cell reference A1 and a Return. Note that you can stack as many commands on a line as you want (up to the 240-character limit). Here you also enter the text to be typed into cell A1 along with a Return.

7. In cell E3, type **{goto}a1˜** Factorial of n˜
8. In cell F3, type **Put in title**
9. In cell E4, type **{goto}a4˜** "n{right}"n!
10. In cell F4, type **Label columns**
11. In cell E5, type **{down}{left}**\-**{right}**\-˜
12. In cell F5, type **Draw line**

In cell E6, you use the /Data Fill command to insert integers 1 to 11 into cells A6..A16.

13. In cell E6, type **'/dfa6.a16˜** 1˜ 1˜ ˜
14. In cell F6, type **Put in n values**

Name cells B6..B16 as **NFAC** so that you can use the {PUT} command to sequentially put the calculated values into the column.

15. In cell E7, type **'/rncnfac˜b6.b16˜**
16. In cell F7, type **Name range for n!**

Here is the first loop created with the {FOR} command. It will execute the cells named FAC 11 times with the value of cell I ranging from 6 to 16.

17. In cell E8, type **{for i,6,16,1,fac}˜**
18. In cell F8, type **Loop over n**

The routine FAC calculates and stores the factorial. First the {CONTENTS} command changes the value of I, the loop counter, into a label and puts it into cell ADDR. Then the {LET} command creates a cell reference by combining the letter *A* and the number in ADDR. It then gets the value referred to by that cell reference and stores it in ARG. This is the value of *n* for which the factorial will be calculated.

19. In cell D10, type **fac**

20. In cell E10, type **{contents addr,i,3,0}**
21. In cell F10, type **Get n**
22. Name cell E10 as **FAC**.
23. In cell E11, type **{let arg,@@(+"A"&@trim(addr))}**

Enter the starting value, 1.

24. In cell E12, type **{put nfac,0,+i-6,1}**
25. In cell F12, type **Starting value**

Loop the value in cell J over the values, 1, 2, ... *n*. In each loop, execute the cells named MULT. This multiplies the value of NFAC in column B by the value of J, which results in the factorial.

26. In cell E13, type **{for j,1,arg,1,mult}**
27. In cell F13, type **Get n!**
28. In cell D15, type **mult**
29. In cell E15, type **{put nfac,0,+i-6,@index(nfac,0,+i-6)*j}**
30. Name cell E15 as **MULT**.

These cells mark the four cells in column E that contain the variables used in the preceding macro.

31. In cell D17, type **i**
32. In cell D18, type **addr**
33. In cell D19, type **arg**
34. In cell D20, type **j**

Name the variables in column E.

35. Execute the /Range Name Labels Right (/**RNLR**) command and select cells D17..D20 to name cells E17 to E20.

This completes the macro. Execute it by holding down the Macro key and typing A. The table will be created, and in 10 to 20 seconds it will look like Figure 4.1.

■ SPREADSHEET UPDATING

Several of the macro commands modify the spreadsheet but do not cause the spreadsheet to be updated. This will not cause a problem, so

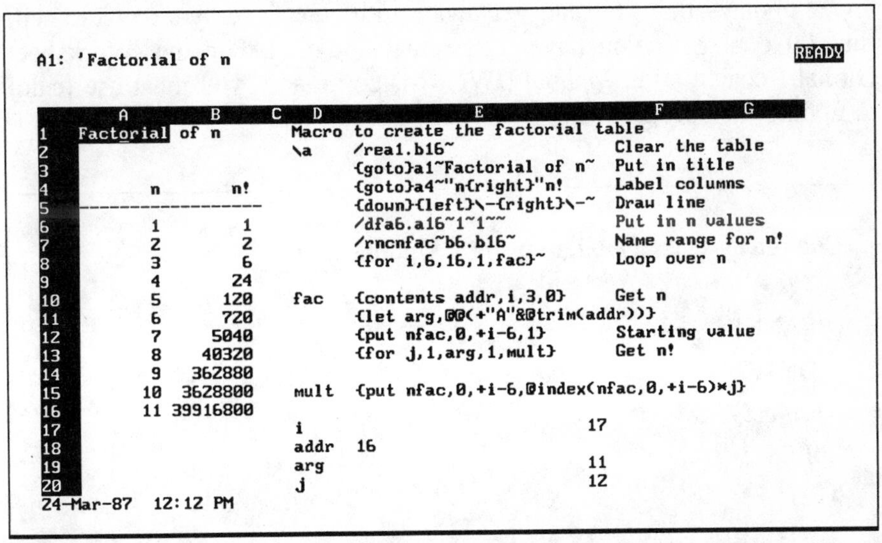

```
A1: 'Factorial of n                                                          READY

     A        B     C  D        E                            F              G
1  Factorial of n      Macro to create the factorial table
2                      \a      /rea1.b16~                    Clear the table
3                              {goto}a1~Factorial of n~      Put in title
4         n       n!           {goto}a4~"n{right}"n!         Label columns
5  ------------------          {down}{left}\-{right}\-~      Draw line
6         1        1           /dfa6.a16~1~1~~               Put in n values
7         2        2           /rncnfac~b6.b16~              Name range for n!
8         3        6           {for i,6,16,1,fac}~           Loop over n
9         4       24
10        5      120   fac     {contents addr,i,3,0}         Get n
11        6      720           {let arg,@@(+"A"&@trim(addr))}
12        7     5040           {put nfac,0,+i-6,1}           Starting value
13        8    40320           {for j,1,arg,1,mult}          Get n!
14        9   362880
15       10  3628800   mult    {put nfac,0,+i-6,@index(nfac,0,+i-6)*j}
16       11 39916800
17                     i                                17
18                     addr    16
19                     arg                              11
20                     j                                12
24-Mar-87   12:12 PM
```

Figure 4.1: A macro to create a table and calculate the factorial of a list of numbers

long as commands used later in a macro do not need updated values. Any cells that you load with a macro command will have the correct values in them whether you update the spreadsheet or not. For example, in cell E11, you use several spreadsheet functions and a string function to create the address of *n*. These functions are calculated by the macro in cell E11, and the result is stored in cell ARG (D19). If, on the other hand, you placed that string equation in cell ARG, you would need to update the spreadsheet before the value could be used by the command in cell E13.

There are two ways for a macro to update the spreadsheet: executing the {calc} key equivalent or, in most cases, executing a Return key equivalent (~). The Return key equivalent (~) can be on the same line as the macro command that causes the need for an update, but the {calc} key equivalent often must be on a separate line to work correctly. Table 4.3 lists the commands that can change the spreadsheet but do not cause updating. This table is different from the one in the *1-2-3 Reference Manual*. By experimenting with the commands, I created the results in this table. I assume that the differences are due to undocumented upgrades. I have noted the differences between the manual and my experience in the table. In any event, if your spreadsheet is not being updated at the correct time, then insert ~ after the command. If that does not work, then insert {calc} in the line after the command. Note that the fewer updates that you can get away with, the faster your macro will run. Of course, if you have set manual updating with the /Worksheet Global Recalculation Manual (/WGRM) command, you must use {calc} to update the spreadsheet.

Command	Update using {calc}	Update using ~
{BLANK}	x	x[1]
{CONTENTS}	x	x[1]
{DEFINE}	x	x[1]
{FILESIZE}	x	
{GET}	x	x[1]
{GETLABEL}	x	x
{GETNUMBER}	x	x
{GETPOS}	x	
{LET}	x	x
{LOOK}	x	x[1]
{ONERROR}[2]		
{PUT}	x	x[1]
{READ}	x	
{READLN}	x	

Notes:

1. A ~ (Return) key equivalent in the same line as each of these commands caused the spreadsheet to be updated, contrary to what the *1-2-3 Reference Manual* said.
2. The command {ONERROR} updated itself when it was executed without a ~ or {calc} key equivalent, contrary to what the *1-2-3 Reference Manual* said.

Table 4.3: Commands that change the spreadsheet but do not cause updating

■ SPEED CONSIDERATIONS

As mentioned in the last section, keeping the number of updates to a minimum will speed up macro execution. The macro in Figure 4.1 takes 13 seconds to complete. If you put a ~ after each {CONTENTS}, {LET}, and {PUT} command, the time increases to 65 seconds due to the unnecessary updating. If you must recalculate often, then turning off window updating and control panel updating with {WINDOWSOFF} and {PANELOFF} will speed up the macro. Turning off window updating decreases the time from 65 seconds to 44 seconds; turning off panel updating as well decreases it to 40 seconds.

■ DEBUGGING

As is the case with all but the simplest codes, macros do not always work correctly the first time they are run. To determine the problem, you need to trace through the macro, step by step. Lotus 1-2-3 provides a Step command to allow you to step through the macro and see what it is doing.

First, remove any {PANELOFF} and {WINDOWSOFF} commands. Second, force the spreadsheet to be updated after every critical operation with ~ or {calc} command key equivalents. These first two steps are needed so that you can see the results of each step in the calculation.

Next, press the Step key. The word *STEP* will appear at the bottom of the screen. Now when you run the macro it will execute only one command at a time, so you can see the effect of each command. Pressing any key will cause the next command to be calculated. When the macro is running, the word *STEP* at the bottom of the screen will change to *SST* (single step) until the macro is completed.

■ PROGRAM MACROS

As well as calculating simple functions, you can create complete programs with macro and spreadsheet commands. The programs can pause for keyboard input, store values, calculate values, test for errors, print error messages, and so on. In this next example, you will examine many of these capabilities.

Calendar Macro This macro will create a calendar for any month in the twentieth century. To figure out what day of the week the first day of the month falls on, you subtract its day number from the day number of a reference day. Calculating modulo 7 of that number will then yield the day of the week. First reset the column width so that the calendar will be correctly proportioned on the screen, label the start of the macro with the macro name \c, enter a title in cell A1, and clear the cells where the calendar will go. Note: You will name all of the required cells later.

1. Set global column width to 4.
2. In cell J1, type **'\c**
3. In cell K1, type **{goto}a1~Calendar Macro~**
4. In cell K2, type **{blank cal}~**

Now label cell K3 **AGAIN**. Suspend the macro and prompt the user to type the month and year in the control panel. Store the returned string in MON.

5. In cell J3, type **again**
6. In cell K3, type **{getlabel "Input the month and year as: MMM-YY: ",mon}**

Convert the date string in MON to a date number and store it in DATNUM. Test for a valid date. If the date is invalid, print an error message and go back to AGAIN (K3). Note that the cell ERR will be located under where the calendar will be printed so that the calendar will erase it when it is created.

7. In cell K4, type **{let datnum,@datevalue(mon)}**
8. In cell K5, type **{if @iserr(datnum)}{goto}err~Incorrect date format~{branch again}**

Test for the month and type the month's name in the cell at column 1, row 0 of the calendar range CAL. You could also do this by indexing an array of month names with the @INDEX function.

9. In cell K6, type **{if @month(datnum)=1}{put cal,1,0, January}**
10. In cell K7, type **{if @month(datnum)=2}{put cal,1,0, February}**
11. In cell K8, type **{if @month(datnum)=3}{put cal,1,0, March}**

12. In cell K9, type **{if @month(datnum)=4}{put cal,1,0,April}**
13. In cell K10, type **{if @month(datnum)=5}{put cal,1,0,May}**
14. In cell K11, type **{if @month(datnum)=6}{put cal,1,0,June}**
15. In cell K12, type **{if @month(datnum)=7}{put cal,1,0,July}**
16. In cell K13, type **{if @month(datnum)=8}{put cal,1,0, August}**
17. In cell K14, type **{if @month(datnum)=9}{put cal,1,0, September}**
18. In cell K15, type **{if @month(datnum)=10}{put cal,1,0, October}**
19. In cell K16, type **{if @month(datnum)=11}{put cal,1,0, November}**
20. In cell K17, type **{if @month(datnum)=12} {put cal,1,0, December}**

Create a string containing the year and put it in the calendar range.

21. In cell K18, type **{put cal,4,0,+"19"&@right(mon,2)}**

Enter the text of the days of the week in row 2 of the calendar range.

22. In cell K19, type **{put cal,0,2,"Sun"}**
23. In cell K20, type **{put cal,1,2,"Mon"}**
24. In cell K21, type **{put cal,2,2,"Tue"}**
25. In cell K22, type **{put cal,3,2,"Wed"}**
26. In cell K23, type **{put cal,4,2,"Thu"}**
27. In cell K24, type **{put cal,5,2,"Fri"}**
28. In cell K25, type **{put cal,6,2,"Sat"}~**

Note the Return key equivalent (~) at the end of the preceding command. It is required to make the spreadsheet update itself, so that the spreadsheet functions in cells K39..K40 will be calculated. You do not need to update the spreadsheet for the next two commands since those functions are calculated within the command and stored in cells K42 and K43 rather than calculated in a cell. Store the starting row and column numbers for the first day of the month and loop over the 31 days possible in a month.

29. In cell K26, type **{let row,3}**

30. In cell K27, type **{let col,daywk-1}**
31. In cell K28, type **{for i,0,30,1,putdat}**~

Routine PUTDAT will be executed 31 times by the previous {FOR} command. Test to see if you have put enough days in this month by seeing if the date number plus the number of days drawn on the calendar is in the next month. If it is in the next month, then break the loop. Otherwise, update the column number to store the next date. If the column number is greater than 7, then it belongs in the next row, so increment the row number and reset the column number to 0. Enter the date in the cell.

32. In cell J30, type **putdat**
33. In cell K30, type **{if @month(datnum+i)>mnth}{forbreak}**
34. In cell K31, type **{let col,col+1}**
35. In cell K32, type **{if col>7}{let col,1}{let row,row+1}**
36. In cell K33, type **{put cal,col-1,row,+i+1}**

This is the end of the program macro; the rest of the cells contain the variables for the program. Cells K38 and K39 determine which day of the week the first day of the month falls on. They do this by subtracting the date number of the first day of the month from a known date (March 1, 1987) that we know is a Sunday. Calculating the modulo 7 of that number and adding 7 if the value is negative yields the current day of the week. All of the rest of the days of the month are inserted relative to that day.

37. In cell J36, type **mon**
38. In cell J37, type **datnum**
39. In cell J38, type **refnum**
40. In cell K38, type **@DATE(87,3,1)-1**
41. Execute the /Range Name Labels Right **(/RNLR)** command for cells K36..K38.
42. In cell J39, type **daywk**
43. In cell K39, type **@IF(@MOD(DATNUM-REFNUM,7)> 0,0,7)+@MOD(DATNUM-REFNUM,7)**
44. In cell J40, type **mnth**
45. In cell K40, type **@MONTH(DATNUM)**
46. In cell J41, type **i**

47. In cell J42, type **row**
48. In cell J43, type **col**
49. Name the macro output cells B3..H12 as **CAL** and C3 as **ERR**.
50. Execute the /Range Name Labels Right (**/RNLR**) command for cells K1, K3, and K30 to name the macro and the labels AGAIN and PUTDAT.
51. Execute the /Range Name Labels Right (**/RNLR**) command and select cells K39..K43 to name the rest of the macro's variables.
52. Hide cells J2..K43.

This macro can now be run by holding down the Macro key and pressing **c**. You will then be asked to enter the month and year. Type them and press Return, and in a few moments the calendar will appear as in Figure 4.2. You can reexecute the macro any number of times to calculate the calendar for different months.

■ SUMMARY

Macros tremendously increase the power of Lotus 1-2-3. With them, many repetitive tasks can be automated. The advanced macro commands form a complete programming language that can be used to perform many calculations that could not be performed with a spreadsheet

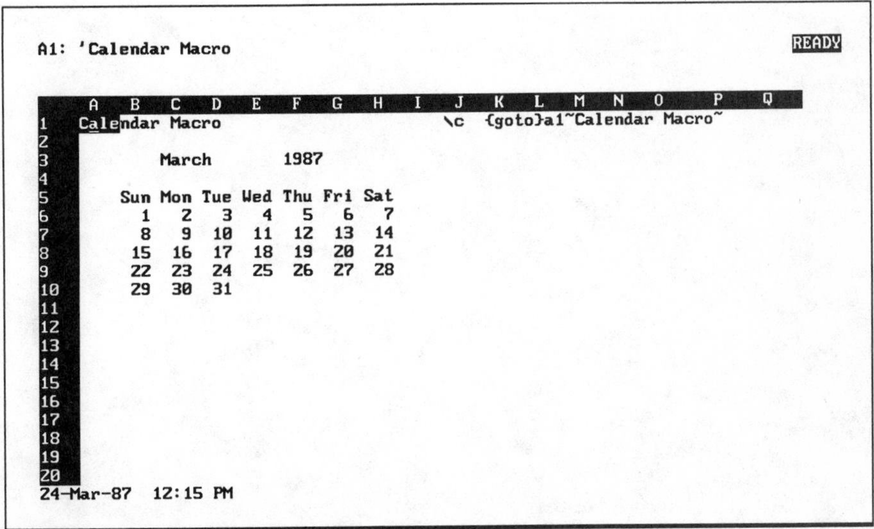

Figure 4.2: Calendar macro created with a macro program

alone. We will use more macros in the coming chapters.

Several books on the market contain many Lotus 1-2-3 macros, including utility macros, business macros, and engineering macros. Complex 1-2-3 macro programs (for instance, a complete accounting package) are also available, and user groups and computer networks offer many more ready-made macros.

■ FOR MORE INFORMATION

For further information about the topics in this chapter, you can consult the following resources.

Macro Program Libraries

A. Simpson, *Simpson's 1-2-3 Macro Library* (Alameda, Calif.: SYBEX, 1986).

R. Flast and L. Flast, *The Complete Book of 1-2-3 Macros* (Berkeley, Calif.: Osborne-McGraw Hill, 1986).

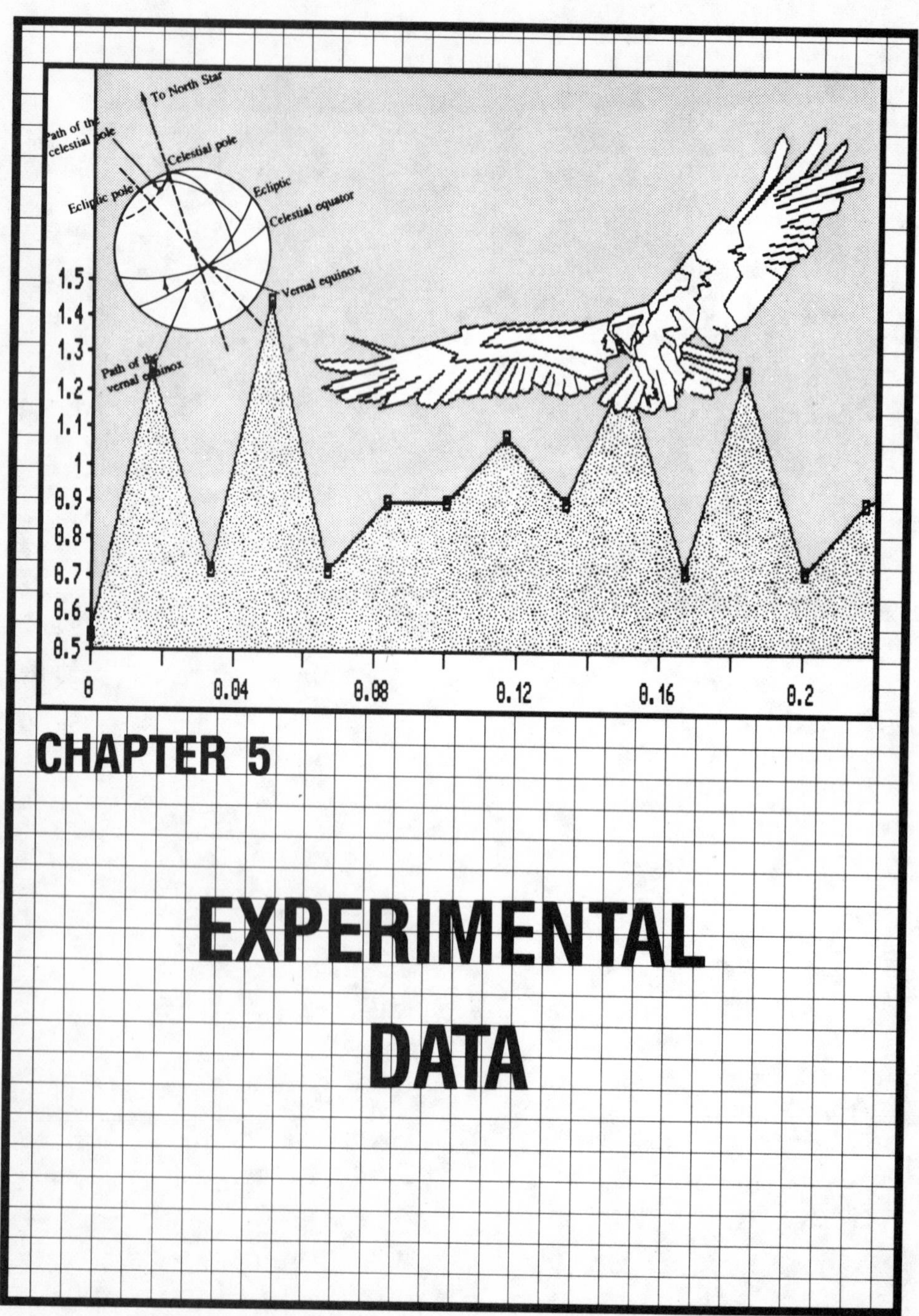

CHAPTER 5

EXPERIMENTAL DATA

Work with experimental data can be as simple as averaging a few numbers or as complex as searching a large database for records that match some criterion. Lotus 1-2-3 can handle each of these cases and most of those in between. Once data is in the spreadsheet, any of the Lotus 1-2-3 functions can be applied to it. For example, many experiments output voltage and current values that are proportional to physical quantities. Using a simple equation and the engineering table format, you can easily convert those voltage and current values into the physical quantities.

INPUT METHODS

Of course, the first thing that you must do is get the data into the spreadsheet. You can choose from among several methods, depending on the format of the data. If the data is in the form of an experimental notebook, then you will have to type it directly into the spreadsheet. If it is already on disk in a text file, then there are a number of ways to get it into the spreadsheet and separate it into the correct cells without having to retype it.

Manual Input

Much experimental data is available only in written form. Notes in an engineering notebook or data tables in reports or journal articles are good examples of printed experimental data. Data in this form must be typed by hand into the spreadsheet, unless you happen to have access to an optical character reader (or a graduate student) that can read the printed characters and turn them into editable text in a disk file.

Entering the data manually can be simplified with a macro. When you enter a table of *X*-*Y* data, for example, you must type the first number, move to the next cell with the arrow keys, type the second number, and so on. The following simple macro eliminates a lot of that typing.

```
{?}{right}{?}{left}{down}{branch \d}
```

Name the macro **\D**. Move to the cell where you want the first data value and press Macro-D. The macro will pause for you to type the first number. When you press Return, it will move one cell to the right and pause for you to type the second number. When you press Return again, it will move left and down so that it is one cell below the first number and then branch back to the beginning of the macro. Thus, all you have to do is type the data in *X*-*Y* pairs, pressing Return between each number, and the data will be entered in two consecutive columns. Any number of columns of data can be entered with a macro similar to this one. Just add the appropriate Move commands to get to the correct cell and use the Pause {?} command wherever you want to insert data. Exit the macro by pressing Break.

Disk-File Input

Data entry is much easier if your data already exists in a disk file. Data of this sort includes that created by numerical simulation computer programs or received from another person or computer on disk or over the telephone. There are several methods you can use to read such data and insert it into the spreadsheet.

Computer modeling of physical phenomena and devices produces large amounts of data that has to be analyzed and plotted. So long as that data is written into an ASCII data file (a text file printable with the DOS PRINT or TYPE command), you can easily load it into the spreadsheet for further analysis. If the data is in a binary file, then you have to write a small computer program to read that binary file and write an ASCII file. For easy conversion, the ASCII file should have the data in the form of a table, with vertically aligned columns of data values or text.

Terminal-emulation programs make your computer behave like a terminal for communications with another computer. You use these programs to receive the results of a calculation or other data from a mainframe computer or data from another person at a remote desktop computer. Most terminal-emulation programs have the capability to receive and store data in ASCII files. Terminal-emulation programs are also useful for connecting two computers with incompatible storage media (such as an IBM PC and an Apple Macintosh) and allowing them to share ASCII files.

File Import and Data Parse Commands

Reading data with the /File Import (/FI) command and then sorting it with the /Data Parse (/DP) command is generally the easiest way to read a text file into a spreadsheet and parse it into separate cells. There are two versions of the /File Import (/FI) command. If you are interested only in the numbers in a text file, the /File Import Numbers (/FIN) command will read and parse that file into separate cells on the spreadsheet. To use /FIN, place the cursor in the upper-left cell of the range that will receive the data from the text file. Execute the command /File Import Numbers (/FIN) and type the file name at the prompt. The command reads the text file until it finds a number; it stores that number in the first cell in the range. It then continues reading until it finds another number and stores that number in the cell to the right of the first one. When it reads a Return character, it moves back to the first column and down one row before it continues looking for numbers.

Spark Gaps For example, consider the text file in Figure 5.1, which consists of some spark-gap data. The text file was printed on the monitor with the DOS TYPE command. If you read this file with the /File Import Numbers (/FIN) command, the spreadsheet will look like Figure 5.2. Note how it skipped all of the text in the file and picked out only the numbers, including the *1-2-3* in the title. The table is complete, with all of the numbers in the correct locations, except for the list of electrode diameters, which are shifted over by one column.

```
A>type b:fig5-1.doc
Figure 5.1
Sample data file for reading into Lotus 1-2-3

           Spark-Gap Length (cm)

 Peak    I    Electrode Diameter (cm) I
Voltage I----------------------------I
 (KV)    I   2.5     5     10     20  I
---------------------------------------
   5          0.13  0.15  0.15  0.16
  10          0.27  0.29  0.30  0.32
  15          0.42  0.44  0.46  0.48
  20          0.58  0.60  0.62  0.64
  25          0.76  0.77  0.78  0.81
  30          0.95  0.94  0.95  0.98
  35          1.17  1.12  1.12  1.15
  40          1.41  1.30  1.29  1.32
  45          1.68  1.50  1.47  1.49
  50          2.00  1.71  1.65  1.66

A>_
```

Figure 5.1: Spark-gap sizes—a text file printed with the DOS TYPE command

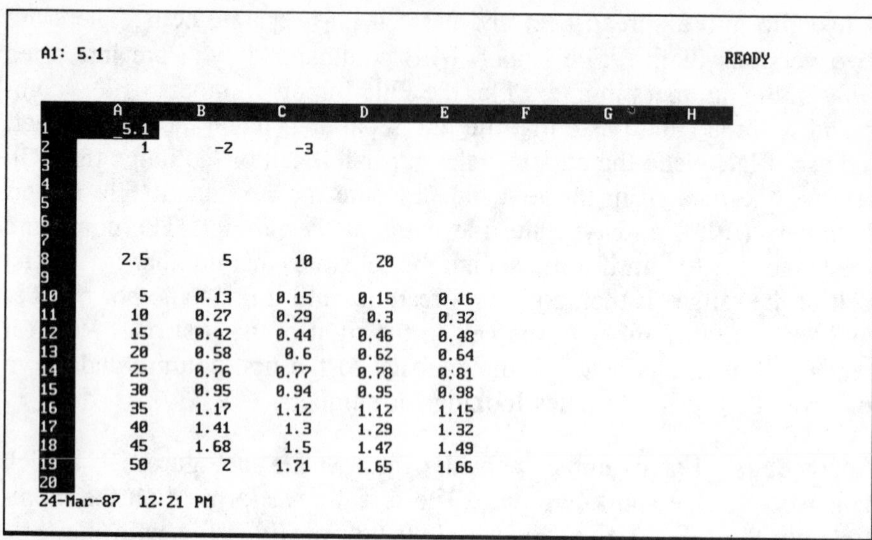

A1: 5.1 READY

	A	B	C	D	E	F	G	H
1	5.1							
2	1	-2	-3					
3								
4								
5								
6								
7								
8	2.5	5	10	20				
9								
10	5	0.13	0.15	0.15	0.16			
11	10	0.27	0.29	0.3	0.32			
12	15	0.42	0.44	0.46	0.48			
13	20	0.58	0.6	0.62	0.64			
14	25	0.76	0.77	0.78	0.81			
15	30	0.95	0.94	0.95	0.98			
16	35	1.17	1.12	1.12	1.15			
17	40	1.41	1.3	1.29	1.32			
18	45	1.68	1.5	1.47	1.49			
19	50	2	1.71	1.65	1.66			
20								

24-Mar-87 12:21 PM

Figure 5.2: The text file in Figure 5.1 read into Lotus 1-2-3 with the /File Import Numbers (/FIN) command

Elementary Particles Figure 5.3 is a table of elementary particles and some of their characteristics. This is a much more complicated (and slightly out of date) table, containing a mixture of text, numbers, and rational fractions. If you try to load it with the /File Import Numbers (/FIN) command, everything will be out of place (see Figure 5.4). Note how in row 5, the fraction 1/2 is split into two cells: one containing the number 1 and the other containing the number 2. Also, in rows 10, 12, 18, and 20, the zero (0) in the particle name was picked up as a number, but the plus (+) and minus (−) signs in the other rows were not, resulting in these rows being offset by one column. Although this spreadsheet could be patched, the probability of errors is quite high. Clearly, patching is not the way to go in this case.

The second form of the Import command is /File Import Text (/FIT). This form of the Import command reads each line of the text file into consecutive cells in a column of the spreadsheet. Each cell in the column will then contain a complete line of text stored as a long label. Beware of text files created by most modern word processors that perform word wrap at the end of lines. In the text files created by these word processors, a complete paragraph is stored as a long line with a Return character at the end. Thus, the whole paragraph (up to the 240-character limit) would be stored in a single cell.

```
A>type b:fig5-3.doc
Particle Physics: A sample text file for reading into Lotus 1-2-3
 Family    Particle Mass  Spin  Strange   Charge  Lifetime (s)
 ------------------------------------------------------------
           Photon    0      1     0          0    Infinite
 Electron  Electron  1     1/2    -         -e    Infinite
   Family  Neutrino  0     0.5    -          0    Infinite
 Muon      Muon    206.77  0.5    -   -1.6e-19 2.212e-6
   Family  Neutrino  0     0.5    -          0    Infinite
 Mesons    Pion +  273.2   0      0   +1.6e-19 2.55e-8
           Pion 0  264.2   0      0          0    1.9e-16
           Kaon +  966.6   0     +1    1.6e-19 1.22e-8
           Kaon 0  974.0   0      1          0    1.00e-10
 Baryons   Proton 1836.12  .5     0    1.6e-19 Infinite
           Neutron 1838.65 0.5    0          0    1013
           Lambda  2182.8  0.5   -1          0    2.51e-10
           Sigma + 2327.7  0.5   -1    1.6e-19 8.1e-11
           Sigma - 2340.5  0.5   -1   -1.6e-19 1.6e-10
           Sigma 0 2332    0.5   -1          0    1e-20
           Xi -    2580    0.5   -2   -1.6e-19 1.3e-10
           Xi 0    2570    0.5   -2          0    1e-10

A>_
```

Figure 5.3: Particle physics constants—a text file printed with the DOS TYPE command

```
A1: 1                                                              READY

          A         B         C         D         E         F         G         H
1          1        -2        -3
2
3
4          0         1         0         0
5          1         1         2
6          0       0.5         0
7     206.77       0.5 -1.6E-19  0.000002
8          0       0.5         0
9      273.2         0         0  1.6E-19  0.000000
10         0     264.2         0         0         0  1.9E-16
11     966.6         0         1  1.6E-19  0.000000
12         0       974         0         1         0  1.0E-10
13   1836.12       0.5         0  1.6E-19
14   1838.65       0.5         0         0      1013
15    2182.8       0.5        -1         0  0.000000
16    2327.7       0.5        -1  1.6E-19   8.1E-11
17    2340.5       0.5        -1 -1.6E-19   1.6E-10
18         0      2332       0.5        -1         0  1.0E-20
19      2580       0.5        -2 -1.6E-19   1.3E-10
20         0      2570       0.5        -2         0  1.0E-10
24-Mar-87  12:24 PM
```

Figure 5.4: Importing the text file in Figure 5.3 with the /File Import Numbers (/FIN) command—a poor choice for this data file

Figure 5.5 shows the result of reading the data file in Figure 5.3 into Lotus 1-2-3 with the /File Import Text (/FIT) command. Although the data may look like it has been separated into separate cells, each line is actually in a single cell in column A. To be able to access this data, you must first parse it into separate columns. You do this with the /Data Parse (/DP) command. To parse the text, you first have to create format lines that tell Lotus 1-2-3 where the different columns begin and end.

A format line is a long label, the length of the labels being parsed. Text in the format line marks the different fields to be parsed. Data that is white space is marked with an asterisk (*). Data marked with asterisks can also be part of a value or label, if that value or label protrudes into a space marked with asterisks. Label fields are marked with an initial L and filled with greater-than (>) symbols. Value fields are marked with an initial V and also filled with greater-than (>) symbols.

1. Create the disk file shown in Figure 5.3 using a text editor (EDLIN will work if you have nothing better) and name it **FIG5-3.DOC**.
2. Start Lotus 1-2-3 and move the cursor to cell A1.
3. Execute the /File Import Text (/**FIT**) command and type the file name **FIG5-3.DOC** at the prompt.
4. Move to cell A2 and execute the /Data Parse Format-line Create (/**DPFC**) command to create a format line.
5. Execute the Quit (**Q**) command to return to ready mode.

```
A1: 'Particle Physics; A sample text file for reading into Lotus 1-2-3         READY

      A        B        C      D        E         F         G         H
1  Particle Physics; A sample text file for reading into Lotus 1-2-3
2    Family     Particle Mass   Spin  Strange   Charge  Lifetime (s)
3    ----------------------------------------------------------------
4               Photon    0      1       0           0   Infinite
5    Electron   Electron  1     1/2      -          -e   Infinite
6      Family   Neutrino  0     0.5      -           0   Infinite
7    Muon       Muon     206.77 0.5      -   -1.6e-19 2.212e-6
8      Family   Neutrino  0     0.5      -           0   Infinite
9    Mesons     Pion +   273.2   0       0   +1.6e-19 2.55e-8
10              Pion 0   264.2   0       0           0  1.9e-16
11              Kaon +   966.6   0      +1    1.6e-19 1.22e-8
12              Kaon 0   974.0   0       1           0  1.00e-10
13   Baryons    Proton  1836.12  .5      0    1.6e-19 Infinite
14              Neutron 1838.65 0.5      0           0  1013
15              Lambda  2182.8  0.5     -1           0  2.51e-10
16              Sigma + 2327.7  0.5     -1    1.6e-19 8.1e-11
17              Sigma - 2340.5  0.5     -1   -1.6e-19 1.6e-10
18              Sigma 0 2332    0.5     -1           0  1e-20
19              Xi -    2580    0.5     -2   -1.6e-19 1.3e-10
20              Xi 0    2570    0.5     -2           0  1e-10
24-Mar-87   12:25 PM
```

Figure 5.5: Data file from Figure 5.3 loaded into the spreadsheet with the /File Import Text (/FIT) command—all data is in column A

6. Move to cell A5 and execute the /Data Parse Format-line Create (**/DPFC**) command again to create a second format line.

The spreadsheet should now look like Figure 5.6. Lotus 1-2-3 has made its best guess as to the correct format line to use to parse the text by looking at the line immediately below the format line. You have entered two format lines: one for the labels in the table heading and one for the table data. Now edit the format lines to correct the errors in Lotus 1-2-3's guess. The format line in line 2 incorrectly splits the last label into two labels. The second format line at line 5 completely misses the first column of labels and incorrectly marks the last column of values as a label. The last column is a special case, containing labels and values. If you mark it as a value column, the values will be converted, and the labels will remain labels.

You are currently at line 5 and in the Data Parse menu.

7. Execute the Format-line Edit (**FE**) command to edit line 5.
8. Use the arrow keys to move to character 3 and type **L>>>>>>>**
9. Move to the last L in the line and change it to **V**.
10. Press Return to end editing and execute the Quit (**Q**) command to return to ready mode.

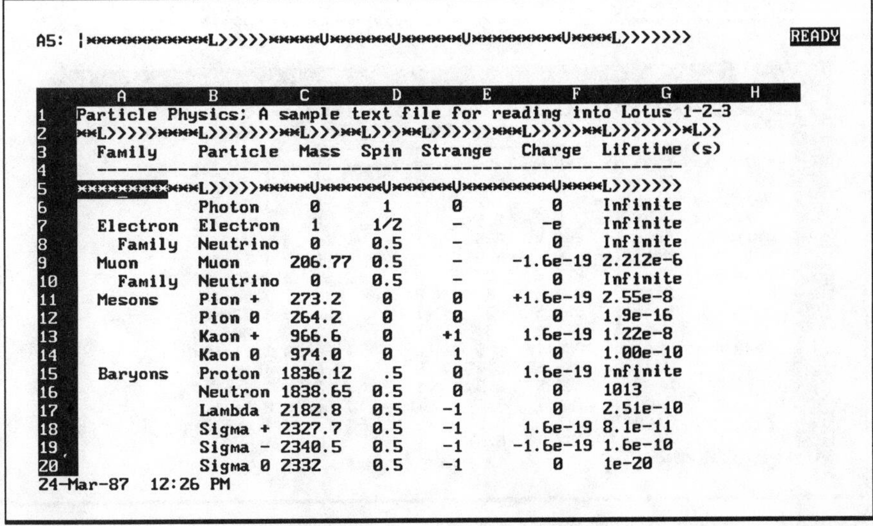

```
A5: |*************L>>>>>*****V******V******V*********V****L>>>>>>>          READY

       A        B        C        D        E        F        G        H
1   Particle Physics; A sample text file for reading into Lotus 1-2-3
2   **L>>>>>****L>>>>>>>**L>>>**L>>>**L>>>>>>***L>>>>>**L>>>>>>>*L>>
3     Family    Particle  Mass  Spin  Strange   Charge  Lifetime (s)
4     ------------------------------------------------------------
5   *************L>>>>>*****V******V******V*********V****L>>>>>>>
6               Photon      0     1     0           0  Infinite
7     Electron  Electron    1    1/2    -          -e  Infinite
8       Family  Neutrino    0    0.5    -           0  Infinite
9     Muon      Muon     206.77  0.5    -   -1.6e-19 2.212e-6
10      Family  Neutrino    0    0.5    -           0  Infinite
11    Mesons    Pion +    273.2   0     0   +1.6e-19 2.55e-8
12              Pion 0    264.2   0     0           0  1.9e-16
13              Kaon +    966.6   0    +1    1.6e-19 1.22e-8
14              Kaon 0    974.0   0     1           0  1.00e-10
15    Baryons   Proton  1836.12  .5     0    1.6e-19 Infinite
16              Neutron 1838.65  0.5    0           0  1013
17              Lambda   2182.8  0.5   -1           0  2.51e-10
18              Sigma + 2327.7   0.5   -1    1.6e-19 8.1e-11
19              Sigma - 2340.5   0.5   -1   -1.6e-19 1.6e-10
20              Sigma 0 2332     0.5   -1           0  1e-20
24-Mar-87  12:26 PM
```

Figure 5.6: Data with initial format lines

11. Move to line 2 and execute the /Data Parse Format-line Edit (/DPFE) command.
12. Move to the last *L in the line and change it to >>.

You are now ready to parse the data. Figure 5.7 shows the spreadsheet with the corrected format lines. Set the input and output ranges and then parse the table. The input range consists of the column of input text, including the format lines. The output range must contain enough columns to include all of the ranges of data that you have marked with the format lines.

13. Execute the Input-column (I) command and select cells A2..A22. You will not parse the data in A1, the title cell.
14. Execute the Output-range (O) command and select cells A2..G22, which will overlay the parsed data on the initial data.
15. Execute the Go Quit (GQ) commands to parse the data and return to ready mode.

The spreadsheet should now look like Figure 5.8. Note that even the fraction in cell D5 has been correctly converted. Any corrections can now be made, and the data can be used in other calculations. There are some zeros in column G due to the numbers being too wide for the

```
A2: |**L>>>>>****L>>>>>>>**L>>>**L>>>**L>>>>>>***L>>>>>**L>>>>>>>>>>>>       READY

       A        B        C        D        E        F        G        H
1  Particle Physics; A sample text file for reading into Lotus 1-2-3
2  **L>>>>>****L>>>>>>>**L>>>**L>>>**L>>>>>>***L>>>>>**L>>>>>>>>>>>>
3   Family    Particle Mass  Spin  Strange   Charge  Lifetime (s)
4  -------------------------------------------------------------
5  **L>>>>>>>**L>>>>>>>***U******U******U*********U****U>>>>>>
6             Photon     0      1     0          0    Infinite
7   Electron  Electron   1     1/2    -         -e    Infinite
8     Family  Neutrino   0     0.5    -          0    Infinite
9   Muon      Muon     206.77  0.5    -   -1.6e-19 2.212e-6
10    Family  Neutrino   0     0.5    -          0    Infinite
11  Mesons    Pion +    273.2   0     0   +1.6e-19 2.55e-8
12            Pion 0    264.2   0     0          0    1.9e-16
13            Kaon +    966.6   0    +1    1.6e-19 1.22e-8
14            Kaon 0    974.0   0     1          0    1.00e-10
15  Baryons   Proton   1836.12  .5    0    1.6e-19 Infinite
16            Neutron 1838.65  0.5    0          0    1013
17            Lambda   2182.8  0.5   -1          0    2.51e-10
18            Sigma +  2327.7  0.5   -1    1.6e-19 8.1e-11
19            Sigma -  2340.5  0.5   -1   -1.6e-19 1.6e-10
20            Sigma 0  2332    0.5   -1          0    1e-20
24-Mar-87  12:29 PM
```

Figure 5.7: Data with corrected format lines

cells. Changing the format to Scientific 1 (S1) or widening the column with /Worksheet Column Set-width (/WCS) will make them visible.

Macro Facility

The Lotus 1-2-3 macro facility has the capability to open text files and read characters or lines of data into the spreadsheet. More complex data importing, such as reading a delimited data file instead of one with the data in columns, can be performed using this capability. A delimited data file is one in which the data is separated by delimiters such as commas and quotation marks rather than being separated by white space and aligned vertically. Although this capability is available, I have not found it necessary to use it, as the /File Import (/FI) and /Data Parse (/DP) commands can usually do the job. *Simpson's 1-2-3 Macro Library* (see "For More Information" at the end of this chapter) contains an excellent example of how to read a delimited data file with a macro program.

Translate Program

Included with the Lotus 1-2-3 program is the translation program TRANS. This program can convert a few specific data file types to valid

```
G11: 0.000000012Z                                                    READY

       A         B          C         D         E         F         G         H
1  Particle Physics: A sample text file for reading into Lotus 1-2-3
2  Family    Particle Mass       Spin      Strange  Charge    Lifetime (s)
3  ------------------------      ------    ------------------ --------
4            Photon           0        1         0         0 Infinite
5  Electron  Electron         1      0.5 -            -e      Infinite
6    Family  Neutrino         0      0.5 -                   0 Infinite
7  Muon      Muon        206.77      0.5 -         -1.6E-19 0.000002
8    Family  Neutrino         0      0.5 -                   0 Infinite
9  Mesons    Pion +       273.2        0         0  1.6E-19 0.000000
10           Pion 0       264.2        0         0         0  1.9E-16
11           Kaon +       966.6        0         1  1.6E-19 0.000000
12           Kaon 0         974        0         1         0  1.0E-10
13 Baryons   Proton     1836.12      0.5         0  1.6E-19 Infinite
14           Neutron    1838.65      0.5         0         0     1013
15           Lambda      2182.8      0.5        -1         0 0.000000
16           Sigma +     2327.7      0.5        -1  1.6E-19  8.1E-11
17           Sigma -     2340.5      0.5        -1 -1.6E-19  1.6E-10
18           Sigma 0       2332      0.5        -1         0  1.0E-20
19           Xi -          2580      0.5        -2 -1.6E-19  1.3E-10
20           Xi 0          2570      0.5        -2         0  1.0E-10
24-Mar-87  12:31 PM
```

Figure 5.8: The completed parsed data file with the cursor in cell G11—the correct number is displayed, even though the spreadsheet shows 0.

Lotus 1-2-3 data files. Table 5.1 lists the programs whose data files currently can be translated. If you need to use data generated in one of these other programs, the TRANS program can directly convert the program's data files without your having to write them to an ASCII text file and then import them into the spreadsheet.

The TRANS program also converts data files from earlier versions of Lotus 1-2-3. A conspicuous omission in the list of translated file types is the Microsoft SYLK (symbolic link) file format. However, the Microsoft spreadsheet programs can write Lotus 1-2-3 version 1A (WKS) files, which can then be converted with the TRANS program to Lotus 1-2-3 version 2.01 files (WK1).

■ STORAGE METHODS

Once you get your data into Lotus 1-2-3, you have to store it so that you can find it when you need it. There are two useful methods for storing and accessing data in Lotus 1-2-3.

Data Table

The simplest data storage method is to use the data table or engineering table, as used in previous chapters. Data for a particular parameter

Translate from:	Translate to:
1-2-3 release 1A	1-2-3 release 1A
1-2-3 release 2 or 2.01	1-2-3 release 2 or 2.01
dBase II	Symphony 1.0
dBase III	Symphony 1.1, 1.2
DIF	
Jazz	
Symphony 1.0	
Symphony 1.1, 1.2	
Visicalc	

Table 5.1: File formats converted with the Lotus TRANS program

are stored in columns, with particular instances of that data in the rows. There is nothing special about this, as it is how scientists and engineers usually store data in laboratory notebooks. Each line contains a particular measurement, with the columns containing the parameters measured. This is how you will store most of your data in a spreadsheet.

Database

For large amounts of data that you need to selectively analyze (for example, by averaging all cells in a column with a particular value on the same row in an adjacent column) the database format is much more flexible. In the Lotus 1-2-3 database, a range of cells is designated as the database. Each column in the database is a field and may contain up to 240 characters of text or values (or formulas). Each row of the range is a database record. Records contain related data. For example, the parameters measured in a single experiment out of many similar experiments would be stored in a single record. The fields contain data of the same type. For example, a particular parameter from many experiments would be stored in the same field in many records, one record for each experiment. As you can see, this is essentially identical to the data table format.

Input Range

The first database record contains field names. These are like the column titles in the data table. They should be simple; they cannot consist of more than one line and cannot be separated from the rest of the database records by blank records or lines.

Criterion Range

The next part of the database is the criterion range. The criterion range consists of a copy of the first database record containing the field names, plus several records for inserting search criteria. Search criteria are labels or values to search for or logical expressions for searching for ranges of values. You can include search criteria under any of the field names to further restrict the search. Criteria placed in the same row are assumed to be connected by a logical AND. Criteria placed in alternate rows are assumed to be connected by a logical OR.

Two wild-card characters—the question mark (?) and the asterisk (*)—are available for searching label fields. The question mark (?) stands for any single character. For example, C?T will match *CAT*, *COT*, and *CUT*. The asterisk (*) matches all of the rest of the characters in the cell (words, numbers, symbols) to the right of its location. For example, C* will match *common*, *creation*, or *continue*. Unfortunately, it cannot match characters to the left of its location. Thus, you cannot search for a single word in a long label using the search string *word*. For 1-2-3 to find a single word, the word must be alone in a single cell or the first word in a cell, or you must know all of the words to the left of that word in the cell and include them in the search string. This limitation makes the Lotus 1-2-3 database a poor choice for a bibliography, since you cannot search a title or abstract for a particular piece of text. Of course, you could write a macro program that performs the search correctly.

Output Range

A few database commands also need an output range, which also consists of a copy of the first database record containing the field names. The output range does not have to contain all of the field names—only those that you want printed in the output range. The output range can consist of either one row or many rows. If your output range consists of only one row, then when the database commands are writing records to this range, they will be written in consecutive rows below the output range. Anything in the way will be overwritten and lost. If you have a multirow output range, then the database commands will write records to it until it is filled and then generate an error. Using multirow output ranges is a way to protect valuable data below the output range.

Database Commands and Functions

1-2-3 offers seven database commands and seven database statistical functions. The database commands are listed in Table 5.2. You use these commands to set up the three database ranges just described and to search the database for records that conform to the search criteria. Located records may be viewed, extracted, or deleted from the database.

The database statistical functions (Table 5.3) perform statistical calculations on the records that match the criteria. These are identical to

Command	Description
/Data Query Input	Set the database range, including the field names in record 1
/Data Query Criterion	Locate the criterion range for searching the database; include the field names
/Data Query Output	Locate the output range; include the field names for the fields to be output
/Data Query Find	Locate and highlight a record that matches the criteria
/Data Query Extract	Locate records that match the criteria and copy them to the output range
/Data Query Unique	Same as extract, but it also eliminates any records in the output range that are the same
/Data Query Delete	Delete records from the database that match the criteria by deleting their rows

Table 5.2: Database commands

the standard statistical functions, except that they are applied only to those records in the range that match the criteria, rather than to the whole range of records. Thus, for example, you can calculate averages or variances of data that have a particular characteristic. See the *1-2-3 Reference Manual* for more information.

Prerace Dehydration in Racing Greyhounds This next example was supplied by Dr. Linda Blythe, DVM, PhD, at the College of Veterinary Medicine at Oregon State University in Corvallis. Dr. Blythe and her coworker Dr. Donald Hansen recently examined prerace weight loss in racing greyhounds. Before greyhound racing begins, the dogs are brought to the racetrack and put in an air-conditioned room known as the *ginny pit*. There they wait until the start of their respective races. During their interval in the ginny pit, some dogs lose several percent of their weight in body fluid. This is due to drooling and panting as the dogs are trained not to urinate or defecate in their cages.

The dogs are weighed when they are brought into the room and again just before their races to ensure that the weight loss has not been excessive. If they have lost more than 3 pounds, they must be examined by a veterinarian before they can race. Loss of an excessive amount of fluids can cause acid/base disturbances that can leave a greyhound with a decreased capacity to handle the hydrogen ions produced during the physical activity of a race.

Name	Description
@DCOUNT(*database,offset,criterion*)	Count the number of non-blank cells in column *offset* for the records that meet the *criterion*
@DSUM(*database,offset,criterion*)	Calculate the sum of the values in column *offset* for the records that meet the *criterion*
@DMAX(*database,offset,criterion*)	Find the maximum of the values in column *offset* for the records that meet the *criterion*
@DMIN(*database,offset,criterion*)	Find the minimum of the values in column *offset* for the records that meet the *criterion*
@DAVG(*database,offset,criterion*)	Calculate the average of the values in column *offset* for the records that meet the *criterion*
@DSTD(*database,offset,criterion*)	Calculate the standard deviation of the values in column *offset* for the records that meet the *criterion*
@DVAR(*database,offset,criterion*)	Calculate the variance of the values in column *offset* for the records that meet the *criterion*

Table 5.3: Database statistical functions

This weight loss is perceived to be a serious problem for some racing greyhounds, so Drs. Blythe and Hansen studied the effect of this loss on racing performance. As data, they had a dog's age, sex, weight before and after being in the ginny pit, race number, race class, post position, and finish position.

Dr. Blythe sent me the data for 489 dogs in 2,552 races, which was far more than I needed for this example. I have included the data for 15 dogs in 100 races in Table 5.4 if you want to recreate the database I used. If not, you can still try the database commands by typing only 10 or 20 records. As you would expect, the results will be different, but the commands will still work. Better yet, use the data from one of your own projects to experiment with the database commands.

1. Change the column widths according to the following table: A = **5**, B = **5**, C = **5**, D = **6**, E = **9**, F = **9**, G = **6**, H = **6**, I = **7**, J = **6**
2. In cell A1, type **Prerace weight loss in racing dogs.**

Create a place for the criterion range, including the range names from the database. Although the criterion range can be anywhere on the spreadsheet, it is simplest to put it either directly above or below the database range.

3. In cell A3, type **Criterion range**
4. In cell A4, type **"Dog**
5. In cell B4, type **"Sex**
6. In cell C4, type **"Age**
7. In cell D4, type **"Race**
8. In cell E4, type **"Init Wt.**
9. In cell F4, type **"Post Wt.**
10. In cell G4, type **"Post**
11. In cell H4, type **"Finish**
12. In cell I4, type **"Class**
13. In cell J4, type **"loss**

Create the database. First enter the field names and then the actual data. You can have no blank or dashed lines between the field names and the data.

Dog	Sex*	Age (mon.)	Race no.	Initial weight (lb.)	Post weight (lb.)	Position Post	Position Finish	Race class*	Weight loss
1	0	58	9	70.5	69.5	8	8	1	1.42%
1	0	58	7	70.5	69.5	9	2	6	1.42%
1	0	58	6	71	70	5	4	6	1.41%
1	0	58	2	72	71.5	1	1	2	0.69%
1	0	58	6	72	71	7	2	2	1.39%
1	0	58	8	72.5	72	5	1	3	0.69%
2	0	29	12	68	67.5	2	5	1	0.74%
2	0	29	9	67	67	2	6	1	0.00%
2	0	29	9	67.5	66.5	6	1	1	1.48%
2	0	29	6	68.5	68	2	6	1	0.73%
2	0	29	6	69	68.5	7	5	1	0.72%
2	0	29	2	69	68.5	4	1	2	0.72%
2	0	29	6	68.5	68	5	5	2	0.73%
3	1	40	12	64	62.5	3	6	1	2.34%
3	1	40	2	64	63	4	9	1	1.56%
3	1	40	6	64	63.5	1	3	1	0.78%
3	1	40	4	64.5	63.5	5	6	1	1.55%
3	1	40	12	65	63	2	2	1	3.08%
3	1	40	2	65	64	5	9	1	1.54%
3	1	40	2	64.5	64	2	1	2	0.78%
4	0	23	12	76	75.5	4	8	1	0.66%
4	0	23	2	76.5	76	9	3	1	0.65%
4	0	23	6	76.5	75.5	8	1	1	1.31%
4	0	23	6	76.5	75.5	9	5	7	1.31%
4	0	23	9	77	76	8	4	1	1.30%
4	0	23	6	77	76	8	2	1	1.30%
4	0	23	9	77	76	1	6	1	1.30%
5	0	24	12	71.5	70.5	5	3	1	1.40%
5	0	24	2	71.5	71	5	2	1	0.70%
5	0	24	9	71	70.5	3	1	7	0.70%

Table 5.4: Prerace dehydration in racing greyhounds—weight loss/performance data (courtesy Dr. L. Blythe, Oregon State University)

Dog	Sex*	Age (mon.)	Race no.	Initial weight (lb.)	Post weight (lb.)	Position		Race class*	Weight loss
						Post	Finish		
5	0	24	6	71.5	71	6	2	7	0.70%
5	0	24	9	71	70	7	2	1	1.41%
5	0	24	9	72	71.5	4	4	1	0.69%
5	0	24	9	71.5	71	8	1	1	0.70%
6	1	47	12	59	58	6	7	1	1.69%
6	1	47	6	58	57.5	2	3	1	0.86%
6	1	47	9	58.5	58	1	4	7	0.85%
6	1	47	6	59	58.5	4	4	7	0.85%
6	1	47	9	58.5	58	1	3	1	0.85%
6	1	47	9	58.5	57.5	6	2	1	1.71%
6	1	47	9	58	57	4	1	1	1.72%
7	0	34	12	72	71.5	7	2	1	0.69%
7	0	34	6	71.5	71	5	9	1	0.70%
7	0	34	9	71.5	71.5	2	3	7	0.00%
7	0	34	6	72	71.5	2	1	7	0.69%
7	0	34	9	72.5	71.5	3	1	1	1.38%
7	0	34	9	71.5	71	8	3	1	0.70%
7	0	34	9	71.5	71	2	5	1	0.70%
8	0	23	12	71.5	71	8	4	1	0.70%
8	0	23	9	72	71.5	8	2	1	0.69%
8	0	23	9	71.5	71	1	9	1	0.70%
8	0	23	11	72	71.5	1	1	2	0.69%
8	0	23	8	72	71.5	8	6	2	0.69%
8	0	23	2	72.5	72	2	4	2	0.69%
8	0	23	2	72	72	9	3	2	0.00%
8	0	23	9	72	71.5	4	6	1	0.69%
9	0	36	12	63.5	62.5	9	1	1	1.57%
9	0	36	2	63.5	63	3	1	1	0.79%
9	0	36	2	63.5	63.5	1	1	2	0.00%
9	0	36	12	64	62.5	9	2	1	2.34%

Table 5.4: Prerace dehydration in racing greyhounds—weight loss/performance data (courtesy Dr. L. Blythe, Oregon State University) *(continued)*

Dog	Sex*	Age (mon.)	Race no.	Initial weight (lb.)	Post weight (lb.)	Position Post	Position Finish	Race class*	Weight loss
9	0	36	12	63	62.5	1	4	1	0.79%
9	0	36	9	63.5	63	5	7	1	0.79%
9	0	36	12	64	63	8	3	1	1.56%
9	0	36	9	63	63	1	9	1	0.00%
10	0	26	11	66	65	1	6	3	1.52%
10	0	26	8	66	65.5	6	9	3	0.76%
10	0	26	5	66	65.5	7	9	3	0.76%
10	0	26	8	66.5	65	6	2	3	2.26%
10	0	26	6	66.5	65.5	3	6	7	1.50%
10	0	26	9	66	64	9	8	7	3.03%
10	0	26	12	67	66	6	3	2	1.49%
11	1	21	11	53.5	52.5	2	1	3	1.87%
11	1	21	5	53	52	1	6	3	1.89%
11	1	21	1	53.5	53	1	4	3	0.93%
11	1	21	1	53.5	53	5	2	3	0.93%
11	1	21	8	53.5	52.5	2	4	3	1.87%
11	1	21	10	53.5	53	2	3	3	0.93%
11	1	21	11	54	53.5	3	9	3	0.93%
11	1	21	5	54	54	2	1	4	0.00%
12	0	28	11	69	68.5	3	4	3	0.72%
12	0	28	8	68	67.5	9	2	3	0.74%
12	0	28	5	69	68.5	5	7	3	0.72%
12	0	28	8	70	69	7	9	3	1.43%
12	0	28	2	68.5	68	2	8	2	0.73%
12	0	28	6	68.5	68	3	8	2	0.73%
12	0	28	12	68	67.5	4	9	2	0.74%
13	1	51	11	62	61.5	4	2	3	0.81%
13	1	51	8	62.5	62	3	6	3	0.80%
13	1	51	7	62	61.5	8	7	6	0.81%
13	1	51	6	62.5	62	4	6	6	0.80%

Table 5.4: Prerace dehydration in racing greyhounds—weight loss/performance data (courtesy Dr. L. Blythe, Oregon State University) *(continued)*

Dog	Sex*	Age (mon.)	Race no.	Initial weight (lb.)	Post weight (lb.)	Position Post	Position Finish	Race class*	Weight loss
13	1	51	11	62.5	62	1	4	2	0.80%
13	1	51	12	62.5	62	7	2	2	0.80%
14	1	33	11	52.5	51	5	8	3	2.86%
14	1	33	5	52.5	52	5	9	3	0.95%
14	1	33	8	52	51	7	7	3	1.92%
14	1	33	12	52	51.5	2	2	3	0.96%
14	1	33	12	52	51	4	9	3	1.92%
14	1	33	12	52	51	5	5	2	1.92%
15	0	25	11	64	63	6	5	3	1.56%
15	0	25	5	64	62.5	2	2	3	2.34%

* Key:

Sex: 0 = male, 1 = female

Race class: 1 (fast) through 5 (slow)
6 and 7 unclassified

Table 5.4: Prerace dehydration in racing greyhounds—weight loss/performance data (courtesy Dr. L. Blythe, Oregon State University) *(continued)*

14. In cell A14, type **Database Range**
15. In cell A15, type **"Dog**
16. In cell B15, type **"Sex**
17. In cell C15, type **"Age**
18. In cell D15, type **"Race**
19. In cell E15, type **"Init Wt.**
20. In cell F15, type **"Post Wt.**
21. In cell G15, type **"Post**
22. In cell H15, type **"Finish**
23. In cell I15, type **"Class**
24. In cell J15, type **"loss**

Calculate the percent weight loss.

25. In cells J16..J115, type/copy **(E16-F16)/E16**
26. Format cells J16..J115 as Percent 2 (**P2**).

Enter the data into the database.

27. In cells A16..I115, type at least 10 or 20 records of the data from Table 5.4.
28. Name cells A15..J115 as **DATABASE**.
29. Name cells A4..J5 as **CRITERION**.

The spreadsheet should look like Figure 5.9. I have used the names DATABASE and CRITERION for the database and criterion ranges. These particular names are not required, but they make using the data base statistical functions more intuitive.

Now that you have a database to work with, you can search it to locate some data of interest. Suppose that you want to know the percentage of male and female dogs in the races. You could use the @DCOUNT function to count the number of males and females and then divide the numbers. However, since the males are marked with 0 and the females with 1, all you have to do is to average the SEX column of the database.

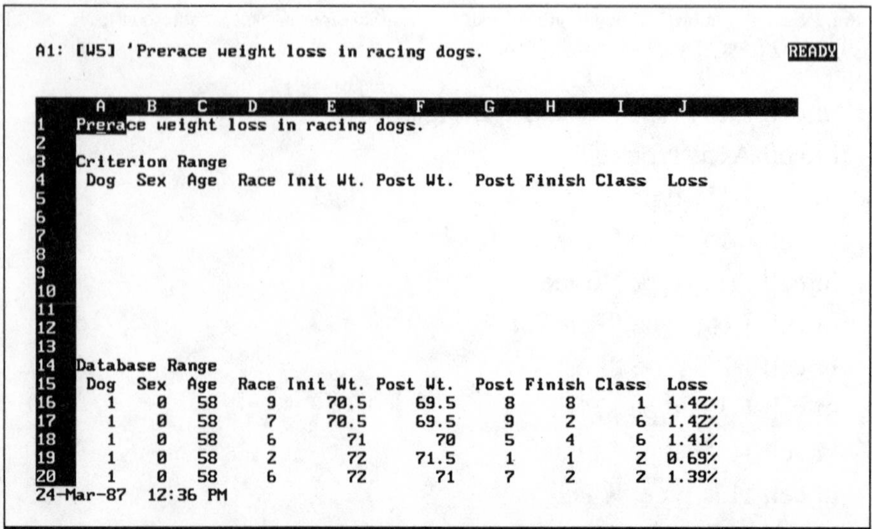

A1: [W5] 'Prerace weight loss in racing dogs. READY

	A	B	C	D	E	F	G	H	I	J
1	Prerace weight loss in racing dogs.									
2										
3	Criterion Range									
4	Dog	Sex	Age	Race	Init Wt.	Post Wt.	Post	Finish	Class	Loss
5										
6										
7										
8										
9										
10										
11										
12										
13										
14	Database Range									
15	Dog	Sex	Age	Race	Init Wt.	Post Wt.	Post	Finish	Class	Loss
16	1	0	58	9	70.5	69.5	8	8	1	1.42%
17	1	0	58	7	70.5	69.5	9	2	6	1.42%
18	1	0	58	6	71	70	5	4	6	1.41%
19	1	0	58	2	72	71.5	1	1	2	0.69%
20	1	0	58	6	72	71	7	2	2	1.39%

24-Mar-87 12:36 PM

Figure 5.9: Prerace dehydration in racing greyhounds—initial database setup

30. In cell E10, type **@DAVG(DATABASE,1,CRITERION)**
31. Format cell E10 as Percentage 2 (**P2**).

As soon as the spreadsheet is recalculated, you will see the figure 34 percent appear (35 percent if you only use the first 20 records), indicating that 34 percent of the dogs are female. Note that an empty criterion range matches the whole database. Now find out how the female dogs are doing at the finish line by finding the percentage of the dogs in the first three places that are female.

32. In cell H5, type **+H16 < 4**

Cell E10 will now hold 30.43 percent (33.33 percent for 20 records). What you have done is to limit the records being averaged to those with dogs in the first three places. You see that the percentage of winning females has decreased slightly.

Since this study is about weight loss, now look at those dogs that win and that have a high weight loss (greater than 2.5 percent of their body weight).

33. In cell J5, type **+J16>0.025**

The percentage in cell E10 will change to 100 (this value is the same for 20 records). This indicates that all of the dogs in the first three places that have high fluid loss are females (see Figure 5.10). You can continue changing the restrictions in the criterion range and see what the results are. You can also count cells that match the criterion with the @DCOUNT command, find the minima or maxima with the @DMIN and @DMAX commands, calculate the standard deviation and variance with the @DSTD and @DVAR commands, and add the values with the @DSUM command.

For any more complicated functions, you must copy the matching records to another part of the spreadsheet, where you can use all of the Lotus 1-2-3 data analysis functions. You do this by designating an input range with the /Data Query Input (/DEI) command and selecting DATABASE as the range, designating the criterion range with Criterion (C) and selecting CRITERION as the range, and selecting an output range using Output (O) and selecting a range as the output destination. The matching data can now be copied to the output range with the Extract (E) or Unique (U) command, where it can be manipulated with other Lotus 1-2-3 functions.

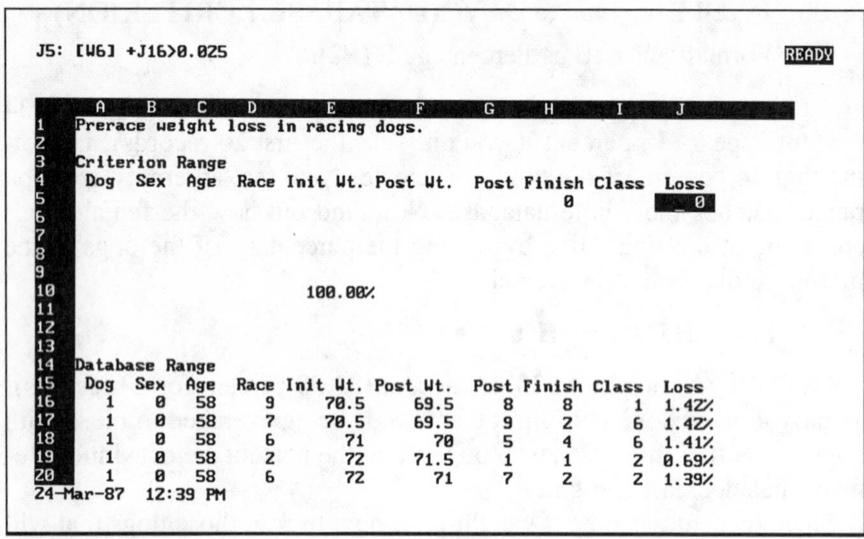

Figure 5.10: Prerace dehydration in racing greyhounds—analysis using database statistical functions

Two other commands—the /Data Sort (/DS) and /Data Distribution (/DD) commands—occasionally are useful with the database format. Executing /Data Sort (/DS) brings up the Sort menu:

Data-range Primary-key Secondary-key Reset Go Quit

This command can sort any set of data and text records, in ascending or descending order, according to a primary and a secondary key. Many columns of data can be sorted according to the values in a single column. For example, you could sort the database range according to the finishing position and the weight loss.

34. Execute the /Data Sort Data-range (/**DSD**) command and select cells A16..J115 as the range.
35. Select Primary-key (**P**), type **H16** to select column H, and select Ascending (**A**) for the sort order.
36. Select Secondary-key (**S**) from the Sort menu, type **J16**, and select Descending (**D**) as the sort order.
37. Execute the Go (**G**) command to sort the database.

The spreadsheet database should now look like Figure 5.11, with all of the records sorted according to the winning position and the weight loss.

A14: [W5] 'Database Range READY

	A	B	C	D	E	F	G	H	I	J
14	Database Range									
15	Dog	Sex	Age	Race	Init Wt.	Post Wt.	Post	Finish	Class	Loss
16	11	1	21	11	53.5	52.5	2	1	3	1.87%
17	6	1	47	9	58	57	4	1	1	1.72%
18	9	0	36	12	63.5	62.5	9	1	1	1.57%
19	2	0	29	9	67.5	66.5	6	1	1	1.48%
20	7	0	34	9	72.5	71.5	3	1	1	1.38%
21	4	0	23	6	76.5	75.5	8	1	1	1.31%
22	9	0	36	2	63.5	63	3	1	1	0.79%
23	3	1	40	2	64.5	64	2	1	2	0.78%
24	2	0	29	2	69	68.5	4	1	2	0.72%
25	5	0	24	9	71	70.5	3	1	7	0.70%
26	5	0	24	9	71.5	71	8	1	1	0.70%
27	8	0	23	11	72	71.5	1	1	2	0.69%
28	1	0	58	2	72	71.5	1	1	2	0.69%
29	7	0	34	6	72	71.5	2	1	7	0.69%
30	1	0	58	8	72.5	72	5	1	3	0.69%
31	11	1	21	5	54	54	2	1	4	0.00%
32	9	0	36	2	63.5	63.5	1	1	2	0.00%
33	3	1	40	12	65	63	2	2	1	3.08%

02-May-87 02:23 PM

Figure 5.11: Prerace dehydration in racing greyhounds—sorted database records

One final database command, the /Data Distribution (/DS) command, uses a set of data values (say, a column in a database) and a set of bins, and calculates the number of data values in each bin (a bin is a minimum value and a maximum value that define a range). This creates data for histogram-like output.

■ SUMMARY

Experimental data is an important resource for scientists and engineers. Managing that resource can be performed with Lotus 1-2-3. In this chapter, we investigated how to enter database data into the spreadsheet and how to store and retrieve it afterward. We also saw how to use the database management capability to analyze experimental data.

■ FOR MORE INFORMATION

For further information about the topics in this chapter, you can consult the following resources.

Spark Gaps

CRC, *Handbook of Chemistry and Physics,* 51st ed. (Cleveland, Ohio: Chemical Rubber Co., 1971), p. E61.

Elementary Particles

D. Halliday and R. Resnick, *Physics* (New York: Wiley, 1967), pp. 551–552.

Reading Delimited Data Files

A. Simpson, *Simpson's 1-2-3 Macro Library* (Alameda, Calif.: SYBEX, 1986).

Prerace Dehydration in Racing Greyhounds

L. L. Blythe and D. E. Hansen, "Factors Affecting Prerace Dehydration and Performance of Racing Greyhounds," *J. Am. Vet. Med. Assoc. 189*, 12 (Dec. 15, 1986): 1572–1574.

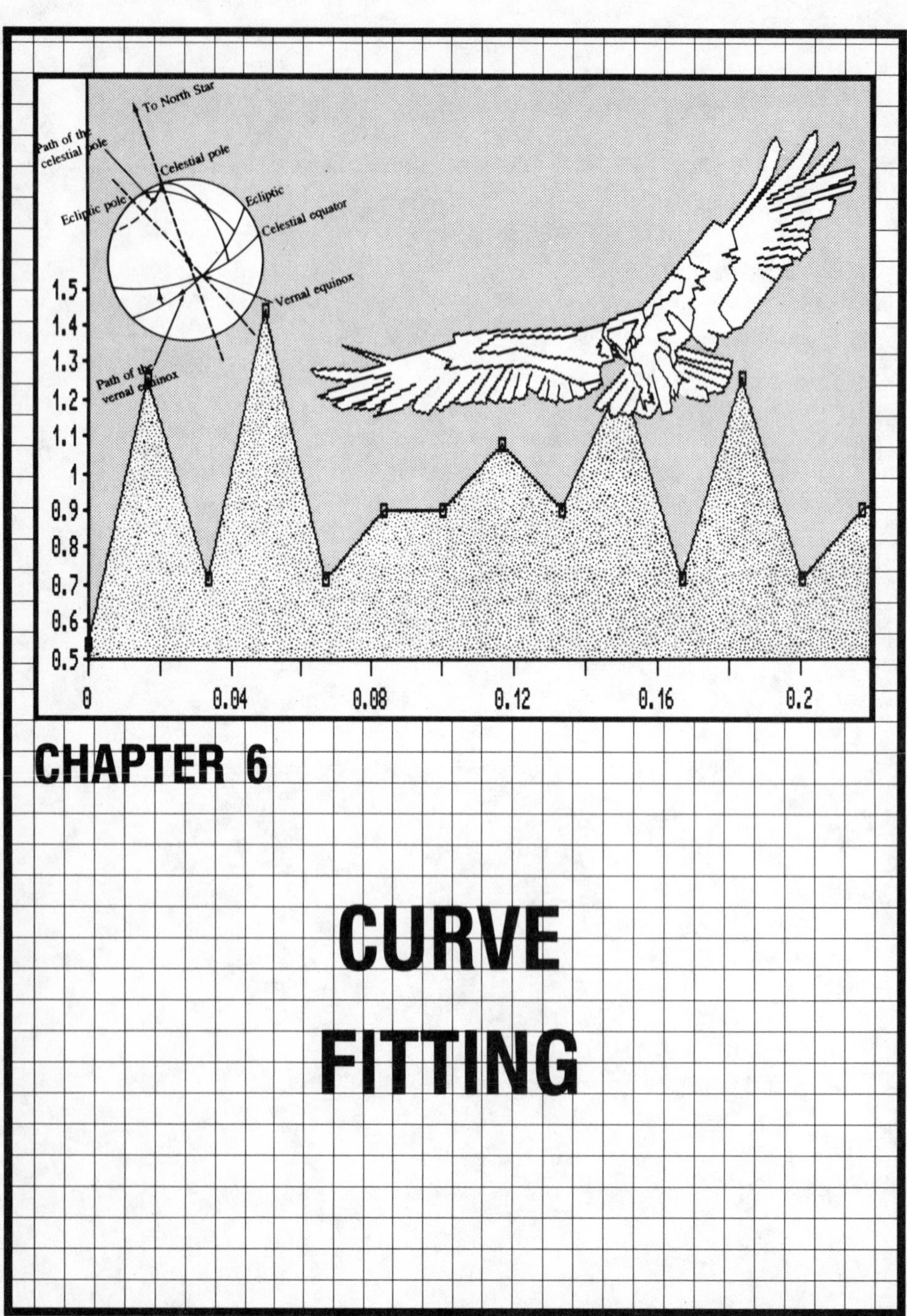

CHAPTER 6

CURVE FITTING

Fitting an analytical equation to a set of data points is a common task of the scientist or engineer. For the scientist, being able to fit a theoretical equation to some experimental data often vindicates a theory. The engineer is more often required to fit some calibration data for an instrument to an analytical equation so that he or she can easily convert the output of the instrument to the physical parameter being measured.

There are three ways to perform curve fitting with Lotus 1-2-3. You can fit most equations to data with the built-in linear regression commands. Linear regression analysis can also be used to fit nonlinear data by suitably transforming the data before it is fit. You can fit more complex equations by manually adjusting the coefficients of the equation until the residual error (the sum of the squares of the differences between the data and the curve) is minimized, or the correlation coefficient is maximized. Finally, for data that does not fit any reasonable equation, you can use table look-up functions and interpolation to calculate values.

BUILT-IN FUNCTIONS

Lotus 1-2-3 has the built-in curve-fitting capability known as *multiple linear regression*. With this capability, you can fit data to either a simple line or a complex polynomial. Most curve-fitting tasks can be accomplished with this easy-to-execute capability.

Regression

When you fit a curve with regression analysis, what you are doing is minimizing the residual square error between the data points and the curve being fit (least squares analysis). The residual square error (E) is found using the equation

$$E = \sum_{i=1}^{n} (y(x_i) - y_i)^2$$

where $y(x_i)$ is the curve being fit, n is the number of data points, and x_i and y_i are the data points being fit to. Lotus 1-2-3 uses multiple linear regression, so it assumes that the curve $y(x_i)$ is of the form

$$y(x_{1,i}, x_{2,i}, \cdots) = A + Bx_{1,i} + Cx_{2,i} + \cdots$$

where A, B, and C are the coefficients of the equation that have to be adjusted to make the curve fit the data. This is done by inserting the function for $y(x_{1,i}, x_{2,i}, \ldots)$ into the equation for the residual error and then setting the derivative of that equation, with respect to each of the coefficients, equal to zero. This results in one equation for each of the coefficients in terms of the other coefficients and the data points, which are then solved for the coefficients. You do not have to worry about any of this when you use 1-2-3, as it is taken care of with the /Data Regression (/DR) commands.

Along with the coefficients of the regression equation, Lotus 1-2-3 also calculates some statistics about the curve fit. It calculates the standard error of the y estimate (S_{yx}), the correlation coefficient (R^2), and the standard errors of the coefficients (S_B, S_C, and so on). The standard error of the y estimate is an estimate of the error in a single value of y calculated with the equation. This can be used, in conjunction with Student's t test, to calculate the confidence limits of the calculated curve. The confidence limit is a band about the calculated curve that contains the true curve with some level of confidence (say, 95 percent). Any good book about statistical methods will show you how to do this. The standard error of the y estimate is calculated with the equation

$$S_{y \cdot x} = \sqrt{\frac{\sum_{i=1}^{n} (y_i - y(x_i))^2}{p}}$$

where p is the degrees of freedom ($p = n - 2$ for a simple linear curve).

The correlation coefficient is a measure of how well the curve fits the data points. It has a range of 0 to 1, with 1 indicating a perfect fit to the data points. Any good curve fit will have a correlation coefficient with a value greater than 0.9. It is calculated with

$$R^2 = 1 - \frac{\sum_{i=1}^{n} (y_i - y(x_i))^2}{\sum_{i=1}^{n} (y_i - \langle y_i \rangle)^2}$$

where

$$\langle y_i \rangle = \frac{\sum_{i=1}^{n} (y_i)}{n}$$

is the average of the y data.

The standard errors in the coefficients are measures of the errors in each of the regression coefficients. The standard error in the first coefficient (S_A) is calculated using the standard error of the y estimate.

$$S_A = \sqrt{\frac{1}{n} + \frac{\langle x \rangle^2}{\sum_{i=1}^{n} (x_i - \langle x \rangle)^2}}\, S_{y \cdot x}$$

Here,

$$\langle x \rangle = \frac{\sum_{i=1}^{n} (x_i)}{n}$$

The main use of the standard errors of the coefficients is to test a coefficient to see if it is statistically 0. Since the coefficients all multiply linear x terms, if $x = 0$, then there is no correlation between that x term and the y data. Using the t value for the required confidence interval $(1 - \alpha)$ and degrees of freedom (p), you calculate

$$|B| > t_{\frac{\alpha}{2},p} S_B$$

If this equation is true, then the coefficient is significant and is not 0. Otherwise, 0 should be used for the coefficient. The rest of the coefficients are handled in a similar manner. A good engineering statistics book will give you a lot more information about how to use these statistics, including a table of t values. In general, if the absolute value of the coefficient is an order of magnitude larger than the standard error of the coefficient, then you can be sure that it is significant. If you have at least 4 degrees of freedom (that is, six data points for a linear fit), the 95 percent confidence interval t value is only about 2.5 and decreases for more degrees of freedom. So if the absolute value of the coefficient is greater than 2.5 times the standard error of that coefficient, the coefficient will still be significant. If it is smaller than that, you will need to get a statistics book and look up the correct values to be sure.

Linear Regression

Linear regression analysis is achieved with the /Data Regression commands (/DR). When you execute that command, the following menu appears:

X-range Y-range Output-range Intercept Reset Go Quit

To select the x values, select X-range (X) and specify the range. Note that the range can consist of more than one column of x values, and the curve-fitting routines will calculate coefficients for each set of values. You select the y values by selecting Y-range (Y) and specifying the range. You also need to select the upper-left cell of the output range. Lotus 1-2-3 will output the results of the regression to a block of cells nine cells tall and a minimum of four cells wide, depending on the number of coefficients that you need to calculate. Make sure that the area you specify has enough room.

The Intercept (I) command allows you to force the line to go through zero or to calculate the zero offset. The Reset (R) command resets all of the input and output ranges, and the Go (G) command executes the regression analysis.

Thermal Conductivity Earlier, you calculated the temperature dependence of the thermal conductivity of silicon from an equation. Silicon is a well-known semiconductor, so an equation for the thermal conductivity was easy to find. Gallium arsenide (GaAs), on the other hand, is not as well known, so you will have to fit the experimental data to some curve.

Table 6.1 contains the experimental data for the temperature dependence of the thermal conductivity of heavily doped, p-type gallium arsenide. First, you will try a simple linear fit of the data. To create your spreadsheet, you need to type this table into the range A5..B17.

1. In cell A1, type **Thermal conductivity of GaAs; Linear Curve Fit**
2. In cell A3, type **"T**
3. In cell B3, type **^K**
4. In cell A4, type **"(K)**
5. In cell B4, type **"(W/cm-K)**
6. Execute the /Data Fill (/DF) command and select cells A5..A17, with a starting value of **250**, a step value of **50**, and the default ending value.
7. In cells B5..B17 type the thermal conductivity values from Table 6.1.

Set up an equation to calculate the y estimates of the linear fit.

T (K)	K (W/cm-K)
250	0.455
300	0.362
350	0.302
400	0.256
450	0.223
500	0.197
550	0.176
600	0.158
650	0.144
700	0.132
750	0.121
800	0.112
850	0.103

Table 6.1: Thermal conductivity of heavily doped gallium arsenide versus temperature

8. In cell C3, type **"K**
9. In cell C4, type **"Est.**
10. Name cells H5 and G11 as **B** and **M**.
11. In cells C5..C17, type/copy **+$M*A5+$B**
12. Format cells C5..C17 as Fixed 3 (**F3**).

Execute the linear regression commands to calculate the linear curve fit of this data. The regression coefficients will then be used by the formulas in cells C5..C17 to calculate the *y* estimates so that these values can be compared to the original data.

13. Execute the /Data Regression X-range (**/DRX**) command and select A5..A17.
14. Execute the Y-range (**Y**) command and select B5..B17.
15. Execute the Output-range (**O**) command and select E4.
16. Execute the Go (**G**) command to calculate the regression parameters and return to ready mode.

The spreadsheet should now look like Figure 6.1. Comparing the linear fit with the experimental data, you can see that you have fit the trend of the data, but have not fit the individual points very well. Checking R^2, you can see that it has a value of 0.875. Figure 6.2 is a plot of the experimental data and the linear curve fit (you should be able to create this graph on your own). As expected, it does not fit very well.

The thermal conductivity of silicon fits the simple equation

$$K = \frac{K_0}{(T - T_0)}$$

where K_0 and T_0 are constants to be determined. However, this equation cannot be used in a linear regression program. But solving it for the temperature, using the equation

$$T = \left(\frac{1}{K}\right)K_0 + T_0$$

yields a linear equation for T in the variable $1/K$, rather than a nonlinear equation for K in the variable T. You can easily rearrange the spreadsheet to calculate $1/K$. You can then use this value as the x-range and T as the y-range.

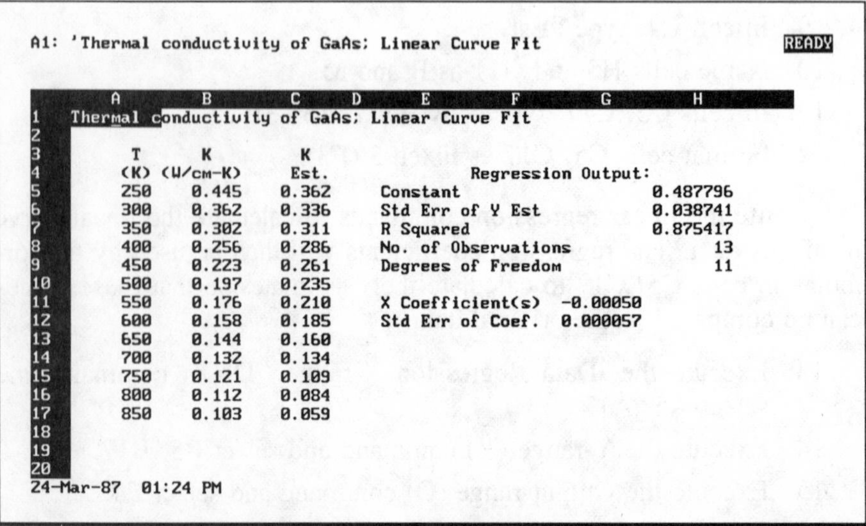

A1: 'Thermal conductivity of GaAs: Linear Curve Fit READY

	A	B	C	D	E	F	G	H
1	Thermal conductivity of GaAs: Linear Curve Fit							
2								
3	T	K	K					
4	(K)	(W/cm-K)	Est.		Regression Output:			
5	250	0.445	0.362	Constant			0.487796	
6	300	0.362	0.336	Std Err of Y Est			0.038741	
7	350	0.302	0.311	R Squared			0.875417	
8	400	0.256	0.286	No. of Observations			13	
9	450	0.223	0.261	Degrees of Freedom			11	
10	500	0.197	0.235					
11	550	0.176	0.210	X Coefficient(s)		-0.00050		
12	600	0.158	0.185	Std Err of Coef.		0.000057		
13	650	0.144	0.160					
14	700	0.132	0.134					
15	750	0.121	0.109					
16	800	0.112	0.084					
17	850	0.103	0.059					
18								
19								
20								

24-Mar-87 01:24 PM

Figure 6.1: Thermal conductivity of GaAs—a linear curve fit

17. Change the width of columns A and E to **6** and **2** respectively.
18. In cell A1, type **Thermal conductivity of GaAs; Linear regression of a formula**

Delete the old regression results.

19. Execute the /Range Erase (/**RE**) command for cells E4..H12.
20. Move cells C3..C4 to D3..D4.
21. In cell C4, type **^1/K**
22. In cells C5..C17, type/copy **1/B5**

Enter the new estimator formula for *K*.

23. Name cells H12 and I6 as **K0** and **T0**.
24. In cells D5..D17, type/copy **+$K0/(A5-$T0)**
25. Format cells C5..D17 as Fixed 3 (**F3**).

Calculate the regression.

26. Execute the /Data Regression X-range (/**DRX**) command and select C5..C17.
27. Execute the Y-range (**Y**) command and select A5..A17.

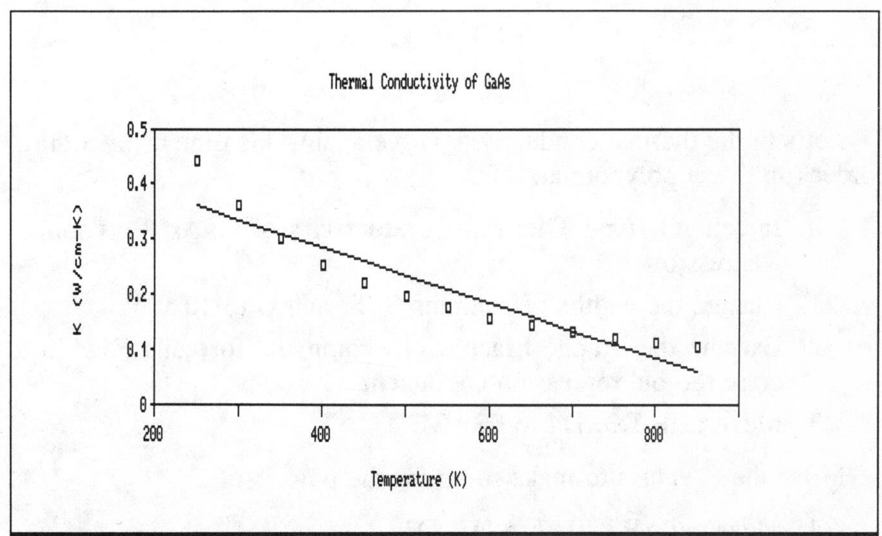

Figure 6.2: Results of fitting the thermal conductivity of GaAs with a line

28. Execute the Output-range (**O**) command and select **F5**.
29. Execute the Go (**G**) command to calculate the regression parameters and return to ready mode.

The spreadsheet should now look like Figure 6.3. Note that the value of R^2 has improved tremendously; it is now 0.998, indicative of a good fit to the data points. Figure 6.4 shows that the regression line now follows the data much better than the linear curve. Note that you have fit a nonlinear curve using a linear curve-fitting program.

Polynomial Regression

Although the Lotus 1-2-3 data regression command is not explicitly set up to perform polynomial regression analysis, you can easily perform it. Polynomial regression fits data with a line of the form

$$y = A + Bx + Cx^2 + \cdots$$

You can fit this equation with a multiple linear regression program by letting

$$x_{1,i} = x_i$$

$$x_{2,i} = x_i^2$$

$$x_{3,i} = x_i^3$$

$$\vdots$$

Let's fit the thermal conductivity curve again, this time using a third-order (up to x^3) polynomial.

30. In cell A1, type **Thermal Conductivity of GaAs; Polynomial Regression**
31. Change the widths of columns E, F, and G to **10**.
32. Execute the /Range Erase (**/RE**) command for cells F5..I13 to erase the old regression coefficients.
33. Move cells D3..D4 to E3..E4.

Move the K values to make room for the powers of T.

34. Move cells B3..B17 to D3..D17.
35. In cell B4, type **"T^2**

A1: [W6] 'Thermal conductivity of GaAs: Linear Regression of a Formula READY

	A	B	C	D	E	F	G	H
1	Thermal conductivity of GaAs: Linear Regression of a Formula							
2								
3	T	K		K				
4	(K)	(W/cm-K)	1/K	Est.				
5	250	0.445	2.247	0.484		Regression Output:		
6	300	0.362	2.762	0.372	Constant			83.17157
7	350	0.302	3.311	0.302	Std Err of Y Est			8.500841
8	400	0.256	3.906	0.255	R Squared			0.998252
9	450	0.223	4.484	0.220	No. of Observations			13
10	500	0.197	5.076	0.194	Degrees of Freedom			11
11	550	0.176	5.682	0.173				
12	600	0.158	6.329	0.156	X Coefficient(s)		80.67974	
13	650	0.144	6.944	0.142	Std Err of Coef.		1.017654	
14	700	0.132	7.576	0.131				
15	750	0.121	8.264	0.121				
16	800	0.112	8.929	0.113				
17	850	0.103	9.709	0.105				
18								
19								
20								

24-Mar-87 01:28 PM

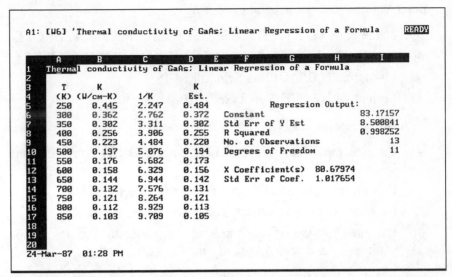

Figure 6.3: Thermal conductivity of GaAs—fitting a nonlinear equation

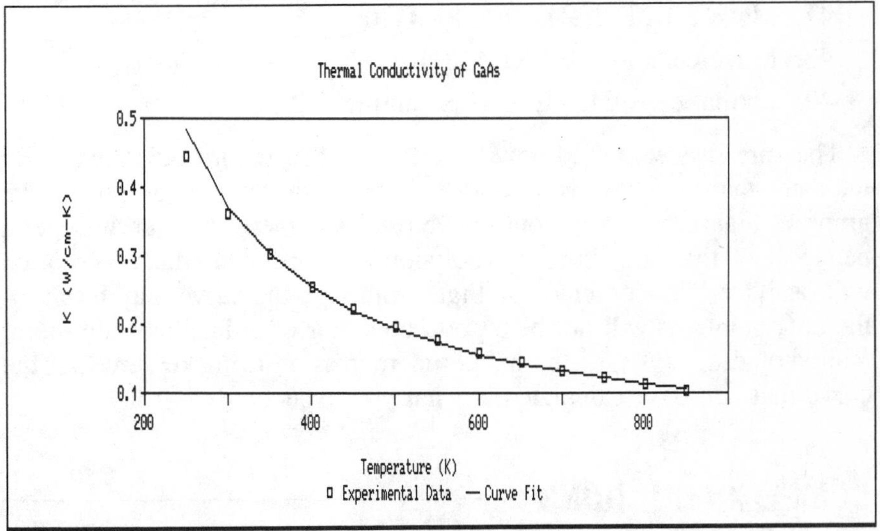

Figure 6.4: Comparison of the experimental data and the nonlinear curve fit

36. In cells B5..B17, type/copy +A5^2
37. In cell C4, type "T^3
38. In cells C5..C17, type/copy +A5^3

Enter the new estimator equation for K.

39. Name cells I6, H12, I12, and J12, respectively, as **A**, **B**, **C**, **D**.
40. In cells E5..E17, type/copy **+$A+$B*A5+$C*B5+$D*C5**
41. Format cells B5..C17 as Scientific 1 (**S1**).
42. Format cells E5..E17 as Fixed 3 (**F3**).

Perform regression analysis.

43. Execute the /Data Regression X-range (**/DRX**) command and select A5..C17.
44. Execute the Y-range (**Y**) command and select D5..D17.
45. Execute the Output-range (**O**) command and select F5.
46. Execute the Go (**G**) command to calculate the regression parameters and return to ready mode.

The output of the regression analysis appears off the spreadsheet, so rearrange it to fit.

47. Move cells F12..J13 to C19..G20.
48. Move cells I6..I10 to H6..H10.
49. Format cells E19..G20 as Scientific 2 (**S2**).

The spreadsheet should now look like that in Figure 6.5. Again, R^2 indicates that the curve is a good fit to the data, as you can see by the graph in Figure 6.6. You could have used a higher order curve to get a better fit of the data, but with polynomial regression, the curve often will oscillate if the order is too high. Although the curve may hit all of the data points, it will not be a good predictor of points between them. You should always plot the results of regression to make sure that the curve that you have calculated is what you expect.

■ COMPLEX FUNCTIONS

If a function cannot be linearized into the form required for linear regression, then you cannot use the linear regression commands to determine the best fit of an equation to the data. For example, the exponential function

$$y = Ae^{Bx}$$

A1: [W6] 'Thermal conductivity of GaAs: Polynomial Regression READY

Thermal conductivity of GaAs: Polynomial Regression

T (K)	T^2	T^3	K (W/cm-K)	K Est.		
250	6.2E+04	1.6E+07	0.445	0.440	Regression Output:	
300	9.0E+04	2.7E+07	0.362	0.366	Constant	1.077851
350	1.2E+05	4.3E+07	0.302	0.306	Std Err of Y Est	0.003893
400	1.6E+05	6.4E+07	0.256	0.259	R Squared	0.998970
450	2.0E+05	9.1E+07	0.223	0.222	No. of Observations	13
500	2.5E+05	1.3E+08	0.197	0.193	Degrees of Freedom	9
550	3.0E+05	1.7E+08	0.176	0.172		
600	3.6E+05	2.2E+08	0.158	0.156		
650	4.2E+05	2.7E+08	0.144	0.144		
700	4.9E+05	3.4E+08	0.132	0.134		
750	5.6E+05	4.2E+08	0.121	0.125		
800	6.4E+05	5.1E+08	0.112	0.114		
850	7.2E+05	6.1E+08	0.103	0.099		

	X Coefficient(s)	Std Err of Coef.
E	-3.62E-03	1.87E-04
F	4.83E-06	3.60E-07
G	-2.27E-09	2.17E-10

24-Mar-87 01:47 PM

Figure 6.5: Thermal conductivity of GaAs—polynomial regression curve fit

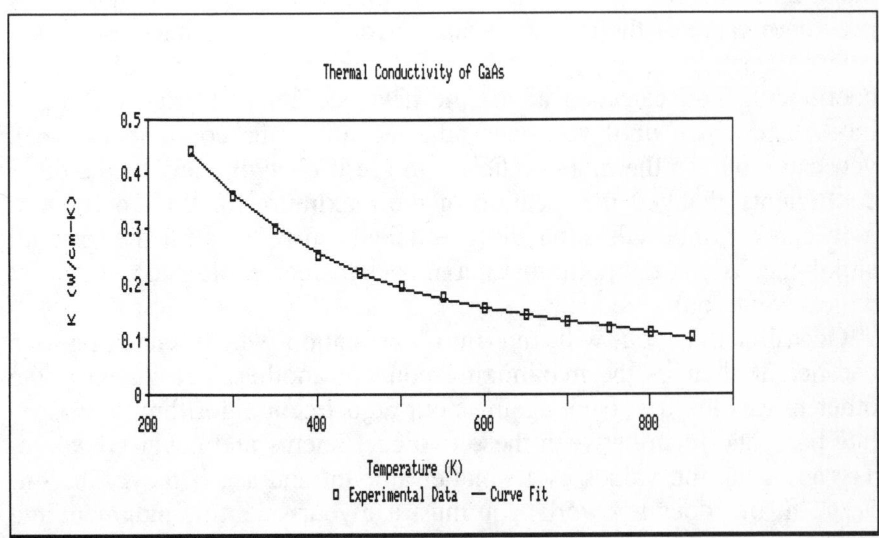

Figure 6.6: Curve fit to the thermal conductivity of GaAs

can be linearized by taking its natural logarithm,

$$\mathrm{Ln}(y) = \mathrm{Ln}(A) + Bx$$

and identifying Ln(A) and B, rather than the A and B of the original equation, as the regression coefficients. On the other hand, a double exponential cannot be linearized unless you know B and D:

$$y = Ae^{Bx} + Ce^{Dx}$$

Another problem arises with equations that can be linearized. Although the calculated coefficients for the linearized equation are the best fit (least square) for that equation, they are usually not the best fit for the original function. For example, regression calculated for the linearized version of the preceding single exponential equation will yield the best values of Ln(A) and B for the logarithmic equation. These will not necessarily be the best values of A and B for the exponential equation, though they will be close.

Manual Adjustments

To fit equations that cannot be fit with regression analysis, you must sequentially adjust the coefficients of the equation until you find the maximum value of the correlation coefficient, which corresponds to the minimum value of the residual square error. To do this, increase or decrease a coefficient until you find the maximum value of the correlation coefficient. You can then adjust the next coefficient to find the maximum, and so on until you have adjusted all of the coefficients. Then you can return to the first coefficient to see if changing any of the other coefficients changed the location of the maximum for this coefficient. You can continue adjusting the coefficients in order until they are all simultaneously at the point that maximizes the correlation coefficient, at which point you are done.

Occasionally, you will run into a situation where changing one coefficient changes the maximizing point of another, but changing the other moves the first back again. Your adjustment algorithm will oscillate back and forth between these two coefficients and never converge. Try adjusting the values by a smaller amount and see if they will converge. If that does not work, you must use your scientific judgment and knowledge of the equation being fit to determine the best values. Bear in mind that there may be two maxima.

Electron Ionization Cross Sections Table 6.2 contains the total cross sections for electron impact ionization of helium versus electron energy. A cross section is an effective area used to determine the probability that a collision will occur between an electron and the atom. If you imagine atoms as a group of small targets that a beam of electrons is trying to hit, the cross section is the target area. The larger the cross

Electron energy (eV)	Cross section (πa_0^2)
150	0.419
175	0.408
200	0.394
250	0.365
300	0.337
350	0.313
400	0.292
450	0.272
500	0.255
550	0.240
600	0.227
650	0.216
700	0.205
750	0.194
800	0.187
850	0.178
900	0.171
950	0.165
1000	0.160

$$\pi a_0^2 = \pi(5.29 \times 10^{-11})^2(\text{m}^2)$$
$$= 8.79 \times 10^{-21}(\text{m}^2)$$

Table 6.2: Experimental total ionization cross section versus energy for helium

section, the easier it is to hit an atom with an electron and the higher the probability that ionization will occur.

From previous experience, I know that the cross section looks like a decreasing exponential in this part of the curve. Therefore, fit it with an equation of the form

$$S(E) = A(1 - e^{-B/E})$$

where S is the cross section in units (πa_0^2), E is the electron energy in eV, and A and B are the coefficients to be determined.

1. In cell A1, type **Electron Ionization Cross Section in Helium**
2. In cell A3, type **"E (eV)**
3. In cell B3, type **S (πa0^2)**
4. In cell C3, type **"S Est.**
5. In cell D3, type **"(y-yx)^2**
6. In cell E3, type **"(y-<y>)2**
7. In cells A4..B22, type the data from Table 6.2.

Create a table of the coefficients to be determined, so that you can easily adjust them.

8. In cell F3, type **"A**
9. In cell G3, type **0.5**
10. In cell F4, type **"B**
11. In cell G4, type **500**
12. Name cells G3, G4, H6, and H7, respectively, as **A**, **B**, **AVEY**, and **FREE**.

Enter the regression equation to calculate the estimated values of y. The next two columns calculate some statistics that you need to calculate the standard error of the y estimate and the correlation coefficient. They are the square of the residual in column D and the square of the scatter in the original data in column E.

13. In cells C4..C22, type **+$A*(1-@EXP(-$B/A4)**
14. In cells D4..D22, type **(B4-C4)^2**
15. In cells E4..E22, type **(B4-$AVEY)^2**

Create a table of the curve-fit statistics.

16. In cell F6, type **Average of y<y>**
17. In cell H6, type **@AVG(B4..B22)**
18. In cell F7, type **Deg. of Freedom**
19. In cell H7, type **@COUNT(B4..B22)-2**
20. In cell F8, type **Std. err of Y est**
21. In cell H8, type **@SQRT(@SUM(D4..D22)/FREE)**
22. In cell F9, type **Cor. Coeff. R^2**
23. In cell H9, type **1-@SUM(D4..D22)/@SUM(E4..E22)**
24. Format cells B4..C22 as Fixed 3 (**F3**).
25. Format cells D4..E22 as Scientific 2 (**S2**).

The spreadsheet should now look like Figure 6.7. To use it, pick some reasonable starting values for *A* and *B* (say, 0.5 and 500, as shown) and enter them in the table (at G3, G4). First, add 0.1 to *A* and then subtract 0.1 from *A* to see which increases the value of the correlation coefficient. Continue adding or subtracting 0.1 from *A* until you find the maximum value of the correlation coefficient. Now adjust *B*, adding and subtracting 100 from it until you maximize the correlation

A1: 'Electron Ionization Cross Section in Helium READY

	A	B	C	D	E	F	G	H
1	Electron Ionization Cross Section in Helium							
2								
3	E (eV)	S (πa0^2)	S Est.	(y-yx)^2	(y-<y>)^2	A	0.5	
4	150	0.419	0.482	3.99E-03	2.43E-02	B	500	
5	175	0.408	0.471	4.00E-03	2.10E-02			
6	200	0.394	0.459	4.22E-03	1.71E-02	Average of y <y>		0.263052
7	250	0.365	0.432	4.53E-03	1.04E-02	Deg. of Freedom		17
8	300	0.337	0.406	4.70E-03	5.47E-03	Std. err of Y est		0.059823
9	350	0.313	0.380	4.51E-03	2.49E-03	Cor. Coeff. R^2		0.551740
10	400	0.292	0.357	4.19E-03	8.38E-04			
11	450	0.272	0.335	4.02E-03	8.01E-05			
12	500	0.255	0.316	3.73E-03	6.48E-05			
13	550	0.240	0.299	3.43E-03	5.31E-04			
14	600	0.227	0.283	3.10E-03	1.30E-03			
15	650	0.216	0.268	2.74E-03	2.21E-03			
16	700	0.205	0.255	2.52E-03	3.37E-03			
17	750	0.194	0.243	2.43E-03	4.77E-03			
18	800	0.187	0.232	2.06E-03	5.78E-03			
19	850	0.178	0.222	1.97E-03	7.23E-03			
20	900	0.171	0.213	1.77E-03	8.47E-03			

02-May-87 05:51 PM

Figure 6.7: Electron ionization cross section in helium—manual curve fit

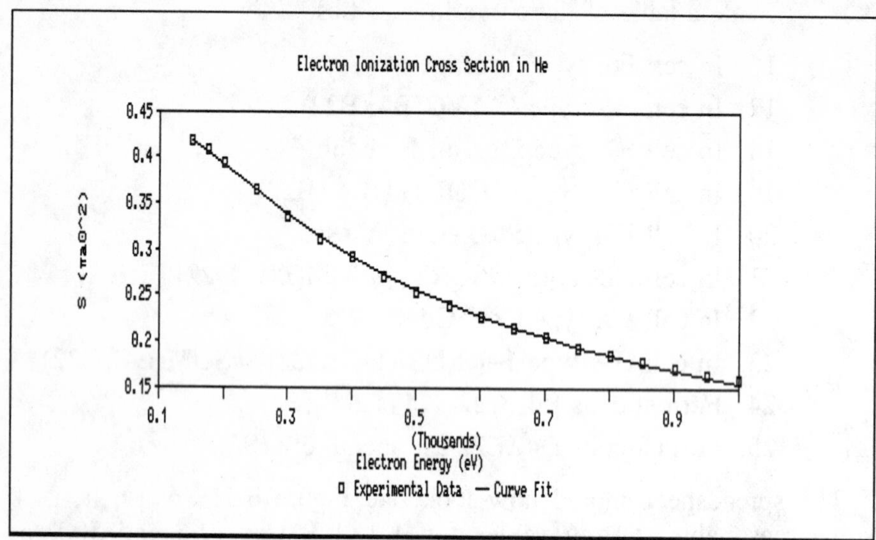

Figure 6.8: Electron ionization cross section in helium—manual curve fit

coefficient. Return to *A* and see if the maximum of the correlation coefficient has changed. Readjust *A* if it has changed. Continue adjusting *A* and *B* until you find the values that maximize the correlation coefficient for both of them.

Next decrease the amount that you add to *A* and *B* by a power of 10. Add and subtract 0.01 to and from *A* and add and subtract 10 to and from *B* until you maximize the correlation coefficient again. Decrease the amount by another power of 10 (0.01 and 1) and repeat the process. When you find the maximum value of the correlation coefficient this time, you will have three-place accuracy in the coefficients ($A = 0.443$, $B = 434$, $R2 = 0.999582$). As you can see from Figure 6.8, the equation is a good fit to the data.

Automatic Adjustments

By using 1-2-3's macro capability, you can automate this search for the maximum of the correlation coefficient. First, name some cells to hold the changes to be added to *A* and *B* and set up a table of values to be used by the macro program.

26. Name cells H3 and H4 as **DA** and **DB** (to stand for delta *A* and delta *B*).

27. In cell F11, type **"DAA**
28. In cell G11, type **+$DA/10**
29. In cell F12, type **"DBB**
30. In cell G12, type **+$DB/10**
31. In cell F13, type **"RSQMAX**
32. In cell F14, type **"TST**
33. In cell G14, type **0**
34. In cell F15, type **"STOP**
35. In cell G15, type **0.0001**
36. Execute the /Range Name Labels Right command and select F11..F15 to name cells G11..G15.
37. Name cell H9 as **RSQ**.

Enter the macro. The first command initializes the value of the maximum value of the correlation coefficient found (RSQMAX) to 0 and prints the flashing label *WORKING* in cell G1. By moving the cursor to cell G1, you make the label flash every time the spreadsheet is updated.

38. In cell I1, type **'\a**
39. In cell J1, type **'{let g1,WORKING:string} {let RSQMAX,0} {goto}G1~**

This is the top of the iteration loop. First clear the value of TST, a variable that you will use to determine whether any of the changes that you made in *A* or *B* have resulted in an increase in RSQ. Next, increase *A* by *DA*, update the spreadsheet, and see whether RSQ has increased. If it has increased, update the maximum value (RSQMAX), set the value of TST, and branch to CONT. If it has not, then decrease the value of *A* by twice *DA* and test RSQ again. If this does not increase RSQ, then change *A* back to its original value.

40. In cell I2, type **"top**
41. In cell J2, type **'{let tst,0}{let A,+A+DA}**
42. In cell J3, type **'{calc}**
43. In cell J4, type **'{if rsq>rsqmax}{let rsqmax,rsq}{let tst,1} {branch cont}**
44. In cell J5, type **'{let A,+A-2*DA}**
45. In cell J6, type **'{calc}**

46. In cell J7, type '**{if rsq>rsqmax}{let rsqmax,rsq}{let tst,1} {branch cont}**
47. In cell J8, type '**{let A,+A+DA}**

Starting with cell CONT, perform the same procedure for *B*.

48. In cell I9, type "**cont**
49. In cell J9, type '**{let B,+B+DB}**
50. In cell J10, type '**{calc}**
51. In cell J11, type '**{if rsq>rsqmax}{let rsqmax,rsq}{let tst,1} {branch cont2}**
52. In cell J12, type '**{let B,+B-2*DB}**
53. In cell J13, type '**{calc}**
54. In cell J14, type '**{if rsq>rsqmax}{let rsqmax,rsq}{let tst,1} {branch cont2}**
55. In cell J15, type '**{let B,+B+DB}**

After changing and testing both coefficients, check whether any of the changes resulted in an increase in RSQ by seeing whether TST has been set to 1. If it has been set, then branch back to TOP and adjust *A* and *B* again. If TST is not set, then decrease the values of *DA* and *DB* by a power of 10 and test the value of *DA* to see whether you have reached the STOP value. If you have not, then branch back to TOP and continue adjusting *A* and *B*. If you have reached the STOP value, then change cell G1 to DONE.

56. In cell I16, type "**cont2**
57. In cell J16, type '**{if tst,1}{branch top}**
58. In cell J17, type '**{let DA,+DAA}**
59. In cell J18, type '**{let DB,+DBB}**
60. In cell J19, type '**{if DA > STOP}{branch top}**
61. In cell J20, type '**{let G1,DONE:string}~**
62. Name cells J1, J2, J9, and J16, respectively, as **\A**, **TOP**, **CONT**, and **CONT2**.

To run the macro, first set the initial guesses of *A* and *B* (say, .5 and 500), set the initial step size in *DA* and *DB* (.1 and 100), and set the stopping criteria for *A* in cell STOP (.0001). Press Macro-A to start the macro and then wait until it finishes. This macro has to update the spreadsheet many times, so it runs slowly. It will take three to five minutes to complete.

The spreadsheet should now look like Figure 6.9, with the macro shown in Figure 6.10. Note that the spreadsheet has converged to slightly different values of *A* and *B* (0.442 and 436, compared to 0.443 and 434) The value of the correlation coefficient is also slightly smaller ($R^2 = 0.999559$ compared to 0.999582). The difference is small, and both curves fit the data quite well. If you were to plot this curve, you would not be able to tell the difference between it and the one in Figure 6.8. What has happened is that the macro program has found a local maximum near the actual maximum. If the local maximum is too far away from the actual maximum, you will have to restart the macro program with different starting values of *A*, *B*, *DA*, and *DB*.

Since this calculation takes several minutes to run, I did a timing test to see the effect of using an 8087 math coprocessor in the system. Without the math coprocessor, the calculation took 318 seconds to run. With the coprocessor, it only took 205 seconds, or 64 percent of the time that it took without the coprocessor. The increase in speed (the inverse of the time) is 55 percent.

```
A1: 'Electron Ionization Cross Section in Helium                        READY

        A        B          C        D        E         F         G         H
1   Electron Ionization Cross Section in Helium             DONE
2
3    E (eV) S (πa0^2)  S Est. (y-yx)^2 (y-<y>)^2         A       0.442    0.0001
4      150     0.419    0.418 1.34E-06 2.43E-02         B         436       0.1
5      175     0.408    0.405 6.73E-06 2.10E-02
6      200     0.394    0.392 3.86E-06 1.71E-02 Average of y <y>  0.263052
7      250     0.365    0.365 7.31E-08 1.04E-02 Deg. of Freedom         17
8      300     0.337    0.339 2.77E-06 5.47E-03 Std. err of Y est 0.001874
9      350     0.313    0.315 3.32E-06 2.49E-03 Cor. Coeff. R^2   0.999559
10     400     0.292    0.293 1.94E-06 8.38E-04
11     450     0.272    0.274 5.10E-06 8.01E-05       DAA  0.00001
12     500     0.255    0.257 4.81E-06 6.48E-05       DBB     0.01
13     550     0.240    0.242 3.79E-06 5.31E-04    RSQMAX 0.999559
14     600     0.227    0.228 1.65E-06 1.30E-03       TST        0
15     650     0.216    0.216 1.63E-12 2.21E-03      STOP   0.0001
16     700     0.205    0.205 8.66E-09 3.37E-03
17     750     0.194    0.195 7.30E-07 4.77E-03
18     800     0.187    0.186 1.66E-06 5.78E-03
19     850     0.178    0.177 4.09E-07 7.23E-03
20     900     0.171    0.170 1.66E-06 8.47E-03
24-Mar-87  01:58 PM
```

Figure 6.9: Electron ionization cross section in helium

```
I1: '\a                                                          READY

     I       J       K       L       M       N       O       P
1   \a        {let g1,WORKING:string}{let RSQMAX,0}{goto}G1~
2        top {let tst,0}{let A,+A+DA}
3            {calc}
4            {if rsq>rsqmax}{let rsqmax,rsq}{let tst,1}{branch cont}
5            {let A,+A-2*DA}
6            {calc}
7            {if rsq>rsqmax}{let rsqmax,rsq}{let tst,1}{branch cont}
8            {let A,+A+DA}
9       cont {let B,+B+DB}
10           {calc}
11           {if rsq>rsqmax}{let rsqmax,rsq}{let tst,1}{branch cont2}
12           {let B,+B-2*DB}
13           {calc}
14           {if rsq>rsqmax}{let rsqmax,rsq}{let tst,1}{branch cont2}
15           {let B,+B+DB}
16     cont2 {if tst,1}{branch top}
17           {let DA,+DAA}
18           {let DB,+DBB}
19           {if DA>STOP}{branch top}
20           {let G1,DONE:string}~
24-Mar-87  01:59 PM
```

Figure 6.10: Macro that performs automatic curve fit

■ TABLE LOOKUP AND INTERPOLATION

Often you will have data that no reasonable function will fit well. In this case, the best method to use is a data table and a table lookup function. A table lookup function looks up and interpolates values in the table for a particular value of x. Essentially you are fitting a simple curve to a few of the data points in the neighborhood of the point that you are interested in, rather than fitting a complicated curve to the whole data set.

As you saw previously, table lookup is accomplished with the @HLOOKUP and @VLOOKUP functions. The interpolation method must be coded explicitly as a macro or as cell formulas. Many interpolation methods are available, differing in the equation used to estimate the value of the function between two known data points. The most common method is linear interpolation. The simplest method is just to use the table lookup functions and to accept the value returned rather than interpolating between values in the table. In many cases, this may be sufficient, in which case you will save yourself a lot of work. Other common methods involve fitting quadratic and cubic curves to three or four data points. More complicated functions are splines and Chebyshev polynomials. Consult a good applied numerical analysis text for more information about these functions.

Linear Interpolation

Linear interpolation is probably the most common interpolation method. It consists of simply connecting the two data points on either side of the value being interpolated with a straight line. If the data points are not far apart, linear interpolation works just fine. It is also simple to implement compared to higher-order functions.

The interpolation formula for linear interpolation is

$$y = \frac{(x - x_2)}{(x_1 - x_2)} y_1 + \frac{(x - x_1)}{(x_2 - x_1)} y_2$$

where x_1, x_2, y_1, and y_2 are the data points from the table, and x, the value being interpolated, is between x_1 and x_2.

Steam Tables Steam tables are tables of temperature, pressure, density, enthalpy, and entropy for saturated steam and water, superheated steam, and compressed water. Saturated steam and water is a mixture of steam and water at a temperature and pressure at which the two coexist in equilibrium. The saturation line on a graph of temperature and pressure divides the graph into all-water and all-steam regions (Figure 6.11). Superheated steam data points are those pressure and temperature points above the saturation line in the direction of increasing temperature. Compressed water data points are those pressure and temperature points above the saturation line in the direction of increasing pressure.

Steam tables are used by engineers that design and operate energy transportation and conversion equipment that employs steam as the working fluid. This equipment includes steam engines, steam turbines, steam and hot water heating systems, and nuclear reactors. Steam tables are also used by scientists that need to know the properties of hot pressurized water and steam.

For example, in a pressurized water reactor (PWR), if the pressure decreases to the saturation line, the water will flash into steam. The temperature and pressure in the reactor will then move along the saturation line until either the pressure is increased to the point that the water stops boiling into steam, or all of the water is boiled away. Since it is

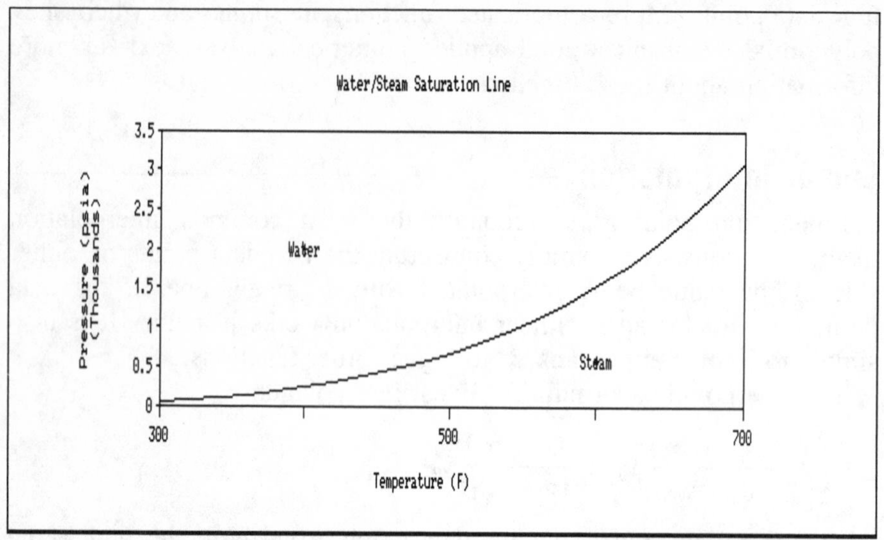

Figure 6.11: Pressure and temperature saturation line for a steam-water mixture—above the line is all water, below the line is all steam; only on the saturation line can steam and water coexist.

not good to have your cooling water boiling away inside a reactor, reactor engineers and operators need to know where the saturation line is so that they can design and operate the reactor with an adequate safety margin. A representative pressurized water reactor operates at around 600° F and 2250 psi, well away from the saturation line.

In the next example, you will build a spreadsheet that calculates the saturated pressure for a given temperature. The spreadsheet will use a table lookup function and linear interpolation to calculate the pressure. First you will enter the data for the steam table from Table 6.3. You will also include an index column so that you can access data above and below the value found by the table lookup function.

1. In cell A1, type **Steam table: Saturated steam/water: Linear Interpolation**
2. In cell A3, type **"Temp.**
3. In cell B3, type **"Press.**
4. In cell C3, type **"index**
5. In cell A4, type **"(F)**
6. In cell B4, type **"(psia)**

Temperature (F)	Pressure (psia)*
300	67
320	90
340	118
360	153
380	196
400	247
420	309
440	382
460	467
480	566
500	681
520	812
540	963
560	1133
580	1326
600	1543
620	1787
640	2060
660	2366
680	2709
700	3094

*psia = pounds per square inch absolute

Table 6.3: Pressure and temperature saturation line for a water and steam mixture

Enter the temperature data, the index column, and the pressure data. The index column starts with 0 to match the indexing scheme of the @INDEX function.

7. In cells A5..A25, enter values from 300 to 700 in steps of 20.
8. In cells C5..C25, enter values from 0 to 20 in steps of 1.
9. In cells B5..B25, type the pressure values 67 psi through 3094 psi in Table 6.3.
10. Name cells A5..C25 as **STEAM**.

Create a table to perform the linear interpolation.

11. In cell E3, type **'Linear Interpolation**
12. In cell D4, type ' (5 spaces) **Temperature**
13. In cell F4, type ' (2 spaces) **Output Pressure**
14. In cell D5, type **"Input**
15. In cell E5, type **"Index**
16. In cell F5, type **"Calc.**
17. In cell G5, type **"True**
18. In cell H5, type **"Error**

Pick some random temperature values to enter for the linear interpolation. Enter the true pressure values in column G so that you can compare them with the interpolated values.

19. In cell D6, type **510**
20. In cell D7, type **520**
21. In cell D8, type **302**
22. In cell D9, type **622**
23. In cell D10, type **538**
24. In cell D11, type **456**

The table lookup and interpolation equations are too large to fit in one cell, so put the table lookup function in one cell and the interpolation function in the next. For each temperature value, the @VLOOKUP function does not return a pressure but the value of the index. You then use this index with the @INDEX command to access the pressure and temperature values needed for the linear interpolation function in column F.

25. In cells E6..E11, type/copy **@VLOOKUP(D6,$STEAM,2)**
26. In cells F6..F11, type/copy **(D6-@INDEX($STEAM,0,E6 +1))*@INDEX($STEAM,1,E6)/(@INDEX($STEAM,0,E6)**

-@INDEX($STEAM,0,E6+1))+(D6-@INDEX ($STEAM,0,E6))*@INDEX($STEAM,1,E6+1)/(@INDEX ($STEAM,0,E6+1)-@INDEX($STEAM,0,E6))

27. In cell G6 type **744.5**
28. In cell G7 type **812**
29. In cell G8 type **69**
30. In cell G9 type **1812.8**
31. In cell G10 type **946.9**
32. In cell G11 type **448.7**

Calculate the error in the interpolated values.

33. In cells H6..H11 type **(G6-F6)/G6**
34. Format cells H6..H14 as Percent 1 **(P1)**.

The spreadsheet should now look like Figure 6.12. Note that for the six random test values, the maximum error is only about one half of a percent. For a smooth function like this, linear interpolation works quite well. Remember, though, that the derivative of linearly interpolated functions is not continuous, but has sharp changes at each data point in the table. In most cases this is not a problem. But I have run into a case

```
A1: 'Steam table: Saturated steam/water: Linear Interpolation                READY

       A        B        C        D        E        F        G        H
1   Steam table: Saturated steam/water: Linear Interpolation
2
3     Temp.    Press.    index          Linear Interpolation
4      (F)     (psia)            Temperature      Output Pressure
5      300        67        0     Input    Index    Calc.     True     Error
6      320        90        1      510       10     746.5    744.5     -0.3%
7      340       118        2      520       11       812      812      0.0%
8      360       153        3      302        0      69.3       69     -0.4%
9      380       196        4      622       16    1814.3   1812.8     -0.1%
10     400       247        5      538       11     947.9    946.9     -0.1%
11     420       309        6      456        7       450    448.7     -0.3%
12     440       382        7
13     460       467        8
14     480       566        9
15     500       681       10
16     520       812       11
17     540       963       12
18     560      1133       13
19     580      1326       14
20     600      1543       15
24-Mar-87  02:08 PM
```

Figure 6.12: Steam table and steam and water saturation line—table lookup function and linear interpolation

where the discontinuities in the derivative of the input data caused discontinuities in the output data of a simulation code that used a table lookup function to create the input. Until I tracked down the cause of the discontinuities, I thought that I had found some new physical process. If you need an interpolation with a continuous derivative, then a spline curve would be more appropriate (and a lot harder to implement, of course).

Cubic Interpolation

You can also use quadratic and cubic interpolation. Cubic interpolation is more accurate than quadratic interpolation, not only because it uses a higher-order curve, but more important, it is more symmetrical about the range being interpolated. Cubic interpolation fits a third-order curve to four data points in a row, with the interpolation being between the center two points. The interpolation equation, in Lagrangian form, is

$$y = \frac{(x - x_2)(x - x_3)(x - x_4)}{(x_1 - x_2)(x_1 - x_3)(x_1 - x_4)} y_1 + \frac{(x - x_1)(x - x_3)(x - x_4)}{(x_2 - x_1)(x_2 - x_3)(x_2 - x_4)} y_2$$

$$+ \frac{(x - x_1)(x - x_2)(x + x_4)}{(x_3 - x_1)(x_3 - x_2)(x_3 - x_4)} y_3 + \frac{(x - x_1)(x - x_2)(x - x_3)}{(x_4 - x_1)(x_4 - x_2)(x_4 - x_3)} y_4$$

where x_1, x_2, x_3, x_4, y_1, y_2, y_3, and y_4 are consecutive x and y values from a table. To get the best value for y, the value being interpolated, x, should lie between x_2 and x_3.

So that you can compare cubic interpolation to linear interpolation, put the cubic interpolation on the same spreadsheet as the linear interpolation. First you need to create a table of the temperature and pressure values that surround the value being interpolated, since these will not all fit in a single cell as the linear interpolation did. Otherwise, the setup of this function is the same as for linear interpolation. You locate the index of the data with the @VLOOKUP function and then use that index value and the @INDEX function to collect the values from the table.

35. In cell A1, type **Steam table: Saturated steam/water: Linear & Cubic Interpolation**
36. In cell E13, type **Cubic Interpolation**

37. Name cells D14, E14, E17..E20, and F17..F20 according to the following list:

D14 **T**	E14 **N**	E17 **TE1**	F17 **PR1**
		E18 **TE2**	F18 **PR2**
		E19 **TE3**	F19 **PR3**
		E20 **TE4**	F20 **PR4**

38. In cell D15, type **Interpolation values for the cubic**
39. In cell E16, type **"Temp.**
40. In cell F16, type **"Press.**
41. In cell D17, type **"1**
42. In cell E17, type **@INDEX($STEAM,0,$N-1)**
43. In cell F17, type **@INDEX($STEAM,1,$N-1)**
44. In cell D18, type **"2**
45. In cell E18, type **@INDEX($STEAM,0,$N)**
46. In cell F18, type **@INDEX($STEAM,1,$N)**
47. In cell D19, type **"3**
48. In cell E19, type **@INDEX($STEAM,0,$N+1)**
49. In cell F19, type **@INDEX($STEAM,1,$N+1)**
50. In cell D20, type **"4**
51. In cell E20, type **@INDEX($STEAM,0,$N+2)**
52. In cell F20, type **@INDEX($STEAM,1,$N+2)**

Insert the test temperature in cell D14 and the correct value for comparison in cell G14. You will use one of the temperatures from the linear interpolation list so that you can compare them. Cell E14 contains the table lookup function that finds the index value, and cell F14 calculates the interpolation.

53. In cell D14, type **510**
54. In cell E14, type **@VLOOKUP(T,$STEAM,2)**
55. In cell F14, type **(T-TE2)*(T-TE3)*(T-TE4)*PR1/((TE1-TE2)*(TE1-TE3)*(TE1-TE4))+(T-TE1)*(T-TE3)*(T-TE4)*PR2/((TE2-TE1)*(TE2-TE3)*(TE2-TE4))+(T-TE1)*(T-TE2)*(T-TE4)*PR3/((TE3-TE1)*(TE3-TE2)**

***(TE3-TE4))+(T-TE1)*(T-TE2)*(T-TE3)*PR4**
/((TE4-TE1)*(TE4-TE2)*(TE4-TE3))

56. In cell G14, type **744.5**
57. In cell H14, type **(G14-F14)/G14**
58. Format cells H6 . . H14 as Percent 3 (**P3**).

The spreadsheet should now look like Figure 6.13. Note that the error has decreased by an order of magnitude over the linear interpolation value. This decrease may not seem important, since linear interpolation worked so well with this curve; however, for more nonlinear curves the increased accuracy may be significant. Also, the discontinuity in the derivative at the data points is much smaller with cubic interpolation.

■ SUMMARY

In this chapter, we saw how to fit curves to data points. With Lotus 1-2-3, the simplest method is to use the /Data Regression (/DR) commands, which can perform multiple linear regression. As this chapter

```
A1: 'Steam table: Saturated steam/water: Linear & Cubic Interpolation       READY

        A        B        C        D        E        F        G        H
1   Steam table: Saturated steam/water: Linear & Cubic Interpolation
2
3     Temp.    Press.   index          Linear Interpolation
4      (F)     (psia)              Temperature     Output Pressure
5      300        67        0    Input    Index     Calc.      True     Error
6      320        90        1     510        10     746.5     744.5   -0.269%
7      340       118        2     520        11       812       812    0.000%
8      360       153        3     302         0      69.3        69   -0.435%
9      380       196        4     622        16    1814.3    1812.8   -0.083%
10     400       247        5     538        11     947.9     946.9   -0.106%
11     420       309        6     456         7       450     448.7   -0.290%
12     440       382        7
13     460       467        8          Cubic Interpolation
14     480       566        9     510        10    744.25     744.5    0.034%
15     500       681       10 Interpolation values for the cubic
16     520       812       11             Temp.     Press.
17     540       963       12       1       480       566
18     560      1133       13       2       500       681
19     580      1326       14       3       520       812
20     600      1543       15       4       540       963
24-Mar-87  02:10 PM
```

Figure 6.13: Steam table and steam and water saturation line—linear and cubic interpolation

shows, by suitably transforming our equations, we can fit many nonlinear equations using multiple linear regression, including the popular polynomial regression curve fit. For more complicated equations, we can use an algorithm that searches for the coefficients that give the best fit to some experimental data. We can also automate this algorithm with a macro program. Finally, we can use the table lookup function and interpolation to fit data that does not fit a known function or that is too much trouble to fit to a known function.

■ FOR MORE INFORMATION

For additional information about the topics in this chapter, you can consult the following resources.

Statistical Methods and t Tests

C. Lipson and N. J. Sheth, *Statistical Design and Analysis of Engineering Experiments* (New York: McGraw-Hill, 1973).

R. M. Bethea, B. S. Duran, and T. L. Boullion, *Statistical Methods for Scientists and Engineers* (New York: Marcel Dekker, 1975).

Thermal Conductivity in Gallium Arsenide

Maycock, "Thermal Conductivity of Silicon, Germanium, III-V Compounds and III-V Alloys," *Solid State Electronics 10* (1967): 161–168.

Electron Ionization Cross Sections

D. Rapp and P. Englander-Golden, "Total Cross Sections for Ionization and Attachment in Gases by Electron Impact: I. Positive Ionization," *J. Chem. Physics 43,* 5 (Sept. 1, 1965): 1464–1479.

Curve-Fitting Functions and Methods

C. Gerald, *Applied Numerical Analysis* (Reading, Mass.: Addison-Wesley, 1978).

Steam Tables

C. A. Meyer, *Thermodynamic and Transport Properties of Steam* (New York: American Society of Mechanical Engineers, 1967).

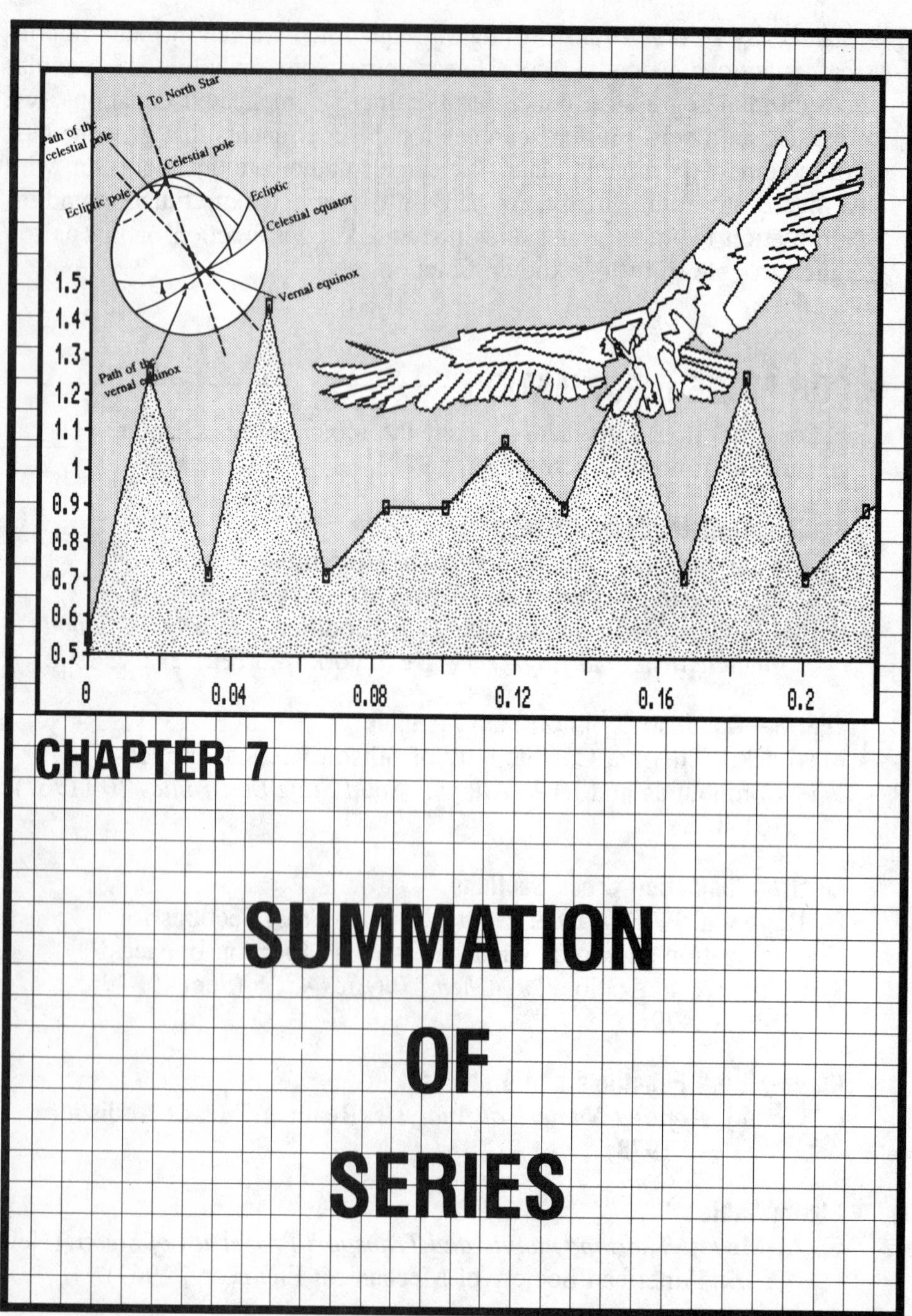

CHAPTER 7

SUMMATION OF SERIES

Many important science and engineering functions are available only as series formulas. Differential equations that do not have closed-form analytic solutions often have solutions in the form of a series. Bessel functions, Legendre polynomials, and Laguerre polynomials are good examples of series solutions to differential equations.

You can use a spreadsheet in three ways to calculate the value of a series formula. First, you can calculate a series term by term in consecutive cells and then sum these cells. Second, you can use the macro language to write a macro program that calculates the series term by term and sums the series. Last, you can use the spreadsheet iterative capability to iterate the series, one term per iteration.

SPREADSHEET METHOD

The simplest method you can use to sum a series is to calculate the terms in consecutive cells and then add them. This approach is straightforward, but it can consume a lot of spreadsheet space if numerous terms are used. For most series, you can find a recursion relation to calculate each term using the previous term. Using a recursion relation will significantly reduce the number of calculations you need to perform, especially when a series involves factorials.

Bessel Functions A Bessel function ($J_n(x)$) is the solution to the differential equation (Bessel's equation)

$$x^2\frac{d^2y}{dx^2} + x\frac{dy}{dx} + (x^2 - n^2)y = 0$$

with $y = J_n(x)$. Bessel's equation is encountered in many physical problems. For example, the solution to the wave equation in cylindrical coordinates results in Bessel's equation. Bessel functions are also solutions to a class of definite integrals:

$$J_n(x) = \frac{1}{\pi}\int_0^{\pi} \cos(nv - x\sin(v))dv$$

Although Bessel functions are defined for any value of n, most commonly n is an integer value. A series solution exists for the integer

Bessel functions:

$$J_n(x) = \sum_{s=0}^{\infty} \frac{(-1)^s}{s!\,(n+s)!}\left(\frac{x}{2}\right)^{n+2s} = \sum_{s=0}^{\infty} G_s(n, x)$$

For noninteger values of n, a gamma function ($\Gamma(n + s + 1)$) must be substituted for the factorial involving n ($(n + s)!$).

You can find the recursion relation for the series terms ($Gs(n,x)$) by inspection. It is

$$G_s(n, x) = G_{s-1}(n, x)\frac{(-1)}{s(n+s)}\left(\frac{x}{2}\right)^2$$

where

$$G_0(n, x) = \frac{x^n}{2^n n!}$$

Using this recursion relation, you can calculate all of the terms in the series without explicitly calculating any but the first factorial. Each term is created from the previous term by multiplying by the recursion factor.

In the following spreadsheet, you will calculate values of the Bessel function with integral values of n. You will sum only the first 10 terms, which yields accurate values of $J_n(x)$ for values of x up to 7 or 8.

1. Change the global column width to **10** with the /Worksheet Global Column-width 10 (**/WGC10**) command.
2. Set the width of column A to **7**.
3. In cell A1, type **Bessel Function; Spreadsheet method**

Enter the values of n, $n!$, and x. For this spreadsheet, you will enter the value of the factorial ($n!$) rather than calculate it.

4. In cells A6, B3, and B4, type the labels **"x**, **"n**, and **"n!**
5. Name cells C3 and C4 as **n** and **n!**.

Sum the terms of the series to get the value of the Bessel function.

6. In cell A7, type **"Jn(x)**
7. In cell B7, type **@SUM(B10..B20)**

Calculate the first 10 terms of the series for the values of the summation variable s. In cell B10, insert the value of the zero-order term.

In cells B11..B20, use the recursion relation to calculate the rest of the terms.

8. In cell A9, type **"s**
9. In cell B9, type **"Terms**
10. In cell B10, type **+B6^$N/(2^$N*$N!)**
11. In cells B11..B20, type/copy **+B10*(-1)*B$6^2/(4*$A11 *($N+$A11))**
12. Execute the /Data Fill (**/DF**) command and select cells A10.. A20 as the fill range, **0** as the start value, and **1** as the step.
13. Format cells B10..B20 as Scientific 2 (**S2**).

To use the spreadsheet, enter the value for *x* (0.5), up to a maximum of 8, in cell B6 and the values for *n* (1) and *n*! (1) in cells C3 and C4. When the spreadsheet is updated, the value of the Bessel function will be in cell B7. Note that the size of the terms decreases rapidly, indicating rapid convergence of the series. Your spreadsheet should now look like Figure 7.1.

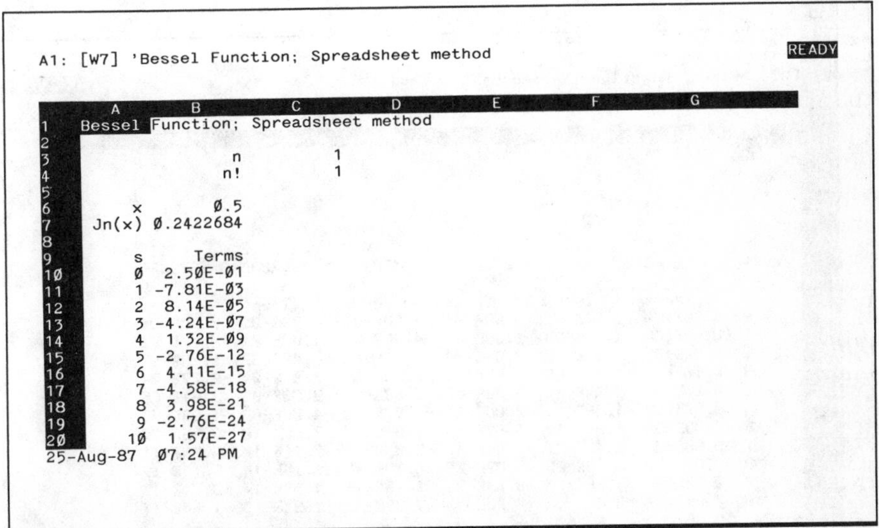

```
A1: [W7] 'Bessel Function; Spreadsheet method                    READY

     A      B         C         D         E         F         G
1  Bessel Function; Spreadsheet method
2
3               n         1
4              n!         1
5
6        x      Ø.5
7    Jn(x) Ø.2422684
8
9        s     Terms
10       Ø  2.5ØE-Ø1
11       1 -7.81E-Ø3
12       2  8.14E-Ø5
13       3 -4.24E-Ø7
14       4  1.32E-Ø9
15       5 -2.76E-12
16       6  4.11E-15
17       7 -4.58E-18
18       8  3.98E-21
19       9 -2.76E-24
20      1Ø  1.57E-27
25-Aug-87  Ø7:24 PM
```

Figure 7.1: Bessel function using the spreadsheet method

Using this format, you can calculate the Bessel function for an entire set of x values. Note that the appropriate parts of the cell references have been locked, so that the formulas in cells B10..B20 can be copied into the cells to their right, and these formulas will reference the correct cells.

14. Copy cells B9..B20 into C9..AB20.
15. Execute the /Data Fill (/DF) command for cells B6..AB6, with a starting value of **0** and a step of **0.3**.

Your spreadsheet should now look like Figure 7.2. Here you have calculated the Bessel function for $n = 1$ and for a series of values of x up to about 8. Figure 7.3 is a plot of these values. If you want to calculate the Bessel function for larger values of x, you will have to increase the number of terms in the series to get adequate convergence.

■ MACRO METHOD

The second way to calculate the value of a series summation is to write a computer program using the macro language. The algorithm is much the same as the one you would use if you were to calculate the series summation using a high-level language such as BASIC.

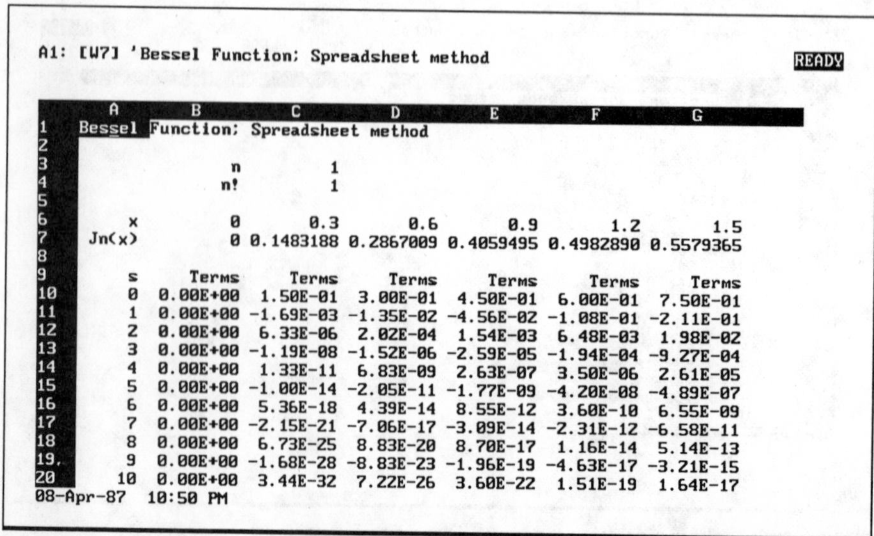

A1: [W7] 'Bessel Function: Spreadsheet method   READY

	A	B	C	D	E	F	G
1	Bessel Function: Spreadsheet method						
2							
3		n	1				
4		n!	1				
5							
6	x	0	0.3	0.6	0.9	1.2	1.5
7	Jn(x)	0	0.1483188	0.2867009	0.4059495	0.4982890	0.5579365
8							
9	s	Terms	Terms	Terms	Terms	Terms	Terms
10	0	0.00E+00	1.50E-01	3.00E-01	4.50E-01	6.00E-01	7.50E-01
11	1	0.00E+00	-1.69E-03	-1.35E-02	-4.56E-02	-1.08E-01	-2.11E-01
12	2	0.00E+00	6.33E-06	2.02E-04	1.54E-03	6.48E-03	1.98E-02
13	3	0.00E+00	-1.19E-08	-1.52E-06	-2.59E-05	-1.94E-04	-9.27E-04
14	4	0.00E+00	1.33E-11	6.83E-09	2.63E-07	3.50E-06	2.61E-05
15	5	0.00E+00	-1.00E-14	-2.05E-11	-1.77E-09	-4.20E-08	-4.89E-07
16	6	0.00E+00	5.36E-18	4.39E-14	8.55E-12	3.60E-10	6.55E-09
17	7	0.00E+00	-2.15E-21	-7.06E-17	-3.09E-14	-2.31E-12	-6.58E-11
18	8	0.00E+00	6.73E-25	8.83E-20	8.70E-17	1.16E-14	5.14E-13
19	9	0.00E+00	-1.68E-28	-8.83E-23	-1.96E-19	-4.63E-17	-3.21E-15
20	10	0.00E+00	3.44E-32	7.22E-26	3.60E-22	1.51E-19	1.64E-17

08-Apr-87   10:50 PM

Figure 7.2: Bessel function for multiple values of x

Legendre Polynomials Legendre polynomials ($P_n(x)$) are often encountered in central-force problems (electromagnetics), defined in spherical coordinates. For example, an electric dipole consists of two charges of magnitude, $+q$ and $-q$, located at $+a$ and $-a$ in a coordinate system. The potential this dipole yields at large distances ($r >> a$) from the dipole is described with a Legendre polynomial,

$$\Phi = \frac{2aq}{4\pi\varepsilon_0} \frac{P_1(\cos(v))}{r^2}$$

where ϵ_0 is the free-space dielectric constant, and r and θ are the coordinates in a spherical polar coordinate system.

Legendre polynomials are solutions to the differential equation

$$(1 - x^2)\frac{d^2y}{dx^2} - 2x\frac{dy}{dx} + n(n + 1)y = 0$$

with $y = P_n(x)$. The series representation of the Legendre polynomials is

$$P_n^{(x)} = \sum_{s=0}^{n/2} \frac{(-1)^s(2n - 2s)!}{2^n s!(n - s)!(n - 2s)!} x^{n-2s}$$

which has a finite number of terms in the summation.

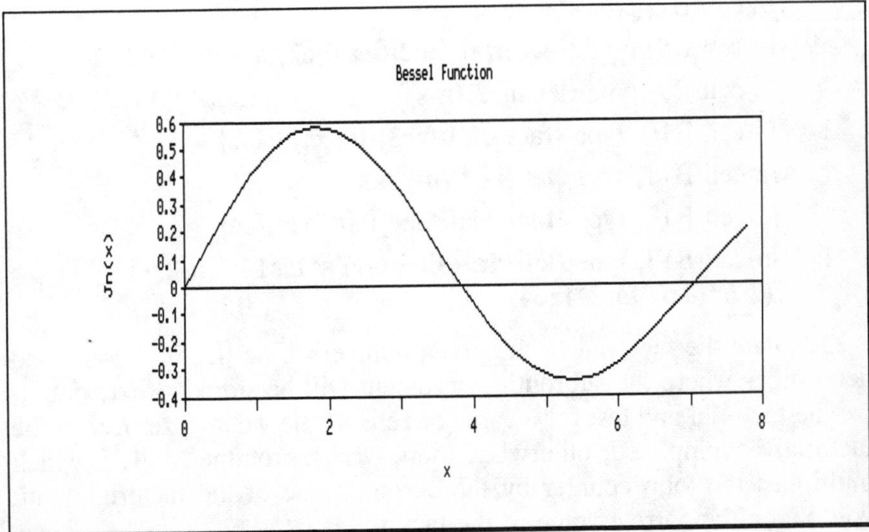

Figure 7.3: Bessel function $J_n(x)$

In the following spreadsheet, you will calculate the series formula from the previous section using a macro program. You will also calculate the factorials for each term explicitly, rather than using a term-recursion relation.

1. Change the width of column A to **10**.
2. In cell A1, type **Legendre Polynomials: Macro Program Method**

Enter the macro program and name it \L. The macro program has four parts: the initial summation loop over the terms, the calculation of the term, and a two-part factorial subroutine. First, initialize the value of the summation variable (PN) and loop over the $n/2$ terms of the series.

3. In cell A3, type **"\L**
4. In cell B3, type **{let Pn,0}{for s,0,n/2,1,legen}~**

Calculate the four factorials needed for each term; then calculate the term and add it to the summation variable (PN).

5. In cell A5, type **"legen**
6. In cell B5, type **{let fac1,(2*n-2*s)}**
7. In cell B6, type **{factorial fac1}{let fac1,fac}**
8. In cell B7, type **{let fac2,s}**
9. In cell B8, type **{factorial fac2}{let fac2,fac}**
10. In cell B9, type **{let fac3,(n-s)}**
11. In cell B10, type **{factorial fac3}{let fac3,fac}**
12. In cell B11, type **{let fac4,(n-2*s)}**
13. In cell B12, type **{factorial fac4}{let fac4,fac}**
14. In cell B13, type **{let Pn,+Pn+(-1)^s*fac1*x^(n-2*s) /(2^n*fac2*fac3*fac4)}**

Calculate the factorial of the given numbers. The {Define} command determines where the subroutine argument will be stored. Next, initialize the factorial and test for a value of zero. If the value is zero, then the factorial is completed; otherwise, loop over the routine MULT, which multiplies the loop counter by the current value of the factorial, until you obtain the correct value of the factorial.

15. In cell A15, type **"factorial**
16. In cell B15, type **{define num:value}**
17. In cell B16, type **{let i,@int(num)}{let fac,1}**
18. In cell B17, type **{if i<1}{return}**
19. In cell B18, type **{for j,1,i,1,mult}**
20. In cell A20, type **"mult**
21. In cell B20, type **{let fac,+fac*j}**
22. Execute the /Range Name Labels Right (**/RNLR**) command and select cells A3..A20 to name the macro labels.

Designate locations for storing the program variables.

23. In cells F2..F4, F7..F11, and F16..F19, respectively, type the labels **"x, "n, "Pn(x), "s, "fac1, "fac2, "fac3, "fac4, "num, "fac, "i,** and **"j**
24. Execute the /Range Name Labels Right (**/RNLR**) command and select cells F2..F19 to name the macro variables.

To execute the macro, place the values of x (0.3) and n (3) in cells G2 and G3 and press Macro-L. The value of the Legendre polynomial will be calculated and placed in cell G4. Your spreadsheet should now look like Figure 7.4.

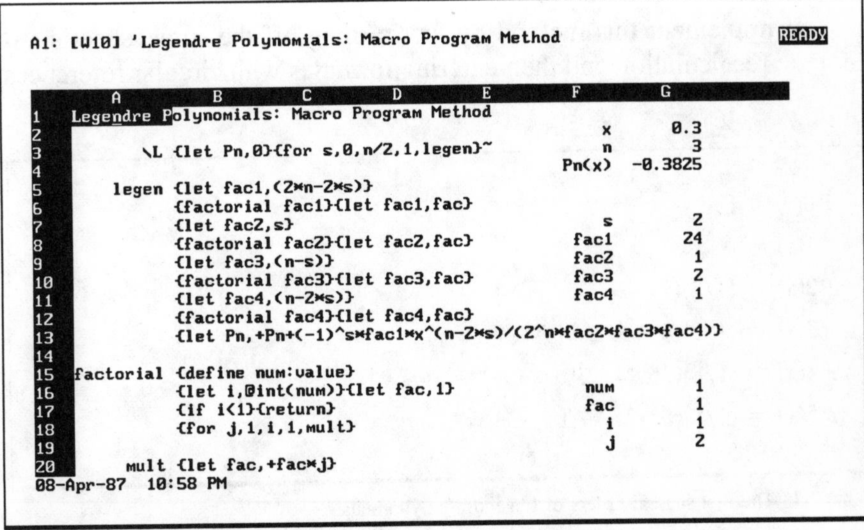

Figure 7.4: Legendre polynomials calculated with a macro program

The series function for the Legendre polynomials yields a finite series rather than an infinite series; that is, the upper limit of the summation is fixed at a value of $n/2$. Thus, you know how many terms to calculate to get the correct value. For an infinite series, you will need to test each term to determine where the series converges.

The Legendre polynomials can also be calculated more simply using the recurrence formulas

$$(2n + 1)xP_n(x) = (n + 1)P_{n+1}(x) + nP_{n-1}(x)$$

where $P_0(x) = 1$ and $P_1(x) = x$. Using this formula, the values of any order of Legendre polynomial can be calculated, without having to calculate a factorial. Table 7.1 contains the analytic equations for the first six Legendre polynomials, obtained by successively applying the recurrence formula.

■ ITERATION METHOD

The method of summing series formulas that is potentially the most powerful and also the most difficult to implement, uses the spreadsheet iteration capability. The spreadsheet can be iterated (repeatedly recalculated) by using circular references. This method causes the spreadsheet to calculate and add a new term to the series every time the worksheet is recalculated.

You implement this method by first turning off the spreadsheet's automatic recalculation and then entering formulas with circular references

$P0(x) = 1$

$P1(x) = x$

$P2(x) = (1/2)(3x^2 - 1)$

$P3(x) = (1/2)(5x^3 - 3x)$

$P4(x) = (1/8)(35x^4 - 30x^2 + 3)$

$P5(x) = (1/8)(63x^5 - 70x^3 + 15x)$

Table 7.1: The first several orders of Legendre polynomials

into the spreadsheet. You use the circular references to implement incrementation of the term index (s) and summation of the terms in the series. Normally, the worksheet calculates independent cells, cells that do not depend on any other cells, working left to right and top to bottom. Dependent cells, cells that contain formulas that have cell references to other cells, are calculated in the same manner, after the cells that they depend on have been calculated. A circular reference occurs when two dependent cells depend on each other. When a circular reference exists, Lotus 1-2-3 calculates a value for the first dependent cell it encounters based on the current value of the other dependent cell and then displays the circular-reference error message. Ignore this message and use the values calculated. Since the spreadsheet is calculated from left to right and top to bottom, you can establish the order in which cells in your spreadsheet are calculated.

You can also use the /Worksheet Global Recalculation Columnwise (or Rowwise) (/WGRC) command to force the spreadsheet to be recalculated column by column (or row by row) and ignore any cell dependencies. Either method can be used, but you must take care to ensure that calculations occur in the order that you want.

Sine Series The trigonometric sine function, which also is available as a spreadsheet function (@SIN), can be calculated with a series, as follows:

$$\text{Sin}(x) = \sum_{s=1}^{\infty} \frac{(-1)^{s-1}x^{2s-1}}{(2s-1)!} = \sum_{s=1}^{\infty} G_s(x) \qquad |x| < \infty$$

The first term of the series is x, and the term recursion formula is

$$G_s(x) = G_{s-1}(x)\frac{(-1)x^2}{(2s-1)(2s-2)}$$

In the following spreadsheet, you will calculate the recursion formula at each iteration of the spreadsheet and add it to the series.

1. Set the widths of columns A..D according to the following list:
   A = **17** B = **10** C = **12** D = **9**
2. Execute the /Worksheet Global Recalculation Manual (**/WGRM**) command.
3. In cell A1, type **Sine series: Worksheet iteration method**

Insert the value for which you want to calculate the sine in cell B4.

4. In cell A4, type **"x**
5. In cell B4, type **20**

The initialization flag is used to initialize the calculation. When it is set to 0, the calculation is initialized. Setting it to 1 allows the calculation to begin.

6. In cell C4, type **"Init Flag**
7. In cell D4, type **1**

Cells B6 and B7 form a circular reference that calculates the summation index *s*. At each recalculation of the spreadsheet, the formula in B6 increments the value in B7. The formula in B7 then sets its value to that in B6 in preparation for the next step. The @IF function initializes the value to 1 when the initialization flag is set to 0.

8. In cell A6, type **"s**
9. In cell B6, type **+B7+1**
10. In cell B7, type **@IF(D4,B6,1)**

Calculate the recursion term in cell B8.

11. In cell A8, type **"Recursion term**
12. In cell B8, type **-B4^2/((2*B7-1)*(2*B7-2))**

Calculate the next term in the series by multiplying the recursion term in cell B8 by the previous term in cell B11. The formula in cell B11 then updates its value for the next recalculation. Cells B10 and B11 form another circular reference. The @IF function sets the initial value to *x*, the value of the first term in the series.

13. In cell A10, type **"Term**
14. In cell B10, type **@IF(D4,B8*B11,B4)**
15. In cell B11, type **+B10**

In cell B13, add the new term in the series to the current total. Cells B13 and B14 form the last circular reference. The formula in cell B14 gets the current value of the summation from cell B13 in preparation for the next recalculation. In cell B16, calculate the correct value of the sine for comparison.

16. In cell A13, type **"Sum of terms**
17. In cell B13, type **@IF(D4,B14+B10,B4)**
18. In cell A14, type **"Sin(x)**
19. In cell B14, type **+B13**
20. In cell A16, type **"@SIN(x)**
21. In cell B16, type **@SIN(B4)**
22. Format cells B10 and B11 as Scientific 2 (**S2**).

The spreadsheet should now look like that in Figure 7.5. Although this is a small spreadsheet, its setup is not simple because you must be concerned with the order in which cells are calculated. In contrast to all of the other spreadsheets created so far, changing the order of some of these cells causes the spreadsheet to work incorrectly.

The iteration method works for series requiring any number of terms for convergence. Calculating a series of several hundred terms requires only a few seconds and only a small amount of spreadsheet space. For example, the sine of 30 (radians) requires about 35 terms for convergence. In fact, the series actually diverges for a few terms before converging to the correct value.

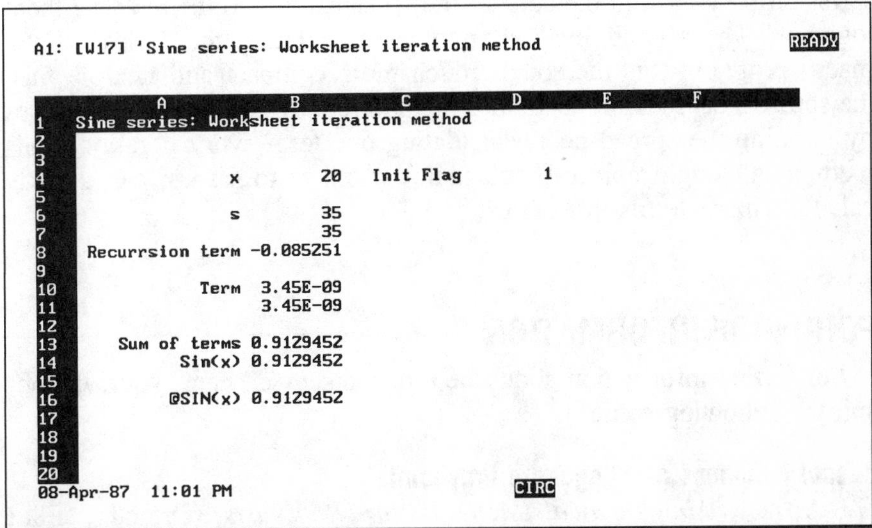

Figure 7.5: Sine of x with the series formula calculated by iterating the spreadsheet

To calculate the series, first set the value of the initialization flag in cell D4 to 0 and set the value of x in cell B4. Pressing Calc initializes the spreadsheet calculation. Next, set the value of the initialization flag to 1. Each time you press Calc, one term of the series will be calculated and added to the series. Continue pressing Calc until the value of the sine of x converges. You can judge whether a series is converging by watching the value of the term and comparing it with the value of the sum of the series.

If the series is converging slowly, you can set up your spreadsheet to iterate it up to 50 times with a single press of the Calc key. You do this by executing the /Worksheet Global Recalculation Iteration (/WGRI) command and setting the number of iterations. Then, when you press Calc, the spreadsheet will be iterated the number of times that you specified. Be careful, though; many series terms decrease rapidly, and numeric underflow could occur if the spreadsheet is iterated too many times.

■ SUMMARY

In this chapter, we investigated three methods for summing a series with a spreadsheet. The simplest, conceptually, requires calculating the series term by term in the cells of the spreadsheet and then adding them together. The second method involves calculating the series with a macro program; this method is much more compact and flexible than the spreadsheet method. The third method requires calculating the series by iterating the spreadsheet, calculating one term every iteration. This method, although more difficult than the others to set up, can quickly calculate many terms in a series.

■ FOR MORE INFORMATION

For further information about the topics discussed here, you can consult the following sources.

Bessel Functions and Legendre Polynomials

G. Arfken, *Mathematical Methods for Physicists* (Orlando, Fla.: Academic Press, 1970), pp. 438, 537.

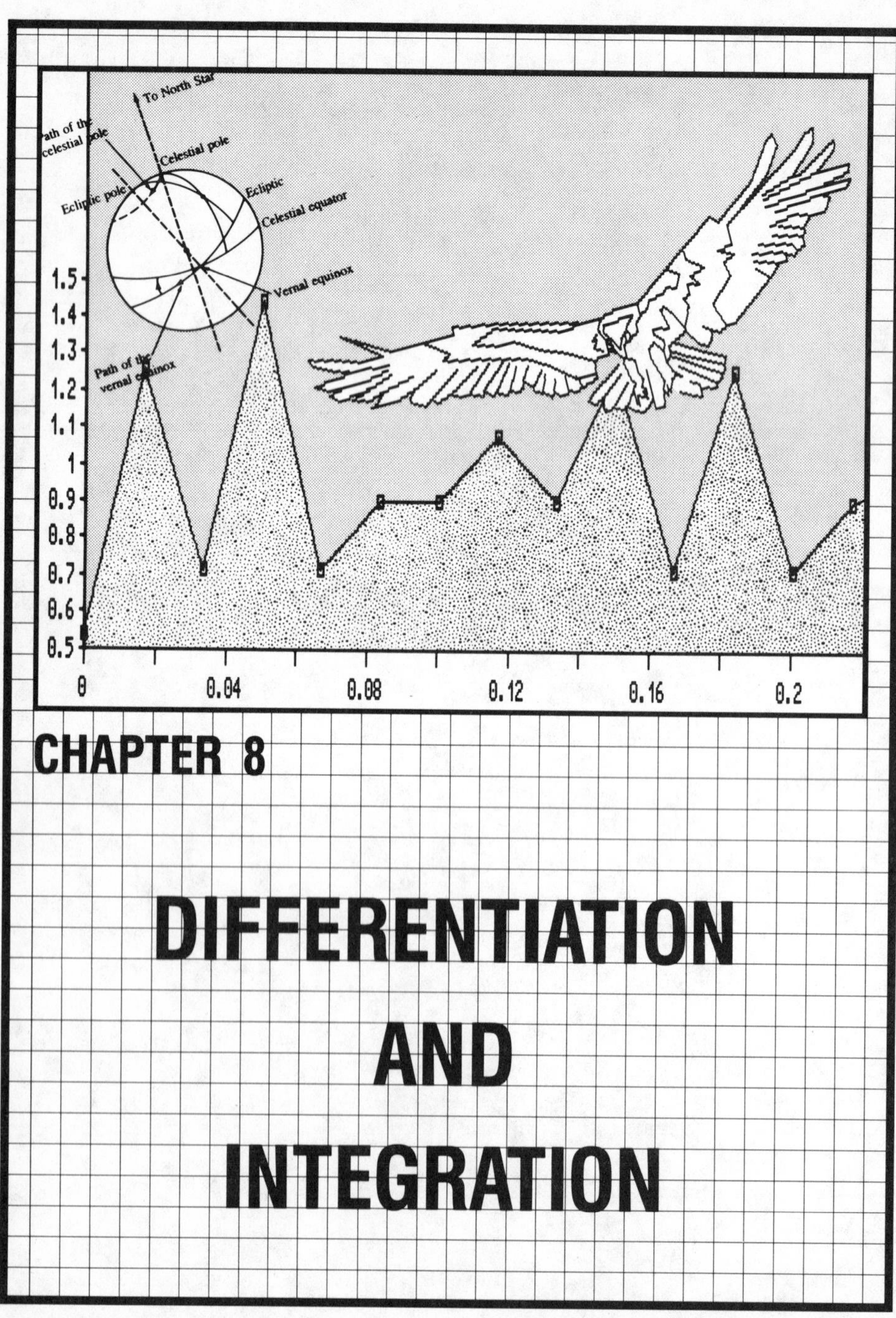

CHAPTER 8

DIFFERENTIATION AND INTEGRATION

Differentiation and integration are usually performed on analytical equations. However, if a function exists only as a set of discrete data points, then you must use numerical differencing and integration techniques to calculate the derivative and the integral. These techniques are usually applied with a short computer program. However, these techniques are easily applied to data in a spreadsheet. In a spreadsheet, you can also see intermediate results, which can often be enlightening, or scary, as the case may be.

■ DIFFERENTIATION

Differentiation of discrete data (or of functions that are troublesome to work out) can be performed using difference formulas. Central difference formulas are the most accurate and the most popular. You can also use forward and backward difference formulas for appropriate problems, such as calculations at the boundaries of a set of data, where a central difference is impossible to calculate.

Difference Formulas

Forward, backward, or central differences predict the derivative at a point based on different sets of data. Forward differences use the data points that come before the point in question to predict the derivative at that point. Backward differences use the points that come after the point in question. Central differences use an equal number of data points before and after the point in question; thus, they yield a more balanced prediction of the derivative.

The difference equation for the first derivative is the same for forward, backward, and central differences. The difference between them is the x value for which the difference formula is predicting the derivative. For example, the first derivative is approximated with

$$\frac{dy}{dx} = \frac{y_2 - y_1}{h}$$

where $h = x_2 - x_1$ is the separation between the data points, and (x_1,y_1) and (x_2,y_2) are consecutive pairs of X-Y data. If this equation is an approximation of the derivative at x_2, then it is a forward difference. If it is an approximation of the derivative at x_1, then it is a backward difference. If it is an approximation of the derivative at the center of the interval between x_1 and x_2, then it is a central difference. Table 8.1 contains the difference formulas for the first several derivatives and the order ($O(h^n)$) of the error associated with them. The formulas all calculate the derivative at the point x_0. The order of the error is the power (n) of the separation between the data points (h) to which the error is proportional. Use this order to compare the relative accuracy of the formulas. The higher the power of h, the more accurate the formula.

Errors

Error in a difference formula results from truncation error and round-off error. The order of the error shown in Table 8.1 is that due to truncation. Truncation error results from predicting the derivative using a few discrete data points rather than a continuous function. Since truncation error is proportional to the separation of the data points (h), it would seem that if you decreased h, you would decrease the amount of

Derivative at x_0	Error	Difference type
$\frac{dy}{dx} = \frac{y_1 - y_0}{h}$	$O(h)$	Forward or backward
$\frac{dy}{dx} = \frac{y_1 - y_{-1}}{h}$	$O(h^2)$	Central
$\frac{d^2y}{dx^2} = \frac{y_2 - 2y_1 + y_0}{h^2}$	$O(h)$	Forward or backward
$\frac{d^2y}{dx^2} = \frac{y_1 - 2y_0 + y_{-1}}{h^2}$	$O(h^2)$	Central
$\frac{d^3y}{dx^3} = \frac{y_3 - 3y_2 + 3y_{-1} - y_0}{h^3}$	$O(h)$	Forward or backward
$\frac{d^3y}{dx^3} = \frac{y_2 - 2y_1 + 2y_{-1} - y_{-2}}{2h^3}$	$O(h^2)$	Central

Table 8.1: Difference formulas for approximating the derivative of a function at point x_0

error. This is true to a point. That point is where roundoff error becomes significant.

Roundoff error results from a computer's not having an infinite number of digits in its numbers. When two nearly equal numbers are subtracted, the difference can be quite small. Divide this difference into one of the original numbers and see how many digits are to the left of the decimal. If the number of digits is comparable to the number of digits in the computer's numbers, then the difference is meaningless. For example, if two numbers with values near 1 are subtracted and the difference is on the order of 1×10^{-14} or less for a computer with 14 digits of accuracy, then the difference is meaningless. Roundoff error decreases with increasing, rather than decreasing, h. Thus, there is a tradeoff between truncation error and roundoff error; however, there will be some optimum, nonzero value of h where the total error is minimized.

Spreadsheet Method

The difference formulas in Table 8.1 are relatively simple, so the best way to apply them to the data is in the spreadsheet rather than with a macro. With the differences in the spreadsheet, you can also keep an eye on the scatter in the differences to see whether the truncation error is getting large.

Free Fall A classic experiment in college freshman physics involves uniformly accelerated motion in free fall. It is performed by dropping a metal weight along a strip of waxed paper. High-voltage alternating current is applied across the weight and a wire behind the paper. Every half cycle of the power supply, a spark is generated between the weight and the wire; this burns a small hole in the paper, marking the position of the weight as it falls. Knowing the frequency of the power supply and the distance between the holes in the paper, you can calculate the velocity and acceleration of the weight.

In a box in my garage, I found some experimental free-fall data that I generated about 15 years ago. The data in Table 8.2 is from that experiment. The sparks were generated at a rate of 60 per second, making the holes in the paper $\frac{1}{60}$ of a second apart. To calculate the velocity, you need to find the first derivative of this data. To find the acceleration due to gravity, you need the second derivative, which should be a constant.

Distance of holes from an arbitrary starting point (cm)
0.00
1.55
3.25
5.30
7.55
10.20
13.05
16.15
19.50
23.15
27.05
31.30
35.72
40.55
45.55
50.80

Note: The holes were generated $\frac{1}{60}$ of a second apart.

Table 8.2: Uniformly accelerated motion of a freely falling weight

Enter some titles and the time between the sparks that generated the holes in the paper.

1. In cell A1, type **Free Fall**
2. In cell C1, type **"DT =**
3. In cell D1, type **1/60**
4. Name cell D1 as **DT.**
5. In cell E1, type **sec.**

Label the column headings.

6. In cells A3..D3, respectively, type the labels **"t**, **"x**, **"dx/dt**, and **"d2x/dt2**
7. In cells A4..D4, respectively, type the labels **"(s)**, **"(cm)**, **"(cm/s)**, and **"(cm/s^2)**

Calculate the time in column A. Note that zero time in this table does not imply zero velocity at the first data point. I skipped the first few data points because they were not clear enough to read accurately. Enter the data from Table 8.2 in column B.

8. In cell A5, type **0**
9. In cells A6..A20, type/copy **+A5+$DT**
10. In cells B5..B20, type the data from Table 8.2.

In column C, calculate the first derivative of the data using a central difference centered on the interval between two points. In column D calculate the second derivative using a central difference centered on each point. Average the acceleration found in column D.

11. In cells C5..C19, type/copy **(B6-B5)/($DT)**
12. In cells D5..D18, type/copy **(B7-2*B6+B5)/($DT^2)**
13. In cell C20, type **"Ave. =**
14. In cell D20, type **@AVG(D5..D18)**
15. In cell E20, type **cm/s^2**
16. Format cells B5..D20 as Fixed 2 (**F2**).
17. Format cells A5..A20 as Fixed 4 (**F4**).

Your spreadsheet should now look like Figure 8.1 minus the regression output in cells E5..H13, which will be discussed in a moment. Column C contains the velocity of the weight, which is graphed in Figure 8.2. As expected, this is uniformly accelerated motion with a relatively smooth curve.

Since the object is freely falling, the acceleration in column D should be a constant and equal to the acceleration due to gravity (980 cm/s^2). As you can see in the spreadsheet and in the graph in Figure 8.3, there is a tremendous amount of scatter in the data, though the average is a reasonable value (951 cm/s^2).

This problem occurred because the random experimental error is magnified each time you take the derivative. You are taking the difference of data that contains random error. The magnitude of the number that you calculate is reduced by the difference because you are subtracting two numbers of similar value, but the error, being random, is not, leaving you with numbers of smaller magnitude but with the same magnitude of error. The relative magnitude of the error, compared to the

```
A1: 'Free Fall                                                          READY

        A          B          C          D        E          F          G         H
1   Free_Fall                DT = 0.016666 sec.
2
3       t          x       dx/dt   d2x/dt2
4      (s)       (cm)     (cm/s) (cm/s^2)
5   0.0000      0.00      93.00    540.00              Regression Output:
6   0.0167      1.55     102.00   1260.00 Constant                              89.65
7   0.0333      3.25     123.00    720.00 Std Err of Y Est                   2.698595
8   0.0500      5.30     135.00   1440.00 R Squared                          0.998716
9   0.0667      7.55     159.00    720.00 No. of Observations                      15
10  0.0833     10.20     171.00    900.00 Degrees of Freedom                       13
11  0.1000     13.05     186.00    900.00
12  0.1167     16.15     201.00   1080.00 X Coefficient(s)   973.2857
13  0.1333     19.50     219.00    900.00 Std Err of Coef.   9.676315
14  0.1500     23.15     234.00   1260.00
15  0.1667     27.05     255.00    720.00
16  0.1833     31.30     267.00   1260.00
17  0.2000     35.75     288.00    720.00
18  0.2167     40.55     300.00    900.00
19  0.2333     45.55     315.00
20  0.2500     50.80     Ave. =    951.43 cm/s^2
08-Apr-87  11:02 PM
```

Figure 8.1: Uniformly accelerated motion: numerical differentiation

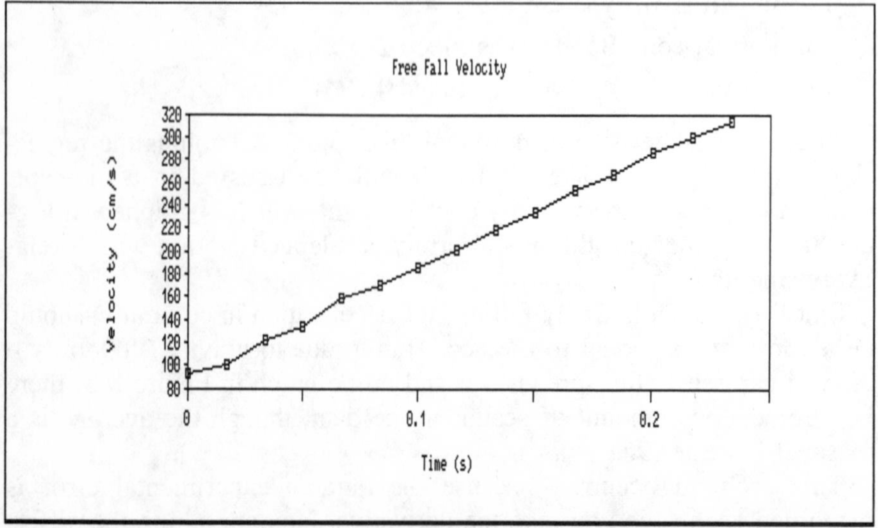

Figure 8.2: Uniformly accelerated motion: velocity of a freely falling object

magnitude of the numbers, increases by the same fraction that the magnitude of the numbers decreases due to the subtraction. To find the second derivative, you subtract the differences, which increases the relative magnitude of the error even more.

Experimental data often must be smoothed before a reasonable approximation of the derivative can be calculated. A good way to smooth data is to fit a known curve to the data and to take the derivative of that curve. Beware when you do this that you do not smooth out any important details. You know that the free fall example should be uniformly accelerated motion, as the velocity data shows, so fit a line to the velocity data. The slope of that line is equal to the derivative of the velocity (the acceleration).

18. Execute the /Data Regression X-range (**/DRX**) command and select A5..A19.
19. Execute the Y-range (**Y**) command and select C5..C19.
20. Execute the Output-range (**O**) command and select E5.
21. Execute the Go (**G**) command to perform the regression and return to ready mode.

The slope of the line through the velocity data (973 cm/s^2) is in cell G12 and is quite close to the correct value of 980 cm/s^2.

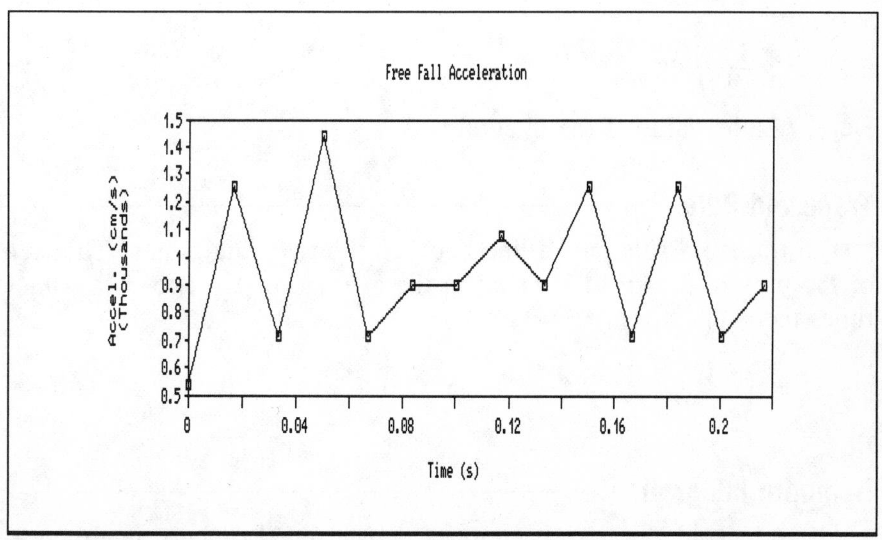

Figure 8.3: Uniformly accelerated motion: acceleration of a freely falling object

■ INTEGRATION

Integrating discrete data involves fitting a function that approximates the real function and whose integral is known to the intervals between the data points. Then you add each of these subintegrals to find the total integral of the curve.

Integration Formulas

There are many integral formulas for discrete data. The most common employ the rectangle rule, the trapezoid rule, Romberg integration, Simpson's rules, and Gaussian quadrature. Each of these rules is more accurate than the last, as it puts a more complicated curve through the data to approximate the function between the data points.

Rectangle Rule

The rectangle rule fills the space between two data points with a rectangle whose height is equal to the value of the function at one of the data points, and whose width is equal to the width of the interval. This would seem like a terrible approximation, but it works quite well. It is also very simple to implement, as all you need to do is to multiply each data value by the separation of the data values and then add them together. This rule is stated as follows:

$$I = \sum_{i=1}^{n-1} y_i(x_{i+1} - x_i)$$

Here, I is the value of the integral.

Trapezoid Rule

The trapezoid rule puts a line between the two data points. The area of the trapezoid formed is equal to the average of the two data values times their separation.

$$I = \sum_{i=1}^{n-1} \frac{(y_i + y_{i+1})}{2}(x_{i+1} - x_i)$$

Romberg Integration

The trapezoid rule can be improved by using Romberg integration. Romberg integration combines two estimates of the integral to get a more accurate estimate of the integral. The first integral uses every value, and the second uses every other value.

$$I_1 = \sum_{i=1}^{n-1} \frac{(y_i + y_{i+1})}{2}(x_{i+1} - x_i)$$

$$I_2 = \sum_{i=1,3,5\ldots}^{n-2} \frac{(y_i + y_{i+2})}{2}(x_{i+2} - x_i)$$

$$I = I_1 + \frac{1}{3}(I_1 - I_2)$$

Simpson's Rules

One of Simpson's rules puts a quadratic (piece of a circle) equation through three data values and then calculates the area. This is known as Simpson's $\frac{1}{3}$ rule. Simpson's $\frac{3}{8}$ rule puts a cubic equation through four data values. Note that Simpson's rules assume equally spaced data points.

$$I = \sum_{i=1,3,5\ldots}^{n-2} \frac{1}{3}(y_i + 4y_{i+1} + y_{i+2})h$$

$$I = \sum_{i=1,4,7\ldots}^{n-3} \frac{3}{8}(y_i + 3y_{i+1} + 3y_{i+2} + y_{i+3})h$$

Here, h is the constant separation between data points.

Gaussian Quadrature

If you are integrating an equation rather than a set of data points, then you can use Gaussian quadrature. Gaussian quadrature is an integration formula in which the value of an integral is found by adding the value of the function at a few specific points. The number of points needed is determined by the order of the curve that you want to fit between the limits. Up to a third-order curve can be calculated with only two values of the function.

$$\int_{-1}^{+1} f(t)dt = f(-0.5773) + f(0.5773)$$

To use the formula with a specific function and specific limits of integration, you must change variables to put your integral into the form shown here. (See the references for higher-order formulas at the end of this chapter.)

Improper Integrals

Often you must integrate functions in which one or both of the limits are infinite or that become undefined somewhere between the limits. For example, many of the "special functions" of physics and engineering (gamma function, error function, and so on) are defined with integrals that have infinity as one of the limits. You can handle these problems in several ways.

The simplest method is to transform the variables of the function so that it no longer has an infinite upper limit. For example, consider the following function:

$$I = \int_0^{\infty} x^2 e^{-x} dx$$

Break it into two integrals.

$$I = \int_0^1 x^2 e^{-x} dx + \int_1^{\infty} x^2 e^{-x} dx$$

Then transform the variables in the second integral with $y = 1/x$.

$$I = \int_0^1 x^2 e^{-x} dx + \int_0^1 \frac{e^{-1/y}}{y^4} dy$$

Now you have two integrals with rational limits. The value of the function at the lower limit is indeterminate (0/0), but the limit is zero, so this will not be a problem.

Many problems with infinite limits converge rapidly to zero as the argument of the function increases toward infinity. (Actually, they must converge rapidly for the value of the function to be finite.) In this case, you can continue integrating the function until the value of the term to be added is much smaller than the value of the integral and then truncate the integral at that point.

The function in the second integral in the preceding equation is indeterminate at the lower limit. You may happen to know that the limit of the function at this value is zero, and you could use this fact to evaluate the integral. If you did not know the value of the function at the limit, or if the value is infinite, as for

$$I = \int_0^1 \frac{dx}{\sqrt{x}}$$

then you need to add a small number ϵ to the lower limit and then calculate the integral. You then reduce the size of ϵ until the value of the integral converges (assuming that it does converge). Note that this is exactly how you would solve the integral analytically.

Spreadsheet Methods

Spreadsheet integration methods are relatively straightforward. Each cell calculates the value of the integral between two of the data points. A final cell then adds these values with the @SUM function.

Gamma Function The gamma function is one of the so-called science and engineering *special functions*. It is used occasionally in physical problems such as normalization of coulomb wave functions and computation of probabilities in statistical mechanics. In fact, you encountered it in the last chapter in the series representation of the Bessel function ($J_n(x)$) for cases when n is not an integer. When n is an integer, the gamma function is equal to the factorial function:

$$\Gamma(n + 1) = n!$$

The gamma function is defined with the integral

$$\Gamma(x) = \int_0^\infty e^{-t} t^{x-1} dt$$

which has no analytic solution. The gamma function is generally listed in a table for various values of x. Figure 8.4 is a plot of the integrand of the gamma function integral. Note that it goes to zero rapidly, so you can truncate the integral at a t value of about 10.

In the following spreadsheet, you will calculate the gamma function by numerically calculating the integration. You will use all of the integration methods discussed so far. The value of the gamma function at

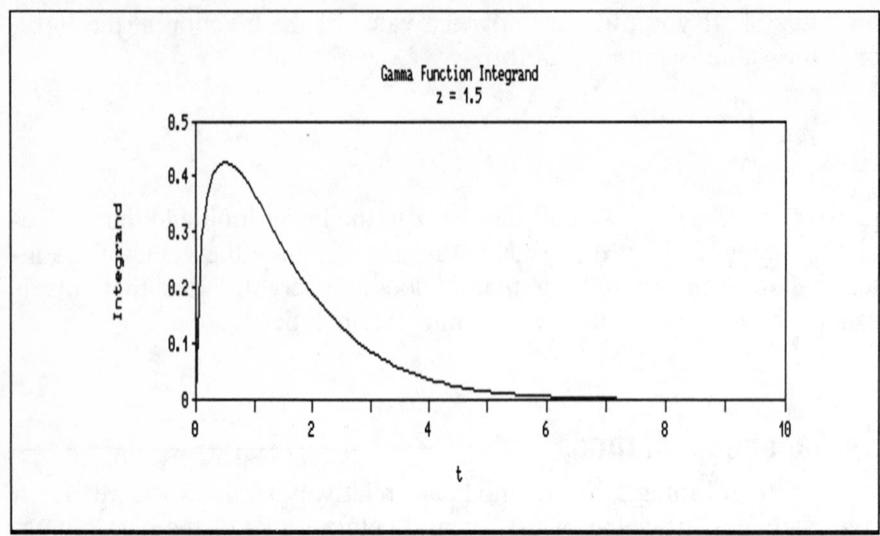

Figure 8.4: A plot of the function integrated to find the gamma function of x for $x = 1.5$

$x = 1.5$ is equal to $\sqrt{\pi/2}$. Use that value of x so that you can compare the integrated results with the correct result.

1. Change the width of column A to **11**.
2. In cell A1, type **Gamma Function**

Insert and name the value to calculate for (Z) and the grid spacing (DT).

3. In cell C1, type **"z =**
4. In cell D1, type **1.5**
5. In cell E1, type **"dt =**
6. In cell F1, type **0.1**
7. Name cells D1 and F1 as **Z** and **DT**.
8. In cells B3..G3, respectively, type the labels **"True, "Rect., "Trap., "Trap.2, "Romberg,** and **"Sim.1/3**

Add the contents of each column to get the total integral for each method. Calculate the error in each method by comparing the calculated integral to the correct value in cell B4. Cell F4 contains the Romberg formula to combine the two trapezoid-rule integrals.

9. In cell A4, type **Integral =**
10. In cell B4, type **@SQRT(@PI)/2**
11. In cells C4..E4, type/copy **@SUM(C8..C102)**
12. In cell F4, type **+D4+(D4-E4)/3**
13. In cell G4, type **@SUM(G8..G102)**
14. In cell A5, type **Error =**
15. In cells C5..G5, type/copy **(C4-$B$4)/$B$4**

In column B, calculate values of the function for each of the 96 values of *t* in column A.

16. In cell A7, type **"t**
17. In cell B7, type **"f(z,t)**
18. In cell A8, type **0**
19. In cells A9..A103, type/copy **+A8+$DT**
20. Format cells A8..A103 as Fixed 3 (**F3**)
21. In cells B8..B103, type/copy **@EXP(-A8)*A8^($Z-1)**

Calculate the rectangle rule.

22. In cells C8..C103, type/copy **+B8*$DT**

Calculate the trapezoid rule twice, once with single spacing and once with double spacing. You need the second evaluation of the trapezoid rule to calculate the Romberg formula in cell F4. Note that the second evaluation of the trapezoid rule uses every other data point, so you zero out every other formula in column E to avoid counting any data point twice.

23. In cells D8..D103, type/copy **+$DT*(B8+B9)/2**
24. In cells E8..E103, type/copy **+$DT*(B8+B10)**
25. In alternate rows in column E (E9, E11, E13 . . . E103), replace the formula with **0**

Calculate Simpson's 1/3 rule. As before, zero out every other value of the formula in column G.

26. In cells G8..G103, type **+$DT*(B8+4*B9+B10)/3**
27. In alternate rows in column G (G9, G11, G13 . . . G103), replace the formula with **0**

Your spreadsheet should now look like Figure 8.5. The values calculated with the rectangle rule and the trapezoid rule are about the same. The Romberg integration decreased the error in the trapezoid rule by about 50 percent—to a value near that calculated with Simpson's rule. In each of these calculations, the range was covered by 96 equally spaced grid points.

You have not yet used the Gaussian quadrature formula in this spreadsheet because it is more accurate and needs fewer grid points. In fact, you will calculate it using only 15 grid points instead of 96. (Actually, you will be using 43 grid points, since third-order Gaussian quadrature calculates two more grid points in each interval.) The layout of this spreadsheet will be the same as that of the preceding one. For comparison, you will calculate the trapezoid rule using the same grid points.

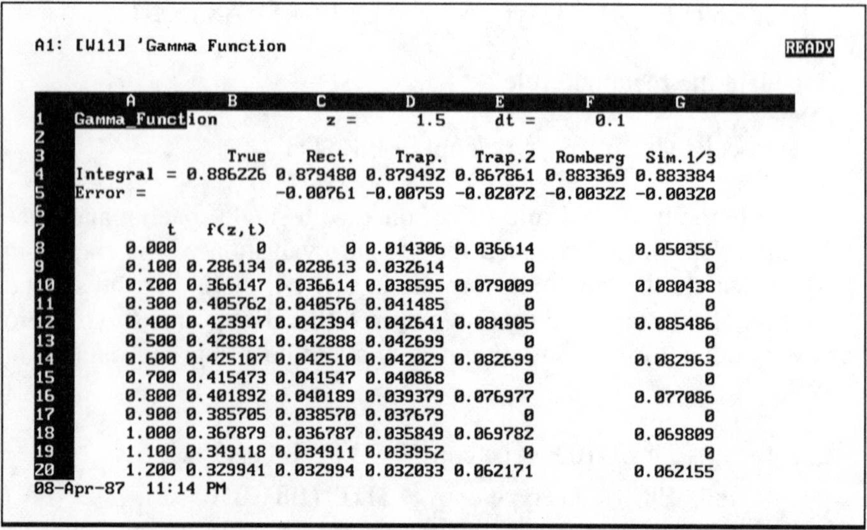

A1: [W11] 'Gamma Function READY

	A	B	C	D	E	F	G
1	Gamma_Function		z =	1.5	dt =	0.1	
2							
3		True	Rect.	Trap.	Trap.2	Romberg	Sim.1/3
4	Integral =	0.886226	0.879480	0.879492	0.867861	0.883369	0.883384
5	Error =		-0.00761	-0.00759	-0.02072	-0.00322	-0.00320
6							
7	t	f(z,t)					
8	0.000	0	0	0.014306	0.036614		0.050356
9	0.100	0.286134	0.028613	0.032614	0		0
10	0.200	0.366147	0.036614	0.038595	0.079009		0.080438
11	0.300	0.405762	0.040576	0.041485	0		0
12	0.400	0.423947	0.042394	0.042641	0.084905		0.085486
13	0.500	0.428881	0.042888	0.042699	0		0
14	0.600	0.425107	0.042510	0.042029	0.082699		0.082963
15	0.700	0.415473	0.041547	0.040868	0		0
16	0.800	0.401892	0.040189	0.039379	0.076977		0.077086
17	0.900	0.385705	0.038570	0.037679	0		0
18	1.000	0.367879	0.036787	0.035849	0.069782		0.069809
19	1.100	0.349118	0.034911	0.033952	0		0
20	1.200	0.329941	0.032994	0.032033	0.062171		0.062155

08-Apr-87 11:14 PM

Figure 8.5: Gamma function: calculating an integral using the rectangle rule, the trapezoid rule, Romberg integration, and Simpson's $\frac{1}{3}$ rule

To use Gaussian quadrature, you first must change variables to make the limits of integration −1 to 1. Do this with the following substitution:

$$t = \frac{(b - a)y + b + a}{2}$$

Here, a is the lower limit, and b is the upper limit. You then insert this equation into the integral for the gamma function:

$$\Gamma(x) = \int_0^{\infty} \mathrm{e}^{-t} t^{x-1} \mathrm{d}t$$

$$= \frac{(b - a)}{2} \int_{-1}^{+1} \mathrm{e}^{-((b-a)y+b+a)/2} \left(\frac{(b - a)y + b + a}{2} \right)^{x-1} \mathrm{d}y$$

In this case, the limits of integration are the grid points between which you are calculating the integral. Note that this method can be used only for integrating a function, not for experimental data.

1. Change the width of column A to **11**.
2. In cell A1, type **Gamma Function**
3. In cell C1, type **"z =**
4. In cell D1, type **1.5**
5. Name cell D1 as **Z**.
6. In cell A3, type **"Integral =**
7. In cell A4, type **Error =**

Enter the grid to use for the integration. You will use a nonlinear grid to place more grid points at the beginning of the grid, where the function changes rapidly, and fewer at the end, where it does not.

8. In cell A5, type **"t**
9. In cells A6..A20, respectively, type the values **0, 0.2, 0.4, 0.6, 0.8, 1, 2, 3, 4, 5, 6, 7, 8, 9,** and **10**
10. Format cells A6..A20 as Fixed 3 (**F3**).

As before, enter the correct value for comparison.

11. In cell B2, type **"True**
12. In cell B3, type **@SQRT(@PI)/2**

Calculate the value of the function. This calculation is not used by the Gaussian quadrature formula, but was included here to show when to truncate the integration. It is used by the trapezoid rule, which is also calculated for comparison.

13. In cell B5, type **"f(z,t)**
14. In cells B6..B20, type/copy **@EXP(-A6)*A6^($Z-1)**

Calculate the Gaussian quadrature formula for each pair of data points and then add these values together in cell C3. Cells C6..C19 calculate the quadrature formula developed for the gamma function.

15. In cell C2, type **'Gaussian**
16. In cell C3, type **@SUM(C6..C19)**
17. In cell C4, type **(C3-$B$3)/$B$3**
18. In cells C6..C19, type/copy **((A7-A6)/2)*(@EXP(-((A7-A6)*(-1/@SQRT(3))+A7+A6)/2)*(((A7-A6)*(-1/@SQRT(3))+A7+A6)/2)^($Z-1)+@EXP(-((A7-A6)*(1/@SQRT(3))+A7+A6)/2)*(((A7-A6)*(1/@SQRT(3))+A7+A6)/2)^($Z-1))**

Calculate the trapezoid rule integration for comparison.

19. In cell D2, type **"Trap.**
20. In cell D3, type **@SUM(D6..D19)**
21. In cell D4, type **(D3-$B$3)/$B$3**
22. In cells D6..D19, type/copy **(A7-A6)*(B7+B6)/2**

Your spreadsheet should now look like Figure 8.6. Note that the Gaussian quadrature integration has only about one fifth the error of the trapezoid rule integration.

Macro Methods

As you might expect, all of these formulas can be implemented as macro programs. The equations remain the same; you just use a {FOR} loop to calculate the parts of the integral and add them together rather than calculating them in separate cells and then adding them with the @SUM function. The macro program is much more flexible than the spreadsheet for integration of functions, as you can change the limits or

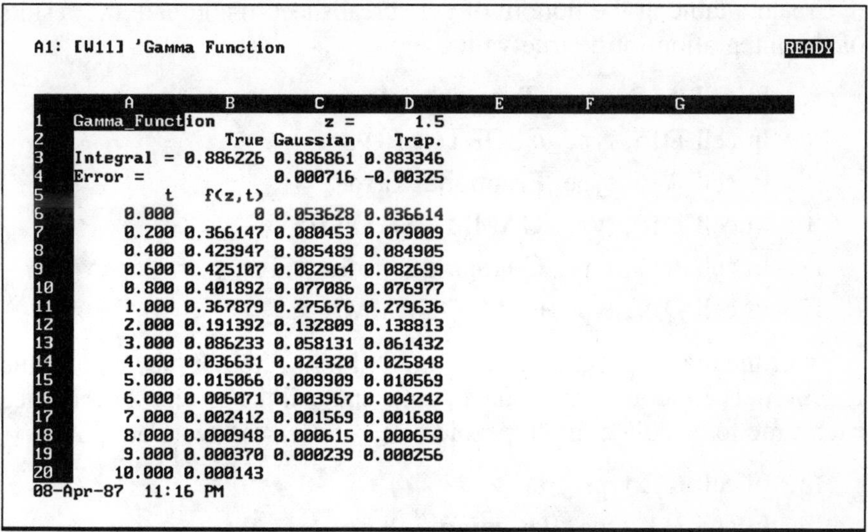

A1: [W11] 'Gamma Function READY

	A	B	C	D	E	F	G
1	Gamma_Function		z =	1.5			
2		True	Gaussian	Trap.			
3	Integral =	0.886226	0.886861	0.883346			
4	Error =		0.000716	-0.00325			
5	t	f(z,t)					
6	0.000	0	0.053628	0.036614			
7	0.200	0.366147	0.080453	0.079009			
8	0.400	0.423947	0.085489	0.084905			
9	0.600	0.425107	0.082964	0.082699			
10	0.800	0.401892	0.077086	0.076977			
11	1.000	0.367879	0.275676	0.279636			
12	2.000	0.191392	0.132809	0.138813			
13	3.000	0.086233	0.058131	0.061432			
14	4.000	0.036631	0.024320	0.025848			
15	5.000	0.015066	0.009909	0.010569			
16	6.000	0.006071	0.003967	0.004242			
17	7.000	0.002412	0.001569	0.001680			
18	8.000	0.000948	0.000615	0.000659			
19	9.000	0.000370	0.000239	0.000256			
20	10.000	0.000143					

08-Apr-87 11:16 PM

Figure 8.6: Gamma function: integral formula solved with Gaussian quadrature

the step width by simply changing a variable rather than having to add or delete cells. On the other hand, if you are integrating experimental data, then the limits and the step width are fixed and the data are already in cells, so the spreadsheet methods are the simplest to implement.

Gamma Function: Macro Program The following macro program calculates the gamma function, again using the trapezoid rule.

1. In cell A1, type **Gamma Function; Macro Program**

Create a table of the input and output cells.

2. In cells A3 and A4, type the labels **"z** and **"Gamma(z)**
3. Name cells B3 and B4 as **Z** and **GAMMA**.

Create a table of the variables used in the macro.

4. Type the following labels in cells A6..A12, respectively: **"t, "dt, "tstart, "tend, "yone, "ytwo**, and **"fact**
5. Name cells B6..B12 by executing the /Range Name Labels Right (**/RNLR**) command and selecting cells A6..A12.
6. Format cells B10..B12 as Scientific 2 (**S2**).

Create a table at the bottom of the spreadsheet to compare the results of the integration to the true value.

7. In cell A15, type **"True value =**
8. In cell D15, type **@SQRT(@PI)/2**
9. In cell A16, type **'Fractional Error =**
10. In cell D16, type **(GAMMA-D15)/D15**
11. In cell A17, type **'Change due to Last Term =**
12. In cell D17, type **+FACT/GAMMA**

Enter the macro program in column D. First, zero out the value of the function. Then loop over the data points and call the routine TRAP once each time to calculate the trapezoid rule between the two data points.

13. In cell C3, type **"\I**
14. In cell D3, type **'{let gamma,0}**
15. In cell D4, type **'{for t,tstart,tend-dt,dt,trap}~**

Calculate the area of the trapezoid between the data points at T and T + DT. Do this by calculating the value of the function at T (YONE) and T + DT (YTWO), averaging them, and then multiplying by DT. Finally, add the area of the trapezoid to the total area stored in GAMMA.

16. In cell C6, type **"trap**
17. In cell D6, type **'{let yone,@exp(-t)*t^(z-1)}**
18. In cell D7, type **'{let ytwo,@exp(-(t+dt))*(t+dt)^(z-1)}**
19. In cell D8, type **'{let fact,dt*(yone+ytwo)/2}**
20. In cell D9, type **'{let gamma,gamma+fact}**
21. Name cells D3 and D6 as **\I** and **TRAP**.

To run the macro, first place the value of *z* (1.5) in cell B3, the lower limit of the integration (0) in cell B8, the upper limit of the integration (10) in cell B9, and the step width (0.01) in cell B7. Next, press Macro-I; wait about three minutes, and the value of the gamma function will appear in cell B4. The spreadsheet should now look like Figure 8.7. You should also check the value of cell B12, which contains the area of the last trapezoid added to the total. It will help you determine whether you have integrated far enough to be able to truncate the integral without appreciable error.

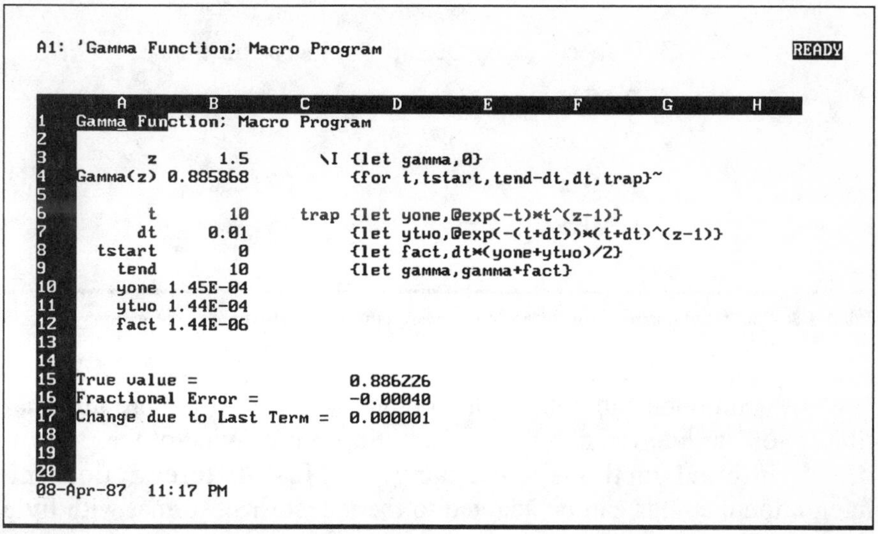

```
A1: 'Gamma Function; Macro Program                                          READY

      A         B         C         D         E         F         G         H
1   Gamma Function; Macro Program
2
3          z       1.5        \I {let gamma,0}
4   Gamma(z) 0.885868            {for t,tstart,tend-dt,dt,trap}~
5
6          t        10      trap {let yone,@exp(-t)*t^(z-1)}
7         dt      0.01           {let ytwo,@exp(-(t+dt))*(t+dt)^(z-1)}
8     tstart         0           {let fact,dt*(yone+ytwo)/2}
9       tend        10           {let gamma,gamma+fact}
10      yone 1.45E-04
11      ytwo 1.44E-04
12      fact 1.44E-06
13
14
15  True value =                 0.886226
16  Fractional Error =           -0.00040
17  Change due to Last Term =    0.000001
18
19
20
08-Apr-87  11:17 PM
```

Figure 8.7: Gamma function macro program

As this is a slow-running macro, I did some timing tests with and without the 8087 math coprocessor. I also compared changing the speed of my system from 4.77 MHz to 7.16 MHz (I have a dual-speed system). As you can see in Table 8.3, the macro runs in nearly half (53 percent) the time when a high-speed processor and an 8087 coprocessor are installed. The speedup due to the 8087 is consistently 46 percent at either processor speed. It is interesting that even though the increase in the processor speed (4.77 MHz to 7.16 MHz) is 50 percent, the increase in spreadsheet calculation speed is only 27 percent.

■ SUMMARY

In this chapter, we calculated numerical derivatives of data and functions. In particular, we looked at spreadsheet methods to calculate forward, backward, and central differences of spreadsheet data. We encountered some of the problems involved in calculating derivatives numerically, particularly those inherent in the difference formula: truncation errors, roundoff errors, and error growth due to differencing.

We also numerically integrated functions and data using spreadsheet and macro methods. These methods are implementations of several standard numerical integration techniques normally applied with a high-level language.

CPU speed	Coprocessor	Macro run time
4.77 MHz	None	350 sec
4.77 MHz	8087	238 sec
7.16 MHz	None	273 sec
7.16 MHz	8087	187 sec

Table 8.3: Speed comparisons for different hardware configurations running the gamma function macro program

Most good books on numerical methods will give you more information if you are interested in the mathematical background of these methods or in other methods and examples. Most differentiation and integration methods can be adapted to the spreadsheet format with little difficulty.

■ FOR MORE INFORMATION

For further information about the topics discussed here, you can consult the following sources.

Science and Engineering Special Functions

G. Arfken, *Mathematical Methods for Physicists* (Orlando, Fla.: Academic Press, 1970).

Numerical Differentiation and Integration

C. Gerald, *Applied Numerical Analysis*, 2nd ed. (Reading, Mass.: Addison-Wesley, 1978).

W. Press et. al., *Numerical Recipes: The Art of Scientific Computing* (Cambridge, Eng.: Cambridge University Press, 1986).

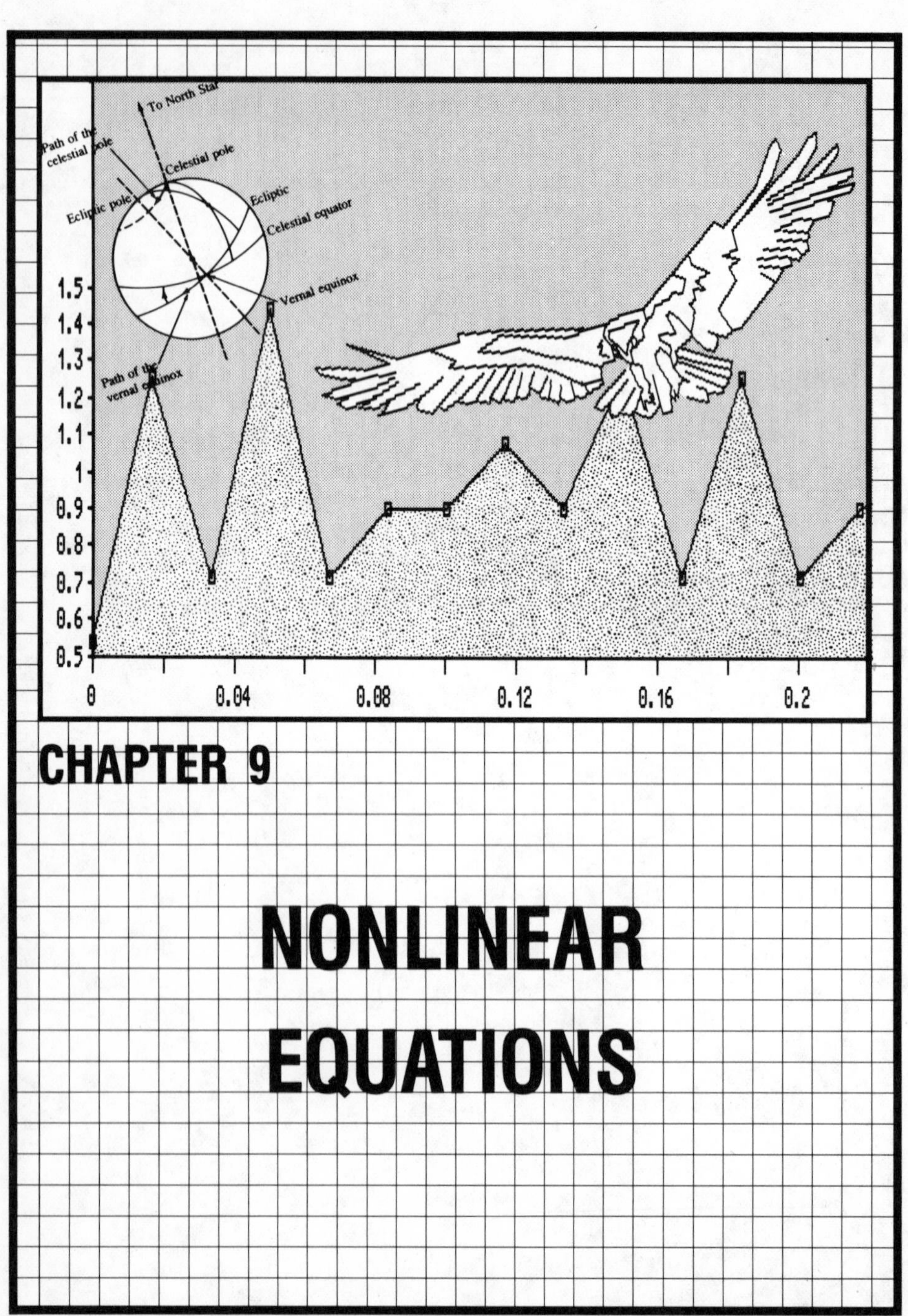

CHAPTER 9

NONLINEAR EQUATIONS

Solving a nonlinear equation is often a frustrating experience. An equation that looks simple can defy solution by any analytical means. Except for polynomials up to order 4 and the simplest transcendental equations (those involving trigonometric or exponential functions), most nonlinear equations cannot be solved analytically. In fact, the solutions of polynomials of orders 3 and 4 are so unwieldy that these solutions are seldom used, even though they exist.

Many numerical methods exist for solving nonlinear equations. The methods are all based on guessing a solution and systematically refining that guess. You try a guess by inserting it into the equation, and you then use the result to try to improve the guess. You repeat this process until you find a root of sufficient accuracy or until the method diverges and you give up and go home for the night, to try again the next morning.

■ SUCCESSIVE APPROXIMATIONS

Although there are a number of simple methods for finding the root of a nonlinear equation, the one most adaptable to a spreadsheet is known as *successive approximations*. To perform successive approximations, you first rewrite the equation in the following form:

$$x = f(x)$$

There are often several ways to rewrite your original equation, any of which are valid for this method, though some may not converge to a solution.

Once you have rewritten the equation, make an initial guess of the value of x. In general, any value of x will do, but the closer your initial guess is to the solution, the faster the problem will converge. Note that for problems with multiple solutions, the initial guess of the value of x determines the solution that you get; to get the other solutions, you use different initial guesses.

Insert the initial value of x into $f(x)$ and calculate a new value of x. This is the new guess of the value of x, which you insert into $f(x)$ again. Continue calculating new values of x in this manner until the value of x converges:

$$x_0 = \text{initial guess}$$

$$x_1 = f(x_0)$$

$$x_2 = f(x_1)$$

$$\vdots$$

$$x_n = f(x_{n-1})$$

Figure 9.1 shows the progress of a solution using this method.

As mentioned, there is often more than one way to convert your nonlinear equation into the form just discussed. Not all converted functions converge to a root. For a function to converge to a root of the original equation, the absolute value of the slope of $f(x)$ must be less than 1.

$$|f'(x)| < 1$$

You could write the derivative of your functions and test them with the preceding condition, but I have found that it is usually faster to just rewrite your equation in the simplest way and try it. If it does not converge, then rewrite it a different way.

Cos(*x*) = *x* A simple, nonlinear, transcendental equation is

$$\text{Cos}(x) - x = 0$$

which can quickly be rewritten into the required form,

$$x = \text{Cos}(x)$$

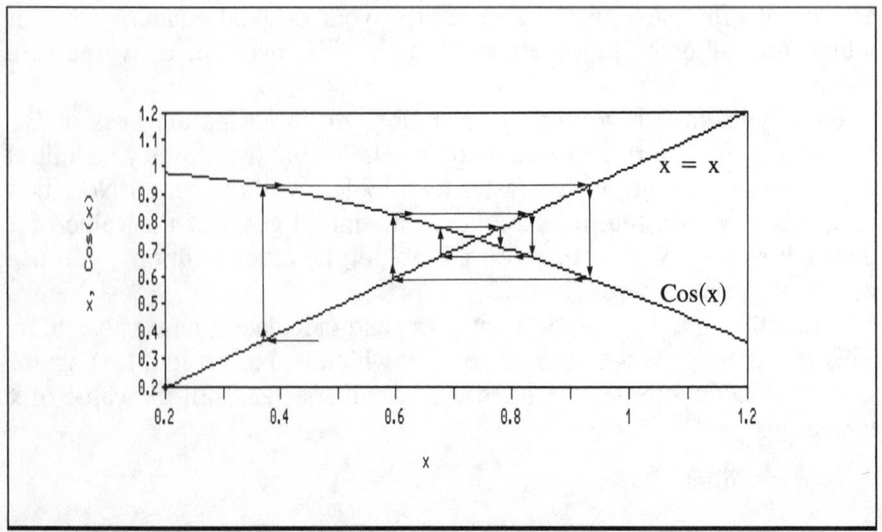

Figure 9.1: Progress of a solution using successive approximations

In this next example, you will solve this equation by successive approximations, using the spreadsheet's iteration capability.

1. Change the width of column A to **16**.
2. Execute the /Worksheet Global Recalculation Manual (**/WGRM**) command.
3. In cell A1, type **x = Cos(x); Successive approximations**

Create a table with the initialization value and the initialization flag. The initialization flag will force the spreadsheet into a predetermined initial state.

4. In cell A3, type **"Initial Value**
5. In cell B3, type **0**
6. In cell A4, type **"Init Flag**
7. In cell B4, type **1**
8. Name cells B3 and B4 as **INIT_VALUE** and **INIT**.

In cell B6, test INIT. If it is 0, then set x equal to the initialization value; otherwise, set x equal to the cosine of x in cell B7. In cell B7, calculate the cosine of the value in cell B6, creating a circular reference.

9. In cell A6, type **"x**
10. In cell B6, type **@IF($INIT = 0,$INIT_VALUE,B7)**
11. In cell A7, type **"Cos(x)**
12. In cell B7, type **@COS(B6)**

Calculate the difference between x and $\cos(x)$ to help determine when the calculation has converged sufficiently.

13. In cell A9, type **"Difference**
14. In cell B9, type **+B7-B6**
15. Format cell B9 as Scientific 1 (**S1**).

Set up a second circular reference to count the number of iterations.

16. In cell A11, type **"Iteration**
17. In cell B11, type **@IF($INIT=0,0,B12+1)**
18. In cell B12, type **+B11**

To perform the calculation, first set the value of the initialization flag in cell B4 to **0** and press Calc to initialize the problem. Next, change the value of the initialization flag to **1** and press Calc again. Each time you press Calc, the calculation will be iterated, calculating the next value of x. Continue pressing Calc until the value of x converges to sufficient accuracy. You can test the accuracy by comparing the value of x to the difference between x and f(x) in cell B9. The spreadsheet should now look like Figure 9.2, with the converged value of x in cells B7 and B8.

If this calculation had not converged, then you would rewrite the equation in the equivalent form (arc-cosine),

$$x = \text{Cos}^{-1}(x)$$

and try again.

■ UNDER RELAXATION

In some situations, a function is so nonlinear that successive approximations will not result in convergence. Extreme nonlinearity is often caused by inflection points in the curve near the root that cause the value of x to change too much at each iteration. You can correct for this problem by decreasing the change in x between steps by a fractional

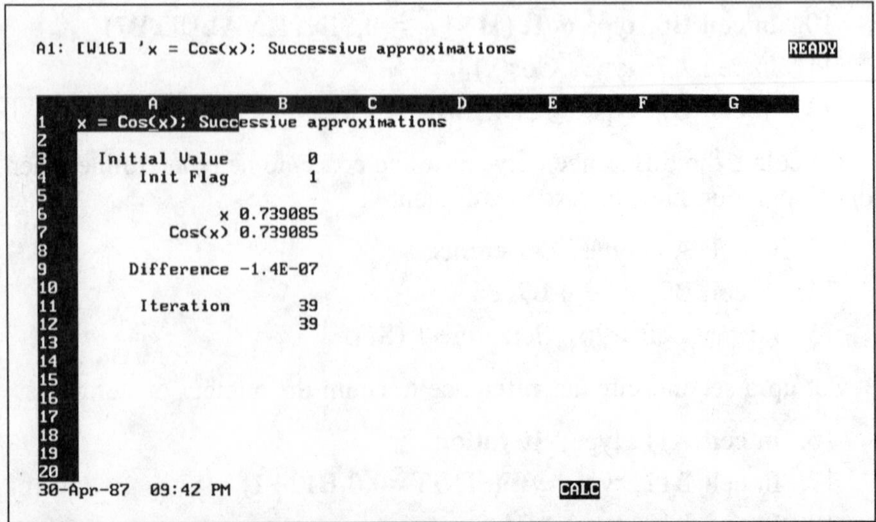

Figure 9.2: Successive approximations method used to find the root of the equation Cos(x) = x

amount (c). This is known as *under relaxation*. The iteration of successive values of x proceeds as follows:

$$
\begin{aligned}
x_0 &= \text{initial guess} \\
x_1 &= x_0 + c\Delta x_0 \\
x_2 &= x_1 + c\Delta x_1 \\
&\vdots \\
x_n &= x_{n-1} + c\Delta x_{n-1}
\end{aligned}
$$

Here, $\Delta x_n = f(x_n) - x_n$ is the change in x for this iteration, and c is the relaxation factor ($0 < c < 1$). Using a value of $c = 1$ is equivalent to using the successive approximation method. Using values of c greater than 1 is known as *over relaxation*. This method can be used to speed up the convergence of some slowly converging problems. Inserting the value for Δx_n into the equation for x_n,

$$x_n = cf(x_{n-1}) + (1 - c)x_n$$

gives the iteration equation to use in the calculation.

Electron Temperature in GaAs The electron temperature in gallium arsenide (GaAs) due to acceleration by an electric field has been calculated by solving a combination of the conservation equations for energy and momentum. This solution is complicated by the fact that GaAs has two conduction bands with different mobilities (that is, electrons can move faster in one band than in the other). The result is

$$Te = T + \left(\frac{2}{3}\right)\frac{\tau q E^2 \mu}{k}(1 + Re^{-\varepsilon/(kTe)})^{-1}$$

where Te is the electron temperature, T is the ambient temperature (300 K), τ is the lifetime for relaxation of energy from the electrons to the crystal lattice (10^{-12} s), q is the electron charge (1.6×10^{-19} coul), E is the electric field, k is Planck's constant (1.38×10^{-23} J/K), μ is the electron mobility in the lower electron conduction band (0.85 m^2/V-s), ϵ is the energy difference between the upper- and lower-conduction bands (0.31 eV), and R is the splitting factor for splitting electrons between the upper- and lower-conduction bands (94.1). This equation is already in the form that you want for the successive approximation method, so try that method with values of the electric field between 10^2 and 10^8 V/m.

1. Set the width of column C to **10**.
2. In cell A1, type **Electron temperature in GaAs; Successive approximations**
3. Execute the /Worksheet Global Recalculation Manual (/WGRM) command.

Create a table of the coefficients of the equation.

4. In cell A3, type **"DELT_E**
5. In cell B3, type **0.31*E4**
6. In cell C3, type **J**
7. In cell D3, type **"K**
8. In cell E3, type **1.38E-23**
9. In cell F3, type **J/K**
10. In cell A4, type **"TAU**
11. In cell B4, type **1.0E-12**
12. In cell C4, type **s**
13. In cell D4, type **"Q**
14. In cell E4, type **1.6E-l9**
15. In cell F4, type **COUL**
16. In cell A5, type **"U**
17. In cell B5, type **0.85**
18. In cell C5, type **m^2/V-s**
19. In cell D5, type **"T**
20. In cell E5, type **300**
21. In cell F5, type **K**
22. In cell D6, type **"R**
23. In cell E6, type **94.1**
24. Execute the /Range Name Labels Right (/**RNLR**) command and select cells A3..A5; then execute **/RNLR** again and select cells D3..D6.

Create a table of the initial value and the initialization flag.

25. In cell A7, type **Initial value**
26. In cell C7, type **300**

27. In cell A8, type **Init Flag**
28. In cell C8, type **1**
29. Name cells C7 and C8 as **INIT_VALUE** and **INIT**.

Type the list of electric field values to solve the equation for.

30. In cell B11, type **^E**
31. In cell B12, type **^(V/m)**
32. In cell B13, type **1E2**
33. In cell B14, type **1E3**
34. In cell B15, type **1E4**
35. In cell B16, type **1E5**
36. In cell B17, type **1E6**
37. In cell B18, type **1E7**
38. In cell B19, type **1E8**

In column C test the initialization flag. If the problem is initializing, then use the initial value; otherwise, set it equal to the function in column D. In column D, calculate the function.

39. In cell C11, type **^Te**
40. In cell C12, type **^(K)**
41. In cells C13..C19, type/copy **@IF($INIT=0,$INIT_VALUE, D13)**
42. In cell D11, type **^f(Te)**
43. In cell D12, type **^(K)**
44. In cell D13..D19, type/copy **+$T+(2/3)*$TAU*$Q*B13^2 *$U/($K*(1+$R*@EXP(-$DELT_E/($K*C13))))**
45. Format cells B13.D19. as Scientific 2 (**S2**).

To operate this spreadsheet, set the initialization flag in cell C8 to **0** and press Calc. Set the initialization flag to **1** and press Calc. These functions will now be calculated once, each time you press the Calc key. The spreadsheet will now look like Figure 9.3.

After five or so iterations, all of the functions except the fifth one will have converged. At a field of 10^6 V/m, the temperature is alternating between a value of 6.76×10^3 and 4.17×10^2 K. Plotting $f(Te)$ versus Te, as in Figure 9.4, you can see the cause of the problem. The function has two plateaus that it alternates between. Note that the slope of the function is greater than 1 to the left of the intersection, which violates our convergence condition.

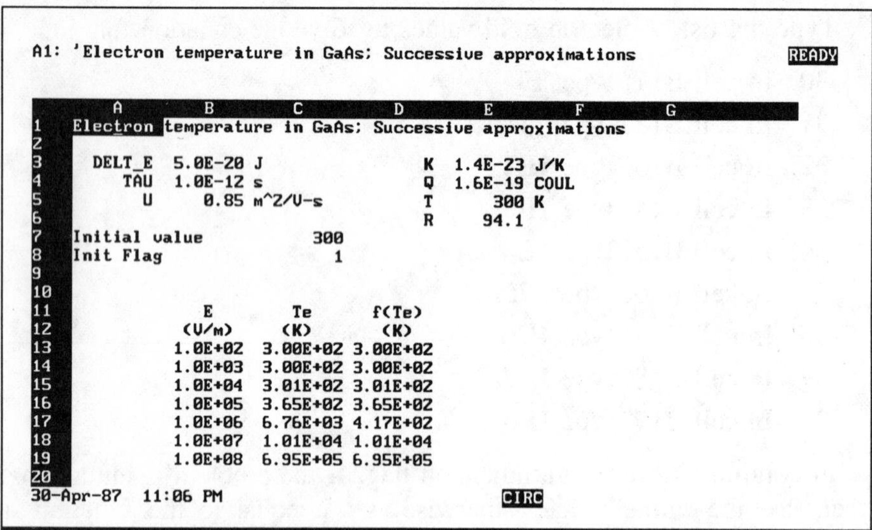

A1: 'Electron temperature in GaAs; Successive approximations READY

Electron temperature in GaAs; Successive approximations

DELT_E	5.0E-20 J		K	1.4E-23 J/K
TAU	1.0E-12 s		Q	1.6E-19 COUL
U	0.85 m^2/V-s		T	300 K
			R	94.1
Initial value		300		
Init Flag		1		

E (V/m)	Te (K)	f(Te) (K)
1.0E+02	3.00E+02	3.00E+02
1.0E+03	3.00E+02	3.00E+02
1.0E+04	3.01E+02	3.01E+02
1.0E+05	3.65E+02	3.65E+02
1.0E+06	6.76E+03	4.17E+02
1.0E+07	1.01E+04	1.01E+04
1.0E+08	6.95E+05	6.95E+05

30-Apr-87 11:06 PM CIRC

Figure 9.3: Electron temperature in GaAs: successive approximations

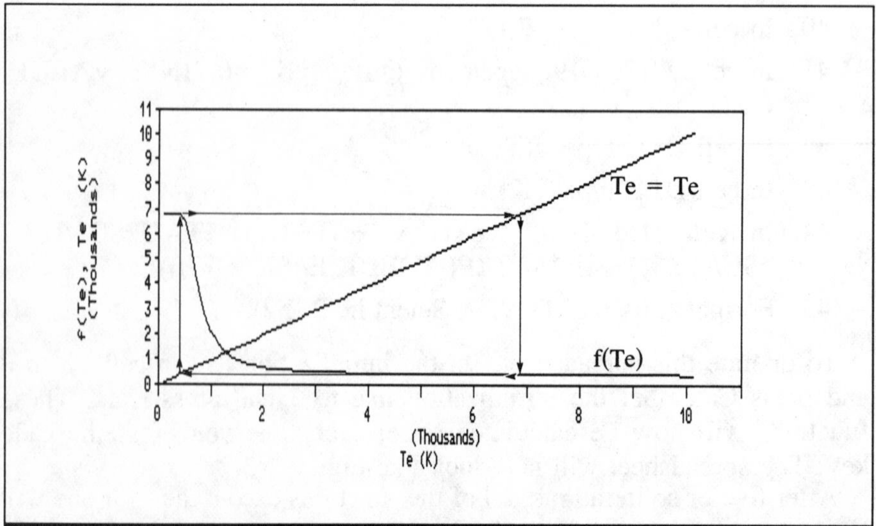

Figure 9.4: Electron temperature in GaAs: plotting $F(Te)$ versus Te at a field of 10^6 V/m to determine the cause of nonconvergence

To correct this problem, use the under-relaxation method.

46. Change cell A1 to **Electron temperature in GaAs; Under relaxation**

Enter a relaxation factor of 0.5 and calculate the new values of *Te* using the under-relaxation equation.

47. In cell A9, type **Relaxation Factor**
48. In cell C9, type **0.5**
49. Name cell C9 as **C**.
50. Change cell D11 to **C*F(Te)+(1-C)*Te**
51. Change cells D13..D19 to **+$C*($T+(2/3)*$TAU*$Q*B13^2 *$U/($K*(1+$R*@EXP(-$DELT_E/($K*C13)))))+(1-$C) *C13**

Now when you iterate the calculation, it quickly converges for all values of the electric field, as shown in Figure 9.5.

■ NEWTON'S METHOD

No discussion of the solution of nonlinear equations would be complete without mentioning Newton's method. The methods that you have

```
A1: 'Electron temperature in GaAs; Under relaxation                    READY

        A        B        C        D        E        F        G
1   Electron temperature in GaAs; Under relaxation
2
3    DELT_E  5.0E-20 J                  K  1.4E-23 J/K
4       TAU  1.0E-12 s                  Q  1.6E-19 COUL
5         U     0.85 m^2/V-s            T      300 K
6                                       R     94.1
7   Initial value              300
8   Init Flag                    1
9   Relaxation Factor          0.5
10
11               E          Te    C*F(Te)+(1-C)*Te
12            (V/m)        (K)       (K)
13          1.0E+02   3.00E+02  3.00E+02
14          1.0E+03   3.00E+02  3.00E+02
15          1.0E+04   3.01E+02  3.01E+02
16          1.0E+05   3.65E+02  3.65E+02
17          1.0E+06   1.28E+03  1.28E+03
18          1.0E+07   1.01E+04  1.01E+04
19          1.0E+08   6.95E+05  6.95E+05
20
30-Apr-87  09:54 PM                                        CALC
```

Figure 9.5: Electron temperature in GaAs: under-relaxation method

been using all converge linearly to the roots of the equations. Newton's method, on the other hand, converges quadratically, yielding much precision in the solution with fewer iterations of the spreadsheet. However, to implement Newton's method you must analytically calculate the derivative of the function.

To use Newton's method, first write your equation as a function equal to 0.

$$g(x) = 0$$

Second, analytically calculate the derivative of the function.

$$g'(x) = \frac{dg(x)}{dx}$$

Finally, calculate the approximations to x.

$$x_0 = \text{initial guess}$$

$$x_1 = x_0 - \frac{g(x_0)}{g'(x_0)}$$

$$x_2 = x_1 - \frac{g(x_1)}{g'(x_1)}$$

$$\vdots$$

$$x_n = x_{n-1} - \frac{g(x_{n-1})}{g'(x_{n-1})}$$

The main drawback of Newton's method is that you must analytically determine the derivative of your function. Although taking the derivative of a function is usually straightforward, it is not always simple. For the electron temperature of GaAs, the function and its derivative are

$$g(Te) = T - Te + \left(\frac{2}{3}\right)\frac{\tau q E^2 \mu}{k}(1+Re^{-\varepsilon/(kTe)})^{-1}$$

$$g'(Te) = -1 - \left(\frac{2}{3}\right)\frac{\tau q E^2 \mu \varepsilon R e^{-\varepsilon/(kTe)}}{k^2 Te^2}(1+Re^{-\varepsilon/(kTe)})^{-2}$$

Modify the spreadsheet to use Newton's method instead of the underrelaxation method.

52. In cell A1, type **Electron temperature in GaAs; Newton's method**
53. Execute the /Range Erase (**/RE**) command for cells A9..C9.

Put the new iteration equation into cells D13 to D19.

54. In cell D11, type **Te-g(Te)/g'(Te)**
55. In cells D13..D19, type/copy **+C13-($T-C13+(2/3)*$TAU *$Q*B13^2*$U/($K*(1+$R*@EXP(-$DELT_E /($K*C13)))))/(-1-(2/3)*$TAU*$Q*B13^2*$U*$DELT_E *$R*@EXP(-$DELT_E/($K*C13))/(($K*C13)^2*(1+$R* @EXP(-$DELT_E/($K*C13)))^2))**

The spreadsheet should now look like Figure 9.6. This spreadsheet works just like the previous ones. Set the value of the initialization flag to **0** and press Calc. Reset the initialization flag to **1** and press Calc again. Each time you press Calc, the spreadsheet is iterated another time.

The increase in speed over the under-relaxation method is dramatic. Under relaxation required 16 iterations of the spreadsheet to converge the calculations to three-place accuracy. Newton's method required only 4 iterations. The successive approximation method needed 5 iterations to converge all but one equation, and that equation would not converge at all.

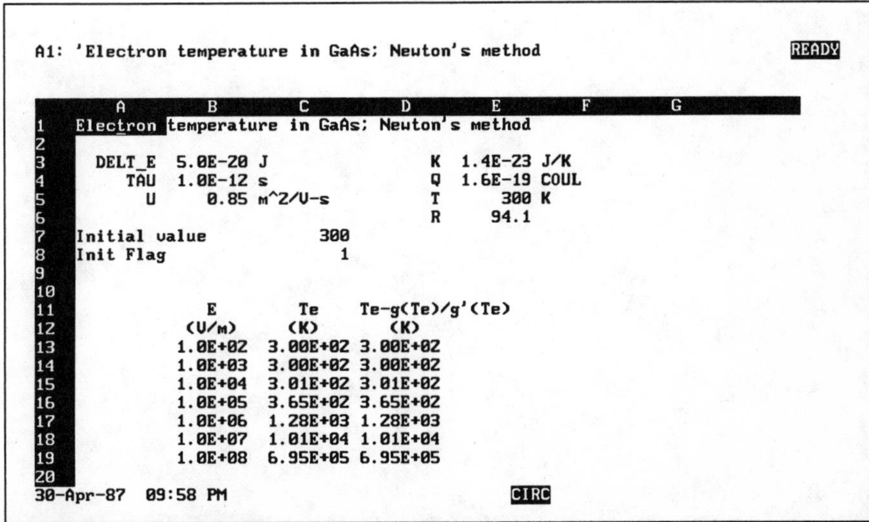

```
A1: 'Electron temperature in GaAs; Newton's method                    READY

     A        B         C         D         E         F         G
1  Electron temperature in GaAs; Newton's method
2
3    DELT_E  5.0E-20 J                     K  1.4E-23 J/K
4       TAU  1.0E-12 s                     Q  1.6E-19 COUL
5         U     0.85 m^2/V-s               T      300 K
6                                          R     94.1
7  Initial value            300
8  Init Flag                  1
9
10
11                E        Te    Te-g(Te)/g'(Te)
12             (V/m)      (K)        (K)
13           1.0E+02  3.00E+02 3.00E+02
14           1.0E+03  3.00E+02 3.00E+02
15           1.0E+04  3.01E+02 3.01E+02
16           1.0E+05  3.65E+02 3.65E+02
17           1.0E+06  1.28E+03 1.28E+03
18           1.0E+07  1.01E+04 1.01E+04
19           1.0E+08  6.95E+05 6.95E+05
20
30-Apr-87  09:58 PM                                CIRC
```

Figure 9.6: Electron temperature in GaAs: Newton's method

■ SUMMARY

In this chapter, we have examined three different methods for solving nonlinear equations with a spreadsheet: successive approximations, under relaxation, and Newton's method. The first two methods will probably solve most of your problems, and Newton's method will usually solve the rest. Several other problem-solving methods can be used; however, those examined in this chapter are the easiest to implement using Lotus 1-2-3.

■ FOR MORE INFORMATION

For further information about the topics discussed here, you can consult the following sources.

Numerical Methods for Solving Nonlinear Equations

C. Gerald, *Applied Numerical Analysis*, 2nd. ed. (Reading, Mass.: Addison-Wesley, 1978).

W. H. Press et. al., *Numerical Recipes: The Art of Scientific Computing* (Cambridge, Eng.: Cambridge University Press, 1986).

Electron Temperature in GaAs

S. M. Sze, *Physics of Semiconductor Devices*, 2nd. ed. (New York: Wiley, 1981), p. 647.

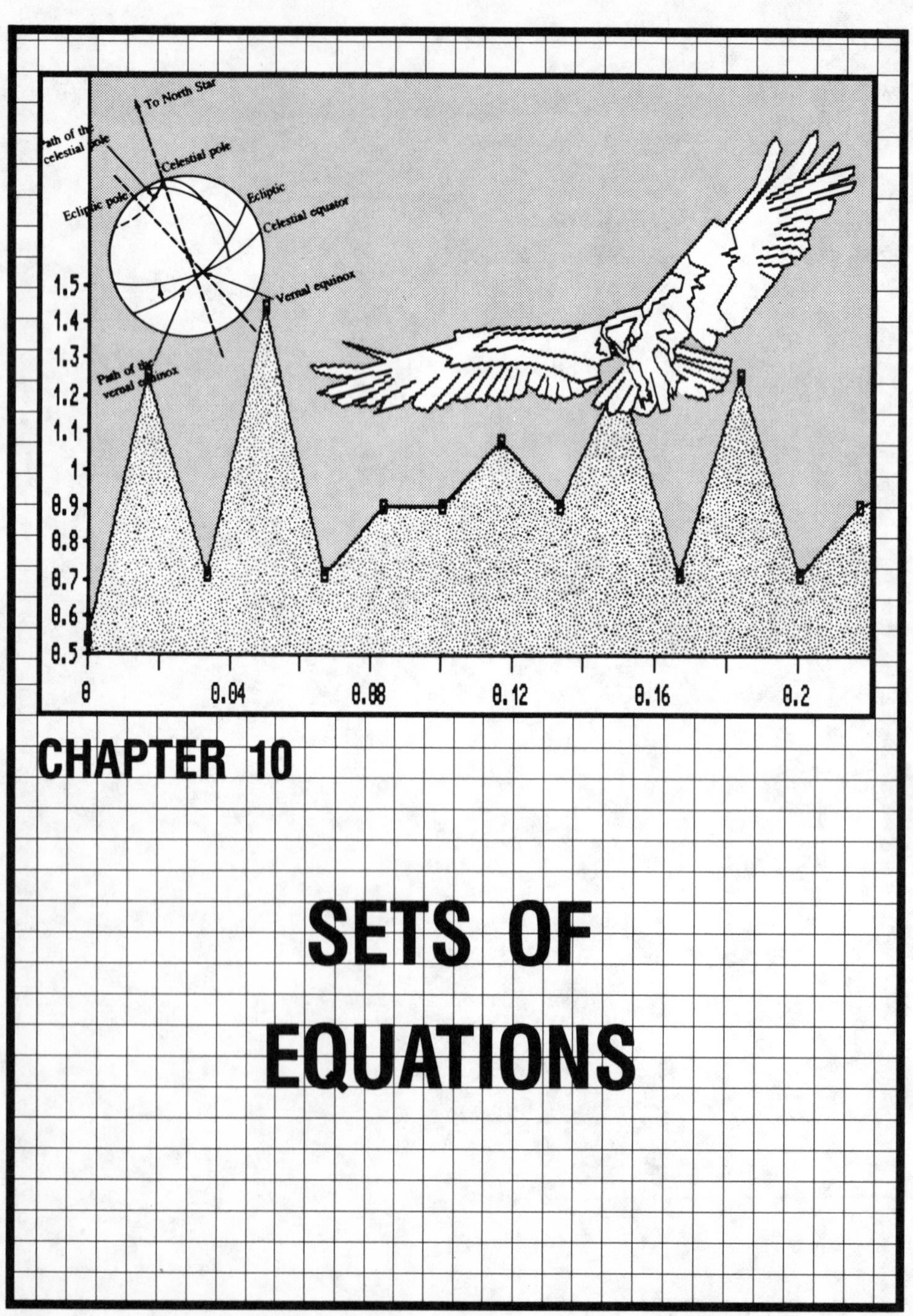

CHAPTER 10

SETS OF EQUATIONS

Many problems in science and engineering result in sets of equations that have to be solved simultaneously. Numerical solutions of partial differential equations, steady-state potentials in electrical networks, and concentration equations for multiple, coupled, chemical reactions are examples of problems that require solving a set of simultaneous equations. Most of these problems result in sets of linear equations, for which there are several good solution methods. If the equations are nonlinear, then relaxation methods will usually work, though they can be difficult to get to converge.

LINEAR EQUATIONS

Most problems that involve simultaneous equations result in sets of linear equations. This is lucky because linear equations are the most straightforward to solve. You can solve most of them with the Lotus 1-2-3 built-in matrix commands. These matrix commands can handle inversion and multiplication of matrices of up to 90 by 90 elements.

The Gauss-Seidel iteration and over/under relaxation methods also work well in a spreadsheet and can be used for linear and nonlinear equations. Gauss-Seidel iteration is the multiequation form of the successive approximations method used with single equations in the last chapter. As you might expect, over/under relaxation is the multiequation analog of the single-equation under-relaxation method.

Matrix Methods

Matrix solutions to sets of linear equations are the simplest to implement with Lotus 1-2-3. First, you must write your set of simultaneous equations in matrix format, as follows:

$$\mathbf{Ax} = \mathbf{b}$$

Here, **A** is the coefficient matrix, **x** is the vector of unknowns, and **b** is the result vector. To solve this matrix equation, multiply both sides from the left by the inverse of **A**:

$$\mathbf{A}^{-1}\mathbf{Ax} = \mathbf{A}^{-1}\mathbf{b}$$

This becomes

$$\mathbf{x} = \mathbf{A}^{-1}\mathbf{b}$$

and you have the solution. Although this seems simple as an abstract equation, calculating the inverse of a matrix is usually not a trivial matter. Luckily, Lotus 1-2-3 has the capability to do this built in: in the /Data Matrix Inverse (/DMI) command.

Three Equations with Three Variables For example, consider the set of linear equations

$$-8x_1 + x_2 + 2x_3 = 0$$

$$5x_1 + 7x_2 - 3x_3 = 10$$

$$2x_1 + x_2 - 2x_3 = -2$$

whose solution is $x_1 = 1$, $x_2 = 2$, $x_3 = 3$. These can easily be put in matrix format.

$$\begin{vmatrix} -8 & 1 & 2 \\ 5 & 7 & -3 \\ 2 & 1 & -2 \end{vmatrix} \begin{vmatrix} x_1 \\ x_2 \\ x_3 \end{vmatrix} = \begin{vmatrix} 0 \\ 10 \\ -2 \end{vmatrix}$$

You can solve this problem easily in a spreadsheet.

1. In cell A1, type **Solving sets of equations; Matrix inversion**
2. In cell B3, type **Ax = b**

Enter the coefficient matrix **A** and the result vector **b**.

3. In cell A5, type **Input Matrix (A)**
4. In cells A6..C8, type the contents of matrix **A**:

   Row 1: **−8 1 2**

   Row 2: **5 7 −3**

   Row 3: **2 1 −2**

5. In cell E5, type **Result Vector (b)**
6. In cells E6..E9, respectively, type the contents of the result vector: **0 10 −2**

Invert matrix **A** and then multiply vector **b** by the inverse of **A**.

7. In cell A10, type **Inverse matrix (1/A)**
8. In cell E10, type **Solution Vector x = (1/A)b**

9. Execute the /Data Matrix Invert (/**DMI**) command and select cells A6..C8 as the input and cells A11..C13 as the output.
10. Execute the /Data Matrix Multiply (/**DMM**) command, select cells A11..C13 as the first matrix ($\mathbf{A}^{-1}$), E6..E8 as the second matrix (**b**) and E11..E13 as the output (**x**).

The spreadsheet should now look like Figure 10.1, with the solution values 1, 2, and 3 for x_1, x_2, and x_3 in cells E11..E13, respectively.

Gauss-Seidel Iteration

Gauss-Seidel iteration is a form of the Jacobi method for solving sets of equations. It is similar to the successive approximations method used in the last chapter. First, solve each of the simultaneous equations for one of the variables, which results in one equation for each variable. To decrease the size of the roundoff error, try to solve for the variables with the largest coefficients. Pick a set of initial guesses of the values of the variables. Insert them into the equations and calculate a new set of values. Put these values back into the equations and calculate another set of values. Continue this process until the values converge.

If you were to calculate all of the new values using only the old values, you would be using Jacobi iteration. However, since the equations

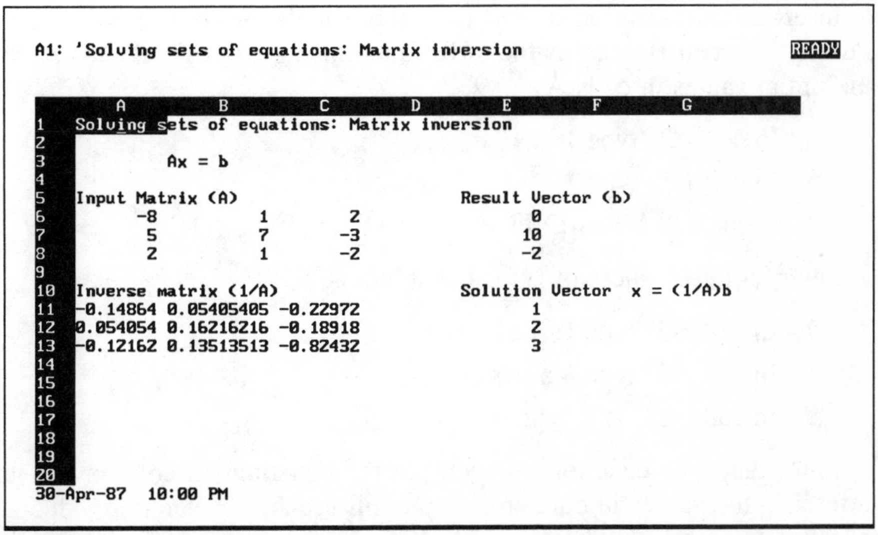

```
A1: 'Solving sets of equations: Matrix inversion                       READY

      A         B         C         D         E         F         G
1   Solving sets of equations: Matrix inversion
2
3            Ax = b
4
5   Input Matrix (A)                      Result Vector (b)
6       -8         1         2                   0
7        5         7        -3                  10
8        2         1        -2                  -2
9
10  Inverse matrix (1/A)                  Solution Vector  x = (1/A)b
11  -0.14864 0.05405405 -0.22972                 1
12  0.054054 0.16216216 -0.18918                 2
13  -0.12162 0.13513513 -0.82432                 3
14
15
16
17
18
19
20
30-Apr-87  10:00 PM
```

Figure 10.1: Solving simultaneous linear equations with the Lotus 1-2-3 matrix commands

are calculated in order, some of the new values are available before you finish calculating each of the equations. If you use these new values as soon as they are available rather than waiting for the next iteration, then you are using Gauss-Seidel iteration.

Applying Gauss-Seidel iteration to the preceding problem, first solve the equations for each of the variables.

$$x_1 = \left(\frac{1}{8}\right)(x_2 + 2x_3)$$

$$x_2 = \left(\frac{1}{7}\right)(10 - 5x_1 + 3x_3)$$

$$x_3 = \left(\frac{1}{2}\right)(2 + 2x_1 + x_2)$$

Create a spreadsheet to solve these equations using Gauss-Seidel iteration.

1. Execute the /Worksheet Global Recalculation Manual (**/WGRM**) command.
2. Change the width of column B to **11**.
3. In cell A1, type **Solving sets of equations: Gauss-Seidel iteration**

Insert an initialization flag to reset the calculation to a known state. Putting 0 in cell B3 causes the @IF functions in cells B7..B9 to return the initial values in cells A7..A9.

4. In cell A3, type **Init Flag**
5. In cell B3, type **1**
6. Name cell B3 as **INIT**.

Enter an initial guess of 0 for the solution.

7. In cell A5, type **Initial**
8. In cell A6, type **Values**
9. In cells A7..A9, type **0**

Enter the three equations. If you put the equations in column C and reference the values in column B, you will use Jacobi iteration. This is because column B will be calculated before column C, so column B will get the old values, and then column C will use these to calculate the new values. Since you want to use Gauss-Seidel iteration, put the equations in column B so that they can be solved and then referenced in column C.

10. In cell B5, type **Equations**
11. In cell B7, type **(C8+2*C9)/8**
12. In cell B8, type **(10-5*C7+3*C9)/7**
13. In cell B9, type **(2+2*C7+C8)/2**

Reference the equations, creating a circular reference, and perform the initialization test.

14. In cell C5, type **Solutions**
15. In cells C7..C9, type/copy **@IF($INIT=0,A7,B7)**

To use this spreadsheet, set the initialization flag to **0** in cell B3 and press Calc. Once the spreadsheet has been initialized, change the initialization flag to **1** and press Calc again. Each time that you press Calc, the spreadsheet will be iterated once. Continue iterating until the values converge. Your spreadsheet should look like Figure 10.2.

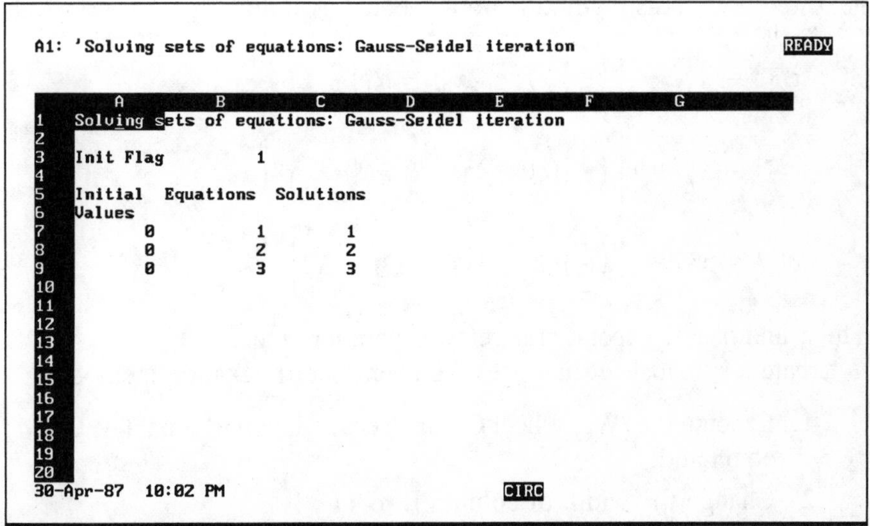

Figure 10.2: Solving simultaneous linear equations: Gauss-Seidel iteration

If you are solving a set of equations that are slow to converge, then execute the /Worksheet Global Recalculation Iteration (/WGRI) command and specify the number of iterations to be performed each time you press Calc. You could also write a macro to recalculate the spreadsheet and then test the change in the solution. If the solution has changed less than some threshold value, quit; otherwise recalculate it again. A macro of this type appears in the next chapter.

Over/Under Relaxation

As was the case with single equations, you can often cause a problem to converge more quickly or more stably by adjusting the amount of correction applied to the values during each iteration. The over/under relaxation method adds the fraction c of the calculated correction to the values during each step. The fraction c can be either greater than or less than 1. If c equals 1, this method is equivalent to the Jacobi or Gauss-Seidel method.

First, calculate a new value for each of the unknowns as you did for the Gauss-Seidel method. Second, instead of using this value in the next iteration, subtract the old value of each unknown to find the change in the unknown. Third, multiply the change in the unknown by c and then add it to the old value of the unknown. This is the value to use in the next iteration. This method is implemented as follows:

$$x_1^{n+1} = x_1^n + c\left[\left(\frac{1}{8}\right)(x_2^n + 2x_3^n) - x_1^n\right]$$

$$x_2^{n+1} = x_2^n + c\left[\left(\frac{1}{7}\right)(10 - 5x_1^n + 3x_3^n) - x_2^n\right]$$

$$x_3^{n+1} = x_3^n + c\left[\left(\frac{1}{2}\right)(2 + 2x_1^n + x_2^n) - x_3^n\right]$$

The n and $n + 1$ superscripts refer to iteration n and $n + 1$.

Create a spreadsheet that uses the over/under relaxation method.

1. Execute the /Worksheet Global Recalculation Manual (**/WGRM**) command.
2. Change the width of column B to **11**.
3. In cell A1, type **Solving sets of equations: Over/Under Relaxation**

This spreadsheet has both an initialization flag and a relaxation factor. The initialization flag sets the calculation to a predefined initial state. The relaxation factor multiplies the change in the values to increase or decrease the amount of correction applied at each iteration.

4. In cell A3, type **Init Flag**
5. In cell C3, type **1**
6. In cell A4, type **Relaxation factor**
7. In cell C4, type **0.5**
8. Name cells C3 and C4 as **INIT** and **C**.

Enter **0** as the initial guess for the solution values. You can insert any reasonable values here; the closer they are to the solution, the faster the equations will converge.

9. In cell A6, type **Initial**
10. In cell A7, type **Values**
11. In cells A8..A10, type/copy **0**

Enter the relaxation equations. These resemble the equations used in the Gauss-Seidel method, except that a relaxation factor controls the amount of change in each value. Create these equations by subtracting the old value from the equation, multiplying by *c*, and then adding the old value to the result.

12. In cell B6, type **Equations**
13. In cell B8, type **+C8+$C*(((C9+2*C10)/8)-C8)**
14. In cell B9, type **+C9+$C*(((10-5*C8+3*C10)/7)-C9)**
15. In cell B10, type **+C10+$C*(((2+2*C8+C9)/2)-C10)**

Create the circular references and perform the initialization.

16. In cell C6, type **Solutions**
17. In cells C8..C10, type/copy **@IF($INIT=0,A8,B8)**

To use this spreadsheet, set the value of the relaxation factor in C4. A value of **0.5** seems to work well for this problem. Different problems will respond differently to the value of the relaxation factor. While any value can be used, I doubt that you could get the spreadsheet to converge with a value greater than about 2. Smaller values are generally more stable but do not converge as fast. Usually, you should start with a value of 1 or 1.5 and see whether the spreadsheet is converging. If it is converging, then increase the value; otherwise decrease it. You do not have to reinitialize the spreadsheet when you change the value of the relaxation factor, so long as the calculated solution values are still reasonable. If the solution values have started to diverge, then you will have to reinitialize the spreadsheet to get them back near the true solution.

Next, set the value of the initialization flag in cell C3 to 0 and press Calc. Change the initialization flag to 1 and press Calc again. Continue pressing Calc until the values converge. When the spreadsheet converges, it should look like Figure 10.3. As mentioned in the last problem, you do not have to sit at your computer and press Calc 50 times each time you want to iterate your equations. By turning on the spreadsheet's iteration capability, you can iterate the spreadsheet up to 50 times each time you press Calc. Just execute the /Worksheet Global Recalculation Iteration (**/WGRI**) command and specify the number of iterations.

■ NONLINEAR EQUATIONS

Probably the most useful method for solving multiple simultaneous nonlinear equations is the over/under relaxation method used in the last section for linear equations. Although the Gauss-Seidel or Jacobi methods may result in convergence, the extra control of the over/under relaxation method is usually needed to get the equations to converge. You apply this method just as you do for the linear equations.

Nonlinear equations may have multiple solutions, so the starting value may be important. If the equations are extremely nonlinear, they may not converge if the initial values are too far from the solution. Try changing those values as well as the relaxation factor if you have trouble getting a solution.

■ ACCURACY AND SCALING

An unfortunate consequence of using matrix and iteration methods to solve simultaneous sets of equations is that the accuracy of the solution can depend on the order in which you solve the equations. You should

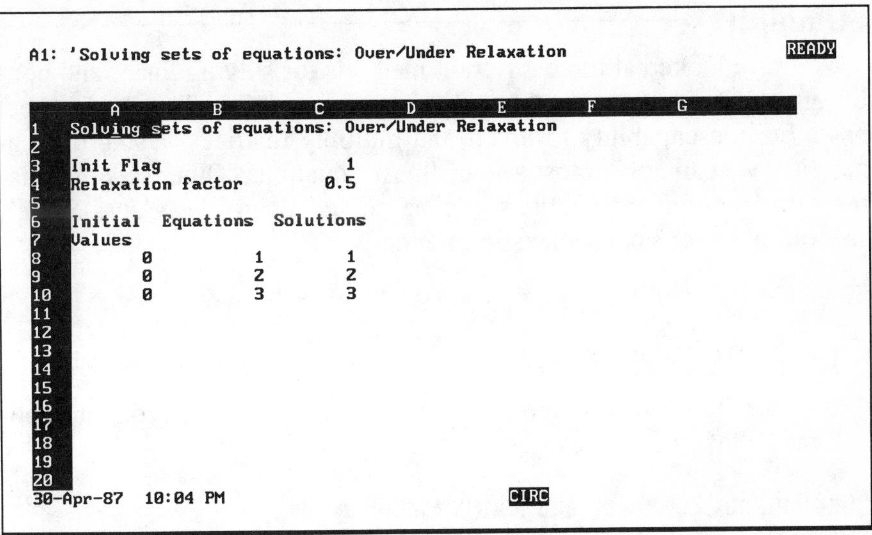

Figure 10.3: Solving simultaneous linear equations: over/under relaxation method

always solve the equations starting with the variable with the largest coefficient (ignoring the sign of the coefficient) relative to the rest of the coefficients in the equation. If you end up with one equation solved for each variable, then you are done, but that is not usually the case, so you will have to use your own judgment to decide which equation to solve for which variable.

When you are using the matrix methods of the first problem, the relative size of the values in the coefficient matrix that you are solving is also important. All of the values in the coefficient matrix should be approximately the same order of magnitude. If one equation has coefficients that are several orders of magnitude larger or smaller than any of the others, then the solution will suffer. To correct this situation, scale the equations by dividing each of the coefficients in an equation by the magnitude of the largest coefficient in that equation. When you scale an equation, do not forget to also scale the result (that is, the *b* values on the right sides of the equations).

If you have trouble getting a solution, review matrix methods in a good numerical methods book. Of course, if your matrix is singular (that is, it has a zero on the diagonal), you will never get a solution.

■ SUMMARY

We have looked at three different methods for solving linear and nonlinear sets of simultaneous equations with Lotus 1-2-3. This spreadsheet has a built-in capability to invert and multiply matrices. Using this capability, we can solve most sets of linear equations. Other sets of equations and nonlinear equations can be solved using the Gauss-Seidel, Jacobi, and over/under relaxation methods.

■ FOR MORE INFORMATION

For more information about the topics discussed here, you can consult the following sources.

Simultaneous Equations and Matrix Methods

C. Gerald, *Applied Numerical Analysis*, 2nd. ed. (Reading, Mass.: Addison-Wesley, 1978).

W. H. Press et. al., *Numerical Recipes: The Art of Scientific Computing* (Cambridge, Eng.: Cambridge University Press, 1986).

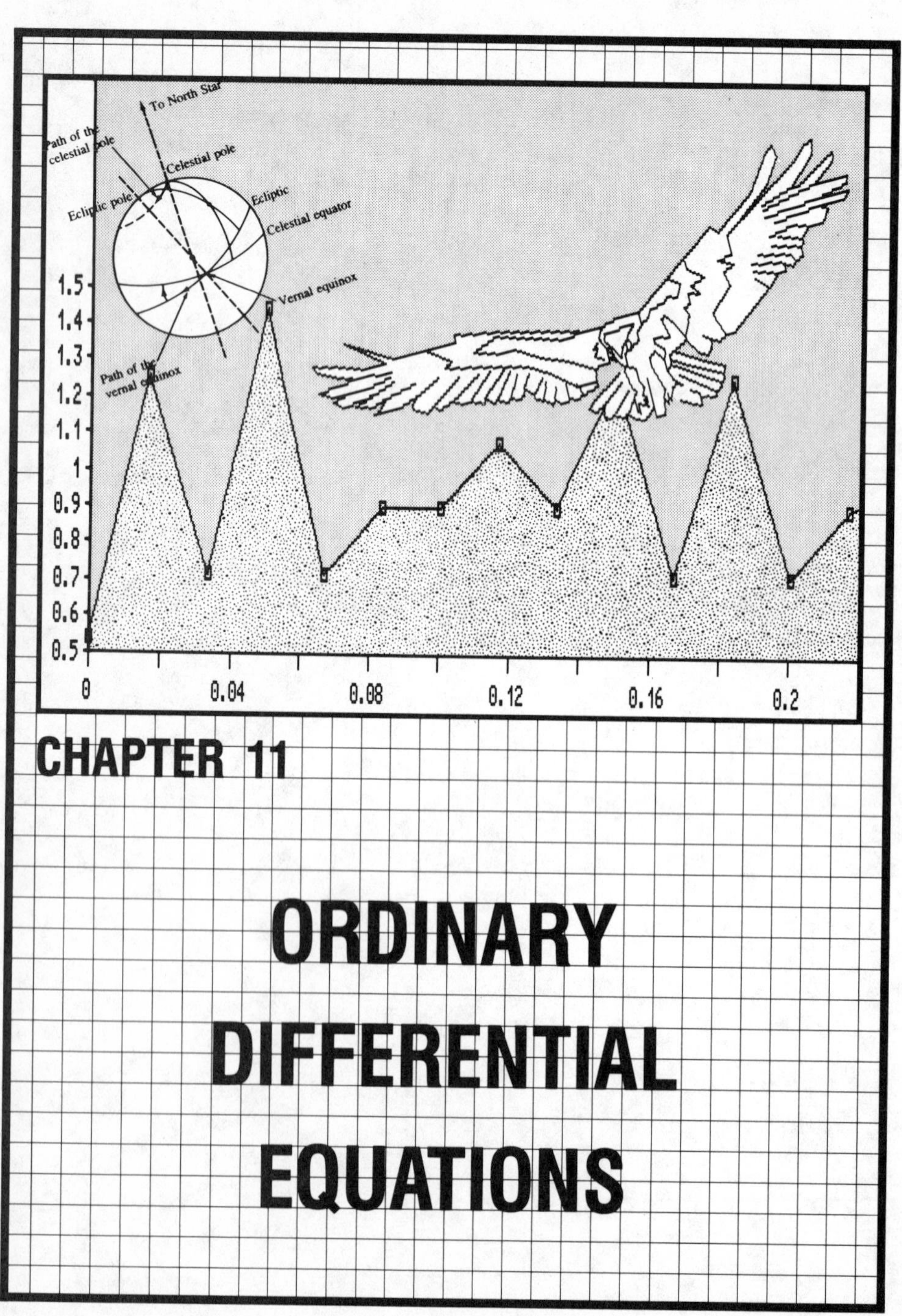

CHAPTER 11

ORDINARY DIFFERENTIAL EQUATIONS

Now comes the fun stuff. Most people do not think of a spreadsheet program when they have to solve a differential equation. However, a spreadsheet, with its dynamically linked cells and iterative capability, can do an excellent job of solving many differential equations. Two kinds of problems involving ordinary differential equations are readily solved on a spreadsheet: initial-value problems and boundary-value problems. The differential equations for initial-value problems and boundary-value problems can be the same; the difference is in the boundary conditions available.

INITIAL-VALUE PROBLEMS

Initial-value problems are those in which the known boundary conditions are all at one boundary of the problem. The goal is to integrate the differential equation from that (known) boundary to the other. Differential equations with time derivatives are often of this type: You know the value of the solution now (the known boundary) and have to integrate the differential equation for some time into the future (the unknown boundary). There are many ways to solve these equations. In this section, you will examine four of the most popular solution methods: the Taylor series method, the Euler and modified Euler methods, and the Runge-Kutta method.

An Initial-Value Ordinary Differential Equation Consider the following first-order ordinary differential equation:

$$(1 + x^2)^{1/2} \frac{\mathrm{d}u(x)}{\mathrm{d}x} + u(x) = x \qquad x > 0$$

$$u(0) = 0$$

This is an initial-value problem because the boundary condition is known at only one location. Actually, first-order, ordinary differential equations with one variable should have only one boundary condition. If there were more than one boundary condition, the problem would be overspecified and possibly unsolvable. Second- and higher-order differential equations, of course, require more boundary conditions to be solved. The problem is to calculate the value of u over the range $x = 0$ to 0.2. For this problem, I happen to know that the analytical solution is

$$u(x) = \frac{1}{2}\left[x - \frac{\text{Ln}(x + \sqrt{1 + x^2})}{(x + \sqrt{1 + x^2})}\right]$$

which you will use to evaluate the effectiveness of the different solution methods. Figure 11.1 shows this solution over the range $x = 0$ to 0.2.

Taylor Series Method

One of the more popular methods for solving an initial-value problem is the Taylor series method. Consider the Taylor series expansion of some function $u(x)$ about the value x_0:

$$u(x) = u(x_0) + \frac{(x - x_0)}{1!}u'(x_0) + \frac{(x - x_0)^2}{2!}u''(x_0) + \frac{(x - x_0)^3}{3!}u'''(x_0) + \frac{(x - x_0)^4}{4!}u''''(x_0) + \cdots$$

Here, I have used the notation

$$u'(x) = \frac{du(x)}{dx},\ u''(x) = \frac{d^2u(x)}{dx^2},\ \ldots$$

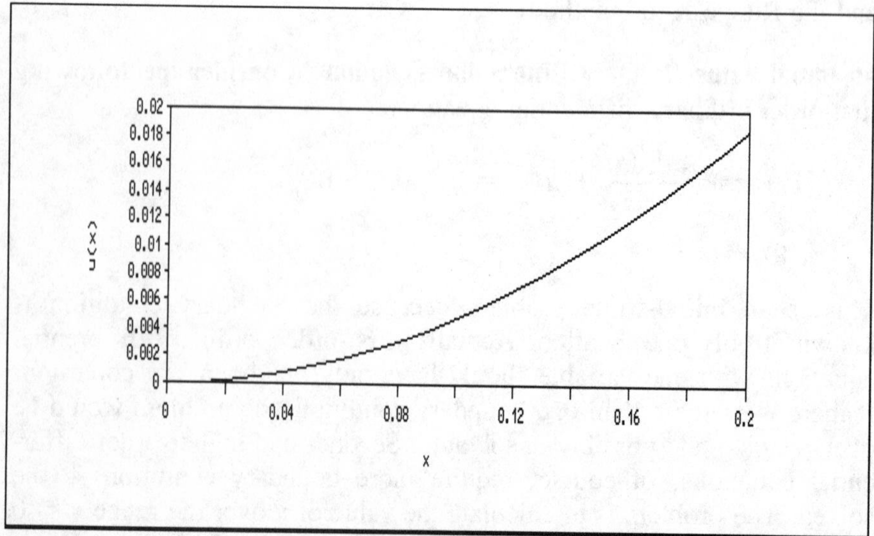

Figure 11.1: Analytic solution to an initial-value problem

If we let $h = (x - x_0)$, then the equation becomes

$$u(x) = u(x_0) + \frac{h}{1!}u'(x_0) + \frac{h^2}{2!}u''(x_0) + \frac{h^3}{3!}u'''(x_0) + \frac{h^4}{4!}u''''(x_0) + \cdots$$

Looking at the differential equation, you will note that for $x_0 = 0$, you know the values of the first two terms of the Taylor series—you know the first from the boundary condition and the second from the differential equation. They are

$$u(0) = 0$$

$$u'(x) = \frac{(x - u(x))}{(1 + x^2)^{1/2}}$$

By successively taking derivatives of the equation for the first derivative, you can get values for the higher-order derivatives,

$$u''(x) = \frac{(1 - u'(x))}{(1 + x^2)^{1/2}} - \frac{x(x - u(x))}{(1 + x^2)^{3/2}}$$

$$u'''(x) = -\frac{u''(x)}{(1 + x^2)^{1/2}} - \frac{2x(1 - u'(x)) + x - u(x)}{(1 + x^2)^{3/2}} + \frac{3x^2(x - u(x))}{(1 + x^2)^{5/2}}$$

$$u''''(x) = -\frac{u'''(x)}{(1 + x^2)^{1/2}} + \frac{3xu''(x) - 3(1 - u'(x))}{(1 + x^2)^{3/2}} + \frac{9x^2(1 - u'(x)) + 9x(x - u(x))}{(1 + x^2)^{5/2}} - \frac{15x^2(x - u(x))}{(1 + x^2)^{7/2}}$$

from which you get

$$u(0) = 0$$

$$u'(0) = 0$$

$$u''(0) = 1$$

$$u'''(0) = -1$$

$$u''''(0) = -2$$

Insert these values into the first five terms of the Taylor expansion and then truncate the expansion after the fifth term. This creates the approximation function

$$u(h) = \frac{h^2}{2} - \frac{h^3}{6} - \frac{h^4}{12}$$

which can be used to calculate values of the differential equation for different values of h, so long as h is small. Use the Taylor expansion to calculate the values of $u(x)$ for $x = 0$ to 0.2.

1. Change the widths of columns A..D according to the following list: A = 7, B = **12**, C = **11**, D = **11**
2. In cell A1, type **Ordinary Differential Equations; Taylor series method**

Enter the x-range data and calculate the value of the analytic solution to the problem for use as a comparison.

3. In cell A3, type **^x**
4. Execute the /Data Fill (**/DF**) command and select cells A5..A25 as the range; set the starting value to **0**, set the step to **0.01**, and accept the default upper limit.
5. Format cells A5..A25 as Fixed 2 **(F2)**.
6. In cell B3, type **^u(x)**
7. In cell B4, type **^Analytical**
8. In cells B5..B25, type/copy **0.5*(A5-@LN(A5+@SQRT(1+A5^2))/(A5+@SQRT(1+A5^2)))**

Use the Taylor expansion to calculate the solution of the partial differential equation. Compare this value with the correct value in column B.

9. In cell C3, type **^u(x)**
10. In cell C4, type **^Taylor**
11. In cells C5..C25, type/copy **+A5^2/2-A5^3/6-A5^4/12**
12. Format cells B5..C25 as Scientific 2 (**S2**).
13. In cell D3, type **^Error**
14. In cell D4, type **^%**
15. In cells D6..D25, type/copy **(B6-C6)/B6**
16. Format cells D6..D25 as Percent 5 (**P5**).

Your spreadsheet should now look like Figure 11.2. Note that the solution is extremely accurate for these small values of x. If you try larger values of x (say, 0 to 2), the error will be quite large. You must use values of h (x in this case, since $x_0 = 0$) that are less than 1 for this method to be accurate. Note that for the Taylor series method, h is measured from x_0 and is not the step size that will be used in the rest of these problems. To calculate values of u over longer distances, you must recalculate the values of the derivatives at the end of the current step so that you can take another step beyond that point.

Euler and Modified Euler Methods

One of the major difficulties with the Taylor series method is that you must analytically calculate several derivatives of your equation. While some equations may have simple derivatives, others, such as the one used in the preceding example, do not. The Euler method eliminates calculation of these derivatives by truncating the Taylor series at the first derivative term. To make the Euler method work, you must use small steps (h) and recalculate the value of the first derivative at each step.

$$u(x + h) = u(x) + hu'(x)$$

A1: [W7] 'Ordinary Differential Equations: Taylor series method READY

	A	B	C	D	E	F	G
1	Ordinary Differential Equations: Taylor series method						
2							
3	x	u(x)	u(x)	Error			
4		Analytical	Taylor	%			
5	0.00	0.00E+00	0.00E+00				
6	0.01	4.98E-05	4.98E-05	0.00001%			
7	0.02	1.99E-04	1.99E-04	0.00011%			
8	0.03	4.45E-04	4.45E-04	0.00037%			
9	0.04	7.89E-04	7.89E-04	0.00088%			
10	0.05	1.23E-03	1.23E-03	0.00174%			
11	0.06	1.76E-03	1.76E-03	0.00303%			
12	0.07	2.39E-03	2.39E-03	0.00486%			
13	0.08	3.11E-03	3.11E-03	0.00731%			
14	0.09	3.92E-03	3.92E-03	0.01049%			
15	0.10	4.83E-03	4.83E-03	0.01451%			
16	0.11	5.82E-03	5.82E-03	0.01946%			
17	0.12	6.90E-03	6.89E-03	0.02547%			
18	0.13	8.06E-03	8.06E-03	0.03263%			
19	0.14	9.31E-03	9.31E-03	0.04106%			
20	0.15	1.07E-02	1.06E-02	0.05089%			

14-May-87 11:19 PM

Figure 11.2: Solution to an initial-value problem using the Taylor series method

Create a spreadsheet to calculate the differential equation using the Euler method. You can use the spreadsheet that you set up for the Taylor series example since the layouts of the two spreadsheets are similar.

1. Change the widths of columns A..F according to the following list: A = **7**, B = **12**, C = **11**, D = **11**, E = **11**, F = **9**.
2. In cell A1, type **Ordinary Differential Equation; Euler and modified Euler methods**

Enter the x-range of data and calculate the value of the analytic solution to the problem to use as a comparison. These two columns are identical to those in the Taylor series problem, so you can reuse part of that spreadsheet if you want to.

3. In cell A3, type **^x**
4. Execute the /Data Fill (**/DF**) command and select cells A5..A25 as the range; set the starting value to **0**, set the step to **0.01**, and accept the default upper limit.
5. Format cells A5..A25 as Fixed 2 (**F2**).
6. In cell B3, type **^u(x)**
7. In cell B4, type **^Analytical**
8. In cells B5..B25, type/copy **0.5*(A5-@LN(A5+@SQRT(1+A5^2))/(A5+@SQRT(1+A5^2)))**

Calculate the solution of the equation using the Euler method.

9. In cell C4, type **^Euler**
10. In cell C5, type **0**
11. In cells C6..C25, type/copy **+C5+(A6-A5)*(A5-C5)/@SQRT(1+A5^2)**
12. Format cells B5..C25 as Scientific 2 (**S2**).

Your spreadsheet should now look like Figure 11.3. As you can see, the accuracy of this method is not very high. Since you are using the slope (the derivative) at the beginning of a step to determine the value at the end of the step, the method will be in error every time, and the error is additive and will grow as you continue to integrate. A better way to estimate the value of the next point is to use the average slope over a step:

$$u(x + h) = u(x) + h\frac{(u'(x) + u'(x + h))}{2}$$

```
A1: [W7] 'Ordinary Differential Equation; Euler and modified Euler methods READY

      A          B              C          D       E       F       G
1   Ordinary Differential Equation; Euler and modified Euler methods
2
3      x        u(x)
4            Analytical      Euler
5     0.00    0.00E+00     0.00E+00
6     0.01    4.98E-05     0.00E+00
7     0.02    1.99E-04     1.00E-04
8     0.03    4.45E-04     2.99E-04
9     0.04    7.89E-04     5.96E-04
10    0.05    1.23E-03     9.90E-04
11    0.06    1.76E-03     1.48E-03
12    0.07    2.39E-03     2.06E-03
13    0.08    3.11E-03     2.74E-03
14    0.09    3.92E-03     3.51E-03
15    0.10    4.83E-03     4.37E-03
16    0.11    5.82E-03     5.32E-03
17    0.12    6.90E-03     6.36E-03
18    0.13    8.06E-03     7.49E-03
19    0.14    9.31E-03     8.71E-03
20    0.15    1.07E-02     1.00E-02
14-May-87  08:41 PM
```

Figure 11.3: Solution to an initial-value problem using the Euler method

The difficulty with this approach is that you do not know the value of the slope at the end of the step. The modified Euler method uses the Euler method to make an initial estimate of the solution. This initial estimate is then used to calculate the value of the slope at the end of the step. Using the average value of the slopes, you can now calculate a better value for the solution. You could apply this method again to try to improve the solution, but using more than one or two iterations will not gain you any accuracy, as the error in the method will be as large as any increase in accuracy gained by iteration.

Recalculate the spreadsheet using the modified Euler method. First calculate the initial prediction of the solution using the Euler method.

13. In cell D3, type '(4 spaces)**Modified Euler**
14. In cell D4, type **^Predicted**
15. In cells D6..D25, type/copy **+E5+(A6-A5)*(A5-E5)/@SQRT(1+A5^2)**

Use that initial prediction to calculate the average slope and to calculate a corrected value of the solution. Compare that value to the analytic solution.

16. In cell E4, type **^Corrected**
17. In cell E5, type **0**

18. In cells E6..E25, type/copy **+E5+((A6-A5)/2)*((A5-E5)/@SQRT(1+A5^2)+(A6-C6)/@SQRT(1+A6^2))**
19. Format cells D5..E25 as Scientific 2 (**S2**).
20. In cell F3, type **^Error**
21. In cell F4, type **^%**
22. In cells F6..F25, type/copy **(B6-E6)/B6**
23. Format cells F6..F25 as Percent 2 (**P2**).

Your spreadsheet should now look like Figure 11.4. Note that the solution has improved tremendously, with the error staying at about a quarter of a percent. You can use the modified Euler method to solve for large values of x, so long as you take small steps to get there.

Runge-Kutta Method

The current method of choice for most initial-value problems is the fourth-order Runge-Kutta method. The fourth-order Runge-Kutta method uses a combination of four estimators of the solution to calculate an accurate value of the solution. The development of the method is a bit too involved, mathematically, to present here, so I will only state the result. If you are interested in the background of this problem, any

A1: [W7] 'Ordinary Differential Equation; Euler and modified Euler methods READY

	A	B	C	D	E	F	G
1	Ordinary Differential Equation; Euler and modified Euler methods						
2							
3	x	u(x)		Modified Euler		Error	
4		Analytical	Euler	Predicted	Corrected	%	
5	0.00	0.00E+00	0.00E+00		0		
6	0.01	4.98E-05	0.00E+00	0.00E+00	5.00E-05	-0.33%	
7	0.02	1.99E-04	1.00E-04	1.49E-04	1.99E-04	-0.29%	
8	0.03	4.45E-04	2.99E-04	3.97E-04	4.47E-04	-0.27%	
9	0.04	7.89E-04	5.96E-04	7.42E-04	7.91E-04	-0.26%	
10	0.05	1.23E-03	9.90E-04	1.18E-03	1.23E-03	-0.26%	
11	0.06	1.76E-03	1.48E-03	1.72E-03	1.77E-03	-0.25%	
12	0.07	2.39E-03	2.06E-03	2.35E-03	2.40E-03	-0.25%	
13	0.08	3.11E-03	2.74E-03	3.07E-03	3.12E-03	-0.25%	
14	0.09	3.92E-03	3.51E-03	3.89E-03	3.93E-03	-0.25%	
15	0.10	4.83E-03	4.37E-03	4.79E-03	4.84E-03	-0.24%	
16	0.11	5.82E-03	5.32E-03	5.78E-03	5.83E-03	-0.24%	
17	0.12	6.90E-03	6.36E-03	6.87E-03	6.91E-03	-0.24%	
18	0.13	8.06E-03	7.49E-03	8.04E-03	8.08E-03	-0.24%	
19	0.14	9.31E-03	8.71E-03	9.29E-03	9.34E-03	-0.24%	
20	0.15	1.07E-02	1.00E-02	1.06E-02	1.07E-02	-0.23%	

14-May-87 09:57 PM

Figure 11.4: Solution to an initial-value problem using the Euler and modified Euler methods

good numerical methods book will describe it. The development of a step with the Runge-Kutta method is as follows:

$$u(x + h) = u(x) + \frac{1}{6}(k_1 + 2k_2 + 2k_3 + k_4)$$

Here,

$$k_1 = hu'(x, u(x))$$

$$k_2 = hu'\left(x + \frac{h}{2}, u(x) + \frac{k_1}{2}\right)$$

$$k_3 = hu'\left(x + \frac{h}{2}, u(x) + \frac{k_2}{2}\right)$$

$$k_4 = hu'(x + h, u(x) + k_3)$$

Recalculate the spreadsheet, this time using the Runge-Kutta method. This problem uses the same differential equation and setup as the last two problems.

1. Change the widths of columns A..H according to the following list, A = **7**, B = **11**, C = **9**, D = **9**, E = **9**, F = **9**, G = **9**, H = **9**
2. In cell A1, type **Ordinary Differential Equations; Runge-Kutta method**

Enter the x-range of data and calculate the value of the analytic solution to the problem to use as a comparison. These two columns are identical to those in the Taylor series and Euler method problems, so you can reuse parts of those spreadsheets if you want to.

3. In cell A3, type **^x**
4. Execute the /Data Fill (**/DF**) command and select cells A5..A25 as the range; set the starting value to **0**, set the step to **0.01**, and accept the default upper limit.
5. Format cells A5..A25 as Fixed 2 (**F2**).
6. In cell B3, type **^u(x)**
7. In cell B4, type **^Analytical**
8. In cells B5..B25, type/copy **0.5*(A5-@LN(A5+@SQRT (1+A5^2))/(A5+@SQRT(1+A5^2)))**

Calculate the values of the four estimators. These estimators will be used to advance to the next step.

9. In cell C3, type **^k1**
10. In cells C5..C24, type/copy **(A6-A5)*(A5-G5)/ @SQRT (1+A5^2)**
11. In cell D3, type **^k2**
12. In cells D5..D24, type/copy **(A6-A5)*((A5+(A6-A5)/2)-(G5+C5/2))/@SQRT(1+(A5+(A6-A5)/2)^2)**
13. In cell E3, type **^k3**
14. In cells E5..E24, type/copy **(A6-A5)*((A5+(A6-A5)/2)-(G5+D5/2))/@SQRT(1+(A5+(A6-A5)/2)^2)**
15. In cell F3, type **^k4**
16. In cells F5..F24, type **(A6-A5)*(A6-(G5+E5))/ @SQRT (1+A6^2)**

Calculate the solution of the problem by combining the values of the estimators. Compare the solution to the analytic result.

17. In cell G3, type **^u(x)**
18. In cell G5, type **0**
19. In cell G6..G25, type/copy **+G5+(1/6)*(C5+2*D5+2 *E5+F5)**
20. Format cells B5..G25 as Scientific 2 **(S2)**.
21. In cell H3, type **^Error**
22. In cell H4, type **^%**
23. In cells H6..H25, type/copy **(B6-G6)*100/B6**
24. Format cells H6..H25 as Scientific 1 **(S1)**.

Now you see some real improvement in accuracy in Figure 11.5. Although this method does require five spreadsheet columns, the largest error is 3×10^{-6} percent. This is several orders of magnitude better than the other three methods.

Higher-Order Equations

Boundary-value problems are not always first-order differential equations. Often they are second- or third-order equations. To solve these

A1: [W7] 'Ordinary Differential Equations; Runge-Kutta method READY

	A	B	C	D	E	F	G	H
1	Ordinary Differential Equations; Runge-Kutta method							
2								
3	x	u(x)	k1	k2	k3	k4	u(x)	Error
4		Analytical						%
5	0.00	0.00E+00	0.00E+00	5.00E-05	4.97E-05	9.95E-05	0.00E+00	
6	0.01	4.98E-05	9.95E-05	1.49E-04	1.49E-04	1.98E-04	4.98E-05	-1.3E-06
7	0.02	1.99E-04	1.98E-04	2.47E-04	2.47E-04	2.95E-04	1.99E-04	-6.3E-07
8	0.03	4.45E-04	2.95E-04	3.44E-04	3.44E-04	3.92E-04	4.45E-04	-4.2E-07
9	0.04	7.89E-04	3.92E-04	4.40E-04	4.39E-04	4.87E-04	7.89E-04	-3.1E-07
10	0.05	1.23E-03	4.87E-04	5.34E-04	5.34E-04	5.81E-04	1.23E-03	-2.5E-07
11	0.06	1.76E-03	5.81E-04	6.28E-04	6.28E-04	6.74E-04	1.76E-03	-2.1E-07
12	0.07	2.39E-03	6.74E-04	7.21E-04	7.20E-04	7.66E-04	2.39E-03	-1.8E-07
13	0.08	3.11E-03	7.66E-04	8.12E-04	8.12E-04	8.57E-04	3.11E-03	-1.5E-07
14	0.09	3.92E-03	8.57E-04	9.02E-04	9.02E-04	9.47E-04	3.92E-03	-1.4E-07
15	0.10	4.83E-03	9.47E-04	9.92E-04	9.91E-04	1.04E-03	4.83E-03	-1.2E-07
16	0.11	5.82E-03	1.04E-03	1.08E-03	1.08E-03	1.12E-03	5.82E-03	-1.1E-07
17	0.12	6.90E-03	1.12E-03	1.17E-03	1.17E-03	1.21E-03	6.90E-03	-1.0E-07
18	0.13	8.06E-03	1.21E-03	1.25E-03	1.25E-03	1.29E-03	8.06E-03	-9.4E-08
19	0.14	9.31E-03	1.29E-03	1.34E-03	1.34E-03	1.38E-03	9.31E-03	-8.7E-08
20	0.15	1.07E-02	1.38E-03	1.42E-03	1.42E-03	1.46E-03	1.07E-02	-8.1E-08

14-May-87 09:59 PM

Figure 11.5: Solving an initial-value problem using the Runge-Kutta method

higher-order equations, break them into two or more simultaneous differential equations by substituting new variables for the derivatives. For example, consider

$$au''+bu'+cu+d = 0$$

Make the substitution $y = u'$, and you will then have two simultaneous first-order differential equations.

$$u' - y = 0$$

$$ay'+by+cu+d = 0$$

To solve these equations, use the same methods shown in this section for a single equation, but alternate the solutions of the two equations so that at the end of any step, you have solved both of them.

■ BOUNDARY-VALUE PROBLEMS

Boundary-value problems make up a second class of ordinary differential equations. Whereas initial-value problems have all of the boundary conditions located at one side of the solution space, boundary-value problems have part of the boundary conditions on one side and the rest on the other. Thus, they must satisfy boundary conditions at both boundaries of the problem rather than just one.

There are two well-known methods for solving boundary value problems: the shooting method and the finite difference method. In this section, we will examine both of these methods.

Shooting Method

The shooting method solves boundary-value problems using the methods used to solve initial value problems. You guess values for the unknown boundary conditions at one of the boundaries (side 1) to change the problem into an initial-value problem. Then you integrate the equations from side 1 to the other side (side 2) with, for example, the modified Euler method. When you have completed the solution, compare the boundary values you calculated at side 2 with those required by the boundary conditions. If they are the same, then you have solved the problem; otherwise you need to change your guess at the unknown boundary values on side 1 and integrate the problem again. Thus, you are "shooting at" the boundary values on side 2 of the solution space by guessing values of the boundary conditions on side 1.

For example, to solve a second-order differential equation, you need two boundary conditions. If this were an initial-value problem, then you would be given the value of the solution and its derivative at one of the boundaries. For a typical boundary-value problem, you would be given only the value of the solution at both sides of the solution space. To integrate this solution to the other side of the solution space using the initial-value problem methods, you would need an estimate of the derivative of the solution at one boundary as well. Given that value, you could integrate the solution to the other boundary and then compare the value of your solution with the value required by the boundary condition. If they are the same, then you are done; otherwise you must try a different estimate of the value of the derivative of the solution. Continue this process until you "hit" the value on the boundary.

Bending in a Uniformly Loaded Beam If you simply support a beam at both ends, as shown in Figure 11.6, it will sag slightly under its own weight. The amount of that sag can be calculated using the following differential equation:

$$\frac{d^2y}{dx^2} = -\frac{m}{EI}$$

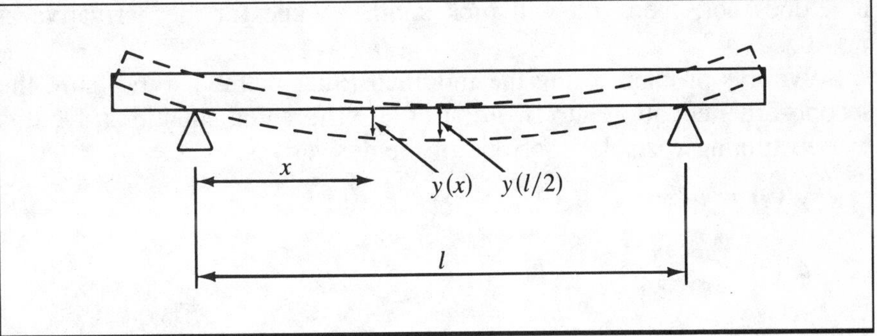

Figure 11.6: A simply supported beam bending under its own weight

Here, y is the displacement, or sag, at point x, I is the moment of inertia, E is the modulus of elasticity (30×10^6 psi for steel), and m is the bending moment. For a beam with a constant cross section,

$$m = \frac{w}{2}x(l - x)$$

where w is the weight per unit length and l is the length. Calculate the sag in a 60 foot piece of an 8-WF-67 steel beam—an 8-inch wide-flange section (a wide I-beam) that weighs 67 pounds per foot. For the orientation with the flange horizontal, the moment of inertia is $I = 271.8 \text{ in}^4$. For small displacements, the analytic solution of this differential equation is

$$y = \frac{wx}{24EI}(l^3 - 2lx^2 + x^3)$$

with the maximum value at the center:

$$y(l/2) = \frac{5wl^4}{384EI}$$

This differential equation has two boundary conditions, one at each end of the beam where it is supported:

$$y(0) = 0$$

$$y(l) = 0$$

To solve it using initial-value problem methods, you need the value and the derivative at one side. You will have to estimate the value of the derivative at $x = 0$, solve the problem, and then see whether $y(l) = 0$.

If it does not, then you will pick another value for the derivative at $x = 0$.

Solve this problem using the modified Euler method. First, split the second-order equation into two first-order differential equations. Do this by substituting variable u for one of the derivatives.

$$y'(x) = u(x)$$

$$u'(x) = -\frac{m}{EI}$$

Normally, using the modified Euler method, you would first calculate the solutions using the standard Euler method,

$$u(x + h) = u(x) + hu'(x)$$

$$y(x + h) = y(x) + hy'(x)$$

and then refine the values using

$$u(x + h) = u(x) + h\frac{(u'(x) + u'(x + h))}{2}$$

$$y(x + h) = y(x) + h\frac{(y'(x) + y'(x + h))}{2}$$

However, in this case you can go directly to the final step since you know the value of $u'(x + h)$ exactly from the differential equation. Create a spreadsheet to solve these equations, given an initial estimate of the value of $u(0)$.

1. Change the width of column F to **13**.
2. In cell A1, type **Deflection of a Beam; Boundary Value Problem; Shooting Method**

Create a table containing the beam parameters. The weight of the bar in cell B5 is 67 pounds per foot; to convert this to pounds per inch, divide by 12. Include the length in cell B8; to convert it to inches, multiply by 12.

3. In cell A4, type **'8-WF-67 Beam parameters**
4. In cell A5, type **"w**
5. In cell B5, type **67/12**
6. In cell C5, type **lb/in**
7. In cell A6, type **"I**

8. In cell B6, type **271.8**
9. In cell C6, type **in^4**
10. In cell A7, type **"E**
11. In cell B7, type **3.0E7**
12. In cell C7, type **psi**
13. In cell A8, type **"l**
14. In cell B8, type **60*12**
15. In cell C8, type **in**
16. Execute the /Range Name Labels Right (**/RNLR**) command and select cells A5..A8.
17. Format cell B7 as Scientific 2 (**S2**).

Since you know the analytic solution of this equation, create a second table to show the analytic solution for some value of x (96 inches) and for the maximum deflection at $x = l/2$.

18. In cell E3, type **Analytic solution**
19. In cell E4, type **"x**
20. In cell F4, type **96**
21. In cell G4, type **in**
22. Name cell F4 as **X**.
23. In cell E5, type **"y**
24. In cell F5, type **(W*X/(24*E*I))*(L^3-2*L*X^2+X^3)**
25. In cell G5, type **in**
26. In cell E6, type **"y(l/2)**
27. In cell F6, type **5*W*L^4/(384*E*I)**
28. In cell G6, type **in**
29. Format cells F6 and F7 as Fixed 5 (**F5**).

Span the solution space, from 0 to 720 inches, with a grid of x values spaced every 12 inches.

30. In cell A10, type **^x**
31. In cell A11, type **^(in)**
32. Execute the /Data Fill (**/DF**) command and select cells A12 ..A72, type **0** as the starting value, type **12** as the step, and accept the default ending value.

Calculate the derivative of u for all values of x. You can get this value directly from the differential equation.

33. In cell B10, type **^u'(x)**
34. In cell B11, type **^(1/in)**
35. In cells B12..B72, type/copy **-$W*A12*($L-A12)/(2*$E*$I)**

Calculate the value of $u(x)$ at each step, using the average value of its derivative in the step interval between the values of x. The first value of u is the missing boundary condition. It references cell F9, where you will enter your guesses.

36. In cell C10, type **^u(x)**
37. In cell C11, type **^(in/in)**
38. In cell C12, type **+F9**
39. In cells C13..C72, type/copy **+C12+(A13-A12)*(B12+B13)/2**

Calculate the value of y at each step, using the average value of $u(x)$ in the interval between the values of x. Set the first value of y to 0, which is the known boundary condition at this side of the solution space.

40. In cell D10, type **^y(x)**
41. In cell D11, type **^(in)**
42. In cell D12, type **0**
43. In cells D13..D72, type/copy **+D12+(A13-A12)*(C12+C13)/2**

Create a table to summarize the numerical results, with the value of y at $x = l$ and $x = l/2$. This is also where you will enter your guesses as to the value of $u(0)$. The value shown in cell F9 causes the value of $y(l)$ to equal 0 to four decimal places. It took me about 15 minutes to find that value.

44. In cell E8, type **Numerical solution**
45. In cell E9, type **"u(0)**
46. In cell F9, type **0.01016935**
47. In cell G9, type **in/in**
48. In cell E10, type **"y(l/2)**

49. In cell F10, type **+D42**
50. In cell G10, type **in**
51. In cell E11, type **"y(l)**
52. In cell F11, type **+D72**
53. In cell G11, type **in**
54. Format cells F10 and F11 as Fixed 5 (**F5**).

To use this spreadsheet, enter a guess as to the value of $u(0)$ into cell F9. After the spreadsheet recalculates, check the value of $y(l)$ that is repeated in cell F11 to see if it is 0. If it is not, then try a different value for $u(0)$. Continue changing the value of $u(0)$ until you get $y(l)$ equal to 0 to as many decimal places as you need. When you have completed this process, the spreadsheet should look like Figure 11.7.

Compare the analytic values of the solution in cells F5 and F6 with the numerical solutions in cells D20 and F10, respectively. Note that even though you have hit the boundary value to four places of accuracy, the rest of the solution values have only about three places of accuracy. This loss of accuracy is due to the inherent accuracy of the method. Since the accuracy is proportional to the spacing between the grid points, decreasing this spacing will increase accuracy—until roundoff error becomes significant.

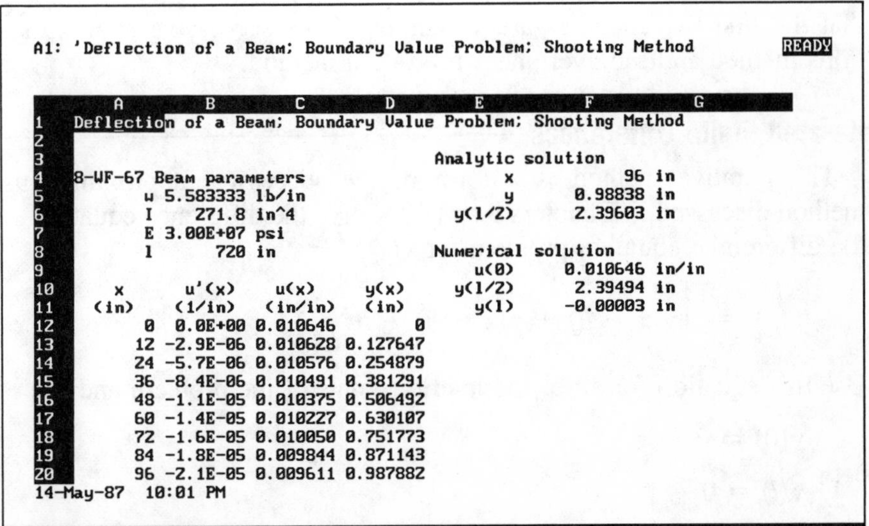

```
A1: 'Deflection of a Beam: Boundary Value Problem: Shooting Method        READY

      A        B         C         D         E          F          G
1   Deflection of a Beam: Boundary Value Problem: Shooting Method
2
3                                       Analytic solution
4   8-WF-67 Beam parameters                   x            96 in
5         w 5.583333 lb/in                    y       0.98838 in
6         I    271.8 in^4                y(l/2)       2.39603 in
7         E 3.00E+07 psi
8         l      720 in                 Numerical solution
9                                          u(0)      0.010646 in/in
10       x       u'(x)     u(x)      y(x)  y(l/2)       2.39494 in
11    (in)      (1/in)   (in/in)     (in)    y(l)      -0.00003 in
12           0 0.0E+00 0.010646         0
13          12 -2.9E-06 0.010628 0.127647
14          24 -5.7E-06 0.010576 0.254879
15          36 -8.4E-06 0.010491 0.381291
16          48 -1.1E-05 0.010375 0.506492
17          60 -1.4E-05 0.010227 0.630107
18          72 -1.6E-05 0.010050 0.751773
19          84 -1.8E-05 0.009844 0.871143
20          96 -2.1E-05 0.009611 0.987882
14-May-87  10:01 PM
```

Figure 11.7: Bending a simply supported beam under its own weight: boundary-value problem solved using the shooting method

Finite Difference Method

Another way to solve this problem is to write the derivatives in the differential equation as central differences, as you did in Chapter 8. By centering each of these differences on the grid points, you will get a set of coupled equations that have to be solved simultaneously. Use the following substitutions for the first and second derivatives:

$$\frac{du}{dx} = \frac{u(x+h) - u(x-h)}{2h}$$

$$\frac{d^2u}{dx^2} = \frac{u(x+h) - 2u(x) + u(x-h)}{h^2}$$

Rewrite the second derivative in the differential equation problem using the central difference substitutions.

$$\frac{y(x+h) - 2y(x) + y(x-h)}{h^2} = -\frac{m}{EI}$$

You will have one of these equations for each of the grid points except for the two at the boundaries, where the values of y are fixed by the boundary conditions.

There are three methods that work well in a spreadsheet to solve a problem in this form: iterative methods, iterative methods with acceleration, and matrix methods. As you review these examples, you will see that the first two methods are variations of the successive approximations method and the over/under relaxation method.

Iterated Finite Differences

The iterative method is a form of the successive approximations method discussed in Chapters 9 and 10. Solve the difference equation in the differential equation problem for $y(x)$.

$$y(x) = \frac{1}{2}\left[y(x+h) + y(x-h) + h^2\frac{m}{EI}\right]$$

Use this equation for all of the interior points of the problem and use

$$y(0) = 0$$

$$y(l) = 0$$

at the endpoints. Create a spreadsheet to solve this problem using the iterative method. The first part of this spreadsheet is the same as was used for the shooting method, so you can reuse part of that spreadsheet if you want.

1. Execute the /Worksheet Global Recalculation Manual (/**WGRM**) command.
2. Change the width of column F to **13**.
3. In cell A1, type **Deflection of a Beam; Boundary Value Problem; Finite difference**

Create the table containing the beam parameters.

4. In cell A4, type **'8-WF-67 Beam parameters**
5. In cell A5, type **"w**
6. In cell B5, type **67/12**
7. In cell C5, type **lb/in**
8. In cell A6, type **"I**
9. In cell B6, type **271.8**
10. In cell C6, type **in^4**
11. In cell A7, type **"E**
12. In cell B7, type **3.0E7**
13. In cell C7, type **psi**
14. In cell A8, type **"l**
15. In cell B8, type **60*12**
16. /I cell C8, type **in**
17. Execute the /Range Name Labels Right (/**RNLR**) command and select cells A5..A8.
18. Format cell B7 as Scientific 2 (**S2**).

Create a second table to show the analytic solution for some value of x (96 inches) and for the maximum deflection at $x = l/2$.

19. In cell E3, type **Analytic solution**
20. In cell E4, type **"x**
21. In cell F4, type **96**
22. In cell G4, type **in**
23. Name cell F4 as **X**.
24. In cell E5, type **"y**
25. In cell F5, type **(W*X/(24*E*I))*(L^3-2*L*X^2+X^3)**

26. In cell G5, type **in**
27. In cell E6, type **"y(l/2)**
28. In cell F6, type **5*W*L^4/(384*E*I)**
29. In cell G6, type **in**
30. Format cells F6 and F7 as Fixed 5 (**F5**).

Span the solution space from 0 to 720 inches with a grid of *x* values spaced every 12 inches.

31. In cell A10, type **^x**
32. In cell A11, type **^(in)**
33. Execute the /Data Fill (/**DF**) command and select cells A12..A72, type **0** as the starting value, type **12** as the step, and accept the default ending value.

Enter the initialization flag so that you can reset the values in the spreadsheet to a known value.

34. In cell A3, type **Init Flag**
35. In cell B3, type **1**
36. In cell C3, type **0**
37. Name cells B3 and C3 as **INIT** and **INIT_VAL**, respectively.

Enter the difference equation and put the boundary values in the first and last cells of the range (B12 and B72). Test the initialization flag to see whether the problem needs to be reset.

38. In cell B10, type **^y(x)**
39. In cell B11, type **^(in)**
40. In cell B12, type **0**
41. In cells B13..B71, type/copy **@IF($INIT=0,$INIT_VAL,0.5*(B14+B12+((A14-A12)/2)^2*$W*A13*($L-A13)/(2*$E*$I)))**
42. In cell B72, type **0**
43. Format cells B12..B72 as Fixed 5 (**F5**).

Make a table of the results of the calculation and specify a place for the macro variables. Get the maximum value of *y* from cell B42. Calculate the change in the calculated values so that you can see the progress of the calculation.

44. In cell E8, type **Numerical solution**
45. In cell E9, type **"y(1/2)**
46. In cell F9, type **+B42**
47. In cell G9, type **in**
48. In cell E10, type **"yold**
49. In cell G10, type **in**
50. Name cells F9 and F10 as **Y** and **YOLD**, respectively.
51. In cell E11, type **"Delta-y**
52. In cell F11, type **+Y-YOLD**
53. In cell G11, type **in**
54. Format cells F9 and F10 as Fixed 5 (**F5**).

Enter a short macro to automatically iterate the spreadsheet until the changes in the calculated solutions become less than 10^{-6}. This macro stores the current value of Y (F9) in YOLD (F10) and then updates the spreadsheet. After the update is complete, test the new value of Y with the saved value in YOLD to see whether the difference is less than 10^{-6}. If it is, then you are done; otherwise the macro branches back to the beginning.

55. In cell D13, type **"\a**
56. In cell E13, type **{let yold,y}**
57. In cell E14, type **{calc}**
58. In cell E15, type **{if @abs(yold-y)>1e-6}{branch \a}**
59. Name cell E13 as **\a**.
60. Execute the /Worksheet Global Recalculation Iteration (**/WGRI**) command and set the number of iterations per recalculation to **10**.

To operate this spreadsheet, set the value of the initialization flag (B3) to **0** and press Calc. After the calculation has been reset, change the initialization flag to **1** and press Macro-A to start the macro's recalculation of the spreadsheet. The macro will continue recalculating the spreadsheet until the value of the solution in cell Y (B42) stops changing significantly, at which point you have the solution. This spreadsheet takes about an hour to converge, so start it running and go to lunch. Your spreadsheet should look like Figure 11.8 after it has converged.

Accelerated Finite Differences

A spreadsheet that converges as slowly as this one is just begging for some acceleration in the same manner that we used over/under relaxation to solve systems of equations. Rewrite the difference equation so that you can control the amount of change in the solution at each iteration. Use the constant multiplier, c, to control the amount of that change.

$$y(x) = y(x) + c\left[\frac{1}{2}\left(y(x+h) + y(x-h) + h^2\frac{m}{EI}\right) - y(x)\right]$$

Enter this change into the existing spreadsheet. First enter the relaxation factor.

61. In cell A2, type **With Relaxation**
62. In cell A9, type **"Relax Fac**
63. In cell B9, type **1.9**
64. Name cell B9 as **C**.

Change the difference formula to incorporate the relaxation factor to control the amount of change in the solution during each iteration. The value of the solution has to be stored in column C so that you can calculate the amount of change during an iteration. Doing this creates a circular reference.

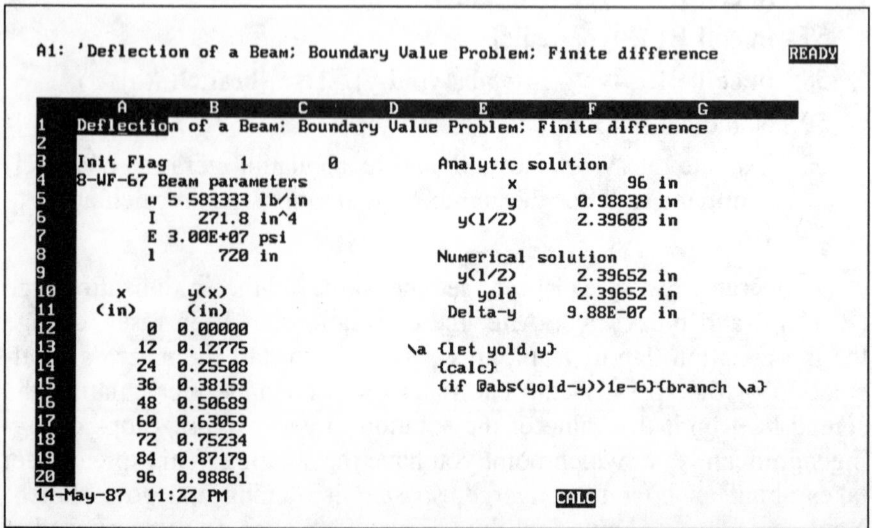

Figure 11.8: Bending a beam: a boundary-value problem solved with iterated finite differences

65. In cells B13..B71, type/copy **@IF($INIT=0,$INIT_VAL, (0.5*(B14+B12+((A14-A12)/2)^2*$W*A13*($L-A13)/ (2*$E*$I))-C13)*$C+C13)**
66. In cells C13..C71, type/copy **+B13**
67. Format cells C13..C72 as Fixed 5 (**F5**).

You operate this spreadsheet in exactly the same manner as the previous one. First, set the value of the initialization flag (B3) to **0** and press Calc. After the problem has been initialized, change the value of the initialization flag to **1** and press Macro-A to start the calculation. This version of the spreadsheet will converge in three-and-a-half minutes, a speedup of nearly sixteen hundred percent! The resulting spreadsheet is shown in Figure 11.9.

If you try to make the spreadsheet converge even faster by using larger values of the relaxation factor (*C*), the spreadsheet will diverge. I tried using a relaxation factor of 2, and the solution values became very large after a few iterations. If your solution diverges, use a smaller acceleration factor. For problems that diverge with iterated finite differences, use an acceleration factor that is less than 1 (deceleration factor) to slow down the change.

```
A1: 'Deflection of a Beam; Boundary Value Problem; Finite difference          READY

         A         B         C         D         E         F         G
 1  Deflection of a Beam; Boundary Value Problem; Finite difference
 2  With Relaxation
 3  Init Flag         1         0              Analytic solution
 4  8-WF-67 Beam parameters                            x          96 in
 5          w 5.583333 lb/in                           y     0.98838 in
 6          I    271.8 in^4                       y(l/2)     2.39603 in
 7          E 3.00E+07 psi
 8          l      720 in                      Numerical solution
 9  Relax Fac       1.9                           y(l/2)     2.39656 in
10      x         y(x)                              yold     2.39656 in
11    (in)        (in)                           Delta-y    9.78E-07 in
12          0  0.00000
13         12  0.12775   0.12775          \a {let yold,y}
14         24  0.25509   0.25509             {calc}
15         36  0.38160   0.38160             {if @abs(yold-y)>1e-6}{branch \a}
16         48  0.50689   0.50689
17         60  0.63060   0.63060
18         72  0.75235   0.75235
19         84  0.87181   0.87181
20         96  0.98863   0.98863
14-May-87  11:24 PM                                    CALC
```

Figure 11.9: Bending a beam: a boundary-value problem solved using accelerated finite differences

Matrix Method

Both of the iteration methods described here work and can be made to converge in a reasonable amount of time. However, what we are solving is a set of linear simultaneous equations that can be solved with the built-in matrix functions. The only restriction is that there must be fewer than 90 equations, because the matrix solver can invert or multiply matrices of up to only 90 × 90 elements.

To use the matrix solver, rewrite the difference equations as matrix equations. Rewrite the example differential equation,

$$\frac{y(x+h) - 2y(x) + y(x-h)}{h^2} = -\frac{m}{EI}$$

as

$$y(x+h) - 2y(x) + y(x-h) = -h^2\frac{m}{EI}$$

with the boundary conditions

$$y(0) = y(l) = 0$$

These can be easily rewritten into a matrix equation,

$$\mathbf{Ax} = \mathbf{b}$$

$$\begin{vmatrix} 1 & 0 & 0 & 0 & 0 & \cdot & \cdot & \cdot & & \\ 1 & -2 & 1 & 0 & 0 & \cdot & \cdot & \cdot & & \\ 0 & 1 & -2 & 1 & 0 & \cdot & \cdot & \cdot & & \\ 0 & 0 & 1 & -2 & 1 & \cdot & \cdot & \cdot & & \\ & & & & \cdot & & & & & \\ & & & & & \cdot & & & & \\ & & & & & & \cdot & & & \\ & \cdot & \cdot & \cdot & & 1 & -2 & 1 & 0 & \\ & \cdot & \cdot & \cdot & & 0 & 1 & -2 & 1 & \\ & \cdot & \cdot & \cdot & & 0 & 0 & 0 & 1 & \end{vmatrix} \begin{vmatrix} x_0 \\ x_1 \\ x_2 \\ x_3 \\ \cdot \\ \cdot \\ \cdot \\ x_{n-2} \\ x_{n-1} \\ x_n \end{vmatrix} = \begin{vmatrix} b_0 \\ b_1 \\ b_2 \\ b_3 \\ \cdot \\ \cdot \\ \cdot \\ b_{n-2} \\ b_{n-1} \\ b_n \end{vmatrix}$$

where

$$b_0 = b_n = 0$$

$$b_i = -h^2\frac{m_i}{EI} \qquad i = 1, 2, 3, \ldots n-1$$

$$m_i = \frac{wx_i}{2}(l - x_i)$$

Once the equations are in this form, the solution is straightforward. Invert matrix **A** and multiply that inverse times the vector **b** to get the solution vector **x**. Create a spreadsheet to solve this problem. The top portion of this spreadsheet is the same as the others in this chapter, so you can reuse that part and save some typing.

1. Change the width of column F to **13**.
2. In cell A1, type **Deflection of a Beam; Boundary Value Problem; Finite difference**
3. In cell A2, type **Matrix method**

Create the table containing the beam parameters.

4. In cell A4, type **8-WF-67 Beam parameters**
5. In cell A5, type **"w**
6. In cell B5, type **67/12**
7. In cell C5, type **lb/in**
8. In cell A6, type **"I**
9. In cell B6, type **271.8**
10. In cell C6, type **in^4**
11. In cell A7, type **"E**
12. In cell B7, type **3.0E7**
13. In cell C7, type **psi**
14. In cell A8, type **"l**
15. In cell B8, type **60*12**
16. In cell C8, type **in**
17. Execute the /Range Name Labels Right (/**RNLR**) command and select cells A5..A8.
18. Format cell B7 as Scientific 2 (**S2**).

Create a second table to show the analytic solution for some value of x (96 inches) and for the maximum deflection at $x = l/2$.

19. In cell E3, type **Analytic solution**
20. In cell E4, type **"x**
21. In cell F4, type **96**
22. In cell G4, type **in**
23. Name cell F4 as **X**.
24. In cell E5, type **"y**
25. In cell F5, type **(W*X/(24*E*I))*(L^3-2*L*X^2+X^3)**

26. In cell G5, type **in**
27. In cell E6, type **"y(l/2)**
28. In cell F6, type **5*W*L^4/(384*E*I)**
29. In cell G6, type **in**
30. Format cells F6 and F7 as Fixed 5 (**F5**).

Span the solution space from 0 to 720 inches with a grid of x values spaced every 12 inches.

31. In cell A10, type **^x**
32. In cell A11, type **^(in)**
33. Execute the /Data Fill (/**DF**) command and select cells A12 ..A72, type **0** as the starting value, type **12** as the step, and accept the default ending value.

Mark a space for the solution vector.

34. In cell B10, type **^y(x)**
35. In cell B11, type **^(in)**
36. In cell C10, type **^b**

Enter b, the right side of the matrix equation, including the boundary conditions.

37. In cell C12, type **0**
38. In cells C13..C71, type/copy **-(A13-A12)^2*$W*A13*($L-A13)/(2*$E*$I)**
39. In cell C72, type **0**

Mark the locations of matrix **A** and its inverse, $\mathbf{A}^{-1}$.

40. In cell D11, type **^A**
41. In cell D74, type **^A^-1**

Enter a small table to retrieve the value of the solution at the point of maximum deflection ($l/2$).

42. In cell E8, type **Numerical solution**
43. In cell E9, type **"y(l/2)**
44. In cell F9, type **+B42**
45. In cell G9, type **in**

Create a macro to fill and solve the matrix. Name cells D12..D172 as A so that you can access the individual components with the {put} command. Fill A with zeros by filling the first element with 0 and then copying it to the rest of the matrix.

46. In cell H1, type **'\m**
47. In cell I1, type **'/rnca~d12.bl72~**
48. In cell I2, type **'{put a,0,0,0}**
49. In cell I3, type **'/cd12.d12~d12.bl72~~**

Loop over all but the first and last rows of the matrix and call the routine MAKEA once for each row. The routine MAKEA will put the values 1, −2, and 1 along the diagonal of the matrix. Put 1 in the first element of the first row and in the last element of the last row of the matrix for the boundary-condition equations.

50. In cell I4, type **'{for j,1,59,1,makea}**
51. In cell I5, type **'{put a,0,0,1}**
52. In cell I6, type **'{put a,60,60,1}~**

Invert the matrix and store the inverse matrix in cells D75..BL135.

53. In cell I7, type **'/dmid12.bl72~d75.bl135~~**

Multiply the inverse matrix times the vector **b** in cells C12..C72 and store the result in cells B12..B72. This is the solution to the problem.

54. In cell I8, type **'/dmmd75.bl135~c12.c72~b12.b72~~**

Enter the routine MAKEA to fill in the diagonal elements of the matrix with the values 1, −2, and 1.

55. In cell L2, type **"makea**
56. In cell M2, type **'{put a,j,j,-2}**
57. In cell M3, type **'{put a,j-1,j,1}**
58. In cell M4, type **'{put a,j + 1,j,1}**

Mark the storage location for the macro variable J and name the macro \A, the routine MAKEA, and the variable J.

59. In cell L6, type **"j**
60. Name cells I1, M2, and M6 as **\A**, **MAKEA**, and **J**, respectively.

The spreadsheet should now look like Figure 11.10, with the macro in Figure 11.11. To use the spreadsheet, simply execute the macro by pressing Macro-A. This macro will take about 10 minutes to calculate a

```
A1: 'Deflection of a Beam; Boundary Value Problem; Finite difference     READY

      A         B         C         D         E         F         G
1  Deflection of a Beam; Boundary Value Problem; Finite difference
2  Matrix method
3                                      Analytic solution
4  8-WF-67 Beam parameters                   x              96 in
5        w 5.583333 lb/in                    y         0.98838 in
6        I    271.8 in^4                y(l/2)         2.39603 in
7        E 3.00E+07 psi
8        l      720 in                 Numerical solution
9                                       y(l/2)         0.00000 in
10       x     y(x)        b
11    (in)     (in)                 A
12       0                 0
13      12          -0.00041
14      24          -0.00082
15      36          -0.00121
16      48          -0.00159
17      60          -0.00195
18      72          -0.00230
19      84          -0.00263
20      96          -0.00295
14-May-87  10:07 PM
```

Figure 11.10: Bending a beam: a boundary-value problem solved with finite differences

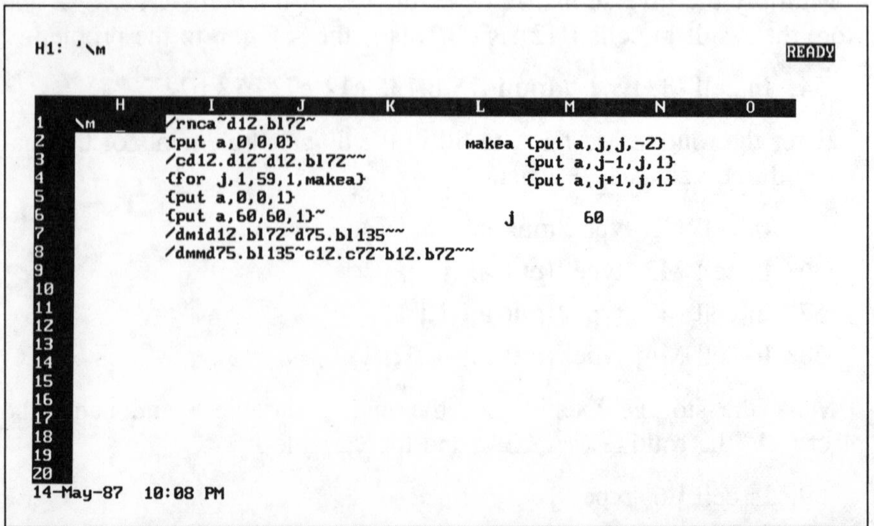

```
H1: '\m                                                            READY

      H       I       J       K       L       M       N       O
1  \m      /rnca~d12.b172~
2          {put a,0,0,0}            makea {put a,j,j,-2}
3          /cd12.d12~d12.b172~~           {put a,j-1,j,1}
4          {for j,1,59,1,makea}           {put a,j+1,j,1}
5          {put a,0,0,1}
6          {put a,60,60,1}~               j          60
7          /dmid12.b172~d75.bl135~~
8          /dmmd75.bl135~c12.c72~b12.b72~~
9
10
11
12
13
14
15
16
17
18
19
20
14-May-87  10:08 PM
```

Figure 11.11: Bending a beam: a macro program to implement a matrix solution to the boundary-value problem finite difference equations

solution. Most of that time is spent inverting the 61 × 61–element matrix **A**. When the calculation is complete, the result will be in column B, as shown in Figure 11.12.

Higher-Order Boundary Conditions

The problem you just solved had Dirichlet boundary conditions; that is, the value of the function was specified at the boundaries. The problem could just as easily have had Neumann boundary conditions, in which the derivative of the function is specified on the boundaries; or it could have had a mix of Dirichlet and Neumann boundary conditions, with the value of the function specified at one boundary and the derivative of the function specified at the other.

To handle such higher-order boundary conditions, add an extra grid point to the problem, just outside the boundary with the derivative boundary condition. Construct a central difference at the boundary using that extra point to set the value of the derivative. For example, in the previous problem, if the boundary condition at $x = 0$ were

$$y'(0) = 0.010646$$

instead of

$$y(0) = 0$$

```
A1: 'Deflection of a Beam; Boundary Value Problem; Finite difference       READY

        A         B          C        D        E            F          G
1   Deflection of a Beam; Boundary Value Problem; Finite difference
2   Matrix method
3                                      Analytic solution
4   8-WF-67 Beam parameters                  x              96 in
5         w 5.583333 lb/in                   y         0.98838 in
6         I    271.8 in^4               y(1/2)         2.39603 in
7         E 3.00E+07 psi
8         l      720 in                Numerical solution
9                                       y(1/2)         2.39656 in
10     x       y(x)        b
11   (in)      (in)             A
12        0        0         0      1        0            0          0
13       12 0.127752 -0.00041      1       -2            1          0
14       24 0.255086 -0.00082      0        1           -2          1
15       36 0.381596 -0.00121      0        0            1         -2
16       48 0.506892 -0.00159      0        0            0          1
17       60 0.630598 -0.00195      0        0            0          0
18       72 0.752352 -0.00230      0        0            0          0
19       84 0.871805 -0.00263      0        0            0          0
20       96 0.988625 -0.00295      0        0            0          0
14-May-87   10:20 PM
```

Figure 11.12: Bending a beam: the result of the matrix solution to the boundary-value problem finite difference equations

you would add another grid point at $x = -h$. You would then write a first-order central difference equation at $x = 0$ and set it equal to 0.010646:

$$\frac{y(h) - y(-h)}{2h} = 0.010646$$

You would use this equation to define the value of the function at the extra grid point, $y(-h)$. At the actual boundary point, you would use the same difference equation that you used in the interior of the problem. Higher-order derivative boundary conditions are handled in exactly the same manner; just insert the difference equation for the higher-order derivative.

Bear in mind that problems with Neumann boundary conditions on all sides may not have a unique solution. If you can add an arbitrary constant to the function in the differential equation and not change the differential equation, then it is possible not to have a unique solution. This will happen when the function appears only in the derivative and not explicitly anywhere else.

The bending-beam problem is just such an equation. If you were to add some value y_0 to the function $y(x)$, the differential equation would not change. If there were no Dirichlet boundary conditions to fix the value of $y(x)$ at some point, then the result would not be unique, and you could add any arbitrary amount to $y(x)$ and the solution would still be correct. Note that physically this amounts to raising or lowering the beam as a complete unit, which has no effect on the amount of bending. The beam will bend the same amount whether it is in the basement or on the roof.

■ SUMMARY

To most people, a spreadsheet may not appear to be a medium for finding numerical solutions to ordinary differential equations. However, we have seen that Lotus 1-2-3 is readily adaptable to their solution. Initial-value problems can be solved on a spreadsheet using the Taylor series, the Euler and modified Euler, and the Runge-Kutta methods. These methods vary in their accuracy and their difficulty to implement.

Boundary-value problems can be solved using the shooting method, in which we pick values of the boundary condition on one side of the problem and then see whether we get the correct result on the other side. Boundary-value problems can also be solved using finite differences, and the resulting difference equations can be solved using iterative or matrix techniques.

■ FOR MORE INFORMATION

For further information about the topics in this chapter, you can consult the following sources.

Bending and Stretching in Structural Materials

S. Timoshenko and D. H. Young, *Elements of Strength of Materials*, 5th. ed. (New York: D. Van Nostrand, 1968).

Numerical Methods for Solving Differential Equations

C. Gerald, *Applied Numerical Analysis*, 2nd. ed. (Reading, Mass: Addison-Wesley, 1978).

W. H. Press, et al., *Numerical Recipes: The Art of Scientific Computing* (Cambridge, Eng.: Cambridge University Press, 1986).

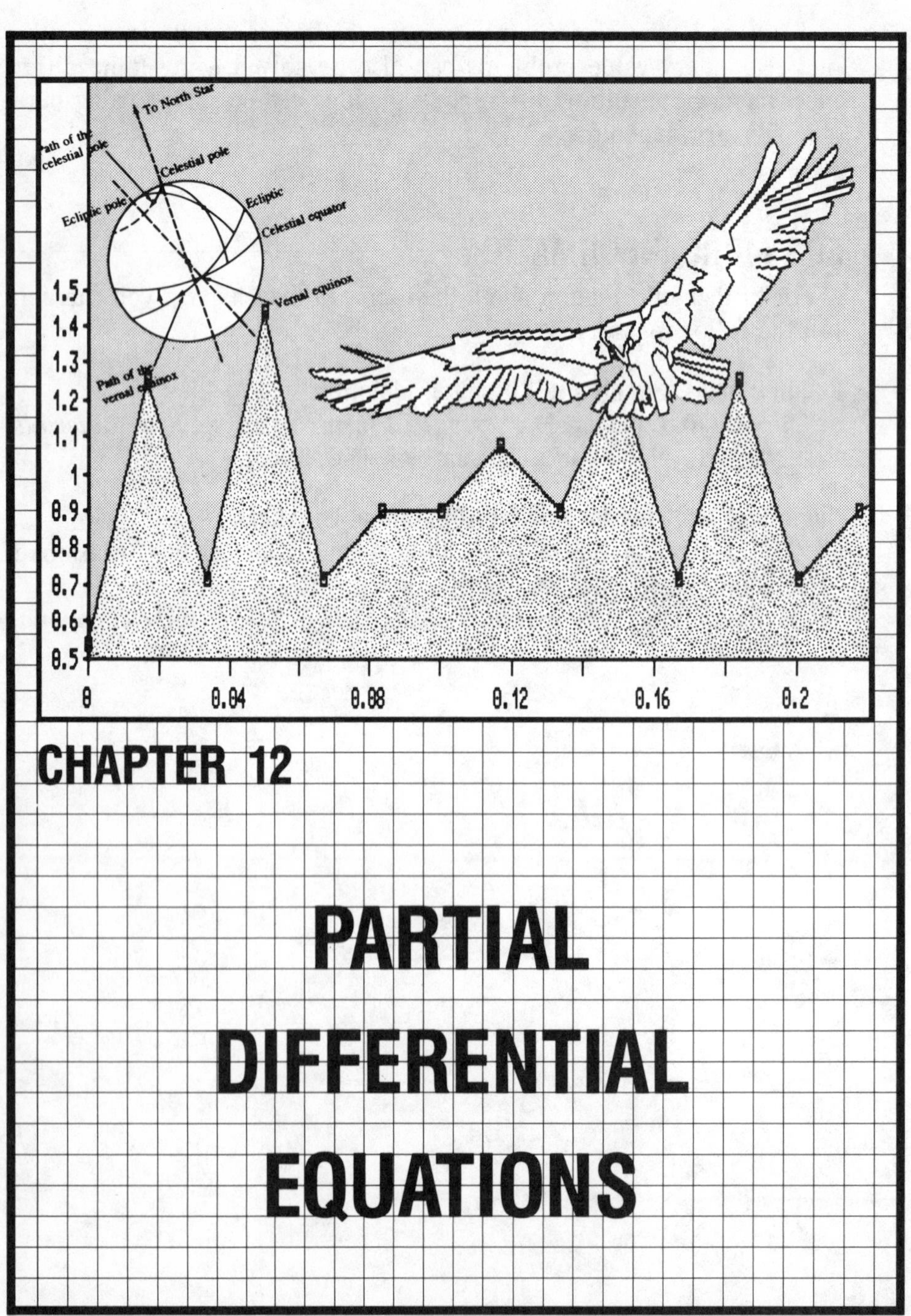

CHAPTER 12

PARTIAL DIFFERENTIAL EQUATIONS

Partial differential equations show up in many important science and engineering problems. Any problem involving a differential process with more than one variable must be described with partial differential equations rather than ordinary differential equations. For a second-order function (u) involving two variables (x,y), there are five different possible differentials:

$$\frac{\partial u}{\partial x}, \frac{\partial^2 u}{\partial x^2}, \frac{\partial u}{\partial y}, \frac{\partial^2 u}{\partial y^2}, \frac{\partial^2 u}{\partial x \partial y}$$

These can be combined into a general partial differential equation:

$$A\frac{\partial^2 u}{\partial x^2} + B\frac{\partial^2 u}{\partial x \partial y} + C\frac{\partial^2 u}{\partial y^2} + D\frac{\partial u}{\partial x} + E\frac{\partial u}{\partial y} + F = 0$$

Each of the coefficients (A–F) can be functions of either of the two variables (x and y) or the function (u).

■ TYPES OF PARTIAL DIFFERENTIAL EQUATIONS

There are three categories of partial differential equations: elliptic, parabolic, and hyperbolic. The equations in these three different categories are distinguished by the relationships of the coefficients of the second-order terms. For example, for the second-order equation with two variables, the category is determined with

$B^2 - 4AC = 0$	Elliptic
$B^2 - 4AC = 0$	Parabolic
$B^2 - 4AC > 0$	Hyperbolic

Since these coefficients are functions of the variables and u, a differential equation can move from one category to another as the variables change.

■ ELLIPTIC PARTIAL DIFFERENTIAL EQUATIONS

Elliptic partial differential equations usually arise from equilibrium problems. Poisson's and Laplace's equations are well-known examples of elliptic partial differential equations. In both of these equations, the coefficient of the cross term (B) is zero, which makes $B^2 - 4AC$ less than zero.

Solving elliptic partial differential equations proceeds in much the same manner as solving iterated finite difference problems involving ordinary differential equations except that you must deal with at least a two-dimensional, rather than a one-dimensional, space.

Poisson and Laplace Equations

Poisson and Laplace equations are generally used for scalar-field problems. You can describe steady-state electrostatic potential with the Poisson equation, which is written as

$$\nabla^2\Phi = -q\frac{\rho}{\epsilon}$$

where q is the electron charge, ρ is the number density of charge carriers, and ϵ is the permittivity. Note that this equation uses the differential operator

$$\nabla \equiv \mathbf{i}\frac{\partial}{\partial x} + \mathbf{j}\frac{\partial}{\partial y} + \mathbf{k}\frac{\partial}{\partial z}$$

where **i**, **j**, and **k** are unit vectors in the x, y, and z directions. This is the definition of the differential operators in three-dimensional cartesian coordinates. The definition differs for other coordinate systems. The square of the ∇ operator is the vector dot product of the operator:

$$\nabla^2 = \nabla \cdot \nabla = \frac{\partial^2}{\partial x^2} + \frac{\partial^2}{\partial y^2} + \frac{\partial^2}{\partial z^2}$$

If no charges are present ($\rho = 0$), then Poisson's equation reduces to the Laplace equation:

$$\nabla^2\Phi = 0$$

Potential between Two Concentric Cylinders Consider two long concentric cylinders of radii a and b in a vacuum (see Figure 12.1). If you apply a voltage across them, then the potential in the space between them will be described with a two-dimensional Laplace equation.

The outer conductor is grounded (0 volts), and the inner conductor is held at 20 volts. The inner diameter, a, is 5 centimeters, and the outer diameter, b, is 15 centimeters. To calculate the potential in the volume between the two cylinders, you will use a two-dimensional Laplace equation because the cylinders are long and the variation in potential in

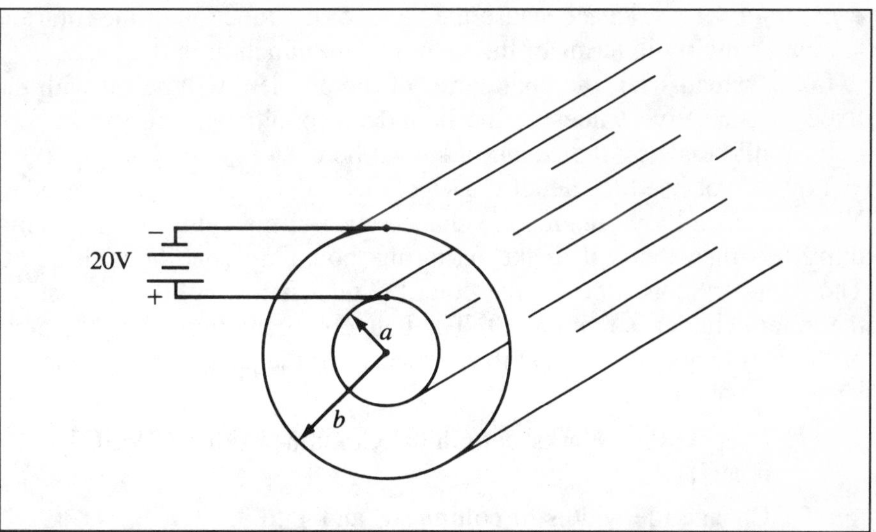

Figure 12.1: Concentric cylinders in a vacuum

the direction parallel to the cylinders' axes can be ignored.

$$\nabla^2\Phi = \frac{\partial^2\Phi}{\partial x^2} + \frac{\partial^2\Phi}{\partial y^2} = 0$$

I solved this problem analytically, so that you can compare the analytical results to those that you calculate. The analytical solution for the potential at some distance r from the center of the cylinders is

$$\Phi(r) = \frac{\Phi_b \mathrm{Ln}(r/a) - \Phi_a \mathrm{Ln}(r/b)}{\mathrm{Ln}(b/a)}$$

To solve the differential equation on the spreadsheet, replace the derivatives in the equation with central differences, centered on the grid point i, j. Assume that the grid spacing (h) is the same in both directions.

$$\frac{\Phi_{i+1,j} - 2\Phi_{i,j} + \Phi_{i-1,j}}{h^2} + \frac{\Phi_{i,j-1} - 2\Phi_{i,j} + \Phi_{i,j-1}}{h^2} = 0$$

Solve this equation for the term at the grid point $\Phi_{\mathrm{i,j}}$.

$$\Phi_{i,j} = (\tfrac{1}{4})(\Phi_{i+1,j} + \Phi_{i-1,j} + \Phi_{i,j+1} + \Phi_{i,j-1})$$

The potential at any grid point is equal to the average of the potentials of the surrounding four grid points. A solution of this form is known as an *explicit finite difference* because the value of the function in the future is known explicitly in terms of the values of the function in the past.

In the spreadsheet, the boundaries of the problem will be set with the fixed or derivative values of the boundary conditions, and the interior points will be set by the equation shown here.

You do not need to model the whole cylinder, but only a slice of it. You will model a 90-degree pie-shaped slice of the cylinder, since anything less than that will make fixing the boundary conditions difficult. The boundary condition for the outer cylinder is fixed at 0, and that for the inner cylinder is fixed at 20. The boundary condition along the edge of the pie-shaped slice is that the derivative of the potential, perpendicular to the boundary, is zero.

1. Execute the /Worksheet Global Column-width 3 (**/WGC3**) command.
2. Change the widths of columns S and T to **9**.
3. Execute the /Worksheet Global Recalculation Manual (**/WGRM**) command.
4. Execute the /Worksheet Global Recalculation Iteration 10 (**/WGRI10**) command.
5. In cell A1, type **Laplace equation between concentric cylinders; Elliptical PDE**

Enter some arrows to locate the x and y axes.

6. In cell C5, type **x --->**
7. In cell B6, type **y**
8. In cell B7, type **'¦**
9. In cell B8, type **'¦**
10. In cell B9, type **'+**

Create a table to contain the values of the potentials for the inner and outer cylinders.

11. In cell S9, type **Applied Potentials**
12. In cell S10, type **"Inner**
13. In cell T10, type **20**
14. In cell S11, type **"Outer**
15. In cell T11, type **0**
16. Name cells T10 and T11 as **INNER** and **OUTER**, respectively.

Enter the outer and inner boundary conditions along the edges of the outer and inner conductors. I drew two concentric circles on grid paper to see what cells to include as part of the boundary. I assumed that any cell that the circle touched was part of the boundary.

17. In cells Q5, Q6, Q7, Q8, P9, P10, P11, P12, O13, N14, N15, M16, L17, J18, K18, G19, H19, I19, C20, D20, E20, and F20, type/copy **$OUTER**
18. In cells G5, G6, G7, F8, E9, F9, B10, C10, and D10 type/copy, **$INNER**

Along the edge of the pie slice, the boundary condition is that the derivative is zero. To insert this boundary condition, insert an extra row of cells (H4..P4 and A11..A19) just outside of the boundary and set their values equal to those in the first row of cells, just inside the boundary (H6..P6 and C11..C19). This will make the derivative zero at the cells on the boundary (H5..P5 and B11..B19). Mark these extra rows with arrows.

19. In cell C4, type **B.C. --->**
20. In cell G4, type **$INNER**
21. In cells H4..P4, type/copy **+H6**
22. In cell Q4, type **$OUTER**
23. In cell A6, type **B.**
24. In cell A7, type **C.**
25. In cell A8, type **'¦**
26. In cell A9, type **'+**
27. In cell A10, type **$INNER**
28. In cells A11..A19, type/copy **+C11**
29. In cell A20, type **$OUTER**

Fill the interior of the region between the cylinders with the finite difference form of the differential equation. Type the equation into cell H5 and then copy it into row H5..P5. Next, copy the row from H5..P5 and insert it into H6..P7. Continue copying the equation in blocks until it fills the entire region.

30. In cells H5..P5, H6..P6, H7..P7, G8..P8, G9..O9, E10..O10, C11..O11, C12..O12, C13..N13, C14..M14, C15..M15, C16..

L16, C17..K17, C18..I18, and C19..F19, type/copy **0.25*(G5+H4+I5+H6)**

Insert the analytic solution along the upper boundary as a comparison. The analytic solution needs the value of the radius at each cell; enter them in a row just below the bottom of the spreadsheet.

31. In cell B3, type **Analytic --->**
32. In cells G3..Q3, type/copy **($OUTER*@LN(G22/5)-$INNER*@LN(G22/15))/@LN(15/5)**
33. Execute the /Data Fill (/**DF**) command and select cells G22..Q22, enter a starting value of **5**, enter a step value of **1**, and accept the default ending value.

Create a simple macro to iterate the spreadsheet until it converges. I chose a cell in the middle of the problem, as far away from the boundary conditions as I could get, to use as the test cell. It is the cell that must undergo the most changing to get to the final value, so I reasoned that it would be nearly the last cell to converge. If you do not accept this reasoning, then you can write your macro to test several cells rather than just one. This macro assumes convergence if the change during a block of 10 iterations (set in step 4) is less than 10^{-3}. Put the macro variable in a cell and calculate the change between iterations to obtain a visual representation of the state of the calculation.

34. In cell S15, type **“JOLD**
35. Name cell T15 as **JOLD**
36. In cell S16, type **“Delta**
37. In cell T16, type **+J12-JOLD**
38. Format cell T16 as Scientific 1 (**S1**).
39. In cell L18, type **‘\a**
40. In cell M18, type **‘{let jold,+j12}**
41. In cell M19, type **‘{calc}**
42. In cell M20, type **‘{if @abs(j12-jold)>1e-3}{branch \a}**

Execute the macro by pressing Macro-A. In a few minutes, it will stop calculating; it should then look like Figure 12.2. Figure 12.3 shows a comparison of the analytic equation in cells G3..Q3 with the values in cells G5..Q5 (the numerical solution on the boundary). The curves in the figure are very similar.

```
A1: 'Laplace equation between concentric cylinders; Elliptical PDE              READY

     A  B  C  D  E  F  G  H  I  J  K  L  M  N  O  P  Q  R     S        T
1   Laplace equation between concentric cylinders; Elliptical PDE
2
3      Analytic --->  20 16 13 11 9. 7. 5. 4. 2. 1.  0
4         B.C.--->    20 16 14 11 9. 7. 5. 4. 2. 1.  0
5         x--->       20 17 14 11 9. 7. 5. 4. 2. 1.  0
6   B.  y             20 16 14 11 9. 7. 5. 4. 2. 1.  0
7   C.  |             20 16 13 11 9. 7. 5. 4. 2. 1.  0
8   |   |          20 18 15 13 10 8. 6. 5. 3. 2. 0.  0
9   +   +       20 20 16 14 12 10 8. 6. 4. 3. 1.  0     Applied Potentials
10  20 20 20 20 18 16 14 12 10 9. 7. 5. 4. 2. 1.  0        Inner       20
11  17 17 17 16 15 14 12 11 9. 7. 6. 5. 3. 2. 1.  0        Outer        0
12  14 14 14 13 13 12 10 9. 8. 6. 5. 4. 2. 1. 0.  0
13  11 12 11 11 10 10 9. 8. 6. 5. 4. 3. 2. 0.  0
14  9. 9. 9. 9. 8. 8. 7. 6. 5. 4. 3. 2. 1.  0
15  7. 7. 7. 7. 7. 6. 5. 5. 4. 3. 2. 1. 0.  0                JOLD 6.850368
16  5. 6. 5. 5. 5. 4. 4. 3. 3. 2. 1. 0.  0                   Delta  6.2E-06
17  4. 4. 4. 4. 3. 3. 2. 2. 1. 1. 0.  0
18  2. 2. 2. 2. 2. 2. 1. 1. 0.  0  0 \a {let jold,+j12}
19  1. 1. 1. 1. 1. 0.  0  0  0          {calc}
20   0  0  0  0  0  0                   {if @abs(j12-jold)>1e-5}{branch \a}
 15-May-87  12:29 AM                             CALC
```

Figure 12.2: Potential between two concentric cylinders: solving a two-dimensional elliptical partial differential equation

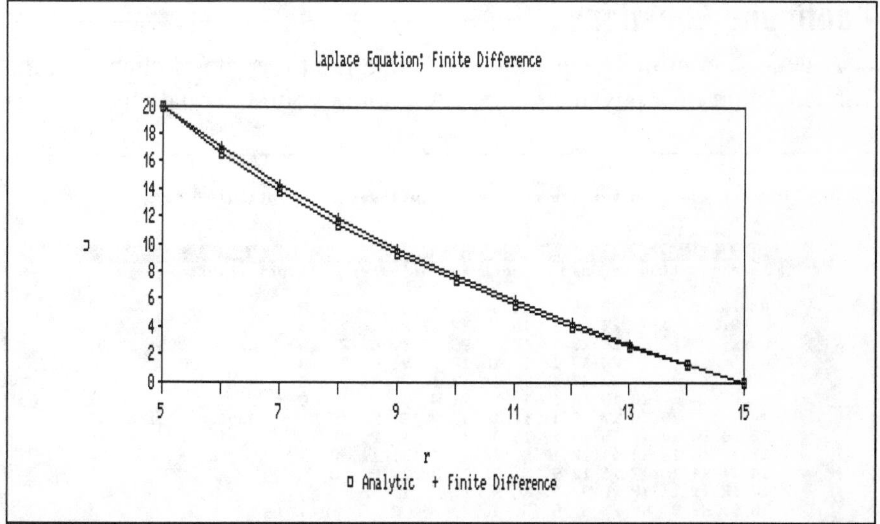

Figure 12.3: Comparison of the finite difference and the analytic solution to the concentric cylinders problem

Once this problem is set up, you can quickly modify it for different potentials on the cylinders by simply changing the value in the table and re-executing the macro. You can also add other conductors to the problem. For example, if you want to insert a wire charged to 25 volts halfway between the two cylinders, all you need to do is replace the difference equation in cell L5 with the value 25 and re-execute the macro. The result is shown in Figure 12.4 and graphed in Figure 12.5. The graph compares the situation calculated with the wire with the analytic solution without the wire.

■ PARABOLIC PARTIAL DIFFERENTIAL EQUATIONS

When the relationship between the coefficients $B^2 - 4AC$ of the general partial differential equation equals 0, the equation is a parabolic partial differential equation. Parabolic partial differential equations show up in problems involving diffusion and fluid flow. In general, they are problems involving the first derivative with respect to time and the second derivative with respect to position of the concentration of some physical quantity (electron density, temperature, chemical concentration, and so forth). The most important of these equations is the continuity equation.

Continuity Equations

A general continuity equation states that the time rate of change in the concentration of a physical quantity in some volume equals the amount

```
A1: 'Laplace equation between concentric cylinders; Elliptical PDE          READY

    A  B  C  D  E  F  G  H  I  J  K  L  M  N  O  P  Q  R      S          T
1   Laplace equation between concentric cylinders; Elliptical PDE
2
3      Analytic --->  20 16 13 11 9. 7. 5. 4. 2. 1.  0
4         B.C.--->    20 18 17 16 16 17 13 9. 5. 2.  0
5         x--->       20 18 17 17 19 25 15 9. 6. 2.  0    Wire at L5; 25 V
6   B. y              20 18 17 16 16 17 13 9. 5. 2.  0
7   C. |              20 17 16 15 14 13 10 7. 4. 2.  0
8   |  |           20 18 16 15 13 12 11 8. 6. 3. 1.  0
9   +  +        20 20 17 15 13 12 10 9. 7. 5. 2.  0       Applied Potentials
10  20 20 20 20 18 17 15 13 12 10 9. 7. 6. 4. 2.  0          Inner      20
11  17 17 17 16 15 14 13 12 10 9. 7. 6. 4. 3. 1.  0          Outer       0
12  14 14 14 14 13 12 11 10 9. 7. 6. 5. 3. 2. 0.  0
13  12 12 12 11 11 10 9. 8. 7. 6. 5. 3. 2. 1.  0
14  9. 10 9. 9. 9. 8. 7. 6. 6. 5. 4. 2. 1.  0
15  7. 8. 7. 7. 7. 6. 6. 5. 4. 3. 2. 1. 0.  0                 JOLD 7.849553
16  6. 6. 6. 5. 5. 5. 4. 3. 3. 2. 1. 0.  0                   Delta  6.6E-06
17  4. 4. 4. 4. 4. 3. 3. 2. 2. 1. 0.  0
18  2. 2. 2. 2. 2. 2. 1. 1. 0.  0  0 \a {let jold,+j12}
19  1. 1. 1. 1. 1. 0.  0  0  0          {calc}
20   0  0  0  0  0  0                   {if @abs(j12-jold)>1e-5}{branch \a}
15-May-87   12:37 AM                          CALC
```

Figure 12.4: Potential between two concentric cylinders, with a wire charged to 25 volts inserted halfway between them in cell L5

of that quantity flowing into the volume, minus the amount that flows out, plus the amount that is created in the volume, minus the amount that is absorbed in the volume. Assuming that the physical quantity moves at some velocity **v**, the partial differential equation can be written as

$$\frac{\partial u}{\partial t} = -\nabla \cdot (u\mathbf{v}) + G - A$$

where the divergence term (the first term on the right) calculates the flow out of (or into) some volume, G is the generation term, and A is the absorption term.

The continuity equation is quite common in many branches of science and engineering. Any substance or physical quantity that can flow from one point to another can probably have that flow described with a continuity equation. It does not matter whether the substance is heat in a solid or tuna cans moving down a conveyor belt—the basic continuity equation is the same.

Transient Heat Flow in a Copper Bar Consider the flow of heat Q in a solid. The velocity at which heat flows through a solid is proportional to the negative of the gradient of the temperature. Substituting the negative gradient of the temperature for the velocity in the continuity equation

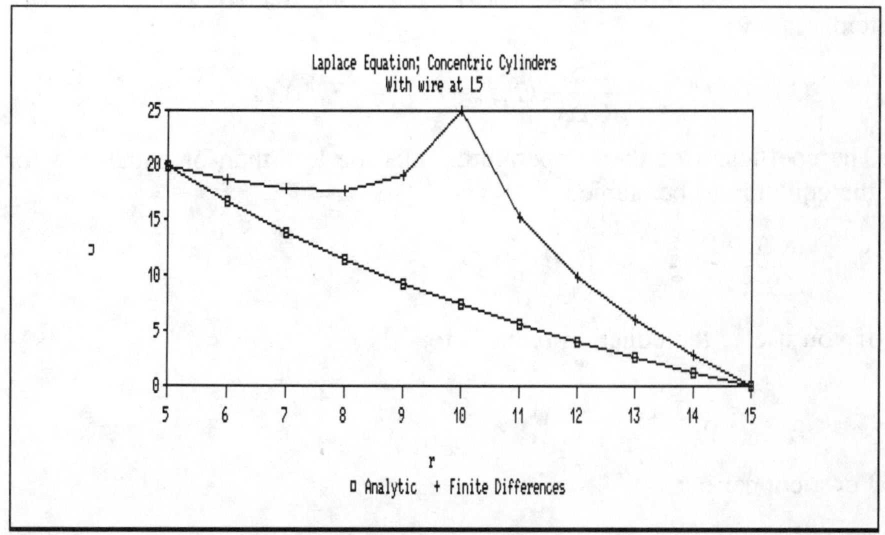

Figure 12.5: Graph of the concentric cylinder problem with a wire charged to 25 volts inserted halfway between the cylinders

and using the chain rule on the time derivative results in this equation:

$$\frac{\partial Q}{\partial T}\frac{\partial T}{\partial t} = \nabla \cdot (K \nabla T) + G - A$$

The derivative of the heat with respect to the temperature is just the heat capacity per unit volume, ρC, where ρ is the density and C is the heat capacity. Inserting these values yields the equation

$$\rho C \frac{\partial T}{\partial t} = \nabla \cdot (K \nabla T) + G - A$$

If you have simple transient heat flow in a metal bar, with no heat generation or absorption mechanisms, the preceding equation reduces to a one-dimensional time-dependent partial differential equation.

$$\frac{\partial T}{\partial t} = \frac{K}{\rho C}\frac{\partial^2 T}{\partial x^2}$$

To solve this equation, first rewrite the derivatives as central differences.

$$\frac{T_i^{n+1} - T_i^n}{\Delta t} = \frac{K}{\rho C}\frac{T_{i+1}^n - 2T_i^n + T_{i-1}^n}{\Delta x^2}$$

Here, Δx and Δt are the spatial and temporal step sizes. The superscript $(n, n - 1)$ indicates the time step. Solve this equation for the future temperature.

$$T_i^{n+1} = T_i^n, + \frac{K \Delta t}{\rho C \Delta x^2}(T_{i+1}^n - 2T_i^n + T_{i-1}^n)$$

The coefficient of the temperatures must be less than or equal to $\frac{1}{2}$ for the equation to be stable.

$$\frac{K \Delta t}{\rho C \Delta x^2} \leq \frac{1}{2}$$

If you use $\frac{1}{2}$, the equation reduces to

$$T_i^{n+1} = \frac{1}{2}(T_{i+1}^n + T_{i-1}^n)$$

For a copper bar,

$$\frac{K}{\rho C} = 1.15$$

This equation fixes the relationship between the time step (Δt) and the spatial grid step (Δx).

$$\Delta x^2 = 2.31\Delta t$$

If the spatial grid step equals 1 centimeter, the time step will be 0.433 seconds.

Consider the problem with a 10-centimeter copper bar, initially at 0° C, with one end held at 0° C and the other at 20° C. Create a spreadsheet to calculate the change in temperature over time for this bar.

1. Execute the /Worksheet Global Column-width 6 (**/WGC6**) command.
2. In cell A1, type **Heat flow in a copper bar; Parabolic partial differential equation**
3. In cell C3, type **Temperature versus position and time.**

Enter the time step using multiples of 0.433 seconds.

4. In cell A5, type **^Time**
5. In cell A6, type **^(s)**
6. Execute the /Data Fill (**/DF**) command and select cells A7..A20; type a starting value of **0**, type a step of **0.433**, and accept the default ending value.

Enter the spatial grid with a grid point every centimeter.

7. In cell E5, type **Position (cm)**
8. Execute the /Data Fill (**/DF**) command and select cells **B6..L6**; type a starting value of **0**, type a step of **1**, and accept the default ending value.

Enter the first boundary condition, a fixed value of 20° C.

9. In cell B7, type **20**
10. In cells B8..B20, type/copy **+B7**

Enter the second boundary condition with a fixed value of 0° C.

11. In cells L7..L20, type/copy **0**

Enter the initial condition of 0° C at t = 0.

12. In cells C7..K7, type/copy **0**

Type the difference equation into the first cell of the range and then copy it into the rest of the range.

13. In cells C8..K20, type/copy **0.5*(B7+D7)**
14. Format cells A7..L20 as Fixed 2 (**F2**).

Your spreadsheet should now look like Figure 12.6, with the resulting temperatures versus position and time. You can easily see the flow of heat down the bar by observing the changes in the temperature.

Iterated Time Steps

In contrast to the method used in the last problem, in which the solution proceeds down the spreadsheet as time increases, you can also calculate a time step by iterating the spreadsheet. The solution uses two rows of cells and a circular reference. One row of cells saves the values of the function from the last step, and the other row of cells calculates the value of the function at a new time step.

Re-create the heat flow problem, this time iterating the time steps. First, change the recalculation mode to manual and rowwise, so that the rows will be recalculated in order.

A1: 'Heat flow in a copper bar; Parabolic partial differential equation READY

	A	B	C	D	E	F	G	H	I	J	K	L
1	Heat flow in a copper bar; Parabolic partial differential equation											
2												
3			Temperature versus position and time.									
4												
5	Time				Position (cm)							
6	(s)	0	1	2	3	4	5	6	7	8	9	10
7	0.00	20.00	0.00	0.00	0.00	0.00	0.00	0.00	0.00	0.00	0.00	0.00
8	0.43	20.00	10.00	0.00	0.00	0.00	0.00	0.00	0.00	0.00	0.00	0.00
9	0.87	20.00	10.00	5.00	0.00	0.00	0.00	0.00	0.00	0.00	0.00	0.00
10	1.30	20.00	12.50	5.00	2.50	0.00	0.00	0.00	0.00	0.00	0.00	0.00
11	1.73	20.00	12.50	7.50	2.50	1.25	0.00	0.00	0.00	0.00	0.00	0.00
12	2.17	20.00	13.75	7.50	4.38	1.25	0.63	0.00	0.00	0.00	0.00	0.00
13	2.60	20.00	13.75	9.06	4.38	2.50	0.63	0.31	0.00	0.00	0.00	0.00
14	3.03	20.00	14.53	9.06	5.78	2.50	1.41	0.31	0.16	0.00	0.00	0.00
15	3.46	20.00	14.53	10.16	5.78	3.59	1.41	0.78	0.16	0.08	0.00	0.00
16	3.90	20.00	15.08	10.16	6.88	3.59	2.19	0.78	0.43	0.08	0.04	0.00
17	4.33	20.00	15.08	10.98	6.88	4.53	2.19	1.31	0.43	0.23	0.04	0.00
18	4.76	20.00	15.49	10.98	7.75	4.53	2.92	1.31	0.77	0.23	0.12	0.00
19	5.20	20.00	15.49	11.62	7.75	5.34	2.92	1.85	0.77	0.44	0.12	0.00
20	5.63	20.00	15.81	11.62	8.48	5.34	3.59	1.85	1.15	0.44	0.22	0.00

15-May-87 12:46 AM

Figure 12.6: Heat flow in a copper bar: a solution to a parabolic partial differential equation

1. Execute the /Worksheet Global Recalculation Manual (/**WGRM**) command.
2. Execute the /Worksheet Global Recalculation Rowwise (/**WGRR**) command.
3. Execute the /Worksheet Global Column-width 6 (/**WGC6**) command.
4. Change the width of columns A and L to **7** and **5**, respectively.
5. In cell A1, type **Heat flow in a copper bar; Parabolic partial differential equation**

Enter the initialization flag. Entering 0 in cell C4 will cause the problem to be initialized, and entering 1 will cause the calculation to proceed.

6. In cell A4, type **Init Flag**
7. In cell C4, type **1**
8. Name cell C4 as **INIT_FLAG**.

Set up a circular reference to calculate the time of the current iteration. The function in cell F3 checks for an initialization iteration and then adds the time step to the current time. Cell G3 stores the time for the next step.

9. In cell E3, type **Time**
10. In cell F3, type **@IF($INIT_FLAG=0,0,G3+0.433)**
11. In cell G3, type **+F3**

Enter the *x* positions across the top of the table.

12. In cell E5, type **Position (cm)**
13. Execute the /Data Fill (/**DF**) command and select cells B6..L6 as the range, **0** as the starting value, and **1** as the step value; accept the default ending value.

Enter the initial condition of 0 and enter the boundary condition of 20 at $x = 0$ and 0 at $x = 10$.

14. In cell A7, type **I.C.**
15. In cells C7..K7, type/copy **0**
16. In cell B7, type **20**
17. In cell B8, type **+B7**

18. In cell B9, type **+B7**
19. In cell L7, type **0**
20. In cell L8, type **+L7**
21. In cell L9, type **+L7**

Enter the finite difference equation in row 8. The formula also checks for an initialization iteration. If the initialization flag equals 0, then the value of the function is set equal to the initial conditions in row 7.

22. In cells C8..K8, type **@IF($INIT_FLAG=0,C7,0.5*(B9+D9))**
23. In cells C9..K9, type/copy **+C8**
24. In cell D10, type **Temperature versus position**
25. Format cells B7..L9, F3, and G3 as Fixed 2 (**F2**).

To operate the spreadsheet, set the initialization flag in cell C4 to **0** and press Calc. Change the value of the initialization flag to **1** and press Calc again. The spreadsheet will show the results after the first time step. Each time you press Calc, the spreadsheet will increment the time step. Press Calc 12 more times and the spreadsheet should look like Figure 12.7, with a problem time of 5.63 seconds. If you compare

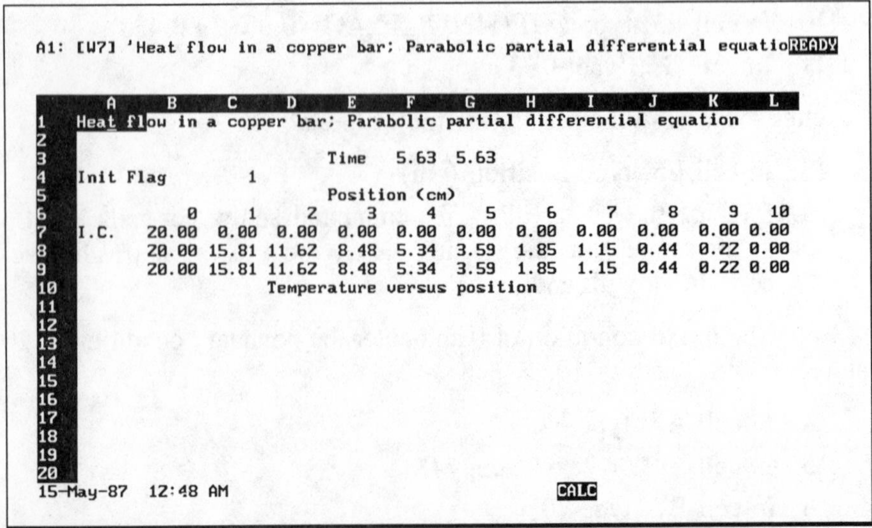

Figure 12.7: Heat flow in a bar: iterated time steps

these results with those in row 20 of Figure 12.6, you will see that they are identical.

One of the benefits of iterated time steps are that you can calculate the results for any number of time steps without using much space on the spreadsheet. For example, to calculate the results after 1000 time steps, the noniteration method in Figure 12.6 would use 1000 lines in the spreadsheet, whereas the iteration method would use no more lines than it does now. To perform 1000 iterations without pressing Calc 1000 times, execute the /Worksheet Global Recalculation Iteration 50 (/WGRI50) command and press Calc 20 times. Each time that you press Calc, the spreadsheet will be iterated 50 times.

Another benefit of the iteration method is that it lends itself to two-dimensional time-dependent calculations. The two spatial dimensions can be represented in the rows and columns of the spreadsheet, and the time dimension can be calculated by iteration. The setup would be similar to that in Figure 12.7, except that you would have three rectangular ranges of cells corresponding to the three rows of cells in the figure. The first range would hold the initial conditions, the second would hold the two-dimensional finite difference equation, and the third would hold the values for the next step.

■ HYPERBOLIC PARTIAL DIFFERENTIAL EQUATIONS

Hyperbolic differential equations are the last category of partial differential equations. In these equations, the relationship between the coefficients in the general equation ($B^2 - 4AC$) is greater than 0, and both variables have second derivatives. Hyperbolic partial differential equations arise in wave mechanics and vibration problems, transport problems (radiation transport for example), diffusion problems, and gas dynamics problems.

The Wave Equation

Probably the most important hyperbolic partial differential equation in modern physics is the wave equation. It consists of second-order derivatives of space and time related by the speed.

$$\frac{\partial^2 y}{\partial t^2} = c^2 \nabla^2 y$$

In this equation, c is the speed of the traveling wave. The wave equation describes both electromagnetic waves in space and waves in a vibrating string.

You will solve the wave equation in the same manner as you solved the previous partial differential equations. Consider a one-dimensional form of the wave equation.

$$\frac{\partial^2 y}{\partial t^2} = c^2 \frac{\partial^2 y}{\partial x^2}$$

First, substitute central differences for the derivatives.

$$\frac{y{^{n+1}_{i}} - 2y^n_i + y{^{n-1}_{i}}}{\Delta t^2} = c^2 \frac{y^n_{i+1} - 2y^n_i + y^n_{i-1}}{\Delta x^2}$$

Then solve the equation for the value of the function at the future time.

$$y{^{n+1}_{i}} = 2y^n_i + y{^{n-1}_{i}} + \frac{c^2 \Delta t^2}{\Delta x^2}(y^n_{i+1} - 2y^n_i + y^n_{i-1})$$

Note that this equation has the added complication that it requires data from two time steps to calculate the value at the future time. This is a problem only during the first time step, in which there is no history yet from which to get the value for y_i^{n-1}. To start the problem, you must somehow estimate the value of this term. If you are given the value of y and its derivative as your initial conditions, then use them in a simple extrapolation to get the value of the function at $-\Delta t$.

$$y{^{n+1}_{i}} = y^n_i - \Delta t \frac{\partial y}{\partial t}$$

If you have other information, then use it to estimate the value of the function at $-\Delta t$.

Vibrating String The oscillations of a vibrating string are described with a one-dimensional form of the wave equation. The boundary conditions are that the ends of the string are held fixed at 0. If the string is plucked, then the extent and location at which the string was pulled and the extent to which it was plucked determine the initial conditions. Assume that you have a 70-centimeter string that is pulled off center by 0.1 centimeter at a point 20 centimeters from one end. The initial conditions would then be

$$y = 0.1\frac{x}{20} \qquad x < 20$$

$$y = 0.1\frac{70 - x}{50} \qquad x > 20$$

For stability, the coefficient in the finite difference equation must equal 1.

$$\frac{c^2\Delta t^2}{\Delta x^2} = 1$$

Setting the coefficient equal to 1 also simplifies the difference equation.

$$y^{n+1}_{i} = y_{i+1}^{n} + y_{i-1}^{n} - y^{n-1}_{i}$$

If you pull the string taut until the wave velocity is 5×10^4 centimeters per second, the relationship between the spatial and temporal steps will be fixed.

$$\Delta x = \sqrt{5 \times 10^4}\ \Delta t$$

If Δx is 10 centimeters, then Δt will be 2×10^{-4} seconds.

You know from the initial conditions that the string is plucked. Therefore, the string is at the maximum extent of an oscillation at the time $t = 0$, which makes the value of the function at the $-\Delta t$ step equal to the value of the function at the first step (at $+\Delta t$).

$$y^{n-1}_{i} = y^{n+1}_{i}$$

Enter this value into the difference equation for the first step only.

$$y^{n+1}_{i} = \left(\frac{1}{2}\right)(y_{i+1}^{n} + y_{i-1}^{n})$$

Create a spreadsheet to calculate the oscillations of the string described here.

1. Execute the /Worksheet Global Column-width 6 (**/WGC6**) command.
2. Change the width of column A to **9**.
3. In cell A1, type **Vibrating String; Hyperbolic equation**
4. In cell C2, type **Displacement of a Plucked String**

Enter the time values with steps of 2×10^{-4} seconds and enter the spatial values with steps of 10 centimeters.

5. In cell A3, type **^Time**
6. In cell A4, type **^(s)**
7. Execute the /Data Fill (**/DF**) command and select cells A5..A35, type a starting value of **0**, type a step value of **0.0002**, and accept the default ending value.
8. Format cells A5..A35 as Scientific 1 (**S1**).
9. In cell B3, type **^B.C.**
10. In cell E3, type **Length (cm)**
11. In cell I3, type **^B.C.**
12. Execute the /Data Fill (**/DF**) command; select cells B4..I4, type a starting value of **0**, type a step value of **10**, and accept the default ending value.

Enter the initial condition of the string being plucked by 0.1 centimeter at a point 20 centimeters from its end. The extension numbers are linear from the point the string is plucked to each end.

13. In cell B5, type **0**
14. In cell C5, type **0.05**
15. In cell D5, type **0.1**
16. In cell E5, type **0.08**
17. In cell F5, type **0.06**
18. In cell G5, type **0.04**
19. In cell H5, type **0.02**
20. In cell I5, type **0**
21. In cell J5, type **'<--- I.C.**

Enter the boundary conditions down both sides.

22. In cells B6..B35, type/copy **+B5**
23. In cells I6..I35, type/copy **+I5**

Enter the special difference equation for the first step with the estimate for the value at $-\Delta t$ contained in it.

24. In cells C6..H6, type/copy **0.5*(B5+D5)**

Complete the problem with the normal difference equation.

25. In cells C7..H35, type/copy **+B6+D6-C5**
26. Format cells B6..I35 as Fixed 2 (F2).

Your spreadsheet should look like Figure 12.8. If you follow the changes in the position of the string, you will note that it is oscillating with a period of 2.8×10^{-3} seconds, or a frequency of 357 Hz. The analytical equation for the oscillation frequency gives exactly the same result:

$$f = \frac{c}{2l} = \frac{5 \times 10^4 \text{ cm/s}}{2 \cdot 70 \text{ cm}} = 357 \text{ Hz}$$

Here, f is the frequency, and l is the length of the string.

■ SUMMARY

In this last chapter, we have looked at solving multidimensional time-dependent partial differential equations with a spreadsheet. Amazingly enough, this is actually rather easy to do. The methods that we have used all involve explicit finite differences equations, in which the value

A1: [W9] 'Vibrating String; Hyperbolic equation READY

	A	B	C	D	E	F	G	H	I	J	K
1	Vibrating	String; Hyperbolic equation									
2				Displacement of a Plucked String							
3	Time	B.C.			Length (cm)				B.C.		
4	(s)	0	10	20	30	40	50	60	70		
5	0.0E+00	0.00	0.05	0.10	0.08	0.06	0.04	0.02	0.00	<---I.C.	
6	2.0E-04	0.00	0.05	0.07	0.08	0.06	0.04	0.02	0.00		
7	4.0E-04	0.00	0.02	0.03	0.05	0.06	0.04	0.02	0.00		
8	6.0E-04	0.00	-0.02	-0.00	0.01	0.03	0.04	0.02	0.00		
9	8.0E-04	0.00	-0.02	-0.04	-0.02	-0.01	0.01	0.02	0.00		
10	1.0E-03	0.00	-0.02	-0.04	-0.06	-0.05	-0.03	-0.02	0.00		
11	1.2E-03	0.00	-0.02	-0.04	-0.06	-0.08	-0.07	-0.05	0.00		
12	1.4E-03	0.00	-0.02	-0.04	-0.06	-0.08	-0.10	-0.05	0.00		
13	1.6E-03	0.00	-0.02	-0.04	-0.06	-0.08	-0.07	-0.05	0.00		
14	1.8E-03	0.00	-0.02	-0.04	-0.06	-0.05	-0.03	-0.02	0.00		
15	2.0E-03	0.00	-0.02	-0.04	-0.03	-0.01	0.00	0.02	0.00		
16	2.2E-03	0.00	-0.02	-0.01	0.01	0.02	0.04	0.02	0.00		
17	2.4E-03	0.00	0.02	0.03	0.05	0.06	0.04	0.02	0.00		
18	2.6E-03	0.00	0.05	0.07	0.08	0.06	0.04	0.02	0.00		
19	2.8E-03	0.00	0.05	0.10	0.08	0.06	0.04	0.02	0.00		
20	3.0E-03	0.00	0.05	0.07	0.08	0.06	0.04	0.02	0.00		

15-May-87 12:50 AM

Figure 12.8: A vibrating string: solution of a hyperbolic partial differential equation

of the function in the future is explicitly determined by the known values of the function in the past.

Finite difference equations can also be written as implicit finite differences equations, in which the value of the function in the future is a function of the value of the function in the past and in the future. The equations thus formed are coupled simultaneous equations that must be solved in a matrix format, a much more complicated calculation than that required by the explicit method.

To those of you who have worked your way to this point, welcome. You have reached the end of the last chapter. I hope that this material will be useful to you, and that you had as much fun working the examples as I had creating them. As is usually the case, I had many more examples than I could possibly squeeze into this book. I hope that the ones that I did include will allow you to extend to your own problems the techniques we developed here.

■ FOR MORE INFORMATION

For further information about the topics in this chapter, you can consult the following sources.

Numerical Methods for Partial Differential Equations

C. Gerald, *Applied Numerical Analysis*, 2nd. ed. (Reading, Mass.: Addison-Wesley, 1978).

W. H. Press et al., *Numerical Recipes: The Art of Scientific Computing* (Cambridge, Eng.: Cambridge University Press, 1986).

General Partial Differential Equations

H. F. Weinberger, *A First Course in Partial Differential Equations* (New York: Blaisdell, 1965).

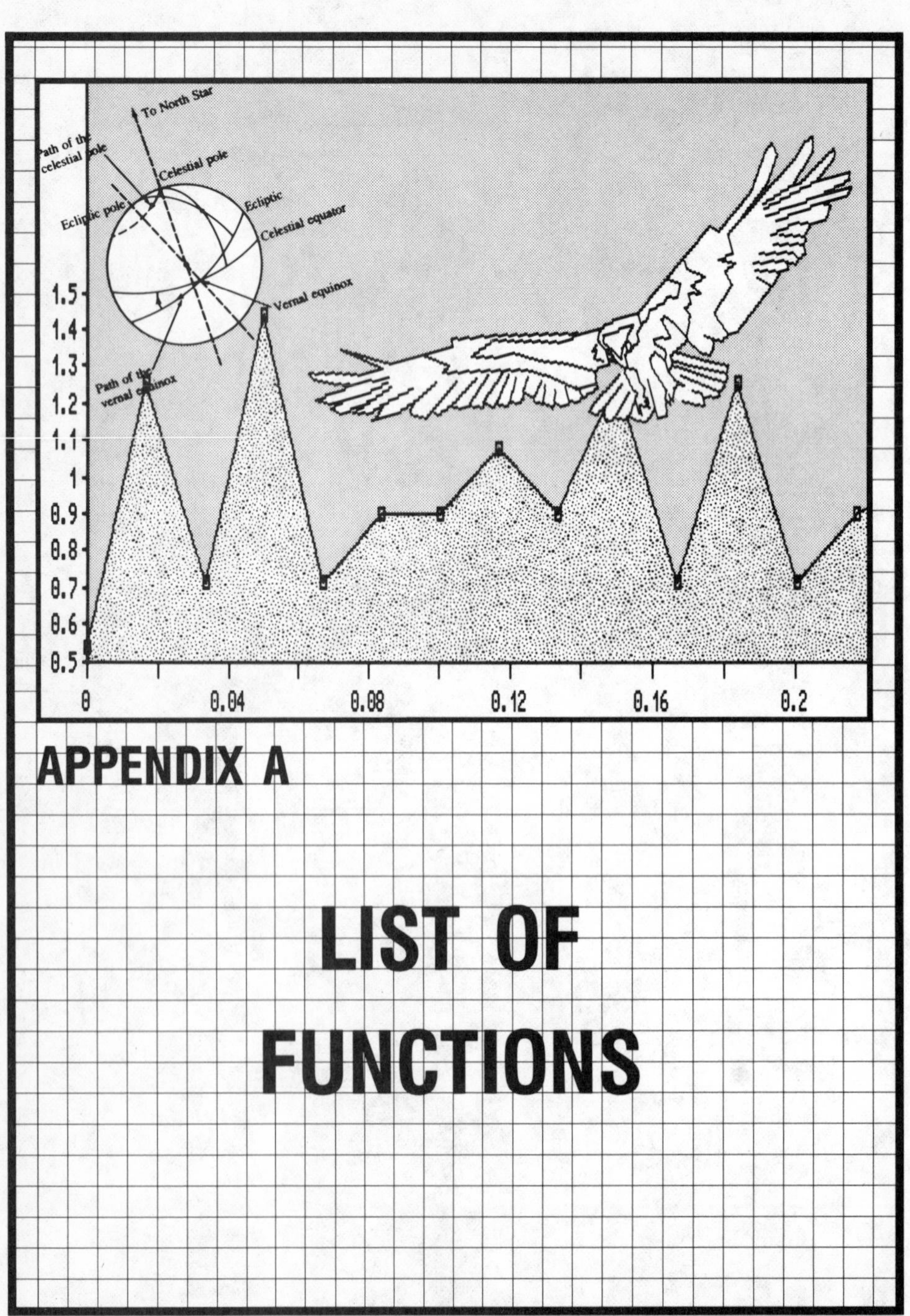

APPENDIX A

LIST OF FUNCTIONS

Following is an alphabetical list of all of the functions in Lotus 1-2-3, with the details of their implementation. A similar list grouped by function and illustrated with numerous examples is contained in the *1-2-3 Reference Manual*.

@@(*ca*) returns the contents (value or label) of the cell referenced by the contents of cell *ca*. This is the double indirection function, which allows you to get the contents of a cell whose reference is in a label or was created with a string formula.

@ABS(*x*) Calculates the absolute value of x.

@ACOS(*x*) Calculates the arc cosine of x, where x is in the range $-1 \ldots +1$. The arc cosine function returns an angle between 0 and π. The inverse trigonometric functions are multivalued, so be careful when you use them to ensure that the angle that you get is the one that you expect. For example, if y is the arc cosine of x, then $-y$ is also the arc cosine of x.

@ASIN(*x*) Calculates the arc sine of x, where x is in the range $-1 \ldots +1$. The arc sine function returns an angle in radians between $-\pi/2$ and $+\pi/2$. The inverse trigonometric functions are multivalued, so be careful when you use them to ensure that the angle that you get is the one that you expect. For example, if y is the arc sine of x, then $\pi - y$ is also the arc sine of x.

@ATAN(*x*) @ATAN2(*x*,*y*) Calculate the arc tangent of x and x/y respectively. The range of x or x/y is $-$I to I. The arc tangent function returns an angle between $-\pi/2$ and $+\pi/2$. The second arc tangent function calculates the arc tangent of x/y and also determines the correct quadrant for the angle. The result is in the range $-\pi$ to $+\pi$. The inverse trigonometric functions are multivalued, so be careful when you use them to ensure that the angle that you get is the one that you expect. For example, if y is the arc tangent of x, then $\pi + y$ is also the arc tangent of x. Using the second form of the function will ensure that you are in the correct quadrant.

@AVG(*list*) Calculates the average of the values in list. This function is equivalent to @AVG(*list*) = @SUM(*list*)/@COUNT(*list*).

@CELL(*att*,*range*) Returns the attribute specified by *att* for the cell in the upper-left corner of *range*. Table 1.9 lists the attributes that may be specified (in double quotation marks) for *att* and the possible returned values.

@CELLPOINTER(*att*) Returns the attribute specified by *att* for the currently highlighted cell. Table 1.9 lists the attributes that may be specified (in double quotation marks) for *att* and the possible returned values.

@CHAR(*x*) Returns the ASCII code that corresponds to the number x. This also includes the extended symbol set ($x > 127$) supplied by Lotus and known as the Lotus International Character Set (LICS). The *1-2-3 Reference Manual* has a complete set of these codes. Note that these extended character codes differ from those in the IBM standard character set, which may cause problems in displaying or printing some of the LICS characters. This function is the inverse of the @CODE function.

@CHOOSE(*x,v0,v1..vn*) Returns the value from the list *v0..vn* selected with the integer value x. If $x = 0$, @CHOOSE returns the value *v0*; if $x = 1$, @CHOOSE returns the value of *v1*; and so on. The contents of the list can be labels, values, or cell references. If x is larger than the number of values in the list or is negative, then this function returns the value ERR.

@CODE(*str*) Returns the ASCII/LICS character code that corresponds to the first character in the string *str*. This function is the inverse of the @CHAR(x) function.

@COLS(*range*) Returns the number of columns in *range*.

@COS(*x*) Calculates the cosine of the angle x, where x is in radians. If x is in degrees, then multiply it by the function @PI and divide by 180 to convert it to radians. This function does not give exactly 0 at odd multiples of $\pi/2$. What it does give is an extremely small number near the limit of the precision of the spreadsheet; for example,

@COS(@PI/2) = − 1.8E − 18

@COUNT(list) Returns the number of nonblank cells in list, if list is a cell-range reference. Any single references will be counted, even if they are blank. For example, @COUNT(B5.B7,B10,B12) counts only the nonblank cells in the range B5 to B7, but counts cells B10 and B12, even if they are blank.

@CTERM(*int,fv,pv*) Returns the number of periods required for the present value (*pv*) to grow to the future value (*fv*) at the given interest rate (*int*) per period. This is a solution to the simple compound interest formula and is equivalent to

@CTERM(*int,fv,pv*) = @LN(*fv*/*pv*)/@LN(1 + *int*).

@DATE(*yr,mo,da*) Returns the date number for the given values of the year (*yr*), month (*mo*), and day (*da*). Years that can be specified range from 0 for 1900 to 199 for 2099. Months range from 1 to 12, and days range from 1 to 31, depending on the number of days in a month. If the number of days you enter is too large for the given month, the function will return ERR.

@DATEVALUE(*str*) Returns the date number for the date contained in the string *str*. The dates contained in the strings must be formatted in one of the standard Lotus 1-2-3 formats (see the /Range Format Date command in the *1-2-3 Reference Manual*).

@DAVG(*database,column,criterion*) Calculates the average of the values in the *column* of the *database* for *records* that satisfy the *criterion*.

@DAY(*n*) Returns a value between 1 and 31 that is the day of the month from the day number *n*. The function ignores fractional parts of *n*.

@DCOUNT(*database,column,criterion*) Returns the number of nonblank cells in the *column* of the *database* of records that satisfy the *criterion*.

@DDB(*c,s,life,per*) Uses the double-declining-balance method to calculate the current period's (*per*) depreciation on an asset with a cost *c*, a salvage value *s*, and a lifetime *life*.

@DMAX(*database,column,criterion*) Finds and returns the maximum value in the *column* of the *database* for records that satisfy the *criterion*. The function ignores blank cells and counts cells filled with labels as 0.

@DMIN(*database,column,criterion*) Finds and returns the minimum value in the *column* of the *database* of records that satisfy the *criterion*. The function ignores blank cells and counts cells filled with labels as 0.

@DSTD(*database,column,criterion*) and @DVAR(*database,column, criterion*) Calculate the population standard deviation and population variance of the values in the *column* of the *database* of records that satisfy the *criterion*.

@DSUM(*database*,*column*,*criterion*) Returns the sum of the values in the *column* of the *database* of records that satisfy the *criterion*. The function ignores blank cells and counts labels as 0.

@ERR Returns the value ERR.

@EXACT(*str1*,*str2*) Returns TRUE or FALSE, depending on whether the strings *str1* and *str2* are identical. Case (upper or lower) and accents are significant in this function, in contrast to functions that use the equal (=) operator, which ignore case and accents.

@EXP(1) Returns the value of **e**, the base of the natural logarithms (approximately 2.718282).

@EXP(*x*) The exponential function. Calculates **e** to the power x, where **e** is the base of the natural logarithms (approximately 2.718282). Theoretically, x can take on any value, but if x is greater than 230 (but less than 710), @EXP(x) will be greater than 10^{99}, and Lotus 1-2-3 will not be able to display it, though it will be maintained internally and can be used in other calculations. If x is equal to or greater than 710, then the result will be larger than 10^{308}, and the calculation will overflow, causing a value of ERR to be returned in the cell.

@FALSE Returns the logical value FALSE, or 0.

@FIND(*sstr*,*str*,*n*) Returns the character position (0 origin) of the first occurrence of the search string *sstr* in the string *str*. The search starts at character position *n*.

@FV(*pmt*,*int*,*term*) Returns the future value of an ordinary annuity with equal payments (*pmt*) compounded at *int* interest rate per period for *term* periods. It is equivalent to

@FV(*pmt*,*int*,*term*) = *pmt** ((1 + *int*)^*n* − 1)/*int*

@HLOOKUP(*x*,*range*,*r*) Returns the value of a cell in *range* in row *r*, with the column selected by sequentially searching the values in the first row of *range* until the largest value that is less than or equal to *x* is found. The row number *r* is a zero-base number that specifies what row in *range* to use (not the spreadsheet row number). If *r* is 0, then the values in the first row are used (the same row used to index the column). The values in the first row of *range* must be in ascending order, since the function searches the values of the first row from left to right. If *x* is smaller than the first value in row 1 of *range*, the function returns the value ERR. If *x* is larger than the last value in the first row in *range*, then the function returns the value in the last column.

@HOUR(*n*) Returns a value between 0 and 23 that is the hour specified by the day number *n*. The function ignores any integer parts of *n*.

@IF(*test*,*x*,*y*) The conditional value @IF statement. The @IF statement calculates the value of *test*, and if it is TRUE, it returns the value *x*. If the value of *test* is FALSE, then it returns the value *y*. This function actually responds simply to 0 (for FALSE) and not 0 (for TRUE). Therefore, any value of *test* other than 0 will cause the @IF statement to be TRUE and return the value *x*.

@INDEX(*range*,*c*,*r*) Returns the contents of the cell at the intersection of row *r* and column *c* in *range*. This function returns the value ERR if *r* or *c* is larger than the number of rows or columns, respectively, in *range*, or if *r* or *c* is negative. The row and column specifiers are zero-based indexes into *range* (that is, the first row is row 0, and the first column is column 0).

@INT(*x*) Returns the integer part of *x*. It returns the largest integer that is less than or equal to *x*, with the same sign as *x*.

@IRR(*guess*,*range*) Returns the internal rate of return (interest rate) for the initial investment and payments listed in *range*. The first value in *range* is the initial investment and must be negative. The remaining values in *range* are the payments on the investment, where positive values represent the return on investment and negative values represent additional investments. A reasonable *guess* is needed to start the calculation. Note that the results are usually multivalued, and different values of *guess* may give different final results.

@ISERR(*x*) A logical test of the type of value in *x*. It returns TRUE if *x* contains the value ERR; otherwise it returns FALSE. ERR is returned when a function or formula contains a numerical error such as division by 0.

@ISNA(*x*) A logical test of the type of value in *x*. It returns TRUE if *x* contains the value NA (not available); otherwise it returns FALSE. A cell has the value NA when it contains the function @NA or refers to a cell that contains the value NA. This value is usually placed in cells that you have not yet filled with values, but to which your functions already refer. Your functions do not return a value until you replace all of the cells containing @NA.

@ISNUMBER(*x*) A logical test of the value x. It returns TRUE if x is a value or blank; otherwise it returns FALSE.

@ISSTRING(*x*) A logical test of the value x. It returns TRUE if x contains a string, including an empty string; otherwise it returns FALSE.

@LEFT(*str*,*n*) Returns the left n characters of the string *str*.

@LENGTH(*str*) Returns the length in characters of string *str*.

@LN(*x*) Returns the natural logarithm (base **e**) of x. The natural logarithm is the inverse of the exponential function (that is, x = @LN(@EXP(x))) and returns the base **e** logarithm of x. The value x must be greater than 0, or the function will return the value ERR.

@LOG(*x*) Returns the common logarithm of x (base 10).

@LOWER(*str*) Returns the string *str* with all letters converted to lowercase.

@MAX(*list*) Finds and returns the maximum value in list. The function ignores blank cells and counts cells filled with labels as 0.

@MID(*str*,*n*,*m*) Returns the substring m characters long starting at character position n, from the string *str*. If n is beyond the end of the string or is 0, the function returns the empty string. If $n + m$ is greater than the length of the string, then the function returns only characters up to the end of the string.

@MIN(*list*) Finds and returns the minimum value in *list*. The function ignores blank cells and counts cells filled with labels as 0.

@MINUTE(*n*) Returns a value between 0 and 59 that is the minute specified by the day number n. The function ignores any integer parts of n.

@MOD(*x*,*y*) Calculates the y modulus of x (in other words, it returns the remainder of the division of x by y). For example, if x is 23 and y is 5, then @MOD(23,5) is 3—the remainder of quotient 23/5. This function is used especially to determine when a number is an even multiple of another number ((@MOD(x,y) = 0) and to map angles larger than 360 degrees back into the range 0 to 360.

@MONTH(*n*) Returns a value in the range 1 to 12 that is the month of the year from the day number *n*. The function ignores fractional parts of *n*.

@N(*range*) Returns the value of the upper-left cell in *range*. If the upper-left cell contains a label, then its value is 0.

@NA Returns the value NA (not available). This function is useful when you are building a spreadsheet and some values are not available. If you leave a cell blank, its value is assumed to be 0, so any calculations that use those cells yield erroneous results. Placing @NA in any cells that are missing data causes formulas that use these values to show the value NA, thus marking them as incomplete.

@NOW Returns the day number of the current date and time.

@NPV(*int,range*) Returns the present value of an ordinary annuity with interest rate *int*, where the payments are regular but not all of equal value. Store the amount of each of the payments in *range*.

@PI Returns the value π (approximately 3.1415926), the ratio of the circumference of a circle to its radius.

@PMT(*prin,int,term*) Returns the payment required to pay off the principle (*prin*) in an account (an ordinary annuity) bearing compound interest (*int*) in *term* payments. (This calculates your car payment or house payment.) This function is equivalent to

@PMT(*prin,int,term*) = *prin***int*/(1 − (1 + *int*)(1/*term*))

@PROPER(*str*) Returns *str* with the first letter of each word capitalized and all others lowercase.

@PV(*pmt,int,term*) Returns the present value of an ordinary annuity. This is the amount of money that you must have on account now, compounding at interest rate *int* for *term* periods (simple compound interest), to equal an annuity of *term* equal payments (*pmt*). The annuity also bears interest at the rate *int*.

@RAND Returns a random number in the range 0 to 1. It uses the same set of random numbers every time you start Lotus 1-2-3, so you can repeat any random-number experiment. Be aware that the value of @RAND changes every time you recalculate the spreadsheet, so your numbers continually change. To work with a fixed set of random numbers, calculate them in a column and then use the /Range Value command to copy the values to another column where you can use them.

@RATE(*fv*,*pv*,*term*) Returns the interest rate per period for the present value (*pv*) to grow to the future value (*fv*) in *term* periods. This solution to the simple compound interest rate formula is equivalent to

@RATE(*fv*,*pv*,*term*) = (*fv*/*pv*)^(1/*int*) − 1.

@REPEAT(*str*,*n*) Returns a string that contains the string *str* repeated *n* times.

@REPLACE(*str1*,*n*,*m*,*str2*) Deletes *m* characters of string *str1* starting at character position *n* and then inserts string *str2* starting at character position *n*. It then returns this modified string.

@RIGHT(*str*,*n*) Returns the right *n* characters of string *str*.

@ROUND(*x*,*n*) Rounds a number to *n* decimal places. If *n* is 0, @ROUND returns *x* rounded to an integer. Negative values of *n* are allowed; in this case, *x* is rounded *n* places to the left of the decimal point.

@ROWS(*range*) Returns the number of rows in *range*.

@S(*range*) Returns the string value of the upper-left cell in *range* as a string. If the cell contains a value, the function returns the empty string.

@SECOND(*n*) Returns a value between 0 and 59 that is the second specified by the day number *n*. This function ignores any integer parts of *n*. Fractions of a second cannot be calculated with this function.

@SIN(*x*) Calculates the sine of the angle *x*, where *x* is in radians. If *x* is in degrees, then multiply by the function @PI and divide by 180 to convert *x* to radians. This function does not give exactly 0 as a result for integer values of π, except when $x = 0$. What it does give is an extremely small number, near the limit of the precision of the spreadsheet (approximately 10^{-16}); for example,

@SIN(2*@PI) = − 2.5E − 16

@SLN(*c*,*s*,*life*) Returns the current period's depreciation on an asset with cost *c*, salvage value *s*, and lifetime *life*, using the straight-line depreciation method. This function is equivalent to

@SLN(*c*,*s*,*life*) = (*c* − *s*)/*life*

@SQRT(*x*) Returns the square root of *x* for *x* ΓE 0. Negative values of *x* cause this function to return the value ERR.

@STD(*list*) Calculates the population standard deviation of the values in *list*. The standard deviation function is equivalent to @SQRT (@VAR(*list*)). To calculate the sample standard deviation, use

std (sample) = @SQRT(@COUNT(*list*)/
(@COUNT(*list*) − 1))*@STD(*list*)

@STRING(*x*,*n*) Returns the value of *x* as a string with *n* decimal places using the fixed numeric format. This is the inverse of the @VALUE function.

@SUM(*list*) Returns the sum of the values in *list*. This function ignores blank cells and counts labels as 0.

@SYD(*c*,*s*,*life*,*per*) Uses the sum-of-the-years digits method to return the current period's (*per*) depreciation on an asset with cost *c*, salvage value *s*, and lifetime *life*.

@TAN(*x*) Calculates the tangent of angle *x*, where *x* is in radians. If *x* is in degrees, then multiply it by the function @PI and divide by 180 to convert it to radians. This function does not go to infinity at odd multiples of $\pi/2$. What it does give is either an extremely large number, near the limit of precision for the spreadsheet (approximately 10^{15}), so the results can be used in other calculations without causing an overflow error; for example,

@TAN(3*@PI/2) = 5.4E + 15

@TERM(*pmt*,*int*,*fv*) Returns the number of periods required for an ordinary annuity with *pmt* payments and *int* interest to grow to future value *fv*.

@TIME(*hr*,*min*,*sec*) Returns the time number (fraction) for the specified hour (*hr*), minute (*min*), and second (*sec*).

@TIMEVALUE(*str*) Returns the time number (fraction) for the time specified in string *str*. The format of the time in *str* must be one of the Lotus 1-2-3 time formats (see the *1-2-3 Reference Manual*).

@TRIM(*str*) Returns the string *str* with leading and trailing blanks removed and any internal multiple blanks replaced with single blanks.

@TRUE Returns the logical value TRUE or 1.

@UPPER(*str*) Returns the string str with all letters converted to uppercase.

@VALUE(*str*) Returns the value of string *str*. If *str* is a reference to a cell containing a value, the value is returned as is. If *str* is empty or the null string, it returns 0. The string *str* can contain any number in standard or scientific format. It can also contain mixed numbers with integer fractions (for example, $3\frac{1}{7}$), which it converts to decimal fractions. Any other characters, except blanks, cause it to return the value ERR.

@VAR(*list*) Calculates the population variance of the values in *list*. The variance function is calculated with the equation

$$\text{@VAR}(list) = \sum_{i=0}^{n} \frac{(v_i - \langle v \rangle)^2}{n}$$

where v_i are the values in *list*, $\langle v \rangle$ is the average of the values in *list*, and n is the number of values in *list*. To calculate the sample variance, change the value of n to $n - 1$ by using

var(sample) = (@COUNT(*list*)/(@COUNT(*list*) − 1))*@VAR(*list*)

@VLOOKUP(*x*,*range*,*c*) Returns the value of a cell in *range* in column *c*. The row is selected by sequentially searching the values in the first column of *range* until the largest value that is less than or equal to *x* is found. The column number is a zero-base number that specifies what column in *range* to use (not the spreadsheet column coordinate). If *c* is 0, then the values in the first column are used (the same column used to index the row). The values in the first column must be in ascending order down the column, since the search proceeds from top to bottom in that column. If *x* is smaller than the first (top) value in the first column, the function returns the value ERR. If the value of *x* is larger than the last (bottom) value in column 1, the function uses the values in the last column.

@YEAR(*n*) Returns a value between 0 (1900) and 199 (2099) that is the year specified by the day number *n*. This function ignores fractional parts of *n*.

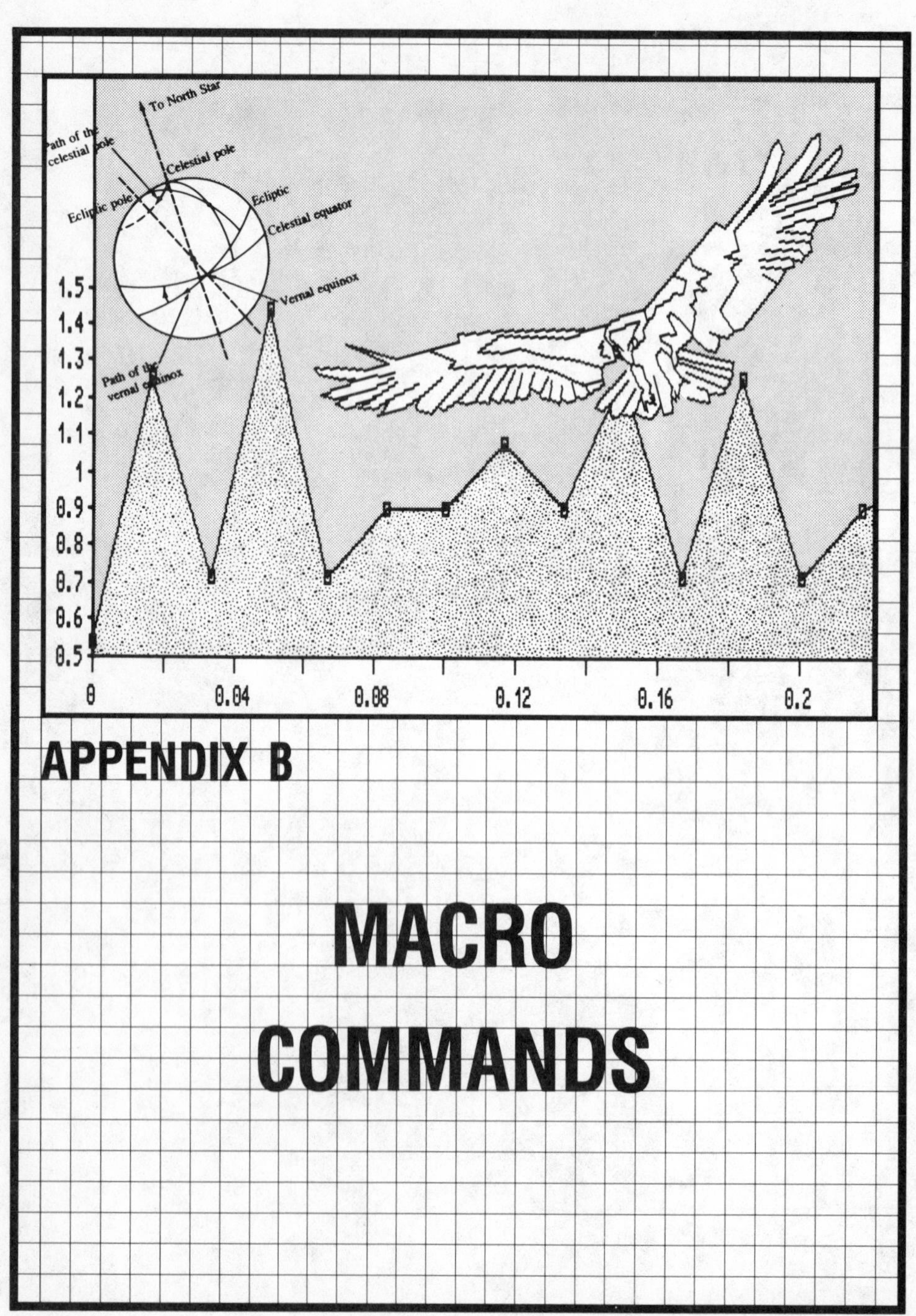

APPENDIX B

MACRO COMMANDS

■ This appendix contains an alphabetical list of the Lotus 1-2-3 macro commands and macro key equivalents. All of the macro commands and all but one of the key equivalents are entered into the spreadsheet as labels and surrounded with braces. The one exception is the key equivalent for the Return key (~), which is part of a label, but is not surrounded by braces. The macro key equivalents represent the nonprinting soft keys on the keyboard; they perform the same action as the keys that they represent. This appendix lists the most common key or key combination for each soft key; check your manual to see which combination is the correct one for your particular computer.

The macro commands extend the macro language, making it not a simple replay of keystrokes but a complete programming language, with variable assignment statements, disk and keyboard input and output, and program flow control. I have listed the macro key equivalents in lowercase and the macro commands in UPPERCASE letters. Note, however, that case is not important in the spreadsheet. Variables appear in *italics*.

Lotus also provides a set of /X commands to maintain compatibility with previous versions of Lotus 1-2-3. All of these have equivalent macro commands, so they are not listed here.

{abs} Key equivalent of the Abs key (F4). Pressing this key cycles a cell reference through all possible combinations of absolute, relative, and mixed cell references.

{backspace} or {bs} Key equivalent of the Backspace key. Moves the cursor to the left one space and erases the character that occupied that space.

{BEEP *tone*} Sounds the keyboard bell. The *tone* argument determines the tone of the bell. The allowed values of *tone* are 1, 2, 3, and 4. If no argument is given, 1 is assumed.

{bigleft} Key equivalent of the Big Left key combination (Ctrl-←). Moves the cursor one page left on the spreadsheet or five characters left in edit mode.

{bigright} Key equivalent of the Big Right key combination (Ctrl-→). Moves the cursor one page right on the spreadsheet or five characters right in edit mode.

{BLANK *range*} Erases the contents of the cells in *range*.

{BRANCH *location*} Continues macro execution at the cell *location*. This command is equivalent to GOTO in BASIC or FORTRAN.

{BREAKOFF} Disables the Break key. Caution: Use this only if you are sure that you will not have to interrupt a macro. With {BREAKOFF} implemented, you can stop a macro only by rebooting the computer.

{BREAKON} Enables the Break key that was disabled with {BREAKOFF}.

{calc} Key equivalent of the Calc key (F9). Causes the spreadsheet to be recalculated.

{CLOSE} Closes the currently open disk file.

{CONTENTS *location1,location2,width,format*} Changes the value in the cell at *location1* into a string in *location2*. You can optionally specify the *width* and *format* of the converted number.

{DEFINE *location1,location2,...*} Use this command as the first statement in a subroutine to specify the location(s) for storing subroutine arguments. The *location* arguments are the cell addresses where the subroutine arguments are to be stored. The arguments are stored as strings unless you append *:value* to *location,* in which case they will be evaluated and stored as values.

{delete} or {del} Key equivalent of the Delete key (Del). Deletes the character currently under the cursor and moves all text to its right one character left.

{DISPATCH *location*} An indirect branch operation. Branches to the cell specified at *location*.

{down} Key equivalent of the Down Arrow key (↓). Moves the cursor down one cell.

{edit} Key equivalent of the Edit key (F2). Changes the spreadsheet to edit mode.

{end} Key equivalent of the End key (End). Used in conjunction with other keys to move to the limits of the spreadsheet.

{escape} or {esc} Key equivalent of the Escape key (Esc). Used to cancel actions and to back up levels in the command tree.

{FILESIZE *location*} Gets the size of the currently open disk file and stores it at *location*.

{FOR *counter,start,stop,step,routine*} Executes *routine* for each value of *counter* beginning with the value *start*, terminating with the value *stop*, and stepping with the value *step*.

{FORBREAK} Terminates a {FOR} loop prematurely.

{GETLABEL *prompt,location*} Prints the *prompt* string in the control panel and waits for a string to be typed. The string is stored at *location*.

{GETNUMBER *prompt,location*} Prints the *prompt* string in the control panel and waits for a value to be typed. The value is stored at *location*.

{GETPOS *location*} Gets the current read or write position in the currently open disk file.

{GET *location*} Gets a single character from the keyboard and stores it in *location*.

{goto} Key equivalent of the Goto key (F5). Used to move the cursor to a particular cell.

{graph} Key equivalent of the Graph key (F10). Displays the current graph.

{home} Key equivalent of the Home key (Home). Moves the cursor to cell A1.

{IF *condition*} If condition is true, executes the remainder of the contents of this cell; otherwise skips to the next cell in the macro.

{INDICATE *string*} The first five characters of *string* are used as the mode indicator in the upper-right corner of the screen. The indicator does not change until you change it. To reinstate the normal indicators, specify {INDICATE} without an argument.

{left} Key equivalent of the Left Arrow key (←). Moves the cursor one cell or one character to the left.

{LET *location,contents*} Sets the cell at *location* equal to *contents*. *Contents* can be a value, string, or formula.

{LOOK *location*} If a key has been pressed on the keyboard, stores it at *location*; otherwise erases *location*.

{MENUBRANCH *location*} Executes the custom menu at *location* and branches according to the selection.

{MENUCALL *location*} Executes the custom menu at *location* and executes a subroutine call according to the selection.

{name} Key equivalent of the Name key (F3). Allows you to select a previously named range for input where a range is expected.

{ONERROR *location1,location2*} If a Lotus 1-2-3 error condition occurs, then branches to *location1*. Optionally, stores the error message at *location2*.

{OPEN *file,access*} Opens the disk file *file* for access specified with the *access* argument. The *access* argument can specify R (Read), W (Write), or M (Modify). Read permits the file only to be read. Write creates a new file for output, deleting any file with the same name. Modify is a combination of read and write.

{pgdn} Key equivalent of the Page Down key (PgDn). Moves the cursor down one page.

{pgup} Key equivalent of the Page Up key (PgUp). Moves the cursor up one page.

{PANELOFF} Disables control panel updating during macro operation. Speeds up macro execution.

{PANELON} Enables control panel updating that was disabled with {PANELOFF}.

{PUT *range,column,row,contents*} Sets the cell at *column* and *row* in *range* equal to *contents*. *Contents* can be a value, string, or formula.

{query} Key equivalent of the Query key (F7). Reexecutes the most recently executed /Data Query (/DQ) database command.

{QUIT} Terminates a macro.

{READ *bytes, location*} Reads *bytes* characters from a disk file and stores them at *location*.

{READLN *location*} Reads a line of data from the currently open disk file and stores it at *location*.

{RECALC *range,condition,iteration*} Recalculates the formulas in *range* row by row. Optionally, tests *condition* and recalculates the cells *iteration* times if *condition* is false.

{RECALCCOL *range,condition,iteration*} Recalculates the formulas in range column by column. Optionally, tests *condition* and recalculates the cells *iteration* times if *condition* is false.

{RESTART} Breaks out of a subroutine call chain. Discards the stack containing the locations for all subroutine returns.

{RETURN} Returns from a subroutine. A blank or numeric cell also causes a return.

{right} Key equivalent of the Right Arrow key (→). Moves the cursor one cell or one character to the right.

{*routine-name*} Begins execution of *routine-name* as a subroutine.

{SETPOS *pos*} Sets the current read or write position in the currently open disk file.

{table} Key equivalent of the Table key (F8). Reexecutes the /Data Table (/DT) command to recalculate a table when the input data or formula is changed.

{up} Key equivalent of the Up Arrow key (↑). Moves the cursor up one cell.

{WAIT *date-number*} Suspends macro operation until *date-number*.

{window} Key equivalent of the Window key (F6). Moves the cursor from one window to another when the spreadsheet is split into two windows.

{WINDOWSOFF} Suspends screen updating during macro operation. This can speed up execution of a macro that involves many spreadsheet updates.

{WINDOWSON} Enables screen updating that was disabled with {WINDOWSOFF}.

{WRITE *string*} Writes *string* to the currently open disk file. *String* can be quoted text or a cell reference.

{WRITELN *string*} Writes a line of text to the currently open disk file. *String* can be quoted text or a cell reference.

{{} Key equivalent of the Left Brace key ({). Enters a left brace in a label that will not be interpreted as a macro command.

{}} Key equivalent of the Right Brace key (}). Enters a right brace in a label that will not be interpreted as a macro command.

{~} Key equivalent of the ~. Enters a tilde in a label that will not be interpreted as a Return key equivalent.

{?} Halts macro execution to await keyboard input. The macro will be resumed when Return is pressed.

~ Key equivalent of the Return or Enter key. Use this to enter Returns in macros.

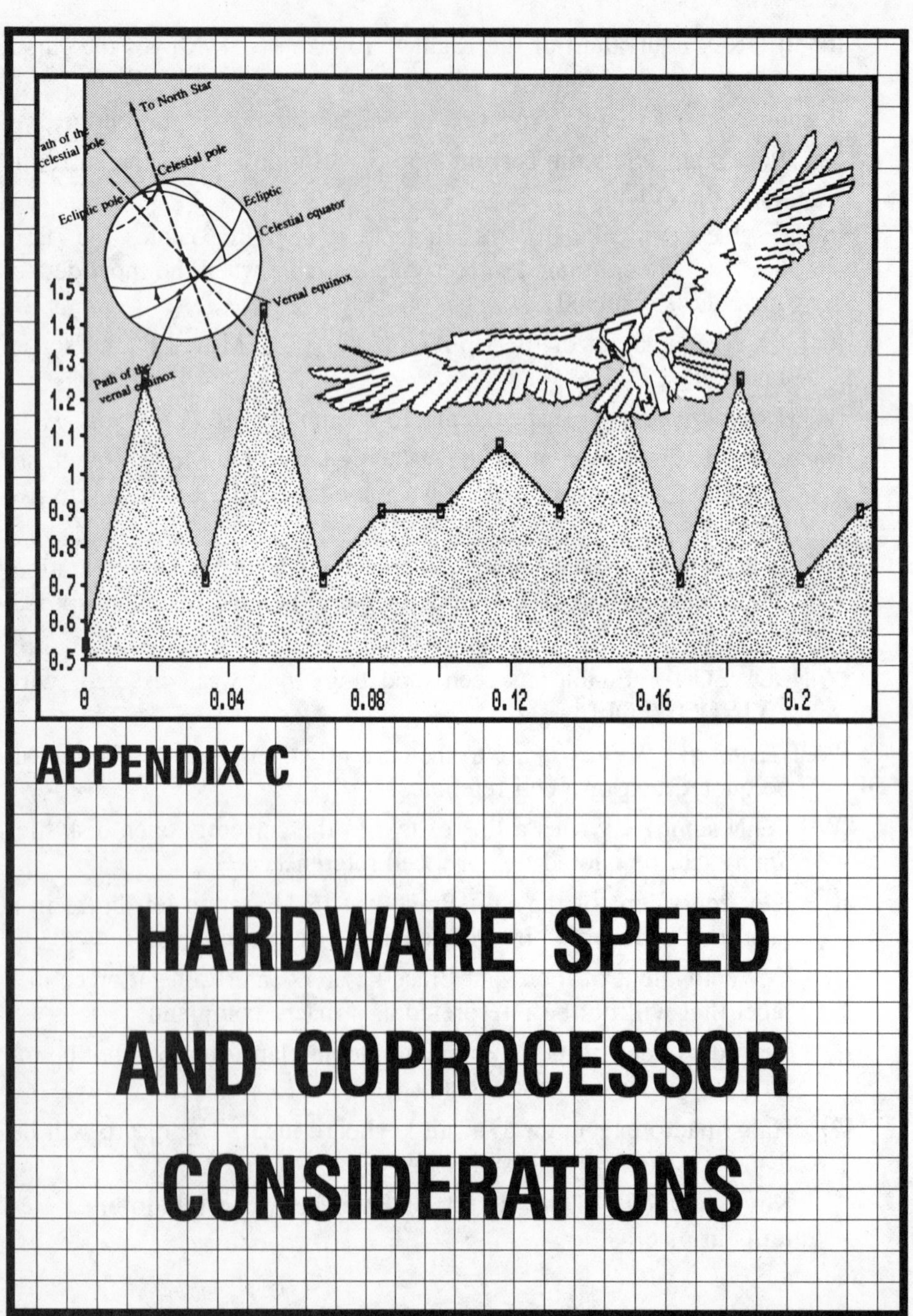

APPENDIX C

HARDWARE SPEED AND COPROCESSOR CONSIDERATIONS

Processor speed and the availability of a math coprocessor are two hardware considerations that affect the speed of Lotus 1-2-3 calculations. The raw processor speed is a measure of how fast the processor can execute instructions. An 8087 math coprocessor is a specialized processor for performing floating-point calculations. Without a math coprocessor, floating-point calculations must be performed using only the integer mathematics available in the CPU. Performing floating-point calculations using integer mathematics requires many calculations to produce a single floating-point result. If a math coprocessor is available, then floating-point calculations can be executed with a single instruction.

The basic IBM PC configuration includes a 4.77 MHz central processor (CPU) and no 8087 math coprocessor. You can increase processor speed by 50 percent by adding a board containing a processor running at 7.16 MHz and memory capable of running at that speed. Adding this board effectively replaces your existing processor and memory with those on the board. Some IBM PC-compatible computers come with a high-speed processor built in. For instance, the Tandy 1000 SX has a dual-speed processor that can be configured to run at 4.77 or 7.16 MHz. Adding the math coprocessor is much simpler: just plug the coprocessor chip into the socket provided and set the switches or jumpers to indicate its presence in the system.

These options to increase the speed with which spreadsheets can be calculated are not inexpensive. Adding a board to upgrade the speed can cost several hundred dollars. A math coprocessor chip costs one to two hundred dollars.

To see the effect on Lotus 1-2-3 of processor speed and coprocessor availability, I timed the calculation of several of the slower spreadsheets in this book. The calculations for most of the problems in this book require only a few seconds to perform. Some, however, require several minutes to an hour or more to complete. I performed the timing test using a macro that executed the @NOW function, updated the spreadsheet, executed @NOW again, and subtracted to find the amount of time used to calculate the spreadsheet. For each problem, I ran four tests to compare the operation of each spreadsheet at 4.77 MHz and 7.16 MHz and with and without an 8087 math coprocessor.

Problem 1 is from Chapter 7, where we calculated a curve fit to the electron ionization cross section of helium. We did this using a macro to search for the coefficients of the curve that minimize the mean square difference between the curve and the data points. The results of this calculation were shown in Figure 7.9. This macro does not perform many calculations within itself, but it does cause the spreadsheet to be recalculated many times.

Problem 2 is from Chapter 9, where we calculated the gamma function from its integral formula. We did this using a macro that uses the trapezoid rule to perform the integration. This problem, shown in Figure 9.7, involves many calculations within the body of the macro.

Problems 3, 4, and 5 are from Chapter 12, where we calculated the deflection of a simply supported beam by solving its differential equation. We used three methods to solve the differential equation; all three methods rewrote the equation using finite differences for the derivatives. The first method used successive approximations to solve the set of equations (Figure 12.8). The second method used acceleration to speed up the convergence of the problem (Figure 12.9). The third method used the internal matrix inversion commands (Figure 12.12).

The following table shows how much time it took to calculate the spreadsheet at two different processor speeds with and without the 8087 math coprocessor. The times shown are in hours:minutes:seconds.

		4.77 MHz		**7.16 MHz**	
Problem	**Figure**	**Without 8087**	**With 8087**	**Without 8087**	**With 8087**
1	7.9	00:06:38	00:04:25	00:05:18	00:03:25
2	9.7	00:05:50	00:03:58	00:04:33	00:03:07
3	12.8	01:39:33	01:15:59	01:18:08	01:00:42
4	12.9	00:05:40	00:04:30	00:04:27	00:03:35
5	12.12	00:12:10	00:11:11	00:09:29	00:08:21

To compare these times, I calculated the percent decrease in time needed to solve the problem. I also calculated the percent relative increase in speed (the inverse of the time necessary to solve the problem). The decrease in the time to perform the calculation was as follows:

	Decrease due to processor speed		**Decrease due to 8087 coprocessor**		**Decrease due to both**
	Without 8087	**With 8087**	**4.77 MHz**	**7.16 MHz**	
1	80%	77%	67%	64%	52%
2	78	79	68	68	53
3	78	80	76	78	61
4	79	80	79	81	63
5	78	75	92	88	69

The increase in the speed of the spreadsheet was as follows:

	Increase due to processor speed		Increase due to 8087 coprocessor		Increase due to both
	Without 8087	**With 8087**	**4.77 MHz**	**7.16 MHz**	
1	25%	29%	50%	55%	94%
2	28	27	47	46	87
3	27	25	31	29	64
4	27	26	26	24	58
5	28	34	9	14	46

Increasing the processor speed by 50 percent increased the spreadsheet speed by only about 27 percent. This indicates that something other than the processor is slowing down the spreadsheet (probably writing to graphics memory); otherwise we should see a one-to-one percent increase in spreadsheet speed with processor speed. The greatest increase in speed occurs in problem 5, which uses the internal matrix solver, which should be a CPU-intensive calculation.

Speed increases due to the addition of an 8087 math coprocessor range from 9 percent to over 50 percent. Looking at problem 5, it appears that the internal matrix inversion subroutine makes little use of the math coprocessor. This is a curious situation, as I would have expected the internal matrix inversion subroutine to make heavy use of the math coprocessor. The problems with the greatest increases in speed are those with large macro programs (problems 1 and 2).

The overall increase in speed by using both a math coprocessor and a high-speed CPU ranges from about 50 percent to over 90 percent. The higher value is nearly a doubling of the spreadsheet speed or a halving of the amount of time that it takes to calculate the spreadsheet. Again, the highest increase in speed occurs in the problems that involve large macro programs (problems 1 and 2).

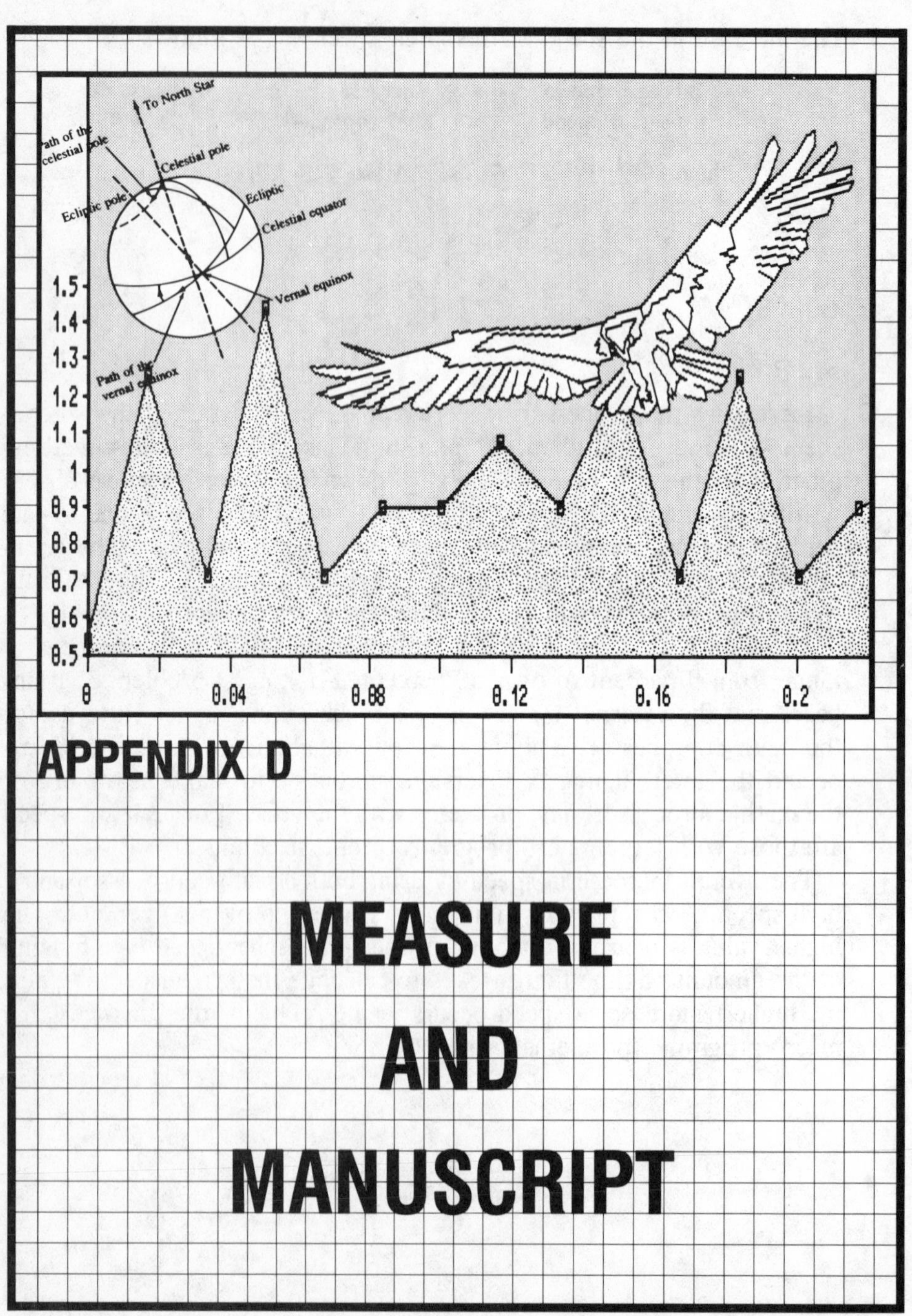

APPENDIX D

MEASURE AND MANUSCRIPT

Lotus has recently introduced two 1-2-3-compatible products for science and engineering applications. Measure, an add-on for the 1-2-3 spreadsheet, and Manuscript, a high-end (that is, full-featured and expensive) scientific word processor. Both of these products serve to enhance the operation and use of Lotus 1-2-3 for scientific and engineering applications. I have not had access to these products for a sufficient length of time to write an in-depth product evaluation, so this appendix is more of a new product review.

In a typical laboratory situation where you are using your computer for data acquisition, you probably have a BASIC program to control a data acquisition board, or an instrument control interface board. The program sets up the board, takes the data, and then writes it to a data file. To manipulate and plot the data, you have either another BASIC program or you read the data into Lotus 1-2-3 and use its functions and graphics. This process involves several steps and a lot of time from data acquisition through data display.

Lotus Measure gives you access to these data acquisition and control boards from within Lotus 1-2-3. Thus, when you perform data acquisition, you can route the data directly into the cells of the Lotus 1-2-3 spreadsheet, then immediately manipulate and plot that data using the spreadsheet functions and commands.

Lotus Measure is installed into Lotus 1-2-3 as another driver in the driver set along with the screen and printer drivers. It is activated simply by pressing Alt and a function key.

Lotus Measure is a software enhancement that adds several new commands to Lotus 1-2-3. These commands control data gathering and instrument control with the data acquisition boards. Lotus Measure currently supports eight data acquisition and control boards:

- the IBM Game Control Adaptor
- the MetraByte DASH-16 data acquisition board
- the National Instruments PC2 and PC2A GPIB boards
- the Hewlett-Packard HP-IB board
- the IBM GPIB board
- the IOtech GP488 board
- a standard RS-232C interface

The IBM Game Control Adaptor and the MetraByte board are for data input only, while the last three boards can also output data for instrument control.

The IBM Game Control Adaptor is normally used to connect a pair of joysticks to an IBM PC for use in game programs. However, it can be used as an inexpensive analog-to-digital converter. The adaptor consists of four digital inputs (the fire buttons) and four analog inputs (the X-Y joystick inputs). The digital inputs detect switch closures and can be used for triggering data acquisition. Each of the four analog inputs requires an external 100K ohm potentiometer (variable resistor) in the circuit. Changing the value of the resistance of the potentiometer changes the value of the analog input on that channel. Note that on compatible computer game control adapters, the details of the analog inputs may be different.

The MetraByte DASH-16 data acquisition board has sixteen analog voltage inputs, four digital inputs, and a counter. Many scientific instruments can be configured to give voltage outputs proportional to the variable being measured; for example, strain gauges, thermocouples, and pressure transducers. You can control up to four DASH-16 boards, for a total of 64 analog inputs, 16 digital inputs, and 4 counters.

The National Instruments GPIB boards, the IBM GPIB board, the IOtech GPIB board, and the Hewlett-Packard HP-IB board are all implementations of the IEEE-488 interface, which is probably the most popular method of interfacing instruments with a controller (the PC). The interface is an 8-bit parallel bus that can connect up to 30 external instruments to the PC. However, Measure can handle a maximum of 15 at one time. Many measuring instruments (digital voltmeters, ammeters, frequency counters, and so on) and control instruments (voltage and current sources, frequency sources, and so on) have an IEEE-488 interface built into them. This is a two-way interface and can be used for instrument setup and control as well as for data gathering.

The RS-232C interface is a standard, asynchronous serial interface that is most often used for connection to a modem or printer; however, it can also be used for connecting to data-gathering instruments that support RS-232C communication.

Lotus has indicated a willingness to work with other manufacturers to expand the number of devices accessible from Measure. Therefore, there may be more accessible boards in the near future.

Reading data directly into a Lotus 1-2-3 spreadsheet is a definite advantage in an experimental situation, and Lotus Measure does it in a straightforward manner. The user interface is nearly identical to that used in Lotus 1-2-3, so setup and learning time is minimal. While

Measure is well designed and useful, it is a bit expensive ($495 list). However, Lotus is planning to sell it through value added retailers, and they will probably discount it when you buy it along with a data acquisition board.

Lotus Manuscript (also $495 list) is a PC-based scientific word processor. What makes it special is that it can directly import Lotus 1-2-3 print files and graphs. Instead of using scissors and glue to paste a Lotus 1-2-3 graph into a report, you can directly import the graph and place it between the text in your document. When you print your report, the figure will be printed in place.

Lotus Manuscript also has a built-in equation formatter and spelling checker; all of these features mean that you must have a hard disk to use it. Manuscript operates as a series of program modules and a memory-resident module manager. There is just too much code to operate on a floppy-disk-based system. You should also have a laser printer such as Apple's LaserWriter to fully access the potential of this program. However, it will do quite well with a dot matrix printer.

Manuscript is not a what-you-see-is-what-you-get word processor. However, it does have a previewer so that you can see the layout of a printed page before printing. This is especially useful because the imported graphic images are not maintained in the document file but are inserted when the file is being printed or previewed.

Graphics of several different formats can be inserted into a Manuscript document. The graphics are not actually inserted into the document. What is done is that the file name containing the graphic is placed into the document. When the document is printed or previewed, the file is opened, and the graphic is printed in its correct position in the document. Lotus Manuscript can import: PIC files from Lotus 1-2-3 and Symphony, BIT and RLE bit-mapped images, GMF graphic metafiles produced by drawing programs such as Lotus Freelance, PS PostScript files, and PDL graphic files produced by Manuscript for the equations.

The equation formatter uses bracketed expressions and keywords to define the relationships between the different parts of an equation. Essentially, a large equation is broken down into several smaller equations. Each smaller equation is then formatted and the formatting commands are surrounded with square brackets. These smaller equations can then be used as parts for writing the formatting of a larger equation, and so on. Functions are set in a Roman font, and variables are set in an italic font. No other character attributes, such as boldface, can be set. You will not see an equation in final form until you print or preview the document, because Manuscript creates the equation as a graphic and then inserts it as it does other graphics at print time.

Previewing is a capability similar to printing, except that the printing is done to the screen rather than to a printer. When you are previewing a document, you can zoom in to the graphics or text to insure that it is being set as you expect it to be. Previewing is the only way to insure that you have formatted your equations correctly without printing the document in final form. Previewing also allows you to check page breaks and figure locations before printing a page.

Both Measure and Manuscript enhance the scientific and engineering aspects of Lotus 1-2-3. If you are using your computer for data acquisition, then Measure will speed the process by storing the acquired data directly into the spreadsheet. For writing a technical report, Manuscript gives you the capability to import your Lotus 1-2-3 graphs and tables directly into your report. Manuscript also has the capability to format equations.

■ INDEX

SYBEX Computer Books are different.

Here is why . . .

At SYBEX, each book is designed with you in mind. Every manuscript is carefully selected and supervised by our editors, who are themselves computer experts. We publish the best authors, whose technical expertise is matched by an ability to write clearly and to communicate effectively. Programs are thoroughly tested for accuracy by our technical staff. Our computerized production department goes to great lengths to make sure that each book is well-designed.

In the pursuit of timeliness, SYBEX has achieved many publishing firsts. SYBEX was among the first to integrate personal computers used by authors and staff into the publishing process. SYBEX was the first to publish books on the CP/M operating system, microprocessor interfacing techniques, word processing, and many more topics.

Expertise in computers and dedication to the highest quality product have made SYBEX a world leader in computer book publishing. Translated into fourteen languages, SYBEX books have helped millions of people around the world to get the most from their computers. We hope we have helped you, too.

For a complete catalog of our publications:

SYBEX, Inc. 2021 Challenger Drive, #100, Alameda, CA 94501
Tel: (415) 523-8233/(800) 227-2346 Telex: 336311

■ 1-2-3 FOR SCIENTISTS AND ENGINEERS — EXAMPLES DISK

If you would like to use the examples and programs in this book but don't want to enter them yourself, you can obtain them on disk. Complete the following order form and return it along with a check or money order for $20.00. California residents please add sales tax.

William J. Orvis
University of California, Livermore
P.O. Box 5504, L-156
Livermore, California 94550

Name ____

Address ____

City/State/ZIP ____

Enclosed is my check or money order.
(Make checks payable to William J. Orvis.)
Please send the *1-2-3 for Scientists and Engineers Examples Disk.*

The University of California is not associated with this offer and is not responsible for any defect in the disk or program.

SYBEX is not affiliated with William J. Orvis and assumes no responsibility for any defect in the disk programs.